DATE DUE

~~OC 2 9 '03~~		
~~OC 2 1 '09~~		
~~AP 3 0 '10~~		

DEMCO 38-296

R

MENTAL DISORDER, WORK DISABILITY, AND THE LAW

EDITED BY
Richard J. Bonnie and John Monahan

THE UNIVERSITY OF CHICAGO PRESS / CHICAGO AND LONDON

ssor and Director of the Institute of Law, Psy-
Virginia. **John Monahan** is the Henry and
r of Psychology and Legal Medicine at the University of Virginia.

The University of Chicago Press, Chicago 60637
The University of Chicago Press, Ltd., London
© 1997 by The University of Chicago
All rights reserved. Published 1997
Printed in the United States of America
06 05 04 03 02 01 00 99 98 97   5 4 3 2 1

ISBN (cloth): 0-226-06450-6

Copyright is not claimed for chapter 1.

The University of Chicago Press gratefully acknowledges a subvention from the John D.
and Catherine T. MacArthur Foundation in partial support of the costs of production
of this volume.

Library of Congress Cataloging-in-Publication Data

Mental disorder, work disability, and the law / edited by Richard J.
  Bonnie and John Monahan.
        p.   cm. — (The John D. and Catherine T. MacArthur Foundation
  series on mental health and development)
    Includes bibliographical references and index.
    ISBN 0-226-06450-6 (alk. paper)
      1. Mentally handicapped—Employment—Law and legislation—United
States.   2. Disability evaluation—Law and legislation—United
States.   I. Bonnie, Richard J.   II. Monahan, John, 1946–
    III. Series.
  KF3469.M46   1997
  344.73′01594—dc20
  [347.3041594]   96-10971
                                                        CIP

⊗ The paper used in this publication meets the minimum requirements of the American
National Standard for Information Sciences—Permanence of Paper for Printed Library
Materials, ANSI Z39.48-1984.

CONTENTS

CONTRIBUTORS

Christopher G. Bell, Jackson, Lewis, Schnitzler, and Krupman, Washington, DC

Julia Benoit, Department of Social Medicine, University of North Carolina at Chapel Hill

Richard J. Bonnie, University of Virginia, School of Law

Jean Campbell, Missouri Institute of Mental Health, School of Medicine, University of Missouri at Columbia

Miriam G. Cisternas, Technology Assessment Group, San Francisco

Norman Daniels, Department of Philosophy, Tufts University

Larry Davidson, Department of Psychiatry, School of Medicine, Yale University

Sue E. Estroff, Department of Social Medicine, University of North Carolina at Chapel Hill

Laura Lee Hall, National Alliance for the Mentally Ill, Arlington, VA

Caroline L. Kaufmann, Department of Sociology, Duquesne University

Marilyn J. Henderson, Center for Mental Health Services, Department of Health and Human Services

William S. Lachicotte, Department of Social Medicine, University of North Carolina at Chapel Hill

Ronald W. Manderscheid, Center for Mental Health Services, Department of Health and Human Services

Laura J. Milazzo-Sayre, Center for Mental Health Services, Department of Health and Human Services

John Monahan, University of Virginia, School of Law

Donald L. Patrick, Department of Health Services, University of Washington at Seattle

Paul Polak, International Development Enterprises, Lakewood, CO

Ellen Smith Pryor, School of Law, Southern Methodist University
John S. Strauss, Department of Psychiatry, School of Medicine, Yale University
Richard Warner, Mental Health Center of Boulder County, Boulder, CO
Edward Yelin, University of California at San Francisco, School of Medicine
Catherine Zimmer, Department of Sociology and Anthropology, North Carolina State University

Work Disability and the Fabric of Mental Health Law: An Introduction

RICHARD J. BONNIE

The basic outline of U.S. social policy relating to work disability is clear: (1) U.S. law does not recognize an individual right to employment, but all people who want to work, including those with disabilities, are entitled to a fair opportunity to participate in the competitive labor market to the full extent of their capabilities. (2) In recognition of the social barriers to full participation, a just society takes special measures to facilitate access to competitive employment for people with disabilities. (3) People who are unable to work due to disability are entitled to a decent level of economic support and to vocational services that might enable them to return to the labor force. Withdrawing from the labor force is not encouraged, lest people who are able to work evade their responsibility to support themselves. (4) Finally, assuming that adequate resources are available, society aims to provide subsidized vocational opportunities for people with disabilities who are not able to compete successfully in the labor market.

An intricate web of statutes and programs implements these work disability policies. First, the fabric of work disability law includes *antidiscrimination statutes,* such as the Americans with Disabilities Act (ADA), that aim to facilitate equal access to employment for those who seek it. The ADA, for example, prohibits employers from discriminating in any aspect of employment against a qualified person with a disability, and obligates the employer to make reasonable accommodations to enable the person to perform essential job functions.

Second, *vocational rehabilitation* (VR) statutes provide rehabilitative services to people with disabilities to enable them to compete in the labor market. The federal VR program provides funds, administered by the states in accordance with federal requirements, for an array of rehabilitative services and employment support to people with disabilities who are potentially employable. In addition, each state has a separate vocational rehabilitation program, under workers' compensation statutes, for people who become disabled in the course of employment.

Third, a complex system of *insurance and social welfare legislation* guarantees benefits to people with disabilities who are unable to work. As already mentioned, state workers' compensation laws (and the analogous federal statutes for veterans and civilian workers) provide income replacement for workers who become totally or partially disabled due to injuries or diseases arising out of employment. The federal Social Security Disability Insurance program (SSDI) pays benefits to workers who have qualified for coverage (usually by working) and who have become disabled. Disability is defined as "inability to engage in any substantial gainful activity by reason of any medically determinable physical or mental impairment which can result in death or has lasted or can be expected to last [at least one year]." Finally, the federal Supplemental Security Income program (SSI) is a social welfare program designed to provide income support for people who have become disabled regardless of whether they have ever worked. Unlike SSDI, the SSI program is means-tested, and it provides benefits lower than the average SSDI benefit. The definition of disability under SSI is the same as under SSDI.

The essays collected here focus on this body of law as it relates to persons with disabilities attributable to mental disorders. Although some of the discussion may apply to persons with mental retardation or other intellectual disabilities, the primary focus is on mental and emotional disorders. The interesting and difficult problems associated with mental disorders have received little attention in the specialized work disability literatures of several pertinent disciplines, including labor economics, social policy, and law. The papers in this volume have been commissioned to provide a picture of the entire landscape pertaining to work disability law and mental disorder. Our goal is to stimulate communication among specialists in the fields of inquiry that touch on this subject. For example, we seek to draw the attention of labor economists to issues relating to participation in the labor force by people with mental disabilities, and to connect the fields of mental health epidemiology and labor economics. From a clinical perspective, we aim to draw the attention of specialists in rehabilitation to the norms of the ADA. We hope, in turn, to stimulate broader interest in the field among students of mental health law.

II

Work disability has been outside the mainstream of scholarship in mental health law. Moreover, the body of existing legal research and scholarship on work disability has been bifurcated, focusing either on access to benefits or on employment discrimination. Entitlement to disability payments under the SSI/SSDI programs has been of interest primarily to mental health advocacy groups who have contested the cost-cutting policies of the Social Security Administration. The broad questions of procedural architecture in disability benefit determinations explored by administrative law scholars have been of little interest to legal theorists specializing in mental health law. Similarly, while disability assessments under the SSI/SSDI systems have been of practical interest to a subset of forensic psychiatrists, they have not interested academic specialists in psychiatry and law.

Recovery under workers' compensation laws for mental injury and consequent disability has been similarly ignored by mainstream scholarship in mental health law. Causation puzzles and concerns about accuracy in compensation determinations have received attention by specialists in tort and injury compensation systems, but connections are rarely drawn to the large thematic issues in mental health law. As with SSI/SSDI determinations, the predominant clinical focus has been on the vagaries of assessing mental impairments and their relation to vocational capacity.

The literature on disability determinations under SSI/SSDI and workers' compensation systems concerns disability as a basis for withdrawal from the labor force. The legal landscape of these topics is far removed, thematically, from the more robust civil rights literature, which emphasizes access to the workforce. Fear of discrimination in the workplace and elsewhere is an overarching concern in mental health law. Legal and ethical restrictions on disclosure of confidential information relating to mental health diagnosis and treatment have been tightened to reduce the risk of discrimination. Moreover, a developing body of antidiscrimination laws, beginning with §504 of the Federal Rehabilitation Act of 1973, and culminating in the ADA, bans unwarranted disadvantage in the workplace. The normative principle underlying these laws is that employment decisions should focus on the person's ability to perform essential job functions, that is, on work-related abilities and disabilities.

A focus on workplace performance raises a wide array of complex issues regarding the job relevance and the clinical assessment of multiple behaviors associated with mental disorders. The assessments focus on what people are able to do rather than what they are not able to do. Until the enactment of the ADA, however, issues relating to work disability and mental disorder were given scant attention in the disability rights literature.

When the John D. and Catherine T. MacArthur Foundation Research Network on Mental Health and the Law resolved to undertake a study of work disability, the ADA had recently been enacted. Notwithstanding extensive discussion of the ADA's employment provisions, however, little attention had been given to the unique issues raised under these provisions for people with mental disabilities. This was soon corrected. The Bazelon Center for Mental Health Law launched a major educational initiative. The American Bar Association Commission on Mental and Physical Disability Law published several important educational documents. The National Institute on Disability and Rehabilitation Research awarded a three-year grant to the Washington Business Group on Health to establish a resource center for employers to facilitate implementation of the ADA in relation to people with mental disabilities. Finally, at the request of Senator Kennedy, the Office of Technology Assessment conducted a major study designed to identify the requisite steps for implementing the employment provisions of the ADA for persons with psychiatric disabilities.

These initiatives have drawn attention to important operational questions regarding the implementation of the ADA and to the many interpretive issues that require judicial clarification. However, these educational and advocacy initiatives have not yet been accompanied by empirical or theoretical research. Moreover, ideas about facilitating labor force participation by people with mental disabilities have not yet been integrated with the body of disability benefit laws that permit people to receive benefits because they are unable to participate in the labor force. As an analytic construct, does work disability have a common meaning across these legal domains? What are the normative aims underlying these various statutory schemes? Are they compatible with one another? Are they being achieved?

III

Advocates for people with mental disorders have been persistently dissatisfied with the operation of work disability laws, and it is not hard to see why. On the one hand, the rate of labor force participation among people with serious mental disorders is very low, even when compared with the rate of labor force participation among people with physical conditions, and there is no evidence that the Americans with Disabilities Act has improved this dismal picture. In something of a self-fulfilling prophecy, the difficulty of placing people with mental disabilities in the workforce apparently leads vocational rehabilitation programs to give them low priority in the allocation of services. On the other hand, even though people with mental disorders represent an increasing fraction of disability benefit recipients, mental disability advocacy groups argue that many seriously disabled people who are unable to compete in the labor market are unfairly denied benefits.

While mental health advocacy groups focus on what they regard as unfair treatment of people with severe mental disorders, other observers insist that work disability laws are too easily manipulated and abused by people who do not have severe mental disorders. As a result, it is argued, people with minor or moderate mental or emotional problems are able to elicit concessions from employers by threatening litigation under the ADA, while malingerers are able to obtain worker's compensation awards or disability benefits so that they won't have to work at all. Concerns about manipulation and abuse are epitomized by claims of work-related stress disorders.

These divergent perceptions invite critical scrutiny. They also expose a moral puzzle that lies at the intersection of work disability law and mental disorder: What is *dis*ability? Where is the line between inability to work and unwillingness to work? How do we know the difference between *can't* and *won't*? Or, in the context of people who seek employment, how do we know the difference between someone who needs an accommodation and someone who simply wants special treatment? Ultimately, attributions of work disability under these various statutes represent contextualized moral judgments about fairness and need.

There is an intriguing connection between legal labels relating to work disability and the entitlements they represent. As Estroff and her colleagues note in chapter 3, "being disabled" or "being on disability" under the SSI/SSDI entitlement programs has become the contemporary equivalent of "being an institutionalized mental patient" in the days before deinstitutionalization. Being "disabled" under the SSI/SSDI programs represents an official declaration that the person is not able to work and has the equivalent of a medical dispensation from working. But this label also carries with it a diminished social status because of the unfavored character of the excuse (for not earning one's own way as a contributing member of society).

By contrast, "disability" under the ADA is invoked as a means of signifying *equal* status. The moral premise of disability rights legislation is that disability is not a proper basis for differential treatment, particularly for exclusionary judgments based on perceived incapacities. From this perspective, being eligible for protection on grounds of disability is not stigmatizing. Despite the intended neutrality of the label, however, the social consequences of labeling under the ADA may not be entirely benign. The problem arises in the context of requests for accommodations. Special exemptions from generally applicable requirements for people with disabilities can evoke resentments similar to those that have plagued race-based affirmative action programs. From this perspective, claiming that one is "disabled" can be interpreted as a manipulative effort to gain unwarranted advantage.

Of course, neither of these legal classifications of disability is objective. Each classification represents a value-laden social judgment. Under the SSI/ SSDI programs, the underlying question is whether the recipient should be excused from working. An answer to this question is implicit in the sequential judgments of evaluating clinicians, application reviewers, administrative law judges, and ultimately of federal district judges. Similarly, the designation of a person as having a disability under the ADA signifies a social judgment that the person is fairly entitled to accommodation in the workplace and that the costs of accommodation should be shifted to the employer. Each of these conclusions is rooted in subtle moral intuitions about the person's degree of control over his or her condition and whether the supposed "impairments" constitute "symptoms" over which the person has no control rather than weaknesses of character or bad habits which he or she should be expected to change.

From this perspective, work disability has much in common with the central thematic issues in mental health law. Like "competence" and "dangerousness," "disability" represents a conflated judgment of clinical fact and moral evaluation. In the end, supposedly objective determinations of "impairment" and work-related "functional capacities" are suffused with subtle moral judgments about choice and responsibility.

IV

Because work disability is a subject of study in many disciplines, one should not be surprised to find varying uses of the same vocabulary. For example, the term *work disability* can refer to a clinical status, a legal status, or an economic status. As a clinical status, work disability refers to impairments of work-related functions. As a legal status, work disability can refer to a normative concept (the criteria that, according to the law, entitle a person to benefits) or to a social fact based on an official decision (actual receipt of benefits). As an economic status, the term *work-disabled* is typically used to refer to nonparticipation in the labor force for reasons of illness or injury, as opposed to other reasons for nonparticipation (such as age).

From both clinical and legal perspectives, one persistent source of confusion is the use of the term *disability* to refer either to a categorical concept or to a dimensional one. For example, a person may have a work-related "disability" for purposes of qualifying for protection under the ADA, but not for purposes of eligibility for workers' compensation; or a person might be disabled for workers' compensation purposes but not for purposes of qualifying for SSI/SSDI benefits. Individually, these statutory definitions reflect separate, contextually determined categorical judgments, but taken together they reveal that, for legal purposes, work disability is a dimensional concept. From a clinical perspective, work-related functional impairments are most sensibly graded in terms of severity, but categories (disabled or not) are typically used for research purposes.

Differences in vocabulary are probably inevitable in a field with diverse normative and empirical agendas, and it would be a mistake to try to impose a uniform mode of discourse. Nonetheless, certain terms have come to have general acceptance; indeed, one could summarize the recent intellectual (and legal) history of the field of work disability by tracing changes in terminology. Many of these changes are attributable to the influence of the "disability rights" movement. For example, it is now generally accepted that "people first" terminology should be used: an individual is not a "disabled person" but rather a "person with [a disability]." Further, "disability" is not a characteristic of the person; instead it is a function of the interaction of the person and the environment—the physical *or* social environment. (A person in a wheelchair does not have a disability if elevators are designed to allow such persons to reach the signals; a person who stutters does not have a disability if listeners patiently await the message.)

The terms *impairment, functional capacity* and ability and *disability* are coming to have generally accepted usage. Objectively speaking, a person may experience impairments of certain functions (as compared with a baseline of nonimpaired functioning) such as impairments of the abilities to move one's legs, to pay attention, or to see. As a result of one of these impairments, the person may have a diminished ability to perform certain job-related functions. Whether the person's ability-impairments (or "activity limitations" in the language of the ADA) actually affect job performance depends not only on the nature of the impairment, but also on the structure and conditions of the workplace and on the alignment of job functions with the person's abilities. This is why disability in general and work disability in particular are said to be contingent concepts, not characteristics of the person.

One other concept should be mentioned. The terms *impairment* and *functional limitation,* which are the predicate terms for the concept of disability, are not necessarily linked with a medical model. It is possible to speak of impairments and functional limitations directly without tying these ideas to any underlying disorder, disease, or condition. The ADA, for example, does not use medical concepts. In contrast, however, disability under the SSI/ SSDI system is linked, definitionally, to a "medically determinable" condition. The idea that a person has an underlying medical condition which causes an impairment is not strictly necessary from a logical standpoint, but the requirement of such a condition often serves the function of anchoring and validating the claim of impairment. Also, when an impairment cannot be seen or measured on its own—as is often the case with mental disorders—the condition (or diagnosis) can also serve as an empirical proxy for the legally operative impairment.

V

This book is organized in four sections. Part 1 begins with a wide-angle lens, focusing on the epidemiology of mental disorders, work disability, and labor force participation. What is the prevalence of work-related disability among people with mental disorders, in general and in relation to specific diagnoses? What proportions of such people are in the labor force? What proportions receive payments under various disability benefit programs, especially SSI/SSDI? Unfortunately, these questions cannot be answered with precise figures based on existing data sources. However, available data regarding prevalence estimates of serious mental disorder and work-related limitations among this population are presented in chapter 1 by Laura J. Milazzo-Sayre, Marilyn S. Henderson and Ronald W. Manderscheid.

In chapter 2, labor economists Edward H. Yelin and Miriam G. Cisternas analyze labor force participation by persons with mental disorders, especially in comparison with persons who have physical disorders. They address the following questions: How does labor force participation by persons with mental disorders compare with labor force participation by other persons with disabilities? What have been the trends in labor force participation among persons with mental disorders? What factors account for changes in the rates of labor force participation? Answers to these questions are potentially of enormous legal significance.

Yelin and Cisternas reach the conclusion that labor force participation is much lower among persons with mental conditions than among people with physical conditions. Although employment among people with mental conditions is affected by general market factors—when demand for labor increases, the proportion of people with disabilities who are employed increases—persons with mental conditions do not get an equal share of the job growth. Yelin and Cisternas also find that mental disability accentuates other labor market disadvantages.

Part 2 focuses on the choices made by individuals who are deciding whether to work or whether to seek disability benefits. The clinical literature on work disability consists primarily of studies of the relationships among diagnosis, work-related functioning, and receipt of SSI/SSDI benefits. What is missing is the perspective of individual choice, that is, of decisions being made by people about working or not working and applying or not applying for benefits. The relation between mental disorder and employment and/or receipt of SSI/SSDI is a product of choices made by the employees or recipients (as well as by employers or benefit administrators). People *choose* to look for work, to stay on a job despite the hardships and difficulties of coping with the symptoms of the disorder or with the insensitivities of others, to stop looking for work, to quit a job, or to seek SSI or SSDI. Although the range of available choices is determined by the overall condition of the labor market, within this probability set people decide how to live their lives.

Virtually all of the empirical literature has focused on persons with severe and persistent mental disorders. Not surprisingly, the available data pertain mainly to those who are outside the competitive labor force, and research samples have typically been drawn from populations in treatment. No systematic clinical studies are available of persons with less severe disorders, especially of those currently in the labor force. Their choices, difficulties, struggles, and adaptations have not been studied—nor have the responses of employers. This is the population most likely to benefit from the ADA, and should be a high priority for research.

The three chapters assembled in part 2 approach the issue of choice from several different angles. In chapter 3, " 'No Other Way to Go': Pathways to Disability Income Application Among Persons with Severe Persistent Mental Illness," Sue E. Estroff, Catherine Zimmer, William Lachicotte, Julia Benoit, and Donald Patrick investigate how clinical impairments, psychological and instrumental dependencies, social characteristics, and the use of mental health services interact to influence the decisions of persons with severe mental illness to apply (or not apply) for SSI/SSDI benefits. In chapter 4, "Mental Disorders, Work, and Choice," John S. Strauss and Larry Davidson focus on the role of working in psychiatric rehabilitation as part of a more general inquiry concerning the process of improvement among people with severe and persistent disorders. They aim to analyze "how the choice to work is facilitated or precluded" for persons with mental disorders, using a series of vignettes to reveal the texture of choice. Finally, in chapter 5, Richard Warner and Paul Polak approach the same question from the perspective of economic choice. In "Economic Opportunities and Disincentives for People with Mental Illness," they present findings from an exploratory study of income, expenditures, and employment among a sample of persons with severe mental illness. Their aim is to see whether and to what extent the low rate of employment among persons with serious mental illness may reflect economic disincentives to work.

Two bodies of law bear on work disability: (1) those governing compensation and benefit systems predicated on determinations that people are unable to work due to mental or physical disability, and (2) antidiscrimination laws such as §504 of the Federal Rehabilitation Act, the ADA, and equivalent state legislation aiming to facilitate access to the labor force by persons with mental or physical disabilities. The enactment of the ADA is bound to highlight and expose the tension arising at the normative borders of these two bodies of law.

Parts 3 and 4 focus on these two bodies of work disability law as they apply to people with mental disorders. Chapter 6, by Ellen Smith Pryor, is the sole chapter in part 3. "Mental Disabilities and the Disability Fabric" presents an integrated analysis of disability benefit statutes and programs, including private disability insurance, workers' compensation, the SSI/SSDI statutes, and the vocational rehabilitation program. Her overall aim is to identify the ways in which these programs differentiate between mental and physical disabilities and to assess whether these differences are justified.

All four chapters in Part 4 address the ADA. In chapter 7, "The Americans with Disabilities Act, Mental Disability, and Work," Christopher Bell, who played a significant role in drafting the ADA, surveys the employment provisions of the act in order to flag the issues that are likely to arise in connection with mental disorders. In chapter 8, Jean Campbell and Carolyn Kaufmann take a look at the ADA from a consumer perspective. In "Equality and Difference in the ADA: Unintended Consequences for Employment of People with Mental Health Disabilities," they explore the possible negative consequences of claiming protection under the ADA for persons with mental disorders. In chapter 9, "Making the ADA Work for People with Psychiatric Disabilities," Laura Lee Hall focuses on what will be needed to achieve effective implementation of the ADA for people with mental disorders. This chapter highlights key issues considered in the 1994 report by the Office of Technology Assessment (OTA) of the U.S. Congress. Finally, in chapter 10, "Mental Disabilities, Equal Opportunity, and the ADA," philosopher Norman Daniels explores the ethical foundations of the ADA, especially as it applies to persons with mental disorders.

PART 1

Mental Disorder and Labor Force
Participation: An Epidemiological Perspective

In qualitative terms, it is easy to describe the empirical relation between mental disorder and work disability. (1) Although a diagnosis of mental disorder must be predicated upon distress or dysfunction, many people with diagnosed mental disorders do not have any significant work-related impairment. (2) Among people with the most serious mental disorders, the most incapacitating symptoms are virtually always associated with work-related impairment. (3) Among people with work-related impairments, the connection to labor force participation is a contingent one: Whether a person's work-related impairment is substantial enough to limit or preclude competitive employment depends on the employment environment and the demands of particular jobs, as well as on the abilities and functional limitations of the individual.

The conceptual connections among mental disorder, work disability, and pertinent legal constructs are also readily drawn. (1) Not all people with mental disorders have a "disability" for purposes of the Americans with Disabilities Act and similar antidiscrimination legislation because many such individuals do not have a significant activity limitation (and are not perceived as having one). (2) Among persons with mental disorders who *do* have sufficient functional limitations to be characterized as having a disability under the ADA, these limitations may not impair job-related abilities at all or may be ameliorated by workplace accommodations. (3) However, among a subset of people with the most severe mental disorders, job-related functional limitations are so pronounced as to preclude "gainful employment" and thereby to make the person eligible for disability benefits under the federal SSI/SSDI programs. In this sense, people who have a "work disability" for purposes of the federal SSI/SSDI program are a subset of those who have a disability for purposes of the ADA, who are in turn a subset of people with diagnosable mental disorders.

Despite the relative clarity of these relationships, their quantitative dimensions have not been well described. Most studies of work-related disability and employment have focused on the most severely disabled people, that is, those in the public services system and recipients of SSI/SSDI benefits. However, we lack studies of the work abilities and experience of the general population which differentiate among people with and without diagnosed mental disorders. Although recent population-based studies of the prevalence of mental disorders have produced some pertinent information, precise data on the prevalence of (and nature of) work-related disability and labor force participation among people with various types of disorders are not available.

The following two chapters aim to summarize and interpret the quantitative information that is now available. In the first chapter, Milazzo-Sayre, Henderson, and Manderscheid summarize pertinent data from the available epidemiological databases in order to provide prevalence estimates of severe mental disorders (the closest proxy for the population covered by the ADA), and to describe the work-related limitations experienced by persons with such disorders. In the next chapter, Yelin and Cisternas use the most comprehensive database now available to analyze labor force participation by persons with mental disorders, especially in comparison with persons who have physical disorders.

1 Serious and Severe Mental Illness and Work: What Do We Know?

LAURA J. MILAZZO-SAYRE, MARILYN J. HENDERSON, AND RONALD W. MANDERSCHEID

This chapter describes efforts to measure the population of persons with what are termed *serious* or *severe* mental illness, presents estimates for this population from various epidemiological and treatment studies, and discusses the involvement of such persons in the employment sector as reported in research studies. Finally, we discuss the implications of this information for vocational rehabilitation programs and suggest ways to improve survey methodology in order to produce more useful information about the population most likely to be affected by the Americans with Disabilities Act (ADA).

Defining Persons with Severe Mental Disorder

Historically, estimation of the number of persons with severe mental disorder has been problematic because of a variety of definitional issues. Prior to the period of deinstitutionalization, this population was viewed as coextensive with residents of state mental hospitals. This concept served to orient much of the definitional work done in the past fifteen years. After deinstitutionalization, it became difficult to enumerate the population because its members were located in a broad range of community and institutional settings, some of which were very difficult to access (e.g., homeless persons on the street). Arriving at a consensual definition of the population is especially difficult because all definitions are, of necessity, different combinations of medical (e.g., diagnostic assessment) and social (e.g., community functioning assessment) criteria.

The major initial effort to define the population was undertaken by Goldman, Gattozzi, and Taube (1981) as part of the development of the *National Plan for the Chronically Mentally Ill* (DHHS 1981). Their definition was based on three criteria: diagnosis, disability, and duration. They provided a detailed definition of the chronically mentally ill population as encompassing "persons who suffer certain mental or emotional disorders (organic brain syndrome, schizophrenia, recurrent depressive and manic-depressive disorders that may become chronic) that erode or prevent the development of their functional capacities in relation to three or more primary aspects of daily life—personal hygiene and self-care, self-direction, interpersonal relationships, social transactions, learning, and recreation—and that erode or prevent the development of their economic self-sufficiency." Duration included functional incapacity that lasted or was expected to last one year or longer. The conceptual and operational work undertaken for the *National Plan* has influenced virtually all subsequent work.

As the definition of the target population and its operationalization have evolved over time, a shift has occurred in the terminology applied to this population as well. Until the middle 1980s, the population was known as the *chronically mentally ill*. Because this was perceived as a pejorative label, new terms were introduced, including *severely and persistently mentally ill* and the *severely disabled mentally ill*. In general, the population referred to by these three phrases was considered to be equivalent. More recently, *persons with serious mental illness* has been introduced into the field and into federal legislation. Although the relationship of this term to the others has not been fully operationalized, some consensus exists that it refers to a somewhat broader population than was encompassed by the terms previously used. Usually, the category is understood to be less restrictive in duration of illness (e.g., it includes persons who have been ill for less than one year) and in the nature and intensity of the disability (e.g., episodic disability is included).

The Center for Mental Health Services (CMHS) of the Substance Abuse and Mental Health Services Administration (SAMHSA) published the current, broader definition of "adults with a serious mental illness" in the Federal Register for 20 May 1993 (vol. 58, no. 96). The CMHS definition includes "persons age 18 and over, who currently or at any time during the past year, have had a diagnosable mental, behavioral, or emotional disorder of sufficient duration to meet diagnostic criteria specified within DMS-III-R, that has resulted in functional impairment which substantially interferes with or limits one or more major life activities" (SAMHSA 1993). This definition is much broader in diagnostic terms than previous definitions discussed, with the emphasis on functional impairment resulting from any diagnosable disorder. It includes a much larger group of persons than those who traditionally have been considered to have severe mental disorder. This broader definition will serve as the basis for the development of standardized methodologies to determine the prevalence and incidence of serious mental illness in adults and serious emotional disturbance in children and adolescents for use by the states.

A technical workgroup, convened by the CMHS, is currently deciding how to operationalize the definition for "serious mental disorder" using data from two major sources: the Baltimore site of the Epidemiological Catchment Area Program (ECA) and the National Comorbidity Study (NCS). The ECA was a major survey sponsored by the National Institute of Mental Health (NIMH) in collaboration with five research sites to collect prevalence and incidence data on mental disorders among adults in the United States population from 1980 to 1985. This was a landmark epidemiological survey that allowed for estimation of discrete diagnoses based on interviews with over twenty thousand respondents using the Diagnostic Interview Schedule (DIS), which can be administered by trained interviewers who are not clinicians. The 1992 NCS was an NIMH-sponsored nationwide sample survey of eight thousand households (including all persons ages 15–54). It was the first survey to administer a structured psychiatric interview to a national probability sample of households in the United States. The NCS, directed by Dr. Ronald C. Kessler of the University of Michigan, employed a revised version of the Composite International Diagnostic Interview, the next generation of the DIS.

The technical work being completed by the CMHS using these two major databases, in collaboration with Dr. Philip Leaf (ECA, Baltimore site) and Dr. Ronald Kessler, will further refine our ability to understand the size and characteristics of the population most likely to be affected by the ADA. Given the current lack of data on this population, however, the analyses that follow focus on the population with "severe" mental disorder. Although this group tends to be a better indicator of the SSI/SSDI population, it currently represents the closest proxy for the group of persons entitled to ADA protection.

Prevalence Estimates from Epidemiological Surveys

To put the size of the population in context, the ECA study indicates that 28% of the U.S. adult population have a diagnosable mental or addictive disorder in a one-year period (51.3 million persons in 1990); that 14.7% of the population receive any mental health service; and that 5.9% of the population receive this care in the specialty mental health/substance-abuse sector. Of those receiving any mental health service, 55% have a current diagnosis, with most of the remaining 45% having had a past diagnosis or having significant psychiatric symptomatology. Twenty-two percent of the population have a mental disorder exclusive of substance use disorders. One-third of those with substance use disorders also suffer from a comorbid mental disorder within the same year. These figures, derived from data collected through the ECA (Bourden et al. 1994), indicate the overall extent of mental and substance use disorders within the adult population.

Data from the ECA also were used to estimate the number of adults with a "severe" mental disorder. An estimated 2.8% of the adult population (approximately 5 million persons in 1990) experience a severe mental disorder in a one-year period. Severe mental disorder is defined here according to the criteria of the U.S. Senate Committee on Appropriations and includes disorders commonly accompanied by psychotic symptoms such as schizophrenia, schizoaffective disorder, manic-depressive disorder, and autism, as well as severe forms of other disorders such as major depression, panic disorder, and obsessive-compulsive disorder. (Detailed methods for operationalizing this definition are provided in the report [National Advisory Mental Health Council 1993].)

Estimates similar to those of the ECA study have emerged recently from the 1992 NCS. Results from this survey indicate that severe mental disorders (defined in accord with the Committee on Appropriations criteria) affect 3.2% of household members 15–54 years of age (National Advisory Mental Health Council 1993).

Prevalence Estimates from Household Surveys

Over time, surveys have been conducted that enable us to provide estimates of the number of persons in households with "severe" mental disorder. In 1978, the Bureau of the Census under the sponsorship of the Social Security Administration (SSA) conducted a Survey of Disability and Work that yielded estimates of persons in households who were severely disabled as a result of mental illness. In this survey, SSA estimated that 1.1 million persons in households in the age range of 20–64 were severely mentally disabled. Estimates were based on fairly narrowly defined criteria for disability, duration, and diagnosis. Disability included limitations in the work/housework dimension; duration included only those currently disabled and/or who had been or were expected to be disabled for twelve months; diagnosis included only self-report of "mental illness" and "nervous or emotional problems" (Ashbaugh et al. 1983).

The 1978 SSA estimates were updated through the 1989 National Health Interview Survey (NHIS), Mental Health Supplement, which was conducted by the National Center for Health Statistics in collaboration with the National Institute of Mental Health (NIMH). This household survey employed a much more flexible definition of "severe mental disorder" than the earlier SSA survey, including "any psychiatric disorder present during the past year that seriously interfered with one or more aspects of a person's daily life" (Barker et al. 1992). Diagnosis was obtained using a checklist of selected mental disorders which included specific severe disorders (schizophrenia, paranoid or delusional disorders other than schizophrenia, manic episodes or bipolar disorder, major depression, severe personality disorders, and Alzheimer's disease). In addition, respondents were asked a separate question regarding the existence of "any other mental or emotional disorder" (not included in the checklist) that seriously interfered with a person's ability to work or attend school, or to manage their daily activities during the past twelve months. Responses to these two questions defined the group of persons diagnosed with severe mental disorders.

Among these persons, disability was measured through questions about activity limitations and receipt of Supplemental Security Income (SSI) or Social Security Disability Insurance (SSDI). Duration was measured by asking about the length of limitation due to the mental disorder. Restrictions placed upon respondents by the way questions were asked during the interviews resulted in the targeting of a more disabled (or severe) population than is conveyed by the term *serious,* even though that term was employed within the survey itself. From this NHIS survey, 3.3 million persons 18 years of age or older within the household population were estimated to have a severe mental disorder, and approximately 2.6 million of these had one or more limitations in daily functioning due to their disorder at the time of interview. These findings for the adult household population, together with findings derived from both institutional and community residential settings, suggest that a conservative estimate of the prevalence of severe mental disorders in the United States would be approximately 4 to 5 million adults, or between 2.1 and 2.6% of the adult population (Barker et al. 1992).

Prevalence of Persons Treated

Information from the Community Support Program (CSP), (formerly a program within the NIMH; currently administered within the CMHS) is useful in understanding the most severely disabled population. The CSP model is intended to provide services to the most severely disabled population of persons with mental disorder. Support systems are set up whereby case managers broker a variety of services, including psychiatric, medical, housing, and social supports (Mulkern and Manderscheid, 1989). In the CSP, duration included "an episode of hospitalization within the last 5 years lasting at least 6 months; or 2 or more hospitalizations within a 12-month period."

As part of the evaluation of this program, the CSP participated in two surveys in 1980 and 1984 that provided initial information about persons served through the program. The 1980 survey tested the Uniform Client Data Instrument (UCDI), which was used to collect data on a random sample of 1,471 persons from the seventeen sites in operation at the time. The 1984 survey was a multisite follow-up using a revised UCDI. The follow-up sample was drawn from eighteen sites and resulted in 1,053 sample cases. [For detailed discussion of each survey's design and procedures, see Mulkern and Manderscheid (1989).] Estimates from these surveys show that approximately 4,288 persons received services through the CSP in 1980, increasing to an estimated 350,000 persons in 1984 as the CSP grew in scope.

The following sections highlight the labor force participation and federal income support of persons with severe mental disorders. Both household (1989 NHIS) and service-based (CSP) estimates are described to illustrate level of disability among persons with severe mental disorders.

Employment Status of Persons with Severe Mental Disorder

Estimates from Service-Based Studies

A majority of persons (75%) with severe mental disorder in the 1984 CSP sample were unemployed (table 1). Of the 25% of clients employed at the time of the survey, a majority held competitive or supported jobs, worked in

Table 1 Employment Status of Clients in the Community Support Program in 1984

Employment	Percent
Currently employed	25
Job type	
Competitive	34
Transitional	13
Work training	10
Sheltered workshop	33
Volunteer	6
Other	4
Job skill level	
Unskilled	73
Semiskilled or skilled manual	14
Clerical	11
Administrative or professional	2
Currently unemployed	75
Actively seeking work	6
Reason unemployed	
Temporary layoff	3
Physical disability	6
Mental disability	76
Retiree, student, or homemaker	13
Other	3
Mean hours worked per week	21.8
Mean months since last job	54.6

Source: National Institute of Mental Health (NIMH), 1984 Survey of Client Support Programs (CSP).

unskilled occupations, and worked on a part-time basis, an average of about 22 hours per week (Mulkern and Manderscheid 1989). This employment figure is nearly identical to the 26% employment rate found in the 1980 CSP survey (Goldstrom and Manderscheid 1982).

The persistence of joblessness among persons with severe mental illness is indicated by the average period of joblessness for the 1984 CSP survey clients: 54.6 months, or approximately four and a half years. As table 1 shows, 76% of these 1984 unemployed clients were currently unemployed due to their mental disability, and only 6% of the unemployed clients were actively seeking work at the time of the study.

Estimates From Household-Based Studies

A significant finding of the 1984 CSP study was the magnitude of unemployment among persons who were severely disabled as a result of mental disorder. It is interesting to compare employment information for this target population enrolled within mental health service programs with information about persons with severe mental disorder identified in a household population. Table 2 presents data from the 1989 NHIS supplement described previously. In this household-based survey, a much lower percentage (29%) of the household population with severe mental disorder was unemployed due to mental disability. The lower percentage among this population is not surprising for two reasons. First, one of the criteria for service within the CSP includes unemployment or difficulty with employment (Ashbaugh et al. 1983); second, a greater proportion of severely disabled persons would predictably be found in a service use population than in a household population. Clearly, however, both the service-based population estimates and the household estimates point to substantial unemployment among persons with severe mental disorder.

Table 2 Current Work-Limitation Status of Persons 18–69 Years of Age with Severe Mental Disorder

Work-Limitation Status	Number (thousands)	Percent
Total	2,874	100
Total with work limitation due to severe mental illness	1,358	47
Unable to work	829	29
Limited in work	529	18
No current work limitation	1,032	36
Does not work for other reasons or work-limitation status unknown	485	17

Source: National Center for Health Statistics (NCHS), 1989 National Health Interview Survey (NHIS).

Table 3 Percent Distribution of Current Work-Limitation Status and Other Limitations of Persons 18–69 Years of Age with Severe Mental Disorder

	Total	Unable to Work	Limited in Work	No Current Work Limitation	Does Not Work for Other Reasons or Work-Limitation Status Unknown
Any other limitation	75	94	91	58	59
Personal care activities of daily living	3	8	3	—	—
Instrumental activities of daily living	23	49	30	5	10
Social functioning	46	70	61	27	31
Coping with day-to-day stress	68	86	80	53	54
Concentrating long enough to complete tasks	46	73	67	21	32

Source: National Center for Health Statistics (NCHS), 1989 National Health Interview Survey (NHIS).

Table 2 shows that of the 2.9 million persons ages 18–69 with severe mental disorder identified in the 1989 Mental Health Supplement to the NHIS, 36% had no current work limitation. This suggests that while labor force participation is an important measure of the severity of disability among persons with severe mental disorder, it is not the only indicator of functional limitations in this population. Table 3 shows that among persons with severe mental disorder who were unable to work due to their mental illness, 94% reported having an additional limitation; 86%, difficulty coping with day-to-day stress; 73%, difficulty with task concentration; 70%, difficulty with social functioning; and almost half (49%), difficulty with instrumental activities of daily living.

Among persons limited in their work activity but not precluded from working due to their mental illness, 91% reported having an additional limitation, with somewhat lower percentages occurring within each limitation category (see table 3). More than half (58%) of persons 18–69 years of age with severe mental disorder and no current work limitation at the time of the study reported having another limitation. For this particular risk group, 53% reported having difficulty coping with day-to-day stress, and 27% had difficulty with social functioning. The degree of difficulty within any limitation can be episodic for this risk-group population; hence, someone who was not experiencing difficulty at the time of the interview might have experienced difficulty at other times.

Federal Support for Persons with Severe Mental Disorder

The experiences of persons with severe mental disorder under the federal income-support programs created to provide assistance to disabled populations should also be examined. In 1984, a majority of clients in the Community Support Program were enrolled in a federal income support program (see table 4). Of these, 20% received Social Security Disability Insurance (SSDI), and 44% received Supplemental Security Income (SSI). In 1980, in comparison, 40% of the CSP clients received SSDI, and 50% received SSI (Goldstrom and Manderscheid 1982). This apparent decrease in the amount of federal income support for CSP clients between 1980 and 1984 should be viewed cautiously, however, due to the dramatic increase in the number of CSP clients during this time period.

Data from the 1989 NHIS indicate that approximately 703,000 (23%) of persons with severe mental disorder in the adult household population received a government disability payment because of their mental illness. Almost 98% of the adults who received such payments had current limitations due to severe mental disorder (Barker et al. 1992). While 46% of those who received disability payments for mental illness reported receiving SSDI and almost 44% reported receiving SSI, 77% of persons currently limited by severe mental illness received no government disability payment at all. We might expect that the disparity between the CSP service population and the NHIS household population in terms of enrollment within SSI/SSDI would be due to the severity of condition within the CSP service population, and to the assistance of service providers in initiating and pursuing the application process. It is unclear from a comparison of these two populations, however,

Table 4 Source of Income for Clients in the Community Support Program in 1984

Income	Percent
Earnings	16
Social Security retirement	11
Social Security Disability Insurance	20
Supplemental Security Income	44
Armed Services disability	3
Social welfare	29
Vocational training	5
Family or spouse	11
Other	11
Mean monthly income	$429

Source: National Institute of Mental Health (NIMH), 1984 Survey of Client Support Programs (CSP).

how persons with severe mental illness fared over time with respect to federal income assistance.

Analysis of data from the Social Security Administration's SSI/SSDI recipient files over the period 1986–1991 (Kennedy and Manderscheid 1992) indicates a larger increase in the number of persons with mental illness on the recipient rolls than in the total number of recipients. Although changes in 1985 to the criteria by which mental illness was assessed made it somewhat easier to obtain benefits, it is clear that increasing numbers of persons with mental illness are relying on federal disability insurance programs for support.

Implications for Vocational Rehabilitation

Epidemiological data depict a sizable population of persons with severe mental disorder, the latest estimate from the NCS being 3.2% of the household population aged 15–54. The data show that this population is beset by a variety of other activity limitations in addition to work-related ones. It is clear that attempts to provide vocational training for this population must take into account social skills, coping mechanisms, and daily living skills. Even when they have gained the vocational skills necessary to fill a position, evidence shows that persons with severe mental disorder may not know how to apply for a job and may lack the interview skills needed to succeed in the application process (Liberman et al. 1987).

Persons with severe mental disorder experience not only functional limitations that affect their capacity to work, but also external barriers to employment opportunities, including stigma and discrimination because of their illness. Mental health workers and vocational rehabilitation counselors, therefore, must be trained to meet the growing needs of persons with mental illness as they attempt to remove the barriers to economic self-sufficiency through implementation of the Americans with Disabilities Act (Zuckerman 1993).

Future Directions

A primary goal of vocational rehabilitation for people with mental disorder is to reduce the functional limitations of the disability and to empower individuals to be gainfully employed. Opportunities to enter the workforce will expand with the implementation of the Americans with Disabilities Act throughout the 1990s. As the mental health field identifies new drugs and other treatments for mental disorders, the number of Americans with psychiatric disabilities who can profit from vocational rehabilitation will increase dramatically. The principles that are important to advancing the vocational situation of this population include access to effective services, consumer involvement, the availability and integration of other services and supports, accommodation in the workplace, and dissemination and utilization of knowledge (Manderscheid 1991).

The CMHS is now assisting states to develop standardized methodologies for estimating the incidence and prevalence of persons with serious mental disorder within their jurisdictions. This initiative is a critical first step in the development of comprehensive public and private service systems for this population. Refinement of diagnostic instrumentation and development of measures of functioning for persons with severe and serious mental disorder through epidemiological studies, such as the ECA Survey and National Comorbidity Study, will provide the mental health field with the research necessary to address critical issues facing persons with severe mental disorder as they participate in and become empowered for the basic tasks of living and employment.

References

Ashbaugh, J. W., P. L. Leaf, R. W. Manderscheid et al. 1983. Estimates of the Size and Selected Characteristics of the Adult Chronically Mentally Ill Population Living in U.S. Households. *Research in Community Mental Health* 3: 3–24.

Barker, P. R., R. W. Manderscheid, G. E. Hendershot et al. 1992. Serious Mental Illness and Disability in the Adult Household Population: United States, 1989. *Advance Data From Vital and Health Statistics,* no. 218. Hyattsville, MD: National Center for Health Statistics.

Bourden, K. H., D. S. Rae, W. E. Narrow et al. 1994. National Prevalence and Treatment of Mental and Addictive Disorders. In R. W. Manderscheid and M. A. Sonnenschein, eds., DHHS Pub. No. (SMA)94-3000. Washington DC: Supt. of Docs., GPO.

SAMHSA. 1993. Substance Abuse and Mental Health Services Administration, Center for Mental Health Services. Children with Serious Emotional Disturbance, and Adults with Serious Mental Illness; Definitions. *Federal Register* 58(96): 29422–29425.

DHHS. 1991. Department of Health and Human Services Steering Committee on the Chronically Mentally Ill. *Toward a National Plan for the Chronically Mentally Ill: Report to the Secretary.* DHHS Pub. No. (ADM)81-1077. Washington DC: Supt. of Docs., GPO.

Goldman, H. H., A. A. Gattozzi, and C. A. Taube. 1981. Defining and Counting the Chronically Mentally Ill. *Hospital and Community Psychiatry* 32(1): 21–27.

Goldstrom, I. D., and R. W. Manderscheid. 1982. The Chronically Mentally Ill: A Descriptive Analysis from the Uniform Client Data Instrument. *Community Support Service Journal* 2(3): 4–9.

Kennedy, C., and R. W. Manderscheid. 1992. SSDI and SSI Disability Beneficiaries with Mental Disorders. In R. W. Manderscheid and M. A. Sonnenschein, eds., DHHS Pub. No. (SMA)92-1942. Washington DC: Supt. of Docs., GPO.

Liberman, R. P., H. E. Jacobs, G. A. Blackwell et al. 1987. Overcoming Psychiatric Disability through Skills Training. In A. T. Meyerson and T. F. Fine, eds., *Psychiatric Disability: Clinical, Legal, and Administrative Dimensions*. Washington DC: American Psychiatric Press.

Manderscheid, R. W. 1991. Vocational Rehabilitation for Persons with Psychiatric Disabilities: A Vision for the Year 2000. Unpublished manuscript.

Mulkern, V. M., and R. W. Manderscheid. 1989. Characteristics of Community Support Program Clients in 1980 and 1984. *Hospital and Community Psychiatry* 40(2): 165–172.

National Advisory Mental Health Council. 1993. Health Care Reform for Americans with Severe Mental Illnesses: Report of the National Advisory Mental Health Council. *American Journal of Psychiatry* 150(10): 1447–1465.

Zuckerman, D. 1993. Reasonable Accommodations for People with Mental Illness Under the ADA. *Mental and Physical Disability Law Reporter* 17(3): 311–320.

2

Employment Patterns among Persons with and without Mental Conditions

EDWARD H. YELIN, AND MIRIAM G. CISTERNAS

The employment prospects of persons with disabilities, including those with mental conditions, have recently moved to the center of public policy concern. Fueled by periodic surges in the number of beneficiaries of disability compensation programs and by the fear that an aging population necessarily brings a pandemic of disability, this concern usually manifests itself negatively in attempts to stem malingering by reducing disability benefits. However, the passage of the Americans with Disabilities Act of 1990 and the more recent reauthorization of the Rehabilitation Act of 1973 put employment issues among persons with disabilities in a more positive light, presenting them in terms of empowerment, independence, and community.

As a result of the renewed interest in employment among all persons with disabilities, we know much more about how such persons fare in work than we did a decade ago, and we know much more about why. Despite the growing interest in employment among persons with mental conditions, however, research in this area has been limited to small-scale clinical studies and some preliminary analyses of community-based data from the five local sites in the Epidemiologic Catchment Area Study (ECA).

In part, the lack of data reflects methodological problems in defining what a mental condition is, in developing ways of collecting such information in a reliable manner, and in finding all those who meet criteria for each condition. But it also reflects the expectation that, as a result of undeserved stigma or objective impairment, society cannot do much to improve the employability of persons with mental conditions.

In this paper we provide some preliminary national data on employment among persons with mental conditions living in the community. In doing so, we take it as a given that the problems of many, if not most, persons with mental disorders, do not necessarily dictate a permanent withdrawal from work. This is not to say that those with severe mental impairments will eventually work; however, the symptoms of most persons with mental conditions are not invariably severe enough to *preclude* work. As evidence, we present data showing that employment rates did change substantially over a relatively short time, though the level of impairment did not. We also take it as a given that volition plays a part in decisions regarding work among persons with mental conditions, but that the level of disability benefits is not the only volitional factor affecting their employment and may not be the most important one.

The contentious debate about the role of disability compensation notwithstanding, changes in the labor market—who works and in what kind of jobs—have a far more profound impact on the employment of persons with disabilities in general and those with mental impairments in particular. Thus, we are concerned to show how changes in the employment of persons with mental conditions correlate with more general trends in the labor market, and what these trends portend for the immediate future.

The Plan of the Essay

To provide first estimates of labor force participation among persons with mental conditions, we draw upon a decade of data from the National Health Interview Survey (NHIS), which is an annual survey of a sample of the U.S. population living in the community. The strength of the NHIS derives from its systematic sampling of the population; its weakness stems from its reliance on self-report measures of mental conditions and disability.

In the section to follow, we discuss how the design of the NHIS affects our estimates of employment among persons with mental conditions. Subsequently, we review the community-based and clinical studies of employment among these persons which suggest that the mental disorder itself may be the most important single factor affecting their work, but indicate that labor market factors, especially work history, profoundly affect their employment prospects. This sets the stage for our analysis of how trends in the overall labor market delimit their work status. In the next section, we describe these overall labor market trends, showing that the expansion of work opportunities during the 1980s did benefit persons with disabilities. We then demonstrate that, *on average,* persons with mental conditions shared in this growth in employment opportunities, although not all of them saw their employment opportunities expand. Turning next to an analysis of how persons with mental conditions fit into more general labor market trends, we show that mental disorders accentuate the separate effects of age, gender, race, and disability status on employment, rendering persons with these conditions even less likely to work than those disadvantaged in the labor market because of age, gender, or disabilities associated with chronic conditions. We conclude by demonstrating that the social and demographic characteristics which place some people at severe disadvantage in the labor market operate even more strongly among those with mental conditions, suggesting that the presence of a mental condition makes a bad employment situation much worse than would be indicated by either the mental condition or the social and demographic characteristics alone.

A Note on Methods

The National Health Interview Survey collects data by structured interview on about one hundred thousand individuals living in forty thousand households in the continental United States. Respondents provide data on medical conditions in two ways. First, they are asked if they have each condition from an explicit checklist. Second, they report whether they are limited in what they do, or have been to a doctor or hospital. If so, they are asked what medical condition resulted in the limitation (hereafter, disability), doctor visit, or hospital admission. Mental conditions are not part of an explicit checklist; thus, the report of these conditions is limited to those with disability or medical encounters (Kovar and Poe 1985). As a result of a one-time supplement, we know that this reduces the prevalence estimates by about 15%, primarily by eliminating the mildest cases (Barker, Manderscheid et al. 1992). This would tend to bias estimates of employment downward, since those without disability or medical encounters would be more likely to work. Similarly, the stigma of mental conditions would result in an underreporting of the prevalence of these conditions. This underreporting would also tend to bias estimates of employment downward, since those who can hide mental disorders probably have mild conditions.

On the other hand, persons with mental conditions are more likely than those with physical conditions to have cognitive problems or to be too mobile for interview, precluding their inclusion in the sample. The omission of such persons would probably bias estimates of employment upward, since persons with cognition problems and those too mobile for interview would be less likely to work. Similarly, persons with mental conditions have high rates of institutionalization, and since the NHIS is limited to those living in the community, it omits those living in institutions, biasing estimates of employment upwards.

We have no way of calculating the extent to which these limitations in the NHIS offset each other. The cautious strategy would be to view the estimates of employment provided here as an accurate indication of labor force participation *among those captured by the NHIS*, but not a true measure of overall employment among those with mental conditions. We do believe the sampling frame of the NHIS captures those persons with mental conditions on whom employment programs would focus, that is, those with disease neither too mild to cause risk of work loss, nor too severe to preclude work.

Although the NHIS includes about one hundred thousand respondents each year, the number with mental conditions is still too small to provide reliable estimates of employment for single years. Fortunately, the NHIS was designed so that researchers can average across years to increase the stability of estimates. To calculate time-trends in labor force participation among persons with mental conditions, we have averaged two five-year periods. To calculate labor force participation rates for persons with mental conditions and different combinations of ages, genders, and races, we have averaged ten years of data. In all analyses, we have used the sampling weights which permit inferences for the entire working age population of the United States.

The NHIS incorporated the ICD-9 definitions of mental conditions (based on the DSM-III) in 1982 (National Center for Health Statistics 1982). Thus, data on the prevalence of mental conditions are only comparable for the ten-year period through 1991, the last year for which public use tapes of the NHIS were currently available when this chapter was written.

What Is Known about Employment among Persons with Mental Conditions

Community-Based Studies

All prior estimates of the employment impacts of mental conditions using community-based data derive from the Epidemiologic Catchment Area (ECA) program (Eaton et al. 1984). The ECA program collected information from a stratified, random sample of persons in five different areas of the country representing a range of living environments: New Haven, St. Louis, Baltimore, Los Angeles, and Durham, North Carolina. Using data from the Durham site, Broadhead et al. (1990) reported labor force participation rates of persons with major depressive disorders, minor depression, and dysthymia, finding that the first two groups were much less likely to work than asymptomatic individuals, and the last group was about as likely to do so.

Using data from all five sites of the ECA study, Johnson, Weissman, and Klerman (1992) reported that persons with depressive disorders and those with depressive symptoms were, respectively, about seven times and three times as likely to lose more than a week of work per year than those with neither depressive disorders or symptoms. Similarly, Mitchell and Anderson (1989) found that symptoms of mental disorder significantly reduce employment rates among older women and men and may, in fact, be the strongest single determinant of employment status among such persons. They also reported that military service increases the probability of alcoholism, drug abuse, and other mental conditions except depression, and that these higher rates entirely account for the lower labor force participation rates of veterans (Anderson and Mitchell 1990). Mullahy and Sindelar (1989) have noted that early onset of alcoholism and other mental health conditions reduce the probability of employment in white collar, service, and blue collar jobs, and reduce long-term earnings. Thus, these first studies using community-based data concur in finding that persons with mental conditions are less likely to work than those without mental conditions, and they have begun the process of explaining why this is so.

Studies Using Clinical Samples

In the largest and most comprehensive of the studies using clinical samples, Wells and colleagues (1989) used data from the Medical Outcomes Study to compare "role" function (work for working-age persons) of persons with and without depressive disorders and symptoms, finding that the groups with depressive disorders and symptoms functioned about 10% more poorly. The similarity of their results and those of the ECA studies suggests that bias due to clinical sampling may be minimal, which in turn suggests that findings from clinical samples may generally apply to the community at large.

Anthony and Jansen (1984) observed that the strongest predictors of work outcomes for those with mental illness are the previous employment history and the work-adjustment skill of the individual. Likewise, Jacobs et al. (1992) reported that a previous work history, especially when combined with a nonpsychotic condition, improves the chance of employment. Of note for the present study, Bacani-Oropilla et al. (1991) found that, among all persons with mental conditions, those with schizophrenic conditions were less likely to work, and those with affective disorders more likely to do so. Yelin and colleagues (1995) also found that persons with anxiety disorders or symptoms had employment rates that were comparable to those of persons without anxiety. Similarly, Vogel and colleagues (1989) found that persons with schizophrenia were likely to experience worsening symptoms in the presence of stressful employment, while the symptoms of those with affective disorders improved. Thus, persons with affective disorders actually may fare well in work, especially if they have established a work history prior to the onset of the condition.

The studies from clinical samples include much more detail about work and work history than the community-based studies, and concur in showing that labor market characteristics largely condition whether an individual will be employed after onset of a mental condition, though the mental condition itself may be the most important single factor. The present paper integrates the two sets of studies by analyzing the impact of the labor market characteristics in the context of a community-based sampling frame.

Labor Market Trends: Quantitative Analysis

In contrast to our major economic competitors, the United States has accommodated substantial growth in the absolute number and proportion of working-age adults in the labor force. In the ten-year period ending in 1991, the labor force participation rate of working-age adults grew by 19%, or almost twice as fast as the 10% growth in the total number of working age adults. This growth provided employment opportunities for 9.3 million more individuals than would have been working had the labor force participation rate not increased. Although the recession has eroded some of these gains, the labor force participation rate remains much higher than at the beginning of the 1980s, and much higher than in any other major industrial power (U.S. Department of Labor 1993).

The increases in the labor force participation rate were not distributed evenly through the population. Instead, they occurred disproportionately among women, especially young women (Yelin 1992). Figure 1 charts the trends in labor force participation. Overall, the labor force participation rate among all U.S. working age adults increased from 68% in 1982, at the end of a severe recession, to a peak of 75% in the years 1988 through 1990, or by 10% in relative terms. It has since receded slightly to 74%—still a 9% increase over the 1982 level.

Men shared in the overall gains, experiencing slightly more than a 6% relative increase in labor force participation rate between 1982 and the years 1987 through 1988, when employment peaked, and 4% after the effects of the recent recession are taken into account. However, the increase in labor

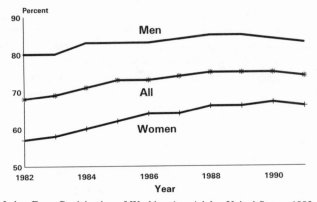

Figure 1 Labor Force Participation of Working-Age Adults: United States, 1982–91.

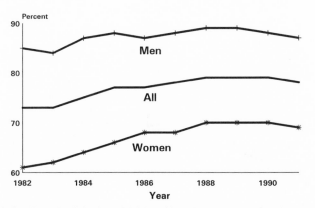

Figure 2   Labor Force Participation of Adults without Disabilities: United States, 1982–91.

force participation occurred disproportionately among women. Labor force participation rates among women increased from 57% in 1982 to 66% in 1991, or by 16% in relative terms. As recently as 1970, only half of working-age women had been in the labor force (U.S. Bureau of the Census 1992). These employment gains among women profoundly altered the composition of the labor force. The ratio of female to male labor force participation rates increased from .71 in 1982 to .80 in 1990 and 1991. As a result, women now make up over 45% of all working-age adults in the labor force.

Employment patterns among working-age adults without disabilities fit these more general labor market trends (figure 2). Among all working-age men without disabilities, labor force participation increased from 85% in 1982 to a peak of 89% in 1988 and 1989, or by 5% in relative terms. Net of the decrease due to the recession, labor force participation among men without disabilities remained 2% higher in 1991 than 1982. Working-age women without disabilities experiencd substantially larger relative growth in employment than men, their labor force participation rates rising from 61% in 1982 to 70% in the years 1988 through 1990. Even after taking the effects of the recession into account, in 1991 women without disabilities were 13% more likely to be in the labor force than in 1982. Overall, working-age persons without disabilities saw their labor force participation rates rise by more than 8% prior to the recent recession, and by about 7% when the impact of the recession is taken into account.

The overall expansion of the labor market did benefit working-age adults with disabilities, especially women (figure 3). Among women with disabilities, the proportion in the labor force rose steadily from 32% in 1982 to 43% in 1990 and 1991, or by 30% in relative terms, roughly twice the rate of increase experienced by women without disabilities. The situation among men with disabilities was more complex. Such men did see their labor force

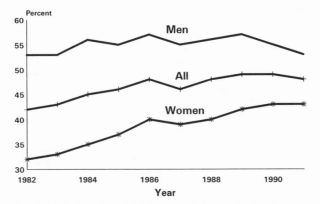

Figure 3 Labor Force Participation of Adults with Disabilities: United States, 1982–91.

participation rates rise by about 8% prior to 1989, though all of the gain has since eroded. Whether another period of economic expansion will again initiate an improvement in their work situation remains to be seen, though in general those displaced from work during the recent recession have had a difficult time finding employment (U.S. Department of Labor 1993).

As a result of the improvement in the employment rate of women with disabilities, the ratio of female to male labor force participation among persons with disabilities increased from .60 in 1982 to .81 in 1991. Prior to the downturn affecting men with disabilities that began in 1989, the ratio had risen to .74, still a substantial increase. Net of the increase among women with disabilities, and the stasis among men with disabilities, overall labor force participation rates among working-age adults with disabilities increased by 17% prior to the recession and by more than 14% over the entire period. These increases were more than twice those experienced by persons without disabilities during this time, and represent a substantial change from prior periods, during which gains among persons with disabilities lagged behind those among persons without disabilities (Yelin 1989).

A growing labor force clearly improves the employment situation of persons with disabilities, at least as gauged by labor force participation rates. The growth in the labor market during the 1980s provided employment to 1.2 million persons with disabilities who would not have been working had labor force participation rates remained at 1982 levels. However, these gains in overall employment were partially offset by the growth of part-time work, especially among those who would have preferred full-time work (data on part-time employment not in table or figures). Among persons with disabilities, the proportion working part-time by choice increased by about 15%; persons without disabilities experienced only a 1% rise in voluntary part-time work (Yelin 1993). At the end of the period, persons with disabilities were

about twice as likely to work part-time by choice as those v
Meanwhile, the proportion of persons with disabilities
involuntarily increased by about 44%, while the propor†
disabilities working part-time involuntarily actually *decreaseu* ⌐ᵣ
end of the period, persons with disabilities were almost two and a halı ⌐⌐
more likely to work part-time involuntarily as those without disabilities.

Thus, although persons with disabilities experienced a greater than proportional share of overall employment growth, they also experienced a greater
than proportional share of the growth in part-time employment, especially in
involuntary part-time employment. Given that part-time work brings fewer
benefits, persons with disabilities were less likely to achieve security from
employment than persons without disabilities.

Labor Market Trends: Qualitative Analysis

The feminization of the labor force, the expansion of employment opportunities for persons with disabilities in general and women with disabilities in
particular, and the growth of part-time work may be seen, positively, as
accommodating the goals of affirmative action. These changes did provide
work for millions who would not otherwise have found employment. However, while certain aspects of the changes in the labor market proved benefi-
cial to some groups, older men, especially older nonwhite men, experienced
job losses. Moreover, the losses came disproportionately in manufacturing
industries which traditionally provided secure full-time employment and relatively high wages, while the gains occurred in service industries providing a
disproportionate share of part-time and low-wage jobs, frequently with poor
benefits.

In addition to changes in the composition of the labor force, and in the
share of jobs in manufacturing and service industries, the very nature of
employment has been in transition. For most of the twentieth century, employers organized work in two tiers. Professionals and managers were paid
on a salaried basis, given more autonomy to do their jobs, and were largely
shielded from layoffs. Production workers were paid hourly wages to do
routine tasks in invariable ways and worked only as much as the economy
allowed (Osterman 1988). Increasingly, employers are melding the two tiers,
requiring production workers to act autonomously to improve productivity,
while no longer providing professionals and managers immunity from layoffs.

The shift to services in the context of job growth pulled persons with
disabilities into the labor force. Service industry jobs are diverse, encompassing both services to individuals, exemplified by the fast-food restaurant
and the large human service organization, and services to business, exemplified by the routine clerical functions of the insurance and banking industries

and the creative work of the advertising copywriter or financial analyst. Employment in jobs providing services to individuals might be difficult for persons with certain mental conditions, requiring continuous and sometimes stressful human contact, and providing services to business might be difficult, too, requiring the use of cognitive skills to solve problems and, perhaps, meet stringent deadlines. If so, and given the unlikely expansion of the job market, the quantitative and qualitative trends in the labor force may work against persons with mental conditions in the years to come.

As we shall see in the next section, in the last decade overall employment patterns among persons with mental conditions fit more general trends in the labor market, increasing the overall proportion in the labor force. However, this overall increase played out differently among persons with mental conditions than among the rest of the population, providing smaller gains to those with disabilities than to those without.

Employment among Persons with Mental Conditions: Both with and against the Tide

Logic suggests that employment among persons with mental conditions must be subject to some of the same forces affecting all working-age adults, including those with physical illness. After all, one would expect employers to make accommodations when labor is scarce, hiring those with little work experience, including those with disabilities or stigmatizing conditions, if no other potential workers are available, and laying off those most recently hired when those with more experience are plentiful.

Logic also suggests that the situations of persons with mental and physical conditions must sometimes diverge. Cognitive and behavioral limitations might be legitimate barriers to employment in jobs with public contact, those requiring split-second decisions, or those with a high level of stress. On the other hand, physical limitations might be legitimate barriers to jobs requiring physical exertion. In addition to technical considerations, the impact of stigma must be considerable, whether due to mental conditions or physical ones like HIV-related illness, though the magnitude of the impact is hard to estimate.

Neither community-based nor clinically based studies provide much guidance in predicting employment patterns among persons with mental conditions, because the former studied only a few areas of the country, and sample sizes were relatively small, especially for estimates of discrete conditions, and most of the latter lacked a control group. Furthermore, public perceptions about the prevalence of mental disorder in the community offer little in the way of signposts. Public perception focuses on the severely ill, especially those with both psychotic and alcohol and drug abuse disorders who may have been institutionalized in the past but who are now homeless. However, deinstitutionalization and rising homelessness are unlikely to alter the number of persons with mental disorders in the labor force, since such persons are unlikely to find permanent jobs even in boom economies.

For the reasons outlined in the section on methods, the estimates of labor force participation provided here do not encompass the universe of persons with mental conditions, since they exclude those with the most and least severe conditions. Even so, the patterns we describe below would not be altered by a fundamental improvement in the sampling frame. Labor force participation rates for persons with and without mental conditions and for persons with mental conditions of different gender, race, and age groupings differ so strikingly that broadening the sampling frame would not change the nature of the patterns observed enough to undermine the results. Thus, while a systematic census of persons with mental conditions would provide better estimates of the actual magnitude of labor force participation, the NHIS provides a reasonable gauge of *relative* employment outcomes, and it encompasses most of those who might work in the years to come.

Persons with Mental Conditions: Cross-Sectional Results

Although researchers tend to study individual conditions in isolation, a significant proportion of persons with chronic disease have more than one. Persons with mental conditions are no exception. According to NHIS estimates, about three million meet NHIS criteria for a mental condition and of these, just under two million also report physical conditions (data not in table). For persons with physical conditions alone, comorbidity worsens functional capacity (Verbrugge, Lepkowski, and Imanaka 1989) and labor force participation (Yelin and Katz 1990). This is *not* true for persons with mental conditions and disabilities (table 1). In the five-year period from 1987–1991, for example, 24% of persons with mental conditions and disabilities but without physical conditions were in the labor force, a significantly lower proportion than the 29% among such persons who also had physical conditions. This result suggests that persons with mental conditions alone and disabilities are different than those with both mental and physical conditions and disabilities.

Although the data provide no clues as to why this may be, one might speculate that the presence of a physical condition reduces the stigma attached to mental conditions. Alternatively, the mental conditions of those with physical conditions may be less severe, perhaps because the mental conditions are due to the physical conditions, as when people with arthritis become depressed because they can no longer work. It also may be that the disability due to a mental condition is sufficient to render the individual unable to work

Table 1 Labor Force Participation Rate of Persons with Mental Conditions, by Disability
Status: United States, 1982–1986 v. 1987–1991

	Period		
	1982–1986	1987–1991	Change (%)
Without physical conditions			
With Disability	.25	.24	−4.0
Without Disability	.72	.76	5.6
Total	.46	.47	2.2
With physical conditions			
With Disability	.27	.29	7.4
Without Disability	.71	.76	7.0
Total	.40	.42	5.0

Source: Authors' analysis of National Health Interview Survey.

or that persons with mental conditions alone cloak their employment problems
in the mantle of disability.

Persons with Mental Conditions: Longitudinal Results

That the expansion in the labor force in the 1980s did benefit persons with
mental conditions is clear. Compared to the period 1982–1986, labor force
participation rates in the years 1987–1991 increased by 2.2% for persons
with mental conditions alone and by 5.0% for those with both mental and
physical conditions (table 1). The employment situation improved substantially for persons with mental and physical conditions regardless of disability
status and for those with mental conditions alone without disabilities. However, labor force participation rates declined for those with mental conditions
alone who report disability. Thus, not only do such persons fare more poorly
at any one point than those with mental and physical conditions with disabilities, but their situation relative to the remainder of those with mental conditions has deteriorated over time. For example, in the 1982–1986 period,
persons with mental conditions alone reporting disabilities were 93% as likely
to be in the labor force as those with both mental and physical conditions
who report disabilities; in the 1987–1991 period, they were only 83% as
likely to be employed. Whether objective impairment or subjective behavior
affects the employment of persons with mental conditions alone who report
disabilities, this group is clearly distinguishable from all others with mental
conditions, having much lower labor force participation rates.

Comparing Employment of Persons with and without Mental Conditions: Cross-Sectional Results

Persons with mental conditions fare much more poorly in the labor market
than those without mental conditions (table 2). In the period 1987–1991, for

Table 2 Labor Force Participation Rate of Persons with and without Mental Conditions, by Disability Status: United States, 1982–1986 v. 1987–1991

	Period		
	1982–1986	1987–1991	Change (%)
With mental conditions			
With Disability	.26	.27	3.9
Without Disability	.71	.76	7.0
Total	.42	.44	4.8
Without mental conditions			
With Disability	.46	.50	8.7
Without Disability	.75	.79	5.3
Total	.71	.75	5.6
Total			
With Disability	.45	.48	6.7
Without Disability	.75	.79	5.3
Total	.71	.75	5.6

Source: Authors' analysis of National Health Interview Survey.

example, persons with mental conditions were only about 59% as likely to be in the labor force as those without (44% vs. 75%). Most of the difference in the labor force participation rate of persons with and without mental conditions occurs among those with disabilities. Only 27% of persons with mental conditions and disabilities reported themselves in the labor force in the period 1987–1991, or slightly more than half the rate for those with disabilities in the absence of mental conditions (50%). Labor force participation rates among persons with mental conditions without disabilities approach those of persons without mental conditions (76% vs. 79% in 1987–1991), and they exceed the average among all working-age adults during that period (75%). Thus, preventing disability or the perception of disability will dramatically improve the probability of employment among persons with mental conditions. In addition, understanding why disability has a greater impact on those with than without mental conditions must become a central concern for those who wish to improve employment prospects among the former group.

Comparing Employment of Persons with and without Mental Conditions: Longitudinal Results

The expansion of the labor force during the 1980s improved the employment situation of persons with and without mental conditions alike (table 2). However, the patterns of improvement in the two groups differed substantially. Comparing the periods 1982–1986 and 1987–1991 we see that persons with mental conditions reporting disabilities experienced smaller growth in labor force participation rates in the years 1987–1991 than those with mental conditions and no disabilities (3.9% vs. 7.0%). In contrast, persons without mental conditions who reported disabilities saw their labor force participation rates increase by 8.7% in relative terms, more than the 5.3% increase among such persons without disabilities.

Thus, the demand for labor benefited all persons with disabilities, but those with mental conditions did not get an equal share of the job growth. However, the demand for labor did help persons with mental conditions and no disabilities, who experienced a larger increase in labor force participation rates than persons without either mental conditions or disabilities.

Summing the trends among persons with and without disabilities, persons with mental conditions generally lagged behind those without mental conditions in employment. Their labor force participation rate increased by 4.8%, or about 86% of the 5.6% increase among those without mental conditions and, owing to the numerical predominance of those without mental conditions, among all working-age persons.

Employment among Persons with Specific Mental Conditions

In table 3, we present estimates of labor force participation rates among persons within subsets of the mental condition category. Since some of the conditions occur rarely, especially among persons who live in the community and choose to respond to surveys, to obtain stable estimates, it was necessary to average the responses from the 1982–1991 NHIS, precluding the analysis of time trends in employment by each subset. We have divided those with mental disorders into two major rubrics, those with all conditions except alcohol and drug abuse disorders and those with such disorders. We have further subdivided the first rubric to show labor force participation rates among persons reporting psychotic and affective disorders. The residual within this rubric includes all those not reporting a discrete diagnosis and those without conditions expected to last six months, the NHIS definition of a chronic disease.

As might be expected, persons with psychotic disorders report substantially

Table 3 Labor Force Participation Rate of Persons with Select Mental Health Conditions: United States, 1982–1991, Ten-year Average

Condition	With Disabilities	Without Disabilities	Total
All mental, except alcohol/drug abuse	.27	.74	.43
Psychotic disorders	.15	.59	.21
Affective disorders	.20	.69	.33
Residual	.33	.76	.51
Alcohol/drug abuse disorders	.24	.61	.34

Source: Authors' analysis of National Health Interview Survey.

lower labor force participation rates than any other subgroup within the mental condition category. Overall, only 21% of such persons were in the labor force during the period 1982–1991. Among those with psychotic disorders and disabilities, only 15% were in the labor force during this time. Since the NHIS omits those living in institutions and undercounts persons with cognitive and behavior problems, the actual labor force participation rate among persons with psychotic conditions is probably lower. Among persons with affective disorders, a third were in the labor force, a much greater proportion than among persons with psychotic disorders. Those in the residual subgroup, most of whom are either mildly symptomatic or have transient conditions, were much more likely to work than others with mental conditions, though they still experience substantially less access to employment than persons without mental conditions with the same disability status (datum about persons without mental conditions not in table 3). Finally, persons with alcohol and drug disorders reported labor force participation rates very similar to those reported by persons with affective disorders, with slightly more than a third of all such persons being in the labor force.

Combining Labor Market Liabilities

After Rosie the Riveter went home at the close of World War II, the labor market was suspended in an equilibrium for close to twenty-five years (Levy 1987). High labor force participation rates among men were matched by low labor force participation rates among women. The equilibrium was maintained by rising real incomes among working men, which reinforced the social norm that women should not enter the labor force unless forced to do so.

Since 1973, however, real wages have been rising very slowly, putting a squeeze on families with one wage earner. Whether the social norm about women's employment changed because of economic necessity or the changed social norm allowed families to respond to economic trends with greater equanimity, women have surged into the labor force in record numbers. While the entrance of women into the labor force no doubt had a salutary economic effect on families, it was partially offset by the exit of men, principally those displaced from industries in decline (U.S. Department of Labor 1988). The surge of women into the labor market continued throughout the 1970s and 1980s; the exit of men abated somewhat in the 1980s, but may have resumed in the last several years (U.S. Bureau of the Census 1992; U.S. Department of Labor 1993).

These changes did not course through the population evenly. Instead, the surge of women was concentrated among young women, and the exit of men was concentrated among older men. Race and disability status accentuated the trends. Young white women experienced a larger than proportional gain in employment than young nonwhite women, and older nonwhite men experienced a larger than proportional loss in employment than older white men. During this period, younger women with disabilities, particularly younger white women with disabilities, rode the expansion into substantially higher labor force participation rates, while the rates for older men with disabilities, particularly older nonwhite men with disabilities, declined sharply.

Although the sample size of the NHIS precludes the analysis of time trends for subgroups of those with mental conditions, aggregating across years allows us to evaluate how mental conditions interact cross-sectionally with gender, age, race, and disability status to affect employment. Not surprisingly, the results indicate that all but a handful of persons with mental conditions fare more poorly in the labor market than similarly situated individuals without mental conditions. In addition, race and disability status operate more powerfully upon those with mental conditions than upon those without, so that those with mental conditions have radically lower rates of employment. Nevertheless, the patterns of employment among persons with mental conditions fit more general patterns, with whites having higher labor force participation rates than nonwhites and persons with disabilities having lower labor force participation rates than those without disabilities.

Table 4, with labor force participation rates by age, gender, and disability status, and table 5, with labor force participation rates by race, gender, and disability status, show the patterns of employment among persons with and without mental conditions. Both tables display absolute labor force participation rates and two sets of ratios, the first comparing the labor force participation rates of persons with and without disabilities within the condition groups (those with and without mental conditions), the second comparing the labor force participation rates of persons with and without mental conditions within disability statuses.

The Combination of Mental Condition and Disability

Every cell in tables 4 and 5 shows that persons with disabilities are less likely to work than those without disabilities. However, disability appears to have a larger impact on the employment of persons with mental conditions than on those without, the ratios of labor force participation rates of persons with and without disabilities being universally lower among persons with mental conditions than among those without. For example, among men 18–44 (table 4), those with mental conditions and disabilities are only 37% as likely to be in the labor force as those without disabilities. Among men of these ages without mental conditions, those with disabilities are 79% as likely to be in the labor force as those without. Similarly, among nonwhite women (table

Table 4 Labor Force Participation Rate of Persons with and without Mental Conditions, by Age, Gender, and Disability Status: United States, 1982–1991, Ten-year Average

	18–44			45–54			55–64		
Group	With Disability	Without Disability	Ratio[a]	With Disability	Without Disability	Ratio[a]	With Disability	Without Disability	Ratio[a]
Men									
With mental conditions	.30	.81	.37	.23	.90	.26	.21	.68	.31
Without mental conditions	.69	.87	.79	.62	.94	.66	.38	.78	.49
Ratio[b]	.44	.93		.37	.96		.55	.87	
Women									
With mental conditions	.32	.71	.45	.27	.67	.40	.13	.46	.28
Without mental conditions	.52	.69	.75	.42	.71	.59	.23	.52	.44
Ratio[b]	.62	1.03		.64	.94		.57	.88	
Total									
With mental conditions	.31	.75	.41	.25	.72	.33	.16	.54	.30
Without mental conditions	.61	.78	.78	.51	.82	.62	.30	.64	.47
Ratio[b]	.51	.96		.49	.93		.53	.84	

Source: Authors' analysis of National Health Interview Survey.
[a]Ratio of labor force participation rates of persons with and without disabilities.
[b]Ratio of labor force participation rates of persons with and without mental conditions.

5), those with mental conditions and disabilities are only 25% as likely to be in the labor force as those without disabilities, far smaller than the ratio of .48 among nonwhite women without mental conditions. Overall, persons with mental conditions reporting disabilities are 36% as likely to be in the labor force as those without disabilities, while persons without mental conditions are 62% as likely to be in the labor force as such persons without disabilities (table 5).

The importance of disability in the employment situation of persons with mental conditions is underscored when we compare their labor force participation rates to those without mental conditions. In every cell in tables 4 and 5, the ratio of the labor force participation rates of persons with and without mental conditions reporting disabilities is less than .71, and the ratio goes as low as .37 (among men 45–54, table 4). Of course, the flip side is that persons with mental conditions but no disabilities fare much better. Compared

Table 5 Labor Force Participation Rate of Persons with and without Mental Conditions, by Race, Gender, and Disability Status: United States, 1982–1991, Ten-year Average

Group	Whites			Nonwhites			Total		
	With Disability	Without Disability	Ratio[a]	With Disability	Without Disability	Ratio[a]	With Disability	Without Disability	Ratio[a]
Men									
With mental conditions	.30	.84	.36	.17	.68	.25	.27	.82	.33
Without mental conditions	.61	.89	.69	.39	.79	.49	.58	.87	.67
Ratio[b]	.49	.94		.44	.86		.47	.94	
Women									
With mental conditions	.29	.69	.42	.16	.64	.25	.27	.68	.40
Without mental conditions	.41	.67	.61	.31	.65	.48	.39	.67	.58
Ratio[b]	.71	1.03		.51	.99		.69	1.02	
Total									
With mental conditions	.29	.75	.39	.17	.66	.26	.27	.74	.36
Without mental conditions	.51	.78	.65	.35	.71	.49	.48	.77	.62
Ratio[b]	.57	.96		.49	.93		.56	.96	

Source: Authors' analysis of National Health Interview Survey.
[a]Ratio of labor force participation rates of persons with and without disabilities.
[b]Ratio of labor force participation rates of persons with and without mental conditions.

to persons without either mental conditions or disabilities, those with mental conditions but no disabilities have at least 86% of the labor force participation rate, and among women 18–44 (table 4) and among white women overall (table 5), those with mental conditions and no disabilities actually have higher labor force participation rates than such women without mental conditions.

Gender, Race, and Age Effects

Among men with mental conditions reporting disabilities, labor force participation rates decline precipitously between ages 18–44 and 45–54 (from 30% to 23%), but then fall much more slowly between ages 45–54 and 55–64 (table 4). Among women with mental conditions reporting disabilities, most of the decline appears to come between ages 45–54 and 55–64, a situation more akin to that experienced by men and women without mental conditions.

Table 6 Ratio of Nonwhite to White Labor Force Participation Rates, by Gender and Disability Status: United States, 1982–1991, Ten-year Average

Gender	Group	With Disability	Without Disability
Men	With mental conditions	.57	.81
	Without mental conditions	.64	.88
Women	With mental conditions	.55	.92
	Without mental conditions	.76	.97

Source: Authors' analysis of National Health Interview Survey.

In absolute terms, women 55–64 with mental conditions reporting disabilities fare the poorest of all the age/gender/disability status groups, with a labor force participation rate of only 13 percent.

Not surprisingly, white men without either mental conditions or disabilities experience the highest labor force participation rate of all the groups defined by race, gender, and disability status, 89%, while nonwhite men with mental conditions reporting disabilities (at 17%) and such nonwhite women (at 16%) have the lowest (table 5).

Table 6 summarizes the interaction of race, disability, and employment. For both men and women, the ratio of nonwhite to white labor force participation rates is lowest for those with mental conditions reporting disabilities. The ratios increase progressively from that among persons without mental conditions reporting disabilities, to that among persons with mental conditions and no disabilities, and, finally, to that among persons without either mental conditions or disabilities. Thus, racial differences in employment are concentrated disproportionately in persons with mental conditions, especially those reporting disabilities.

The interaction among gender, disability, and employment is more complex (table 7). In general, even after the surge of women into the labor force, men have higher labor force participation rates than women (U.S. Department of Labor 1993). However, men with mental conditions reporting disabilities do not differ from such women in their labor force participation rates (the gender ratio in labor force participation rates is 1.00). And, although the ratio of male to female labor force participation rates among persons with

Table 7 Ratio of Male to Female Labor Force Participation Rates, by Disability Status: United States, 1982–1991, Ten-year Average

Group	With Disabilities	Without Disabilities
With mental conditions	1.00	1.21
Without mental conditions	1.49	1.29

Source: Authors' analysis of National Health Interview Survey.

mental conditions without disabilities is 1.21, indicating that males are more likely to work, this gender ratio is smaller than among persons without mental conditions, regardless of disability status. Note that the gender ratio is greatest for men without mental conditions reporting disabilities. Thus, disabilities (or the report of disabilities) profoundly reduce the probability that men with mental conditions will be in the labor force, a finding at odds with the more general picture of employment among men and women, and at odds with the situation among men with disabilities due to conditions other than mental ones.

Summary of Labor Market Interactions

Men with mental conditions in general and especially those with mental conditions and disabilities appear to fare more poorly in the labor market than men without mental conditions. Otherwise, mental conditions intensify the effects of age, race, and disability status on labor force participation. Thus, as labor force participation decreases with age, among persons with mental conditions it does so at earlier ages and to a greater degree. As nonwhites experience lower labor force participation rates than whites, in the presence of mental conditions the racial gap in employment widens. Finally, as persons with disabilities have lower rates of employment than those without, persons with mental conditions reporting disabilities stand an even smaller chance of working.

Is It the Mental Condition, the Social Situation, or Both?

The data presented above provide ample evidence that mental conditions accentuate other labor market disadvantages. One might surmise that persons with mental conditions would fare poorly in employment even in the absence of those conditions because they are likelier to have some of the other characteristics that place them at a disadvantage. Likewise, one might surmise that they would do poorly even in the absence of those other characteristics because of the powerful impact of mental conditions due either to the objective effect of impaired cognitive function or to the stigma of mental illness. In this section, we estimate the impact of the mental conditions in the absence of other labor market liabilities and of the other labor market liabilities in the absence of mental conditions, and then show how the two sets of liabilities combine.[1]

In 1991, 74% of all working-age adults were in the labor force (table 8). Naturally, those with neither mental conditions nor disabilities experienced the highest labor force participation rates, 77% on average. Persons with mental conditions reporting disabilities but no physical comorbidity had the

Table 8 Labor Force Participation of Working-Age Adults, by Mental and Physical Condition, Disability Status, and Social and Demographic Characteristics: United States, 1991

Scenario	Ment. Cond. − Dis. −	Ment. Cond. − Dis. +	Ment. Cond. + Phys. Cond. − Dis. −	Ment. Cond. + Phys. Cond. − Dis. +	Ment. Cond. + Phys. Cond. + Dis. −	Ment. Cond. + Phys. Cond. + Dis. +	Total	Health Gradient[a]
White man 18–44, married, from midwest suburb, > college	.95	.85	.91	.65	.94	.67	.94	1.40
Nonwhite woman 55–64, never married, from northeast central city, < high school	.15	.05	.09	.02	.14	.02	.13	7.50
Total	.77	.51	.67	.26	.76	.28	.74	
Social gradient[a]	6.33	17.0	10.11	32.5	6.71	33.5	7.23	2.96

Source: Authors' analysis of National Health Interview Survey.

[a]Health gradient = ratio of labor force participation rates of persons with no mental conditions and no disabilities to that of those with mental conditions, no physical conditions, and disabilities.

[b]Social gradient = ratio of labor force participation rates of persons in the two scenarios.

lowest labor force participation rate, 26%. Holding constant for social and demographic characteristics, this resulted in a health gradient of 2.96.

In that same year, the labor force participation rate among persons with the matrix of social and demographic characteristics that maximized employment was 94%, a rate more than seven times as great as among those with the characteristics that minimized it. Thus, all else equal, the social and demographic characteristics affect labor force participation rates more strongly than the combination of health characteristics. Although the labor force participation rate of the young white men with mental conditions and disabilities in the first scenario in table 8 is lower than among such men with neither mental conditions nor disabilities, it is still close to the average among all working age adults. In contrast, even those older nonwhite women who have neither mental conditions nor disabilities in the second scenario have only a 15% probability of employment.

In much of the foregoing analyses, we made the assumption that the characteristics which put one at a disadvantage in the labor market—gender, age, race, disability status, and mental conditions—had a cumulative, though additive effect on employment prospects, suggesting that the health gradient has a constant effect across social and demographic characteristics. However, the health gradient is *not constant* across social and demographic characteristics. Instead, the combination of mental health status and disability matters much less to those persons with the characteristics that maximize employment prospects (young white men with more than a college education who are married and living in a midwestern suburb) than to those with the characteristics that minimize them (older nonwhite women with less than a high school education who have never been married and now live in central city in the northeast), the health gradient being 1.40 in the former case, 7.50 in the latter.

Similarly, when mental conditions combine with disabilities, the social and demographic gradient increases. From an average of 7.23 among all working age adults, the gradient rises to 32.5 among persons with mental conditions reporting disabilities but no physical comorbidity (65% vs. 2%) and to 33.5 among those with mental conditions, disabilities, and physical comorbidity (67% vs. 2%).

Should We Have a Mental Health Employment Policy?

Although the health gradient in labor force participation is smaller than the social and demographic gradient, this should not deter us from policies that place a special emphasis on health characteristics. While it is true that the employment prospects of persons with labor market liabilities other than those due to mental conditions and disabilities remain poor, decreasing the impact of the mental conditions and disabilities nevertheless will benefit them immensely. The estimates presented in the second scenario in table 8 indicate that we could increase the probability of labor force participation from 2% to 15% among those with labor market liabilities that extend beyond mental conditions. In particular, we would do well to focus on why those who report disabilities in the presence of mental conditions have such poor labor market prospects in comparison to those with mental conditions not reporting disabilities and in comparison to those with disabilities from physical conditions.

Interpreting the Results and Looking to the Future

We have found that persons with mental conditions reporting disabilities fare particularly poorly in the labor market. No doubt part of this finding is an artifact of reporting. Persons with mild physical conditions need not be limited by them in work. Moreover, physical conditions that do not limit work function are unlikely to be noticed at work. For persons with mental conditions, however, limitation in work activities may be the first sign that they have such a condition and may also alert their colleagues to the condition. Thus, work limitation may precede diagnosis; indeed, it may have resulted in diagnosis in the first place. Thus, the low labor force participation rates of persons with mental conditions and disabilities may be tautological, with problems in coping with work simultaneously leading to diagnosis and loss of employment.

The simple way that the National Health Interview Survey measures activity limitation serves the goal of enumerating overall disability rates well. Given the nature of mental conditions, however, it may be more fruitful to ask more discrete questions about work limitation, for example, how the individual copes with deadlines, supervision, coordination, and communication. One way to do this without dramatically expanding the scope of the survey would be to ask such questions only of those reporting mental conditions. If this were done, it would also make sense to tie the kinds of problems encountered at work with the occupation and industry of the individual and with the specific symptoms experienced. Ultimately, one would want to know the order in which work limitations, symptoms, and change in labor force status occur to determine the extent to which work causes the symptoms to arise or merely exacerbates existing symptoms.

Integrating Mental Health and Labor Market Policy

The labor market may be viewed as a current. During the 1980s, the current flowed swiftly forward, hastening the entry of persons with mental conditions into the labor market, including those with disabilities, as part of the overall employment gains. This general drift notwithstanding, not all with mental conditions were pulled into work equally. Those without physical conditions did not experience job growth proportional to their share of the population, and such persons reporting disabilities actually saw their labor force participation rates fall. In the early 1990s, the labor market current has reversed and, although the data are not yet sufficient to state this with certainty, it appears that this reversal has propelled persons with mental conditions out of work faster than the remainder of the population.

Likewise, at any one point, the probability that an individual will be working is the sum of a matrix of social, demographic, and health vectors, some of which reduce the odds of employment, and some of which increase it. All else equal, mental conditions in the absence of disability reduce the odds slightly, but in the presence of disability, the probability of employment falls dramatically. After relaxing the assumption that all else is equal, the probability can rise to two-thirds for those with mental conditions and disabilities who are without other liabilities or reach very close to zero for those with such liabilities.

The metaphor of the current makes sense in the short term, since labor market trends can and do indicate the limits for public policies designed to overcome liabilities. Increasing the employment of persons with mental conditions was a likely outcome in the expansionist 1980s, but it is much less likely in the contractionist period of the early 1990s. The metaphor breaks down, however, on the assumption that the long-term trend in the proportion of working-age adults actually in the labor market is a given and thus not amenable to public intervention. Labor force participation rates vary widely among nations with comparable standards of living (U.S. Department of Labor 1993), and these nations differ in their orientation to the family, in their proclivity to transfer income from workers to nonworkers, and in the age of eligibility for retirement pensions (Burkhauser and Hirvonen 1989).

More important, the metaphor breaks down on the assumption that, individually or in combination, the liabilities that jeopardize employment can be justified on the basis of capacity for work. Net of education, training, and experience, nonwhites face discrimination in employment. Net of capacity for work, persons with mental conditions face stigma and self-doubt in seeking work and net of stigma, they are limited in functional capacity.

Clearly, any effort to improve the employment situation of persons with mental conditions must determine just how stigma impedes work opportunities. Just as clearly, we will need to establish in a much more systematic fashion what kinds of jobs individuals with specific symptoms and diagnoses of mental conditions can do.

In theory, the Americans with Disabilities Act of 1990 (ADA) takes care of both concerns, banning job discrimination against those with stigmatizing conditions and ensuring that those who can perform the essential functions of a job, regardless of their ability to perform its other functions, must be given a fair chance to compete for work (West 1991). However, the ADA requires individuals alleging discrimination to make claims with the Equal Employment Opportunity Commission (EEOC). Providing statistical evidence of discrimination, such as the data provided in this paper, will not suffice to prove discrimination in individual cases. The expense and difficulty of pursuing legal recourse prohibit all but a few from filing claims with the EEOC. Thus, relatively few persons with disabilities have made use of this legal remedy (ADA Compliance Guide Monthly Bulletin 1993), and if the past experiences of minorities, women, and the elderly are a guide, few are likely to use this remedy in the future (O'Meara 1989).

The labor market, unlike a current, can be diverted from its course. Nations can and do choose labor force participation rates, even if only implicitly. However, the ADA, touching only the tiny fraction of those with mental conditions who have the financial wherewithal and cognitive skills for legal recourse, will not fundamentally alter labor market dynamics. As the experience of the 1980s attests, the rising tide helps, but it only increased the proportion of persons with mental conditions in the labor force by 4.8%, much less than the increase among those without mental conditions. And the rising tide does not help all groups equally, leaving those with labor market liabilities far behind despite the overall expansion of the last decade, and such persons are likely to be the first to lose work in the present era of declining employment opportunities. Those with labor market liabilities may very well need special policies that help them gain access to employment. Persons with mental conditions are certainly one such group.

However, while the low labor force participation rates of persons with mental conditions relative to those without justify special attention to their needs in employment policy, we must remember that the mental condition is rarely their only liability, that it may not be their most important liability, and that mental health policy in the absence of an effective full-employment policy will leave the majority of persons with mental conditions out of work.

Acknowledgments

This study was supported by grants from NIAMS (AR-20684) and the Milbank Memorial Fund.

Note

1. To calculate the interaction among social and demographic characteristics, mental conditions, and employment, we analyzed data from the 1991 National Health

Interview Survey. Specifically, we used logistic regression to estimate the impact of mental conditions with and without physical comorbidity and with and without disability; age; race; census region of the country; residence in central city, suburban, or rural areas; marital status; and education on labor force participation. Using the resulting regression equation, we then estimated labor force participation rates for persons with the social and demographic characteristics that maximized and minimized employment in each of the cells defined by mental condition, comorbidity, and disability status. Those with the highest labor force participation rates are white men 18–44 with more than a college education who are married and living in a midwestern suburb; those with the lowest are nonwhite women 55–64, with less than a high school education, who have never been married and are living in a northeastern central city.

References

ADA Compliance Guide Monthly Bulletin. 1993. ADA Employment Bias Complaints to EEOC Top 11,000. *ADA Compliance Guide Monthly Bulletin* 4(9): 8. Washington, DC: Thompson Publishing Group.

Anderson, K., and J. Mitchell. 1990. Effects of Military Experience on Mental Health Problems and Work Behavior. *Medical Care* 30: 554–563.

Anthony, W., and M. Jansen. 1984. Predicting the Vocational Capacity of the Chronically Mentally Ill. *American Psychologist* 39: 537–544.

Bacani-Oropilla, T., S. Lippman, E. Tully et al. 1991. Patients with Mental Disorders Who Work. *Southern Medical Journal* 84: 323–327.

Barker, P., R. Manderscheid, G. Hendershot et al. 1992. Serious Mental Illness and Disability in the Adult Household Population: United States, 1989. *Advance Data* no. 218.

Broadhead, W., D. Blazer, L. George, C. Tse. 1990. Depression, Disability Days, and Days Lost from Work in a Prospective Epidemiologic Survey. *Journal of the American Medical Association* 264: 2524–2528.

Burkhauser, R., and P. Hirvonen. 1989. United States Disability Policy in a Time of Economic Crisis: A Comparison with Sweden and the Federal Republic of Germany. *Milbank Quarterly* 67 (supp. 2, part 1): 166–195.

Eaton, W., C. Holzer, M. Von Korff et al. 1984. The Design of the Epidemiologic Catchment Area Surveys. *Archives of General Psychiatry* 41: 942–948.

Jacobs, H., D. Wissusik, R. Collier, D. Stackman, and D. Burkeman. 1992. Correlations Between Psychiatric Disabilities and Vocational Outcome. *Hospital and Community Psychiatry* 43: 365–369.

Johnson, J., M. Weissman, and G. Klerman. 1992. Service Utilization and Social Morbidity Associated with Depressive Symptoms in the Community. *Journal of The American Medical Association* 267: 1478–1483.

Kovar, M., and G. Poe. 1985. The National Health Interview Survey Design, 1973–1984, and Procedures, 1975–1983. *Vital and Health Statistics* series 1, no. 18.

Levy, F. 1987. *Dollars and Dreams: The Changing American Income Distribution.* New York: Russell Sage Foundation.

Mitchell, J., and K. Anderson. 1989. Mental Health and the Labor Force Participation of Older Workers. *Inquiry* 26: 262–271.

Mullahy, J., and J. Sindelar. 1989. Life-Cycle Effects of Alcoholism on Education, Earnings, and Occupation. *Inquiry* 26: 272–282.

National Center for Health Statistics. 1982. *Public Use Tape Documentation, National Health Interview Survey.* Hyattsville, Maryland: National Center for Health Statistics.

O'Meara, D. 1989. *Protecting the Growing Number of Older Workers: The Age Discrimination in Employment Act.* Labor Relations and Public Policy Series no. 33. Philadelphia: Industrial Relations Unit.

Osterman, P. 1988. *Employment Futures: Reorganization, Dislocation, and Public Policy.* New York: Oxford University Press.

U.S. Bureau of the Census. 1992. *Statistical Abstract of the United States, 1992.* Washington, DC: GPO, 381–382.

U.S. Department of Labor. 1988. *Labor Force Statistics Derived from the Current Population Survey, 1948–1987.* Washington, DC: GPO.

———. 1993. Tables 4, 6, 7, and 48. *Monthly Labor Review* 116(8): 70, 72–73, 105.

Verbrugge, L., L. Lepkowski, Y. Imanaka. 1989. Comorbidity and Its Impact on Disability. *Milbank Quarterly* 67: 450–484.

Vogel, R., V. Bell, S. Blumenthal, N. Neumann et al. 1989. Work and Psychiatric Illness: The Significance of the Posthospitalization Occupational Environment for the Course of Psychiatric Illnesses. *European Archives of Psychiatry and Neurological Sciences* 238: 213–219.

Wells, K., A. Stewart, R. Hays et al. 1989. The Functioning and Well-Being of Depressed Patients: Results from the Medical Outcomes Study. *Journal of the American Medical Association* 262: 914–919.

West, J. 1991. Introduction. In J. West, ed., *The Americans with Disabilities Act: From Policy to Practice.* New York: Milbank Memorial Fund.

Yelin, E. 1989. Displaced Concern: The Social Context of the Work Disability Problem. *Milbank Quarterly* 67 (supp. 2, part 1): 114–166.

———. 1992. *Disability and the Displaced Worker.* New Brunswick: Rutgers University Press.

Yelin, E., and P. Katz. 1990. Labor Force Participation among Persons with Musculoskeletal Conditions. *Arthritis and Rheumatism* 33: 1205–1215.

———. 1993. Making Work More Central to Work Disability Policy. *Milbank Quarterly* 72: 593–620.

Yelin, E., S. Fifer, S. Mathias et al. 1995. The Impact of a Physician Intervention on Employment among Persons with Previously Untreated and Unrecognized Anxiety. *Social Science and Medicine.* In press.

PART 2

To Work or Not to Work:
The Constrained Choices of Persons
with Serious Mental Disorders

Persons with serious mental disorders are often at a competitive disadvantage in the labor market for many reasons. The onset of mental illness may have interrupted their education and vocational training and deprived them of valuable job experience. They may confront working conditions that exacerbate their symptoms as well as job requirements poorly tailored to their abilities. Employers and coworkers may be at once skeptical and fearful. Finding and retaining competitive employment is, to put it mildly, an uphill battle for many people with serious mental disorders.

What factors influence the employment opportunities of persons with serious mental disorders and their prospects for vocational satisfaction and success? As noted in the preceding chapter, labor participation and employment rates for this population are affected by overall conditions of the labor market. Now we will look at these issues "from the bottom up," so to speak, focusing on choices about working or not working made by individual workers.

Some persons experience such substantial impairments of work-related functioning in so many spheres that competitive employment is a practical impossibility. For most persons with mental disorders, however, competitive employment is possible under some conditions. If the satisfaction of working is very great, a person might be willing to pay a high personal cost in emotional discomfort and inconvenience in order to find or hold a job. Conversely, a person who repeatedly confronts failure and tension in the workplace or low remuneration compared to available benefits may abandon aspirations of employment. An employer may choose to reduce an employee's personal costs by making accommodations that make it easier for the employee to remain in the labor force. Other employers may not be flexible and may be unwilling to hire a person with a mental disability or to make needed accommodations.

Understanding the aspirations, fears, incentives, and obstacles experienced by persons with serious mental disorders is an essential predicate for vocational rehabilitation and for sensible design of work disability policies. As William Anthony has recently written, "the vocational rehabilitation process is, in its most basic form, the process of people with psychiatric disabilities *choosing, getting* and *keeping* a job." Further, "consumer choice must be an integral part of the vocational rehabilitation process" (Anthony 1994, 19). Work may set back therapeutic progress, but it might also enhance the prospects for success. Similarly, progress under the Americans with Disabilities Act (ADA) in reducing barriers to employment will depend on a collaborative effort to understand the desires of applicants and employees and the flexibility to implement the necessary accommodations.

Choice must also be at the center of research on the disability benefit process. Why do people apply for benefits? What disincentives and pressures do they face? To what extent is the expected level of benefits the determinative consideration? From a policy perspective, understanding the political economy of work disability is an essential step in the search for the right mix of incentives, especially in relation to part-time employment.

The three papers in this part, which use very different methodologies, illustrate the kind of bottom-up research that is needed on the decision making of persons with serious mental disorders with regard to seeking employment and seeking work disability benefits. In chapter 3, Estroff and her colleagues focus on choices to seek SSI/SSDI benefits. In chapter 4, Strauss and Davidson explore the therapeutic value of work. Finally, in chapter 5, Warner and Polak focus on the economic incentives and disincentives that shape the work-related choices of persons with serious mental disorders.

References

Anthony, W. A. 1994. The Vocational Rehabilitation of People with Severe Mental Illness: Issues and Myths. *Innovations and Research* 3: 17–23.

3

"No Other Way to Go": Pathways to Disability Income Application among Persons with Severe, Persistent Mental Illness

SUE. E. ESTROFF, CATHERINE ZIMMER, WILLIAM S. LACHICOTTE,
JULIA BENOIT, AND DONALD L. PATRICK

> I have thought a lot about whether I want the tag "disabled." I've decided that by using it I have a lot to gain. . . . Despite the reward of monthly direct credit to my bank account, and the later Medicare coverage, I was humbled; I felt shamed.
>
> (Caras 1994, 323)

> I told him [case manager] that I felt bad about going on disability because I felt like it was giving up. And I didn't like the idea, so I told him I wanted to try to work. . . . I've had two jobs this year that didn't work out for different reasons. I still don't like the idea of having to be on disability, but at this point, I have no other way to go.
>
> (Study participant)

In this chapter, we report results from our work on the subject of disability income in the lives of persons with severe, persistent mental illness. The main questions addressed by the study were (1) How do persons with severe, persistent mental illness come to apply for and receive Supplemental Security Income (SSI) and Social Security Disability Insurance (SSDI)?[1] (2) How do SSI/SSDI applicants and recipients differ from those who did not apply and do not receive? (3) What does getting on disability mean to recipients? (4) What are the roles of clinical, demographic, sociocultural, and service-system factors in the application and receipt process? Our approach involves considering biographical, experiential, cultural, demographic, clinical, and pragmatic elements because we believe that all of these are involved in the process of disablement. We designed this part of the study to investigate how clinical impairments, psychological and instrumental dependencies, social characteristics, and the use of mental health services interact to influence persons with severe mental illnesses to apply for disability income. In this chapter, we focus solely on the application process.

When we examine disability income in the lives of individuals with severe, persistent mental disorders, we also address a cluster of interrelated empirical questions about the heterogeneity of their lives and illness courses. By exploring an identifiable, increasingly common event and process in the lives of the population of concern—application for SSI/SSDI—we may improve understanding of the natural history and periodicity of severe mental illness (see Watt et al. 1983; Zubin et al. 1983; Harding et al. 1987b). Until relatively recently, long-term hospitalization was perhaps the most penetrating intervention and enduring social response to people with major mental illnesses. In our view, being on disability may be the current equivalent to prolonged hospitalization in the depth and duration of its impact on the lives of many individuals with serious psychiatric disorders. Thus, the process of getting on disability deserves equal scrutiny as to its meaning and consequences. Albeit less stigmatizing, we argue that becoming "disabled" is a replacement identity or label and social institution for prolonged psychiatric patienthood, with similar personal costs and material benefits, as described so clearly in the opening quotations.

Before discussing the study and findings, we introduce three conceptual models of the process of applying for disability income and a critical appraisal of current perspectives and research on disability income and disablement. Excerpts from interviews with SSI/SSDI applicants in the study are included in the following discussion to enrich and deepen the points and to demonstrate the usefulness of combining narrative and survey methods.

Conceptual Models of SSI/SSDI Application

Three conceptual models may account for application for disability income, the outcome variable in this analysis. The *impairment* model predicts that those with the most clinically severe impairments and pervasive functional and psychological dependencies will apply for disability income. Clinically assessed physical and/or mental limitations will primarily determine whether a person applies. Some measures of this domain are symptom-scale scores, diagnosis, and days in hospital.

A *labeling* model suggests that application is determined mainly by acceptance of and immersion in a disabled, patient role. That is, labeling oneself as mentally ill and a patient, and being labeled likewise by others, within the context of using services (i.e., being in the patient role surrounded by others who confirm that status), will lead to designation by self and others as disabled, and result in disability income application. Measures include the duration and amount of time spent in the patient role, and the duration and amount of interaction with clinician/service providers who (1) diagnose, label, or otherwise formally designate a person as impaired; (2) provide access to information and assistance regarding benefits; and (3) may encourage and facilitate application and receipt. In this formulation, severity of dysfunction is less important than taking on the patient/disabled role.

Finally, a *needs/resources/dependence* model points to lack of resources, relatively uninfluenced by severity of dysfunction or self-labeling, as the strongest factor motivating application for disability income. From this perspective, an individual already at the social and personal margins would apply once medical or psychiatric problems occur, whatever their type or severity. The lack or abundance of resources prior to and after injury or illness drives the process of getting on disability. In essence, the larger the discrepancy between an individual's needs and available resources, and the greater her dependence on others, the more likely she will be to seek disability income.

These views of the disablement process are both competing and complementary. We introduce impairment, labeling, and needs/resources/dependence as conceptual frameworks rather than as empirical models that will be tested deductively. Instead, these perspectives influenced the selection of research questions and methods, and shaped the way we defined the variables in the analysis. In concluding the chapter, we return to assess their salience in light of the results.

Contextual Considerations

The Social Place of Persons with Disabilities

Individuals with significant physical and mental disabilities are more visible and attract more public concern in Western societies than at any previous time (Strauss and Corbin 1988). The Americans with Disabilities Act of 1989–90 represents the most extensive successful federal legislation directed at the rights of and by the sensibilities of persons with disabilities since 1973. At the same time, and not coincidentally, an increasing number have emerged from relative silence and obscurity to claim a declarative presence in social, political, academic, and clinical discourse (Stubbins 1988).

Both the geographic and social positions of noticeably disabled people have changed markedly in recent decades. Many have relocated physically from the isolated and obscuring architecture of institutions to residence in community and nursing home settings, sometimes with equal invisibility and isolation. Others with severe, sometimes multiple disablements, avoid confinement altogether and remain in public places, often unwelcome and unincorporated into the flow of public social life. Far too many of these persons occupy public spaces only and are without domicile, ironically shifted radically from near complete invisibility to unremitting public gaze.

As public, long-term care institutions have become smaller and decreased in number, their former and potential residents lead their lives in neighborhoods instead of hospitals, political wards rather than psychiatric wards, and walk the streets rather than hospital hallways. Concurrently, advances in medical technology have altered the natural history of physical impairment, prolonging life for neonates, adults, and older individuals who previously would not have survived. As a result, individual financial viability for those who are severely impaired and living outside of institutions is increasingly problematic. The source and amount of money available for housing and health care for a growing number and variety of persons with disabilities are now inescapable concerns for those who shape public health and mental health policy, as well as health and mental health service systems.

The Social Study of Persons with Disabilities

Much of the seminal work on persons with disabilities was conducted in institutional settings, many of them psychiatric, with persons who were categorized primarily as deviant (Goffman 1961). Disability studies inherited many concepts, orientations, and methods which were appropriate for the captive subjects of research in "total" institutions. The token economies once common in psychiatric hospitals have been replacd by actual individual economies in communities, and patient-staff interactions are now as likely to occur in a fast-food restaurant as in a day room, with staff exerting considerably less control over the daily lives of patients. Older analytic perspectives and research tactics are now ill suited to both the dispersed and mobile groups of disabled persons, and the topics that arise as community treatment and living largely replace institutional care and residence. At this juncture, the social science of disability may require its own sort of deinstitutionalization movement.

Another legacy of the institutional origins of studies of deviance and disability is a lack of attention to the political economy of disability and related health and social welfare policies at the societal level, and to the economies of individuals at the personal level. Despite their well-documented drawbacks, institutions have provided for the basic subsistence needs of their residents (Grob 1983). Food, shelter, clothing, and health care, however inadequate, were paid for in large part by the governments that operated large institutions for mentally ill, developmentally disabled, and retarded persons. Veteran's Administration hospitals and homes likewise provided for many persons physically disabled by injuries in the Korean and Vietnam wars. There was, in effect, little reason for social scientists or clinicians to be concerned about individual economies—how severely impaired individuals, with limited vocational skills and even fewer employment opportunities, would survive financially or obtain the basic material resources for living in the community.

Previous research failed to take the economic survival of individuals with disabilities as a starting point, following wherever that might lead.

Most of the recent health economics literature about costs related to disablement and major mental illness focuses on rational expenditures or the financing of service systems (e.g., Chirikos 1989; Rice et al. 1990; McGuire 1991; Scheffler and Frank 1989). Neither type of research illuminates the individual financial exigencies of persons with mental illness or their experiences and efforts in the labor force. As one study participant explained, working may involve a complicated interplay of successes, symptoms, and relapses: "Last year I tried to work. I worked a month. I got in there. I was hired to do one job, and before it ended I was doing six different jobs. It got on my nerves so bad I just couldn't take it no more, so I just quit. I wasn't on any kind of medication then, and next thing I knew, you know, three months later I ended up with a nervous breakdown."

Health economists have been interested in disability income programs and participation since their inception. Summarized incisively by Yelin (1992), the research has been focused primarily on accounting for rising rates of reported and supported disability, and the falling rates of labor force participation at the national level. The main questions are whether there is an actual increase in the number of work-disabled persons, or whether increasing numbers of persons define themselves as disabled in order to withdraw from the labor force, replacing wages with disability-derived income. This debate could be called the "can't versus won't work" or the need vs. choice argument. There is little empirical support for the "replacement," or rational choice, theory that people with a not-necessarily-disabling impairment make a decision to withdraw from the labor force to get on disability, based on a calculation of resources gained and lost (Wolfe and Haveman 1990). Recently, Moffitt and Wolfe (1993) have demonstrated, however, that private insurance coverage in the workplace that was as comprehensive and readily available as Medicaid would induce many single mothers who were welfare recipients to enter the labor force. In essence, Medicaid availability via welfare *and* the lack of health insurance in private sector employment, were influencing single mothers to remain on welfare. Moffitt and Wolfe did not focus their analysis on persons with disabilities, but whether a similar dynamic operates is certainly worthy of exploration.

Clinical outcome research on individuals with disabling conditions is beginning to reflect a shift in the meaning of the term *outcome* away from that of a static, objectively defined end-state occurring after a linear progression to cure (Bond and Boyer 1988). There is increased emphasis on processes or phases of *reconstruction* or *rehabilitation,* based as much on fluctuating subjective states and social indicators as on medical measures of impairment (Anthony 1993). Individual economic viability achieved through various pub-

lic and private means, and self-assessment of satisfaction with such arrangements are also considered to be evidence of successful outcome. The former
emphasis on "independence" as the goal for profoundly impaired persons is
shifting to accommodate various degrees of interdependence. Reliance on
public financial support in the form of disability income may not represent a
failure to achieve independence, but a *means* to lead more autonomous,
self-directed lives.

Economic and health policy concerns about controlling health care and
social welfare expenditures, and increasingly contested resources for long-
term care now make these issues interesting to researchers engaged in analyses at levels other than the individual, and from perspectives different from
the phenomenological. So far, the research enterprise lacks the conceptual
clarity and pragmatic focus needed to inform public policy, clinical practice,
or the social science of disability regarding the influence of individual subsistence strategies on the course and experience of chronic illness. There are
ethnographic and narrative accounts of individuals and small groups of persons with disabilities outside of institutions (Estroff 1985, Edgerton 1967,
Simmons 1965, Williams 1984) on the one hand, and large-scale, quantitative
economic and policy analyses on the other (e.g., Scheffler and Frank 1989).
To date, phenomenological studies of the chronic illness experience have
neglected to examine both individual economies (personal financial survival
strategies) and the political-economic context of income supports and employment opportunities for disabled persons. Similarly, research in the economic
and policy areas of disability remains largely uninformed by the experiential
and individual perspective (Berkowitz 1986). Noticeably lacking are inquiries
that combine quantitative and qualitative methods, micro and macro perspectives, and that bridge the gap between individual experience and aggregate
analyses.

Disability Income and Persons with Severe, Persistent Mental Illness

Individuals with severe, persistent psychiatric disorders face massive challenges to achieving satisfying lives. None is so basic, nor perhaps as perva-
sively unmet, as adequate subsistence. The rate of unemployment is higher
among seriously mentally ill persons than among other disabled groups, and
there is persuasive evidence that employers view persons with known psychiatric disorders with more skepticism and discrimination than persons with
other types of disabilities (Link 1982, Weber and Orcutt 1984, Black 1988).
Despite recent advances in and increased attention to vocational rehabilitation
and employment opportunities, the vast majority, 75%–85%, do not have
real jobs, and even fewer earn sufficient incomes from employment (Noble
1984, Anthony and Jansen 1984).

The resulting lack of earned income creates dire material circumstances and enormous stresses for individuals already plagued with substantial day-to-day difficulties. Such pervasive poverty can challenge even the most optimistic individuals, innovative community treatment programs, and dedicated families in their efforts to increase coping capacities and assist in making life acceptable in quality (Cohen 1993). Having a severe, persistent mental illness very often means a life harshened by the presence of financial and material deficits as well as clinical impairment and social dysfunction.

The Epidemiology of SSI and SSDI

Being on disability has become a way of life for increasing numbers of people with serious mental illness. "Cause everybody else is getting it . . . everybody else that I know that has a similar problem like mine is. . . . They had similar problems and they're living off of disability. . . . I'm pretty much in the same boat as other people I know who are getting it. If they deserve it, then I do. That's just the way I feel." Psychiatric disorders have been the largest diagnostic category among adult disabled SSI recipients since the inception of the program in 1974 (Kochhar 1979), but only since 1987 has the same ranking applied to SSDI. Kennedy and Manderscheid (1992) report that in 1991 the number of individuals with mental disorders exclusive of mental retardation who received SSI and SSDI was 1,154,754, or approximately half of the estimated total target population (Goldman and Manderscheid 1987). Individuals with psychiatric disabilities now represent the largest single diagnostic group of disabled adult recipients in both the SSI and SSDI programs, constituting 28.2% of SSI recipients and 24.5% of SSDI recipients, or about one in four adult recipients under the age of sixty-five (Kennedy and Manderscheid 1992, NASI 1994). They tend to be younger than recipients with other impairments (Kennedy and Manderscheid 1992) and have the longest tenure as SSDI recipients, a mean of 15.6 years compared to that of persons with all other disabling conditions (Hennesey and Dykacz 1989). Over one-third of SSDI recipients who also receive SSI, or dual recipients, have a mental disorder (NASI 1994). This reflects both the youth of mentally ill recipients and their low labor force participation, both of which result in inadequate earnings for full SSDI payments.

At present, the number of persons with disabilities who are beneficiaries of both programs is increasing (Stone 1984; Yelin 1986, 1989, 1992; Chirikos 1989, NASI 1994). The number of psychiatrically disabled beneficiaries in particular is also increasing, at a somewhat higher rate than total program growth. SSI recipiency has increased over 33% in five years, with the SSDI program experiencing a more modest rise of 10% (SSA 1988, 1989, 1990, 1991). Expanded participation in both programs by individuals with mental disorders is especially marked in the 30 to 50 year-old age group (SSA 1988, 1989, 1990, 1991).

The rise in the number of recipients with psychiatric disabilities is not surprising in view of renewed efforts to decrease state psychiatric hospital expenditures (Taube and Goldman 1989), the early 1990s recession, and the widespread, if relatively recent, concerted efforts of community mental health professionals to obtain benefits for those in their care (Cain 1993). Recent amendments to eligibility criteria, spearheaded by advocates and clinicians, have also made SSI and SSDI more accessible to those with psychiatric conditions (Goldman and Gattozzi 1988). Expanded Medicaid and Medicare reimbursement for outpatient psychiatric care and psychosocial rehabilitation services, including case management, have also created incentives for SSI and SSDI enrollment (Adams, Ellwood, and Pine 1989). Disabled SSI recipients are automatically eligible for Medicaid coverage in all but fourteen states, and SSDI recipients under the age of sixty-five are eligible for Medicare, after a two-year waiting period during which they may be covered by Medicaid.

In addition, the explosive growth of energetic and politically influential family and consumer advocacy groups has resulted in wider dissemination of information regarding the availability and usefulness of entitlements. Because family members of mentally disabled persons bear a substantial, enduring financial burden for their support and health care, they may be especially interested in obtaining federal disability benefits.

Thus, there are individual, family, and service-system-centered needs that can be met by SSI/SSDI recipiency among persons with severe, persistent mental illnesses. One of the ongoing ironies of disability policy is the relentless skepticism about the motives and employability of individual disability income recipients (Yelin 1986, 1992; Murphy et al. 1988), coupled with almost complete inattention to the financial and other incentives for providers (Gronfein 1985) and family members for receipt of disability income by patients.

> They [family] glad I got the social security so I would have some kind of income coming in. That Tracy Labor job was paying me like $20 a day. So that wasn't a lot of money to go by, and I didn't have the right clothes to wear. So social security helps me buy clothes, food, and anything else I need.

> He [doctor] said I needed a stable income, and he said that I had to work more on my problems and stuff like that—without worrying about money and worrying about work.

> I figured I was disabled after he [doctor] said that I was disabled to work.

> . . . the doctor up there suggested I get some kind of help for
> her [patient], you know, especially for her medical bills. So, I
> applied for whatever was available . . . and they accepted her
> and she's still getting disability checks. And she helps me with
> the bills. . . . You know, she didn't know what was going on.
> But she does help pay the bills with that, because I feel like
> that's what it's for, because my house payment is $800. . . .
> So without her helping I couldn't make it. That does help out a
> little, and she's not working. . . . I'm surprised they hadn't
> already stopped it, but they said they would reevaluate her some
> day. But I don't feel like she could hold a job now. I know she
> couldn't now, and I don't know if she ever will be.

Neither SSI nor SSDI were meant to wholly replace income for disabled
persons (Berkowitz 1987), but both have become a de facto major or sole
source of support for the target population. The January 1994 average
monthly payment of $641 for SSDI recipients and 1992 payment of $434 for
SSI recipients with no other earnings (Kennedy and Manderscheid 1992,
NASI 1994) places beneficiaries well below the poverty level, at the same
time creating real and imagined obstacles to obtaining or earning more
income.

Meager as this income may be, SSI and SSDI beneficiaries are more fortunate than those with no resources whatsoever, or those solely dependent on
local welfare or state general relief funds, which are universally lower in
amount and less stable. There are also intriguing questions about persons
with severe, enduring psychiatric disorders who do not receive SSI or SSDI—
about one-half of the target population. In one sense, the answer is tragically
clear. Thousands of individuals disabled by psychiatric disorders have no
financial resources and many are homeless (Baxter and Hopper 1982, Koegel
et al. 1988, Calsyn et al. 1993). Many others have few resources except
for those provided by relatives, sporadic earned income, or other makeshift
strategies (Hopper et al. 1985). On the other hand, it is also apparent that a
considerable number of people with disabling conditions navigate community
life without the benefit of public disability income. Little, however, is known
of their subsistence strategies and quality of life.

While receipt of disability income is widely viewed as a characteristic of
an individual, we suggest that it is better conceived of as a result of the
collaboration, needs, and characteristics of various parties with various interests. Taking this view adds increased irony to the social labeling dimensions
of getting on disability and suggests caution in using SSI and SSDI receipt
as indicators of *individual* dysfunction. From our perspective, the epidemiology of SSI and SSDI among persons with severe, persistent mental illness

tells us as much about service-system inadequacies, lack of economic opportunities, and the social forces of isolation, discrimination, and alienation of persons with disabilities.

Disablement in Context and as Process

It is increasingly clear that relatives provide an enormous amount of financial and social support to persons with disabilities in general and with serious mental illness in particular, and that they play important roles as partners in effective services and treatment (Harding et al. 1987; Carpentier et al. 1992; McGuire 1991; Lefley 1987, 1990; Noh and Turner 1987; Cook 1988; Steinwachs et al. 1992; Corbin and Strauss 1987). Yet seldom have relatives been included as participants in research that investigates processes of disablement or recovery, nor has their participation in the process of SSI and SSDI application been assessed. "I'd rather work full hours if I could get social security to let me, because my mother needs it sometimes, because I can't afford to work and pay her that. So I'm trying to find a shortcut way, you know, that I can let her keep some money, and I can take a few dollars and be happy. Because I don't need that much."

Getting on disability occurs within a social network of relatives and mental health providers that must be included in any understanding of the subject (Conrad 1987; Dozier et al. 1987; Jacobson 1986; Sherbourne and Hays 1990). Our research indicates that family members initiated almost as many SSI/SSDI applications as did mental health providers, and that household financial pressures played an important part in the applications process.

> Well, his daddy applied for it . . . my husband filled them out [SSI forms]. . . . And he needed little things, and by me being the only one working, and his daddy wasn't working at the time, it made a big difference—a lot of difference. Cause all I could do was try to pay the bills, and Lord they cut my lights off about five times, you know.

> Because he [patient] couldn't pay his rent. He couldn't buy groceries. He couldn't pay none of his bills. And after I got my bills paid if I'd have any I'd try to help him, you know, what I could . . . just like I told [counselor], I'd done all I could do, and I couldn't keep my house going and hissen too, you know, for I didn't draw that much money. . . . I'm scared they might ask for it back. You don't ever know . . . I think it's going to give him a better outlook on life. At least he doesn't have to come to me and say, "Mama, do you have a dollar? I want to buy a Pepsi."

An Overview of Research on Disability Income and Individuals with Severe, Persistent Psychiatric Disorders

Most of the published information about disability income participation by persons with major mental illness lacks qualitative data or multivariate analysis that models or predicts application. For example, Okpaku (1985) simply describes the clinical and demographic characteristics of individuals referred for psychiatric evaluation for SSI/SSDI. There are numerous descriptions of the characteristics of SSI and SSDI beneficiaries, post-receipt recovery, employment, and the demographics and financial and health status of recipients and nonrecipients (Schmulowitz 1973; McCoy and Weems 1989; Trietel 1979; GAO 1989, 1992; Trout and Mattson 1984). Most of these studies are cross-sectional, and none focuses in sufficient detail on recipients with psychiatric disorders to provide more than clues about the process of disablement. Several authors address various clinical and policy issues related to SSI, SSDI, and the target population (e.g., Lamb and Ragowski 1978; Mechanic 1987; Anderson 1982; Goldman and Gattozzi 1988; Okpaku 1988; Test et al. 1985).

There is no published research of which we are aware that investigates the process of application for SSI/SSDI. As a result, when we review previous work in the area, we must focus on investigations of SSI/SSDI recipients. The findings from recent research about disability income beneficiaries suggest that severity of psychiatric symptoms alone is not a consistent predictor of SSI or SSDI receipt, that receipt has some effects on the capacity and willingness of beneficiaries to work, and that receipt is associated with a mixed picture of functioning in other life domains. Segal and Choi (1991) explored SSI receipt and tenure in a ten-year follow-up of sheltered-care residents, and constructed a model to predict which residents were recipients at follow-up. In this study, recipients and eligible nonrecipients were remarkably similar in diagnosis, demographics, amount of mental health service used, percentage who were employed, and severity of symptoms. Compared to eligible nonrecipients, the current recipients had spent significantly less time in psychiatric hospitals since baseline, were more likely to be seeing a private counselor or psychiatrist, were much more likely to live in sheltered care, and had less informal social support from friends and family. Segal and Choi conclude that recipients were at least as psychiatrically and socially impaired as nonrecipients, and that the prolonged hospitalization of nonrecipients was the only major difference between the two groups. This raises the question of how or if SSI receipt was helpful, beyond perhaps preventing multiple, long-term hospitalizations.

Massel et al. (1990) also found no differences in symptom severity between disability income recipients and nonrecipients, and a surprising comparability in some areas of tested work capacity between the two groups. Work tolerance, performance, and grooming were, however, significantly worse in the recipient group. Jacobs et al. (1992) found that SSI recipients were less successful than SSDI recipients and nonrecipients in their vocational rehabilitation program, a result they attribute to the poorer work histories, earlier age of illness onset, and higher number of hospitalizations among SSI recipients. Perl and Kahn (1983) compared fully financially compensated psychiatrically impaired veterans with those partially compensated or receiving no compensation. The only significant differences between the groups on measures of psychopathology, use of services, locus of control, and self-esteem were that the fully compensated were more hostile, and they spent less time in the hospital in the year following receipt of full compensation; and the partially compensated had higher self-esteem. These findings suggest that factors other than severity of psychiatric impairment influence the receipt of disability income, and that receipt may in turn broadly influence the nature and quality of recipients' lives.

Calsyn et al. (1993) interviewed 288 people who were homeless to determine which were recipients of welfare benefits and examined the welfare records of a subsample of 100 respondents. They used logistic regression to investigate what characteristics or experiences of the respondents were associated with receipt of welfare benefits, including SSI and SSDI. These investigators were not able to analyze SSI and SSDI receipt separately because only 10 respondents were SSI or SSDI recipients. However, their findings are of interest. Having a prior psychiatric hospitalization significantly *lessened* the odds of being a welfare recipient for women and had no effect on welfare receipt among men. Psychiatric symptomatology did not affect welfare receipt for men or women, but the number of agencies the person contacted did. The more agencies contacted, the more likely men and women were to receive benefits. Evidently, the psychiatric hospital did not function as a social service agency in engineering SSI or SSDI applications for these individuals. Because it is not clear when these hospitalizations occurred, it is difficult to take the findings further. The small number of SSI and SSDI recipients among their sample might indicate that receipt of SSI and SSDI helps to prevent individuals from becoming homeless, or it could mean that it is very difficult to get SSI or SSDI benefits if one is homeless. These findings about individuals who are homeless are not inconsistent with those above, that is, that psychiatric impairment and hospitalization do not measurably increase SSI, SSDI, or other benefit receipt.

In perhaps the most comprehensive survey of families of persons with serious mental illness, Steinwachs et al. (1991, 1992) report findings from a sample of 1401 members of the National Alliance for the Mentally Ill

(NAMI). Although this group may be unrepresentative, nearly 50% reported that their severely mentally ill relative received SSI or SSDI, with 19% being dual recipients. Nearly half of the families of persons who did *not* receive SSI or SSDI had never applied, citing their household income as too high as the most frequent reason for not applying for SSI. Their consumer relative's lack of adequate work history most frequently stopped them from applying for SSDI.[2] Only about 15% of the nonapplying families said they "did not want" SSI or SSDI. In a companion survey of 552 of the consumers themselves, Uttaro and Mechanic (1994) report that 51% of these persons with major mental illness said that "keeping busy so you don't get bored or lonely" was an unmet need, and it was the area wherein the most respondents wanted more help. Nearly two-thirds, 60%, said getting or keeping a job was a need, but only 19% wanted more help. Even fewer, 18%, said they wanted more help with SSI, SSDI or other benefits. We may infer from these findings that while obtaining benefits was not a high priority for the consumers, their lives as benefit recipients involved widespread boredom and loneliness.

Pathways to Disability Income: A Prospective Multimethod Investigation

We investigated pathways to disability income application among a cohort of 169 individuals who were early in the course of major psychiatric disorder but had never applied for or received these benefits. The principal goal of the study was to describe how individuals with serious mental illness came to apply for SSI/SSDI, comparing applicants in the cohort to those who did not apply. We were interested in examining the interplay between clinical and social factors that contributed to this critical juncture in the life and illness course of the study participants. By following the cohort prospectively, we sought to observe and analyze the many contributing factors along pathways to formal designation as disabled. Although the approach was largely inductive, the investigation was informed by the impairment, labeling, and needs/resources/dependence models introduced previously. We hypothesized that the psychological, functional, and clinical dependencies of this group, their interactions with service systems and experiences in the labor force, their experiences with and understandings of psychiatric symptoms and labels, and the availability of other social and material resources would play significant roles in their decisions to seek disability income.

Data Collection

Study participants were recruited primarily in four psychiatric hospitals (two state, one university, and one community) and secondarily from two public outpatient mental health programs. All persons admitted to the hospitals from five local counties were screened by our research team for potential eligibility and were then approached about the study. Each was followed for thirty-two months in six waves of interviews. We recruited individuals who were "early and eligible"—early in their careers with major psychiatric disorders, and ostensibly eligible for SSI/SSDI because of a poor work history, earned income below $300 per month (the SSA substantial gainful activity level at the time), and severe symptoms within the last twelve months.

We used a variety of methods to gather data, including the Psychiatric Epidemiology Research Interview (PERI) (Dohrenwend et al. 1980; Dohrenwend, Levav, and Shrout 1983a and b) and Brief Psychiatric Rating Scale (BPRS) (Overall and Gorham 1962; Luckoff, Liberman, and Neuchterlein 1986) to assess level of symptoms and clinical impairment; structured elicitation of information about employment, mental health service use, living situation, and social networks; an interpersonal relationship scale, the Structural Analysis of Social Behavior (SASB) (Benjamin 1993, 1979, 1974); and open-ended questions about explanations of mental illness and self-labeling, among other topics. Five of the six interviews were face-to-face; the last was by telephone. The baseline interview took place in the hospital in most cases, and the follow-ups occurred in whatever setting was most convenient for the participants, usually their homes. Two interviews were largely semistructured, in-depth sessions that were taped, transcribed, and coded for content. Hospital charts and mental health center records were also reviewed. We also interviewed the primary subjects' self-identified most significant other, usually a parent, once during the study.

The original sample consisted of 169 people. For most analyses, the number of respondents ranges from 146 to 110 for two reasons. First, 21 people applied for SSI/SSDI in the six months prior to the baseline interview, making them inappropriate for the multivariate causal analysis; second, some individuals were missing data on some variables.

Measurement of Variables

Table 1 presents univariate statistics for all variables for the six months prior to the baseline interview and the bivariate relationship between each variable and application, controlling for the six-month time period prior to each interview during which the data were collected. The variables are organized by conceptual domains: demographic; clinical; income; work; service system use; social network, social support and dependence; and illness behaviors.

Application. Information about application was primarily self-report, elicited at each interview via questions about the sources and amount of respondents' income. We also learned of applications for SSI/SSDI from interviews

Table 1 Baseline Descriptive Statistics for Study Variables

Application Variable (*N* = 146)	
Applicants	37.7%

Demographic Variables (*N* = 146)	
African-American	30.8%
SES 1	13.7%
SES 2	19.2%
SES 3	17.1%
SES 4	30.8%
SES 5	19.2%
Female	50.0%
Mean age	28.4 years
Married*	10.3%

Clinical Variables (*N* = 143)	
Schizophrenias	41.3%
Affective disorders	33.6%
Personality disorders	16.8%
Other disorders	8.4%
Mean BPRS score**	12.7
Mean PERI AH score	1.3
Mean PERI DM score***	1.9
Mean PERI SP score	2.2
Mean PERI PH score*	1.7
Mean PERI SI score	0.8
Mean PERI CT score*	2.0
Mean PERI FBP score***	1.1
Mean PERI M score	1.2
Newly hospitalized last six months***	91.6%
Median years since first hospitalization	2 years
Median days in hospital last six months*	20 days
Median days in hospital over lifetime**	86 days
Median days in hospital during the study***	20 days

Income Variables (*N* = 110)	
Needs taken care of	
Poorly*	30.9%
Adequately	26.4%
Fairly well	27.3%
Very well	15.5%
Doing worse financially than others***	57.3%
Doing about the same financially as others	33.6%
Doing better financially than others	9.1%
Median earned income per six months**	$1,120

Continued

Table 1 *continued*

Application Variable (N = 146)	
Applicants	37.7%

Work Variables (N = 144)	
No job	19.4%
Working mostly part-time	29.2%
Working mostly full-time	51.4%
Attending school**	16.7%
Median number of days worked during last six months**	53.5 days

Service-System Use Variables (N = 145)	
Non-users*	40.0%
Episodic users	19.3%
Regular users	40.7%
County mental health center users	31.0%
Private therapist users*	29.0%
Median number of outpatient visits during last six months	2 visits
Median number of days as outpatient during last six months	30 days

Social Network, Social Support, and Dependence Variables (N = 119)	
One or more difficulties with daily living*	73.1%
One or more helpers with daily living	55.5%
Listing one or more MHPs in social network	66.4%
Listing one or more MHPs on grid*	24.4%
Living alone**	17.6%
With parent in the household	42.0%
With spouse in the household*	9.2%
With adult child in the household	2.5%
Financially dependent on family***	28.6%
Mean SASB submit coefficient	0.12
Mean SASB control coefficient	0.40
Mean symmetry score	0.69
Mean network size	11.8 members
Network composition	
Median % relatives	64.3%
Median % friends**	25.0%
Median % MHPs	8.3%

Table 1   *continued*

Application Variable (N = 146)	
Applicants	37.7%

Illness Behavior Variables (N = 146)	
Self-labeling	
No	43.8%
Yes	48.6%
Don't know**	7.5%
Explanatory model	
No model	11.6%
Medical model	35.6%
Emotional model*	24.0%
Medical emotional model	8.2%
Other model	20.5%

Note: The asterisks in this table indicate a significant bivariate relationship between application and the explanatory variables, controlling for time period.

*p < .10.
**p < .05.
***p < .01.

with mental health staff and respondents' significant others, but always confirmed these reports with the respondents before considering a person to be an applicant. Among the 146 respondents in the multivariate analyses, 37.7% applied for SSI/SSDI. Figure 1 illustrates the timing of application, most of the applications (36, or 65.5%) occurred between the baseline and second interviews, declining precipitously over the study period.[3] We coded the six-month time periods prior to each interview as dummy variables for the event-history analysis, with the pre-baseline period as the reference category.

Demographic Variables. Almost 31% of the baseline respondents were African-American. We derived the socioeconomic status (SES) index using the Hollingshead and Redlich (1958) two-factor (education and occupation) method for the respondent if he or she had an occupation, or if not, for the respondent's parents if the respondent lived in the parental home. Respondents fell into five groups, with SES 1 the highest group and SES 5 the lowest. Most respondents were ranked in SES 4 (30.8%), with the others fairly evenly spread across the other four groups. The categories of income were dummy coded for multivariate analyses, and SES 5 was the reference category. There were equal numbers of men and women. The average age of respondents was 28.4 years, reflecting our attempt to sample individuals early in their illnesses.

As expected, only 10.3% of the respondents were married. This is the only demographic variable with a significant bivariate relationship with application. Those who were married were significantly less likely to apply for SSI/SSDI.

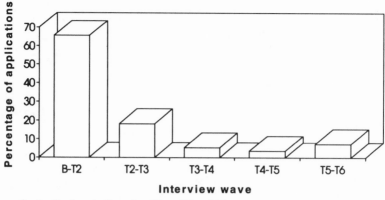

Figure 1 Applications by Interview Wave (N = 146).

Clinical Variables. Diagnosis was based on review of the most recent DSM III-R discharge diagnosis, the admitting or working diagnosis for the baseline hospitalization, and the discharge diagnosis for the baseline hospitalization. In the rare event that there were discrepancies among these, the most frequent diagnosis was assigned. As Table 1 shows, 41.3% of respondents had schizophrenias, 33.6% affective disorders, 16.8% personality disorders, and 8.4% had other psychotic diagnoses. People with a diagnosis of schizophrenia were more likely to apply for SSI/SSDI than individuals in all other diagnostic groups; however, this difference is not statistically significant.

Type and severity of symptoms were measured with two instruments. For the first, we summed eight symptom constructs from the Brief Psychiatric Rating Scale (BPRS) checklist (Overall and Gorham 1962). These were conceptual disorganization, excitement, motor retardation, blunted affect, tension, mannerisms and posturing, uncooperativeness, and emotional withdrawal. At the end of each interview, the interviewer rated the respondent on these dimensions, providing an independent assessment of severity of symptoms. The range for each item is 1–7, where a higher score indicates greater severity. The mean BPRS composite score for the sample is 12.7.

The second method of symptom assessment was a set of eight Psychiatric Epidemiological Research Interview (PERI) subscales that measured primary psychiatric symptoms. These were anti-social history (AH); demoralization (DM); schizoid personality (SP); perception of hostility (PH); suicidality (SI); confused thinking (CT); false beliefs and perceptions (FBP); and mania (M). The PERI is a self-report symptom scale with a one-year referent time frame, and scores have a potential range of 0–4, with higher scores indicating higher severity. The highest mean score in the sample was 2.2 for schizoid personality and the lowest was 0.8 for suicidality.

The significant bivariate relationships across all time periods for the symptom variables are in the expected direction. As the severity of symptoms goes up, measured by higher BPRS scores, higher demoralization, more perceived hostility, more confused thinking, and more false beliefs and perceptions, the likelihood of applying for SSI/SSDI goes up as well.

Almost everyone, 91.6% of the sample, was newly hospitalized in the six months prior to our first interview with them. Across all time periods, being in the hospital in the prior six months increased a respondent's likelihood of application.

The number of years since the first hospitalization ranged from 0 to 24 years, with a median of 2 years. Only 10% of the sample had been first hospitalized 8 or more years ago. We collected data on the number of days spent in the hospital via self-report and review of hospital charts. Based on these data, we computed three measures of hospital days. First, we defined recency as the number of days in the hospital during the previous six months. For the baseline period, the median was 20 days. Second, we defined biographical duration of hospital patient career with number of days in the hospital cumulated over the respondent's lifetime. The median lifetime days in the hospital for our sample is 86 days. Finally, we define an interim measure—between lifetime and past six months—as the number of days in the hospital during the study, which is the same as the prior six months for the pre-baseline period, a median of 20 days. The greater the number of days people spent in the hospital, regardless of how it was measured, the more likely they were to apply for SSI/SSDI.

Income Variables. Income was measured at each interview wave except baseline; we considered finances to be a topic too personal to broach at this initial meeting. In the subsequent interviews, income and finances were discussed extensively, both relatively and absolutely. Income information for the prebaseline six-month period came from the second (time 2) interview. Three questions probed the respondents' assessment of their finances in relation to needs and expectations. The first question asked, "Does the amount of money you (and your family) have take care of your needs poorly, adequately, fairly well, or very well?" Most respondents felt their needs were taken care of poorly (30.9%). This group, in comparison to those who felt their needs were taken care of very well (15.5%), were significantly more likely to apply for SSI/SSDI.

The second question asked, "How well do you think you are doing financially now compared to other people your age—better, about the same, or worse?" The majority of respondents (57.3%) saw themselves as worse off than their peers. Compared to the reference category of those who are financially about the same, those doing worse were more likely to apply.

The last question asked for the respondent's earned income, that is, money they got by working. The median earned income for the period prior to the

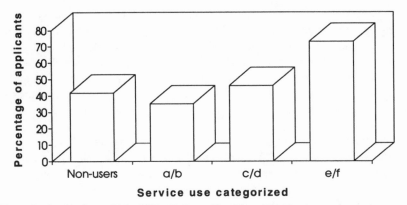

Figure 2 Application and Mental Health Center Use (N = 103). Service system use is categorized as follows: a = 1 to 3 visits ever during study; b = fewer than 1 visit per month; c = 1 to 2 visits per month; d = 2 to 3.5 visits per month; e = 3.5 to 5 visits per month; f = more than 5 visits per month.

baseline interview was $1,120. As expected, as earned income increased, the odds of applying went down. The overall picture is of respondents applying for SSI/SSDI because they evaluate their financial circumstances as meager, inadequate, and below expectations (i.e., in comparison to others like them).

Work Variables. We asked respondents about their work activity repeatedly and intensively. Only 19.4% had no job during the six months prior to our first interview, 29.2% worked mostly part-time, and 51.4% worked mostly full-time. There were no significant differences in application by work pattern. However, those in school (16.7%) were less likely to apply. Median number of days worked six months prior to the baseline interview was 53.5 days. As the number of days worked increased, people were less likely to apply.

Service System Use Variables. Use of mental health center services and private therapists was self-reported. The frequency and pattern of mental health center use, however, were collected from billing records provided by the centers. Figure 2 shows that the heaviest users of community mental health services were the most likely to apply for SSI/SSDI. When we look at pattern of mental health services use, either public or private, differences emerge as well. The 40% of the sample who did not use mental health services at all were more likely to apply for SSI/SSDI than the 40.7% who were regular users or the 19.3% who were episodic users. The respondents who saw private therapists (29%) were less likely to apply than those who received no mental health services.

The median number of outpatient visits per respondent in the six months before the first interview was two visits, whereas the median number of days spent as an outpatient was thirty days. Neither of these variables is associated with application.

Social Network, Social Support, and Dependence Variables. Social network/social support data covering a wide range of topics were gathered at each interview. There was no limit to the number of network members a respondent could list when determining network size. A large portion of the sample had difficulties with daily living (73.1%). However, only 55.5% named one or more people who helped them with their daily lives. Those who did have one or more difficulties with living were more likely to apply for SSI/SSDI. Mental health professionals (MHPs) were often named as part of the respondents' networks; 66.4% listed them as part of their social network, but only 24.4% of the sample considered them one of their closest network members. Those with close relationships with MHPs were more likely to apply.

Few of these respondents lived alone (17.6%). Many lived with their parents (42.0%), and few lived with a spouse (9.2%) or with their own adult child (2.5%). Those living alone were more likely to apply for SSI/SSDI, while those with spouses were less likely to apply. Financial dependence on the family was a variable constructed by comparing earned income with in-kind contributions from others. When in-kind resources exceeded earned income, the person was considered financially dependent. More than a quarter of the sample was financially dependent on family (28.6%). This dependence increased the odds of applying for government assistance.

The Structural Analysis of Social Behavior (SASB) scale (Benjamin 1974, 1979, 1989) requires the respondent to choose another person with whom they rate their own behavior and the other's behavior in relation to themselves. The submit and control coefficients measure enmeshment within this identified relationship. Most respondents chose their mother as the person with whom they rated themselves. The SASB assumes that submission and control work in an interactive, complementary dynamic. The coefficients range from -1 (least controlling or submissive) to 1 (most controlling or submissive). The mean SASB scores for the sample were .40 for control (respondents describe the SO's transitive actions towards them) and .12 for submit (respondents describe themselves in reaction to the SO).

The reciprocity of support from others and to others, which we call symmetry, is the proportion of relationships within which the respondents lend and give material resources to their most significant network members who lend and give back. Symmetry occurred on average for 69% of the relationships.

Social network size ranged from 1 to 30 members with an average of about 12 people. These networks consisted predominantly of relatives (64% on average of respondents' networks). A quarter of these networks consisted of friends, and 8.3% were mental health professionals. As the percentage of

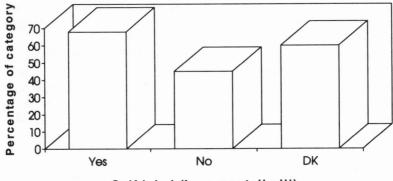

Self-label (I am mentally ill)

Figure 3   Self-Labeling and Application (N = 139).

friends in a network increased, the likelihood of application decreased. That is, respondents whose networks were composed primarily of relatives were more likely to apply.

Illness Behavior Variables. Self-labeling position and explanatory models (respondents' explanation of the nature and workings of their problems) were discussed during each interview. Verbatim responses to a series of structured questions were entered into a text base and coded. Respondents could label themselves as mentally ill (at the baseline interview, 48.6% of the sample), decline to so label (43.8%), or indicate that they did not know if they were mentally ill or not (7.5%). Those who said they did not know were significantly more likely to apply for SSI/SSDI than those who did not label themselves as mentally ill. Surprisingly, the self-labelers were no more likely to apply than the nonlabelers. Figure 3 uses the predominant labeling position taken by a respondent over the entire study and illustrates that although individuals who labeled themselves as mentally ill were more likely to apply for disability income than those who did not self-label, a significant group of people who did not consider themselves mentally ill also applied for SSI/SSDI.

Five types of illness explanations or explanatory models were identified: (1) no model or explanation, (2) a medical/clinical model, (3) an emotional/developmental model, (4) a social model, and (5) some respondents reported they had no problem to explain. Respondents sometimes combined ideas from different models (See Estroff et al. 1991). Only some of the categories had enough respondents for analysis. All other types were combined into the "other model" category. At baseline we found that 11.6% of respondents had no model, 35.6% had a medical model, 24.0% had an emotional model, and 8.2% combined a medical and emotional explanation of their illness.

The only significant difference in application between these groups and those having no model was that the respondents with an emotional model were significantly less likely to apply.

In sum, there are bivariate relationships between application and at least one variable from each domain. Nearly all of these were in the expected direction, anticipated by one or more of the impairment, labeling, and needs/resources/dependence models.

Analysis Techniques

We used text analysis and other qualitative methods along with multivariate statistical techniques to analyze the data. To analyze survey data on the processes of application for SSI/SSDI, we used discrete event-history analysis (Allison 1982, 1984), which uses a unique data structure to take account of the timing of events like application for SSI/SSDI, the focus of our investigation. One record is created for each respondent for each *period* at which they are at risk of *application* for SSI/SSDI. Once application has occurred, no further records are created. Thus, the sample is composed of the number of person periods, not simply the number of persons who experience an event. The result is a set of cases for analysis ranging from 395 to 297, depending on missing data. This data structure allows for changes in the values of explanatory variables over time and uses all information for a respondent up to the time of the event or up to the time of censoring (death or dropping out of the study).

We used logistic regression to estimate effects of the explanatory variables on the log-odds of application for SSI/SSDI. First, we analyzed conceptual domains one at a time. Then we put all of the variables that were significant in the domain analyses into a final model that combined the domains.

Results

During the study period, slightly less than half of the original cohort of 169 (80, or 47.3%) applied for SSI/SSDI, and about one-third (60, or 35.5%) became recipients. There were 28 SSI-only recipients, 24 SSDI-only, and 8 were dual recipients. Of those who applied, 75% became recipients; 67.5% were awarded benefits on the first try. This rate of allowance is considerably higher than the current national rate for all applicants, which is about 35% (NASI 1994, 92). Eight people reapplied at least once, and six eventually became recipients.

Fifteen respondents applied for disability benefits but did not become recipients during the study period. Compared both to recipients ($n = 60$) and those who never applied (n = 89), this group had higher proportions of whites and women, as well as of married, divorced, and separated persons. Compared to recipients, those who were denied included a higher proportion of persons with personality disorders and fewer individuals with schizophrenias; people with affective disorders were slightly overrepresented. In terms of work and income, those who were denied show a profile very similar to those who became recipients, and both groups differ significantly from individuals who never applied. Those who were denied benefits worked on the average more days than persons whose claims were allowed (53 days vs. 32 days), and both groups worked far less than people who never applied (107 days).

Earned income follows the same pattern. Individuals who never applied earned a mean of $571 per month, compared to $191 per month among those denied, and $127 per month among recipients. For each study period and overall, compared to recipients and nonappliers, respondents who were denied benefits had the lowest total income, including earned, other, and in-kind income. These patterns indicate that people who applied for SSI/SSDI but did not become recipients were quite similar to recipients in terms of financial need. Those who did not apply clearly were faring better in the labor force than both successful and unsuccessful applicants.

We also explored the process of application—how and by whom decisions to apply were made, and how the patients in the study participated in the work of the application. Eleven (13.75%) of the 78 applications were initiated by patients. Families initiated 29 (36.25%), mental health staff managed 34 (42.5%), and 6 applications had no identifiable originator. Only about 15% of the patients were involved very actively in the application process itself via making appointments and phone calls and being well-informed of the proceedings. We found that 42.3% were minimally involved, often reporting that they were unaware of applying. About 38% were moderately engaged. Applications initiated by family members were the most likely to result in receipt, but those managed by staff and patients were not far below their 83% success rate. Reconstructing the application process was often difficult because many study participants had only vague recollections of the relevant events. For example, one woman said that she received a letter from Social Security denying her application when she had no idea that she had applied. Upon reflection, she recalled two "nice ladies" coming to talk with her in the hospital one day and asking her a lot of questions about work and money. It was only during our interview that she understood that she had applied for disability income. We asked another person if he had applied for disability: "As far as I know. I might be wrong, but I know that we went into the office looking for SSI. . . . [did case manager help?] Yeah. She thinks that I need to be on SSI or disability also."

Work and Income

Work activity and earned income were of particular interest, given the focus of the study, and the findings are surprising. Table 2 reports that over a period of two years, from two-thirds to three-quarters of the sample reported some work activity. While the research convention recognizes only jobs that last at least two weeks as work, we used a subject-centered definition of working, reasoning that few of them would consider only a two-week job to be "work." Work activity was defined as any self-reported paid employment for any period of time. This may account for the unexpectedly high amount of work activity we encountered, which exceeded what we expected and raised questions about how accurate established views of employment among this population may be. The median days worked per six-month period range from a high of seventy days to a low of thirty-three, and from one-third to one-half of the jobs were full-time. Most of the jobs were service-type, and the median earned income per month reflects this—it is uniformly low. Participants in the study earned from a low of $127 to a high of $220 per month, with the median income per work day stable at between $22 and $23. This profile makes quite clear that the study participants were not giving up on work. They were earning very little but expending considerable and consistent effort to work.

Withdrawal from the labor force is a controversial issue in the disability

Table 2 Work Activity and Earned Income

	Baseline (N = 169)	Time 2 (N = 138)	Time 3 (N = 115)	Time 4 (N = 113)	Time 5 (N = 108)
Work					
No[a]	22.5%	26.1%	29.6%	31.0%	36.1%
Looking for work[b]	55.3%	37.1%	48.5%	15.2%	30.8%
Yes	77.5%	73.9%	70.4%	69.0%	63.9%
Full-time	48.8%	37.0%	44.3%	37.2%	37.0%
Part-time	28.6%	37.0%	26.1%	31.9%	26.9%
Type of Job					
Professional	11.5%	4.0%	9.9%	7.7%	10.1%
Service	65.4%	64.4%	58.0%	57.7%	59.4%
Manual	23.1%	31.7%	32.1%	34.6%	30.4%
More than one job	55.0%	34.1%	33.9%	31.0%	25.9%
Median days worked	45	49	33	70	35
Median earned income/mo.	$162	$145	$133	$220	$127
Median income/workday[c]	$22.70	$22.90	$23.65	$22.90	$23.10

[a]Percentages are of the entire sample.
[b]Percentages of those unemployed only.
[c]Calculated only on those who were gainfully employed during the period. Value equals earned income for entire period divided by days worked during period.

income arena, so we asked the participants why they left each job during the study. People in the study reported that the main reason for job termination was quitting—over half of all terminations were because the individual left the job. In slightly over 10% of terminations, the person was fired. When we probed further about why individuals quit or left a job, they most often said they were laid off. Only about 12% indicated that their mental illness was the reason they left a job, and less than 10% said that problems with the boss caused them to leave. We also asked those who were not looking for work at baseline why they were not. The most frequent answers were because of depression (25%), anxiety (13.5%), and stress (13.5%).

Because of the subtle and often complex reasons for leaving a job or not working, text data are perhaps more instructive than the closed categories above. The following excerpts, each from a different person, convey in often stark terms the apprehensions experienced and obstacles faced by the study participants in work environments.

> [How have people been treating you since you've been out? Do they know you were in the hospital?] [M]y boss at work, he knows that I got the job through Triangle J [supported employed program] because they pay the first month's salary. And he looks at me 57 years old, and having somebody else to pay the first month's salary—you sort of wonder, you know, at the beginning . . . [after describing a problem at work] . . . well, as I said, prejudice against me, or doubts about me, because I was helped, you know, by the state.

> [What kind of help could the system give you?] I need help for training for my occupation depending on the testing and what I can do to try to work around my impairment. I need to identify another occupation and be trained for that so I can support myself. Otherwise I'm going to end up on welfare, and Medicaid, and Social Security, and whatever else is available, and not be able to earn a living. But the help that schizophrenic patients are getting is minimal, because there's really not a whole lot I can do. . . . I can't get insurance. They're not going to hire schizophrenics. . . . Unless the insurance companies got together in the United States and perhaps with government encouragement, and even assistance, created a special industrial insurance package so that in a controlled manner schizophrenics could be trained and be given a job even if they couldn't earn enough of their support . . . those who could work ought to work just because it gives them useful things to do.

> The way this society is set up and the way the mental health is, they could put me in an environment. They can institutionalize me right in here for the rest of my life if they wanted to. And here I am—I just proved—I went down to Florida and got two jobs. Man said he would hire me back any time I come back. I just proved to myself

that I can go down there and work. So, let's say I do live in the car. I've seen tents pitched in the middle of the cities. I mean if you've got to work. I'm able to work. But to pitch a tent out there because I don't have a home, you're weird or something is wrong with you. It's just that I don't have a place to stay is all. I'm willing to work. I'm able to work. I'm able to function. I've proved that.

I've been looking for a part-time clerical job. At the library and Meals on Wheels. And I had two interviews at the library to be a page, put the books up on the shelves, and I didn't get either job. They picked people in junior high school, juniors in high school who worked at Hardee's for the summer. So, it looked like discrimination to me. I mean, I'm a college graduate, and I worked there volunteer. I think there's discrimination, I don't know, for people on disability. It's hard getting a job if you put that on the application.

Well, when I look back on the whole thing now, I see the whole scenario—it is not anything but a wicked scenario. That explains why I probably have had trouble with trying to get a job. First of all, if anybody looked into my background, I was afraid of this from the very beginning with being put in Dorothea Dix [state psychiatric hospital], I told them so. If you tell the truth on your application then your chances of getting a job are next to nothing. It's just one big Catch-22 is what it is.

My status changed once they found out I was in the hospital. Somebody told them, you know. I mean, I was great, good, glorious—coming along just fine 'til they found out that about me. And then I was, you know, the scum of the earth, and my God!—what to do with me.

When I think of trying to apply for jobs that would pay more money, with background checks and things like that, I feel like it would stand in my way, you know. Because, you know with a history of going into mental institutions, people don't hire you. That scares me, you know. I'm going back to try to get my degree, and I don't want that to stand in my way, you know? It'd be all for nothing. I guess that's the main thing that bothers me, that's always going to be in the corner somewhere in the back of my mind, that I'll be rejected because of it, you know.

It's not fair to people who have this illness because we don't, and this is true, you don't get the chance to advance. If you're in the hospital once or twice a year, and your employer knows it, you're not going to get advanced.

Family Interviews

Sixty-four interviews were conducted with the most significant other designated by the patient in the study. These interviews revealed a picture of families with few financial resources who were providing a substantial amount of financial and instrumental support to the patients. Family members were often actively engaged in the SSI/SSDI application process.

Over two-thirds of those interviewed were mothers, and 57.8% lived with the patient. Nearly 60% of the family members interviewed were married, while the remainder were divorced or widowed. Nearly 60% reported that another close relative had been hospitalized with serious psychiatric or substance abuse problems, but only 20% reported ever receiving any outpatient psychiatric services themselves. Nearly 75% had daily contact with the patient, and over 90% saw him or her weekly. Over two-thirds thought the patient was mentally ill. The median yearly household income was approximately $20,000, and over half of those interviewed were currently working full-time. Over two-thirds of the relatives said they were financially responsible for the patient, and 53% rated the financial impact of the patient's problems on their family from moderate to overwhelming. Yet 47% rated the financial impact as none or minimal. About 25% of the household income was reported expended on behalf of the patient by over 80% of those interviewed. The median direct costs on behalf of the patient expended by the family was $416 per month. Over half of the relatives said that their resources met their own needs only adequately or poorly.

As noted above, family members initiated nearly as many of the applications for SSI/SSDI as did mental health professionals. These relatives, primarily parents, engaged in the process of application in large part because they were providing housing and other subsistence to their mentally ill relative and needed financial assistance. Over 70% also felt that their family members could not work or support themselves financially. Only five of those interviewed were representative payees.[4] Among the whole sample of recipients 20% (11) had payees. Their roles ranged from playing the role of banker with minimal supervision of expenditures to daily management of money.

> But it's almost like he's regressed in some ways, like he's a little kid, as far as like with money and stuff . . . like I have to be custodian of his money, and if I say to him here's $20, now make this last a couple of days, or if I give him $5 for a day, he's still going to spend that that day . . . so the only way I can do it is just doling it out.

Others found themselves in the uncomfortable position of being the liaison with employers:

> Well, I had to tell them that he was hospitalized—why he wasn't at work. Maybe I should have lied and said he was at—well, I figured if I told them he was at Rex hospital with a broken arm, they would have called, you know. So what was I going to do? Maybe you shouldn't tell the truth all the time. But how you going

to explain that he's not at work for a couple of weeks or more? I mean you going to lose your job that-a-way. So, I don't know. . . . Now, the boss told me they wanted him. I explained the condition as best I could, and told him that. And of course, he asked, "Is he violent? Has he ever been?" I said, "No, of course not. He's never been violent. There's no problem with that." I never told them that there was—I had seen potential for violence, but he actually never has become violent. And the boss was wanting him to come back to work, and he had started back a couple of days when the big boss came to town and found out about it. Then all of a sudden they didn't need him. . . . And so there's no doubt in my mind that the stigma of mental illness is such that it's very difficult to conquer over.

Family members were also greatly influenced by the prognostic assessments of mental health providers. One mother related the reasons why she initiated an application for disability income for her son:

I told the doctor and the social worker . . . "Now, I want to know specifically is B. lazy, and is that why he won't work? Or is there a real problem, and he is not capable. Now that's what I want to know. Please evaluate him and give me an answer." So this particular doctor told me on the phone, "Ms. V., you are right your son is not capable." . . . Now, it was after that that I took B. down and we filled out the papers . . . to apply for medical disability. . . . So I said [to herself], "Now if he's not capable then that means— they have not told me that he will ever be capable, so I have to go on the assumption that he will never be capable." He can't go on living like this the rest of his life. So, I went down and I said, "Son, then we will go and apply for medical disability." He said, "OK, Mom."

Her son's version of the application process was somewhat different. He said that the application was an "agreement" between him and his mother, but that it was "mainly her suggestion." When asked, "Why does she think that you should apply?" he answered, "Because she doesn't fully understand that there is nothing wrong with me. . . . It's just that I have a few minor problems that are real easy to solve . . . and she sees it as me having a problem I can't solve. In other words, it's like she has a real negative attitude to me . . . she says it's [his inability to work] because there is something wrong with me."

Analysis of Individual Domains

The coefficients in Tables 3–9 are effects on the odds of application for each conceptual domain. For each domain, time-period variables are examined

Table 3 Effects of Demographic Variables on the Odds of Application ($N = 395$)

Explanatory Variables	Model 1	Model 2
Time Periods		
Pre–time 2	0.4129**	0.4167**
Pre–time 3	0.1528***	0.1551***
Pre–time 4	0.1198***	0.1237***
Pre–time 5	0.2716**	0.2907**
Demographic Variables		
African-American	—	0.9303
SES 1	—	0.4688
SES 2	—	0.9587
SES 3	—	0.4869
SES 4	—	0.8806
Female	—	0.8523
Age	—	1.0229
Married	—	0.2218*
Intercept	0.3273***	0.2726**
Model chi-square	25.55***/4df	35.50***/12df
Chi-square change	—	9.95/8df
Applications	55	55

*$p < .10$.
**$p < .05$.
***$p < .01$.

alone in model 1, and with the domain variables in model 2. Significant coefficients greater than 1 reflect increases in the probability of application occurring, with increases in the explanatory variables. Nonsignificant coefficients reflect no effect of the explanatory variable. Fractional significant coefficients reflect decreases in the probability of application occurring, with increases in the explanatory variables.

The time-period variables (pre–time 2 to pre–time 5) refer to the six-month study periods during which subjects applied for disability income. The reference category is the group that applied after the baseline interview and before time 2. The results for each domain indicate that individuals in the study were less likely to apply at each time period after the first, and that different types of people applied at different times. These findings mirror the descriptive pattern; that is, nearly half of all applications took place between the baseline and time-2 interviews, with application frequency declining steadily over the life of the study. The effects of time on application with the introduction of other explanatory variables remain significant for each domain except clinical impairment.

Among demographic variables (table 3), being married significantly low-

Table 4 Effects of Clinical Variables on the Odds of Application ($N = 353$)

Explanatory Variables	Model 1	Model 2
Time Periods		
Pre–Time 2	0.3411**	0.7208
Pre–Time 3	0.1682***	0.2465
Pre–Time 4	0.1321***	0.2587
Pre–Time 5	0.2477**	0.5426
Clinical Variables		
Schizophrenia	—	0.9678
Affective disorder	—	0.5228
Personality disorder	—	0.4491
BPRS score	—	1.0763*
PERI AH score	—	0.8012
PERI DM score	—	2.3691**
PERI SP score	—	0.8015
PERI PH score	—	1.1263
PERI SI score	—	1.0393
PERI CT score	—	0.7468
PERI FBP score	—	1.5218
PERI M score	—	0.6258
Newly hospitalized	—	3.6752**
Years since first hospitalization	—	0.9872
Days in hospital in last six months	—	0.9908
Days in hospital over lifetime	—	1.0019
Days in hospital during the study	—	1.0095*
Intercept	0.3365***	0.0267***
Model chi-square	24.03***/4*df*	58.13***/21*df*
Chi-square change	—	34.10**/17*df*
Applications	51	51

*p < .10.
**p < .05
***p < .01.

ered the odds that a person would apply for disability income. Among clinical impairment variables (table 4), higher scores on the BPRS and PERI demoralization (DM) scales significantly increased the odds of application, as did hospital days during the study period and, as important, a hospitalization in the interview period prior to application (newly hospitalized). In terms of income, those who earned more were significantly less likely to apply, while those who considered themselves to be doing worse financially than others their age were more likely to apply (table 5). Within the domain of work, attending school and more days worked significantly lowered the odds that a person would apply for disability (table 6). The odds of application increased

Table 5 Effects of Income Variables on the Odds of Application ($N = 340$)

Explanatory Variables	Model 1	Model 2
Time Periods		
Pre–time 2	0.3693**	0.3740**
Pre–time 3	0.1341***	0.1742***
Pre–time 4	0.0566***	0.0928**
Pre–time 5	0.1820***	0.3182*
Income Variables		
Needs taken care of		
Poorly	—	2.0007
Adequately	—	1.0990
Fairly well	—	0.8538
Financial status		
Worse than others	—	2.7175**
Better than others	—	1.6158
Earned income	—	0.8229**
Intercept	0.3924***	0.2146***
Model chi-square	30.48***/4df	51.34***/10df
Chi-square change	—	20.86***/6df
Applications	48	48

*$p < .10$.
**$p < .05$.
***$p < .01$.

significantly with the number of outpatient mental health visits during the study (table 7). Respondents who were financially dependent on their families and who reported one or more difficulties in instrumental activities of daily living were significantly more likely to apply. In addition, individuals who rated themselves as submissive and dependent psychologically on their significant other (SASB submit coefficient) were more likely to seek SSI/SSDI. Living with a spouse lowered the odds of application, as did having more MHPs on the network (table 8). Adhering to an emotional explanation of mental illness lowered the odds of application, while individuals who were uncertain about whether they were mentally ill or not were more likely to apply (table 9).

These analyses indicate that applicants for disability income among the cohort fit a profile that might be expected. That is, compared to those who did not apply, the applicants had been hospitalized recently, were faring poorly financially and in the work force, were more impaired clinically, were more dependent on their families psychologically and instrumentally, and were unmarried. Those individuals who were the most disabled in multiple

Table 6 Effects of Work Variables on the Odds of Application ($N = 374$)

Explanatory Variables	Model 1	Model 2
Time Periods		
Pre–time 2	0.4696*	0.5247
Pre–time 3	0.1645***	0.2168**
Pre–time 4	0.1377***	0.1874**
Pre–time 5	0.2157**	0.3013*
Work Variables		
Working mostly part-time	—	1.0167
Working mostly full-time	—	1.5350
Attending school	—	0.2722**
Number of days worked		
During last six months	—	0.9921**
Intercept	0.3091***	0.4638**
Model chi-square	23.36***/4*df*	37.10***/8*df*
Chi-square change	—	13.74***/4*df*
Applications	51	51

*$p < .10$.
**$p < .05$.
***$p < .01$.

life domains were those who turned to SSI/SSDI as a source of material support.

Combined Analysis of Domains

Next, we combined the variables from the domains and created the equations reported in table 10, the full event-history model of application. At least one variable from each domain was significant in the first stage of analysis, and all of these were included in the final analysis. Even within this sample, assembled around SSA eligibility criteria, application was a rare event. The marginal probability of application in this sample was 0.178. Table 10 shows that among all the significant variables from each domain, the significant predictors of application were demoralization; more psychiatric hospital days during the study period; financial dependence on families; whether respondents rated their financial situation as worse than that of others their age; one or more problems in instrumental activities of daily living; and higher rating of oneself as submissive and dependent on significant others.

It is evident that the perceived need for SSI/SSDI, demonstrated by application, is not bounded by demographic or diagnostic factors, but rather by

Table 7 Effects of Service-System Use Variables on the Odds of Application ($N = 392$)

Explanatory Variables	Model 1	Model 2
Time Periods		
Pre–time 2	0.3875**	0.3220***
Pre–time 3	0.1571***	0.1314***
Pre–time 4	0.1233***	0.1107***
Pre–time 5	0.2794**	0.2610**
Service-System Use Variables		
Nonuser	—	1.4202
Episodic user	—	0.6929
County mental health center user	—	2.1885
Private therapist user	—	0.6173
Outpatient visits	—	1.0179*
Days as outpatient	—	0.9980
Intercept	0.3182***	0.2503
Model chi-square	24.71***/4df	34.93**/10df
Chi-square change	—	10.22/6df
Applications	53	53

*$p < .10$.
**$p < .05$.
***$p < .01$.

what might be summarized as dysfunction, dependence, and despair. The analysis suggests that dysfunction, dependence, and despair exert independent and significant effects on decisions to apply for disability income. Those who viewed themselves as comparatively in need financially, who were experiencing clinical and functional difficulties, who felt helpless and in despair about themselves, and who experienced themselves as submissively dependent on their families applied for disability income. The findings therefore suggest that SSI/SSDI benefits are being sought by those for whom the programs were intended.

Discussion

A confluence of social, personal, and clinical conditions interact in complex ways to direct an individual to apply for disability income. It is perhaps as important to note the factors that we expected to be influential that were *not*: amount of work and earned income. These are indicators of considerable interest to those who determine eligibility for SSI/SSDI, and constitute the primary rationale for the programs, that is, that individuals with severe, persisting, or terminal illnesses who cannot work and who lack adequate

Table 8 Effects of Social Network, Social Support, and Dependence Variables on the Odds of Application ($N = 353$)

Explanatory Variables	Model 1	Model 2
Time Periods		
Pre–Time 2	0.3175***	0.3086**
Pre–Time 3	0.1250***	0.1131***
Pre–Time 4	0.1020***	0.0826***
Pre–Time 5	0.2273***	0.2371*
Social Network, Social Support, and Dependence Variables		
One or more difficulties with daily living	—	2.9716**
One or more helpers with daily living	—	0.9794
One or more MHPs in network	—	1.6435
One or more MHPs on grid	—	1.8489
Living alone	—	2.1361
Parent in household	—	0.8258
Spouse in household	—	0.1734*
Adult child in house	—	0.6924
Financially dependent on family	—	2.7394***
SASB submit coefficient	—	2.2058**
SASB control coefficient	—	0.5519
Symmetry	—	0.7839
Social network size	—	1.0101
Percentage of friends in network	—	0.9864
Percentage of MHPs in network	—	0.9484**
Intercept	0.4000***	0.2415*
Model chi-square	30.35***/4*df*	63.68***/19*df*
Chi-square change	—	33.33**/15*df*
Applications	51	51

*$p < .10$.
**$p < .05$
***$p < .01$.

financial resources deserve public financial support. Somewhat surprisingly, amount of earned income and number of days worked do *not* have a strong influence in the final model of application. One possible interpretation is that there was very little variation in earned income among the sample; it was quite low, with the median per month ranging from $127 to $162. Given the universally meager circumstances of the cohort, what prompted application was the person's assessment of relative poverty, that is, whether they were doing worse than others, and how great were the needs of others on whom they were dependent. The findings do not support a view of disabled persons who seek disability income as people who choose not to work. Rather, we

Table 9 Effects of Illness Behavior Variables on the Odds of Application ($N = 376$)

Explanatory Variables	Model 1	Model 2
Time Periods		
Pre–time 2	0.4105**	0.4719*
Pre–time 3	0.1580***	0.1589***
Pre–time 4	0.1455**	0.1634**
Pre–time 5	0.2716**	0.3107**
Illness Behavior Variables		
Self-labeling		
Yes	—	1.3738
Don't know	—	2.7191*
Explanatory model		
Medical model	—	0.6617
Emotional model	—	0.3643*
Medical/emotional model	—	0.7999
Other model	—	0.8351
Intercept	0.3273***	0.3903**
Model chi-square	23.14***/4df	31.16***/10df
Chi-square change	—	8.02/6df
Applications	54	54

*$p < .10$.
**$p < .05$.
***$p < .01$.

provide ample evidence that repeated and continual efforts to work and earn adequate income fail. We find not a failure of will, but of opportunity, circumstance, and ability.

It is also important to recall that this analysis is of pathways to disability income *among* a cohort of individuals with major psychiatric disorders. Perhaps the work and income factors would be salient if the investigation explored application among a cohort that included people without psychiatric diagnoses, or a sample not drawn primarily from psychiatric hospital patients. This analysis helps to identify factors that prompt individuals who are impaired by psychiatric illness to apply for disability income, not to identify appliers from among the general population.

Recent days in hospital (i.e., during the study), which was salient, may play one of several roles here. First, being in the hospital almost always precludes an individual from working or earning income. Hospital days may be a more powerful composite indicator of impairment and inability to work than either of those factors alone. Individuals who applied may have been in the hospital longer because they were more impaired, lacked the resources for discharge, because they were waiting for application and receipt before

Table 10 Effects of Significant Domain Variables Taken Together on the Odds of Application ($N = 297$)

Explanatory Variables	
Time Periods	
Pre–time 2	0.4756
Pre–time 3	0.1651*
Pre–time 4	0.3183
Pre–time 5	0.7834
Demographic Variables	
Married	0.9251
Clinical Variables	
BPRS score	1.0347
PERI DM score	2.0075**
Newly hospitalized	2.5241
Days in hospital during the study	1.0073*
Income Variables	
Financial status	
Worse than others	3.9029***
Better than others	1.4508
Earned income	0.7470
Work Variables	
Attending school	0.4586
Number of days worked during last six months	1.0060
Service-System Use Variables	
Outpatient visits	1.0098
Social Network, Social Support, and Dependence Variables	
One or more difficulties with daily living	2.9562**
Spouse in household	0.2578
Financially dependent on family	2.4244*
SASB submit coefficient	2.4218**
Percentage of MHPs in network	0.9772
Illness Behavior Variables	
Self-labeling	
Yes	0.4698
Don't know	1.0425
Explanatory model	
Medical model	1.4969
Emotional model	0.5438
Medical/emotional model	0.5599
Other model	1.2246
Intercept	0.0055***
Model chi-square	78.63***/26*df*
Applications	45

*p < .10.
**p < .05.
***p < .01.

discharge, or because the longer they stayed in the hospital, the more likely the staff were to initiate an application. The influence of hospital days during the study on application also suggests that individuals who have more and closer recent contact with providers will be urged to apply or assisted with application more than others. Apparently, the decision to apply for disability is more heavily influenced by recent events than longer term trends (i.e., lifetime hospital days).

The finding that financial dependence on family influences application bolsters our argument that getting on disability often happens within and because of a family context, and lends support to the needs/resources/dependence model of application. It is important to view this instrumental dependence in tandem with the significance of self-reported submissiveness reflected in the SASB submit coefficients. First, it is possible that the experience of submissiveness was compounded or even caused by the financial and functional needs of the respondents. In this sense, getting disability income might help to lessen their actual and perceived dependence on others. Second, those who became formally designated as disabled were dependent psychologically and functionally *before* they applied or SSI/SSDI.

Our view is that for the most part, application for SSI/SSDI is something that happened to respondents, not with their help or by their initiative. Pragmatic rather than clinical or more philosophical concerns drive the process, and what this move means to the individual in terms of stigma, loss of self-esteem, or giving up is less important at the time than the material resources that SSI/SSDI can provide for applicants and their social network members. The pessimism or realism of family members about the current and future financial circumstances of their loved ones, influenced often by the prognostications of providers, reflects their needs for immediate financial support as caregivers and their concerns about the future. Disability income addresses these needs.

Similarly, SSI/SSDI receipt serves multiple purposes from the providers' point of view, including potential reimbursement for their services via Medicaid or Medicare, decreased financial stress for the client and family, and access to resources such as housing reserved for clients who are disability income recipients. We found that while outpatient service use was not a significant predictor of application in the multivariate analysis, the rate of application increased incrementally with mental health center service use (figure 2). Those who used the most services were the most likely to apply.

The important point is that SSI/SSDI receipt by a person with a psychiatric disorder plays multiple roles for multiple parties, and meets the needs of many different people and systems. Disability income application and receipt should not therefore be viewed as characteristics of individuals, but as a reflection of them in the context of their daily lives, families, and mental health service systems. In this sense, disability is a relative term, reflecting a gap between needs and resources, expectations and abilities, desires and realities.

The PERI demoralization scale was the only measure of severity of symptoms that distinguished between appliers and nonappliers, yet we are cautious about concluding that symptom severity is implicated in prompting application. The DM scale is like a mini-PERI that includes items that reflect psychotic symptoms (e.g., feeling confused and having trouble thinking), somatization (e.g., bothered by all different kinds of ailments in different parts of your body), and feelings of despair (e.g., feeling completely helpless, hopeless, wondering if anything was worthwhile anymore). This self report measure of multidimensional distress, or what Dohrenwend et al. (1980) refer to as "non-specific or global psychological distress," was a stronger predictor of application than either the separate symptom scales in the PERI, or the interviewer-rated BPRS, which focused more narrowly on symptomatology. The idea behind the DM scale derives from Frank's (1973) concept of demoralization as the experience of combined anxiety, hopelessness, sadness, and poor self-esteem as distinct from psychopathology, yet often associated with and confused with psychopathology. The respondents in this study may well have experienced demoralization as a consequence of their symptoms or their impact on their lives, and their symptoms may have increased as a result of their demoralization. Yet, the DM scale has a significant independent effect on application. This suggests strongly that it is the loss of hope and the experience of lack of competence in daily living—reflected by instrumental and psychological dependence—that together lead to applying for disability income.

The significance of demoralization—both the scale and the concept—for the application process is entirely consistent with the multidimensional conceptual foundations of this investigation. We have sought to explore the extent to which it was possible to illuminate disablement as a process that proceeds at many levels and across many conceptual domains. Our findings demonstrate that this is not only feasible, but indeed necessary.

Conclusions: Dysfunction, Dependence, Despair, and Disablement
Revisiting Impairment, Labeling, and Needs/Resources/Dependence

The results lend some support to each of the three conceptual models of disablement that the project was designed to test. The impairment and needs/resources/dependence models are the most strongly supported, followed by the labeling model. The clinical impairment model predicts that individuals with the most severe symptoms and diagnoses, longer histories of psychiatric disorder, and with more days in hospital will by virtue of the degree of their

impairment apply for and receive SSI/SSDI. The needs/resources/depen-
dence model argues that individuals with the largest gap between their needs
and resources, who are the most dependent on a social network with inadequate resources, will apply for SSI/SSDI. The labeling model considers that
a person who self-labels as mentally ill, who is in frequent and extended
contact with providers (i.e., in the role of a psychiatric patient), who has a
medical illness account, who is a substantial consumer of inpatient and outpatient services, and who has fewer social roles and identities to compete with
that of disabled person or patient will apply for SSI/SSDI. Each of these
perspectives received some empirical support from the event-history analysis
of applications, but none emerges alone as an entirely satisfactory explanation.

For heuristic reasons, we have separated what are probably three component constructs of a more complex model of disablement. Indeed the formal
SSA criteria for eligibility include elements incorporated into each conceptual
model. For example, by design the SSDI program focuses on medical severity
of impairment and ability to return to work, and does not take the financial
resources of the applicant into account; that is, SSDI is not means tested.
SSI is based on the same medical and employability criteria, but does take
other available material resources into account. Thus, we would expect more
SSI recipients to fit the needs/resources/dependence model, while SSDI beneficiaries would be more likely to follow the impairment and labeling formula-
tions. Future analyses of SSI and SSDI recipients will shed some light on
whether this is the case.

We have argued that the loss of self, self-esteem, valued social roles, and
other aspects of a nonpatient identity that accompany self-labeling may lead
to taking on or may reinforce the chronic sick role, resulting in a poorer life
and illness course (Charmaz 1983, 1987; Estroff et al. 1991; Estroff 1989,
1993; Friedland and McColl 1992; Thompson 1988). We were especially
interested to find out whether and how self-labeling influenced application
for SSI/SSDI. We expected that individuals who thought they were mentally
ill would be more likely to apply. Indeed, 68% of the people who consistently
labeled themselves as mentally ill applied, compared to 45% of those who
did not self-label. The interrelations between self-labeling and application do
not present a picture that is linear or simple (see figure 3). For example,
nearly half of the applicants did not consider themselves to be mentally ill.
Since so many applications were initiated by others, this is not surprising.
Possibly, the applicants who did not self-label differentiated between being
disabled and being mentally ill. Disabled is a broader, perhaps more benign,
category with different sociocultural meanings than mental patient or mentally
ill (Caras 1994). Getting disability may represent something distinct from
being sick, and being on disability may be less stigmatizing than being men-

tally ill. Many of the study participants and their families indicated repeatedly that they had pressing basic material needs. In order to survive, no doubt, individuals who resisted or rejected the label of mental illness pragmatically agreed to the disabled designation.

Link (1987) shows that demoralization and expectations of rejection or devaluation by others among former, current, and repeat-contact psychiatric patients results in withdrawal from social interactions, including employment. Thus, the labeled person expects to be rejected, and avoids contact with others, specifically in the workplace. As a result, they earn less or do not work, compounding isolation, demoralization, and poverty. Link (1982) has argued further that "the acquisition of the status of mental patient appears to have a negative impact on a person's chances of getting and keeping a job" (p. 210), and has demonstrated that patient status negatively affects income. In another vein, Thoits (1983) argues that multiple social identities are associated with increased psychological well-being. When one fails or experiences less competence or gratification in a particular identity, such as spouse, one may compensate with success in another arena, such as parenthood or work. The loss or absence of valued and various social interpersonal roles may then lead to prolonged sick-role occupancy, decreased or more fragile well-being, and, we would infer, greater risk for disablement. Her formulation parallels our own (Estroff 1989), which suggests that progressive role constriction and the fusion of identity with illness among persons with major mental illness contributes to, indeed constitutes, chronicity.

At the policy level, the rapid growth of illness-tested welfare programs nationally, the emerging political and social force of disabled persons, and efforts to curb long-term health care costs present difficult resource-allocation questions (Stone 1979, 1984; Berkowitz 1987; Mechanic and Rochefort 1992, IOM 1990; Wolfe and Haveman 1990; Lerman 1985). For example, are we more inclined to pay for supported employment programs so that a person with a serious disability can find and keep a job or to pay for nursing home care? The inevitability of retrenchment in entitlement programs (if not their actual disappearance), the unhappy history of the massive terminations of mentally ill persons from the disability rolls in 1981, and the evidently increasing reliance on SSI and SSDI for basic subsistence among the target population causes concern and increases the need for improved understanding of how SSI and SSDI influence the lives of applicants and recipients.

This is especially important in view of the substantial reliance on SSI and SSDI among the severely mentally ill population and their low termination rate; at present a meager 0.5% of recipients terminate receipt because of improvement or rehabilitation. The repeated attempts of participants in our study to work and the influential role of their dependence on their families in applying for disability income suggest that finding less restrictive ways to support them and their families while they work toward rehabilitation would benefit everyone. Disability income becomes an end rather than a means to restoration when fears of losing needed resources accompany improvement.

Overall, the event-history findings demonstrate that it is a combination of dysfunction, dependence, and despair that direct individuals to disability income. The qualitative data frame these results in a complicated but coherent picture. We learn that no single factor accounts for the pathways to SSI/SSDI application. Rather, individuals who lack material and social resources, who try repeatedly to work but who cannot earn enough, who feel stigmatized by their experiences and by others, and whose social networks cannot support them adequately seek other means of survival. Living on disability is a harsh reality of being mentally ill—seldom, it seems, a personal choice but more a matter of necessity. The many costs of being on disability challenge us to find alternatives to ''no other way to go.''

Acknowledgments

The research reported here was supported by grant number MH 40314 from the National Institute of Mental Health. In the course of this research, we benefited immeasurably from the advice and enthusiasm of Linda K. George, and the extraordinary programming skills and patience of Robert Schwartz. Linda Illingworth, Anna Johnston, and Bob Ruth were the primary interviewers and contributed a great deal to the analysis. We thank also the four participating hospitals and area mental health programs and their staffs for their cooperation, without which the study could not have been conducted or completed. The Department of Social Medicine provided a generous home for the work, and the Sheps Center for Health Services Research offered data management expertise and resources beyond the call of duty. Finally, but most importantly, we thank the primary study participants—patients and their family members—whose candor and willingness to let us chronicle their lives during difficult times cannot be fully repaid. We hope that we have learned what they taught us well enough to help in some ways to ease the many burdens that they bear with courage and dignity.

Notes

1. The Social Security Administration defines disability as ''the inability to do any substantial gainful activity by reason of any medically determinable physical or mental impairment which can be expected to result in death or which has lasted or can be expected to last for a continuous period of not less than 12 months.'' Substantial gainful activity (SGA) was set by the Social Security Administration as over $300 per month in earned income until January 1990, when it was raised to $500 per

month. SGA includes work activity that is done for pay or profit, involving significant physical or mental activity. Supplemental Security Income (SSI) began in 1974 as a program to provide income supports or supplements to aged persons and to blind and disabled adults and children who were not considered to be disabled workers or covered by the Social Security Disability Insurance program (SSDI). SSI and SSDI use the same medical listings of impairments, evaluation criteria for severity of dysfunction, and definitions of disability. SSI is administered by the states, and payments are supplemented in some of these states. Thus, SSI payment levels vary nationally. SSI is means-tested, or income-and-asset-tested, and SSDI is not. SSI eligibility requires no prior paid employment or contribution to the Social Security system. SSDI eligibility includes a prior work requirement, and payment levels are based on the amount of prior work contributions to the Social Security system. Recipients of both SSI and SSDI are required to undergo a continuing disability review every three to five years.

Some individuals receive both SSI and SSDI, and are known as dual recipients. Most dual recipients with psychiatric disabilities have worked at low-paying jobs that did not provide an adequate amount of SSDI payments when their contribution was calculated. In this circumstance, SSI payments supplement the SSDI payment so that it reaches an administratively set minimum level.

2. These results reveal an unfortunately widespread misconception among the families and, presumably, the researchers. An individual does not apply separately for SSI or SSDI. The same application can result in receipt of either or both. It is during the disability determination process that decisions are made about whether a person is eligible and for which program.

3. We were particularly concerned to avoid influencing study participants with regard to applying for SSI/SSDI. We asked about SSI/SSDI at baseline only to make certain that the person was not a recipient. At subsequent interviews, we inquired about SSI or SSDI as part of the income section of the interview and as a final event checklist item. Only when there was an affirmative answer about application did we pursue the topic further. While it is possible that being in the study had some impact, the rate of application following the baseline interview was the highest during the study for other reasons. This was the only time period during which everyone had been hospitalized, a factor which later analyses show has some influence on application. While the number of eligible nonappliers decreased over the life of the study, by the last interview, nearly 15% of the sample remained eligible by income alone and had not applied.

4. When, in the opinion of the Social Security Administration, an individual is not capable of managing money, a representative payee may be appointed to receive and administer the SSI/SSDI payments. The payee may be a family member or another person designated by the recipient.

References

Adams, E. K., M. R. Elwood, and P. L. Pine. 1989. Utilization and Expenditures under Medicaid for Supplemental Security Income Disabled. *Health Care Finance Review* 11(1): 1–24.

Allison, Paul D. 1982. Discrete-Time Methods for the Analysis of Event Histories. In
S. Leinhardt, ed., *Sociological Methodology*. San Francisco: Jossey-Bass, 61–98.
———. 1984. *Event History Analysis: Regression for Longitudinal Event Data*. Bev-
erly Hills, CA: Sage Publications.
Anderson, Jack R. 1982. Social Security and SSI Benefits for the Mentally Disabled.
Hospital and Community Psychiatry 33(4): 295–298.
Anthony, William A. 1993. Recovery from Mental Illness. *Innovations and Research*
2(3): 17–24.
Anthony, William A., and M. Jansen. 1984. Predicting the Vocational Capacity of
the Chronically Mentally Ill: Research and Policy Implications. *American Psychol-
ogist* 39: 537–544.
Baxter, E., and K. Hopper. 1982. The New Mendicancy: Homelessness in New York
City. *American Journal of Orthopsychiatry* 52: 393–408.
Benjamin, Lorna S. 1974. Structural Analysis of Social Behavior. *Psychological
Review* 81: 392–425.
———. 1979. Structural Analysis of Differentiation Failure. *Psychiatry* 42: 1–23.
———. 1993. *Interpersonal Diagnosis of Personality Disorders*. New York: Guilford
Press.
Berkowitz, E. D. 1987. *Disabled Policy*. New York: Cambridge University Press.
Berkowitz, Monroe. 1986. Illness Behavior and Disability. In S. McHugh and T.
Vallis, eds., *Illness Behavior*. New York: Plenum Press, 189–203.
Black, Bertram. 1988. *Work and Mental Illness*. Baltimore: Johns Hopkins University
Press.
Bond, Gary R., and S. L. Boyer. 1988. Rehabilitation Programs and Outcomes. In
J. A. Ciardiella and M. D. Bell, eds., *Vocational Rehabilitation of Persons with
Prolonged Psychiatric Disorders*. Baltimore: Johns Hopkins University Press,
231–263.
Cain, L. P. 1993. Obtaining Social Welfare Benefits for Persons with Serious Mental
Illness. *Hospital and Community Psychiatry* 44(10): 977–980.
Calsyn, Robert J., C. W. Kohfeld, and L. A. Roades. 1993. Urban Homeless People
and Welfare: Who Receives Benefits? *American Journal of Community Psychology*
21(1): 95–112.
Caras, Sylvia. 1994. Disabled: One More Label. *Hospital and Community Psychiatry*
45(4): 323–324.
Carpentier, Normand, A. Lesage, J. Goulet, P. Lalonde, and M. Renaud. 1992.
Burden of Care of Families Not Living with Schizophrenic Relatives. *Hospital and
Community Psychiatry* 43(1): 38–43.
Charmaz, Kathy. 1983. Loss of Self: A Fundamental Form of Suffering in the Chronically Ill. *Sociology of Health and Illness* 5(2): 168–195.
———. 1987. Struggling for a Self: Identity Levels of the Chronically Ill. *Research
in the Sociology of Health Care* 6: 238–321.
Chirikos, T. N. 1989. Aggregate Economic Losses from Disability in the United
States: A Preliminary Assay. *The Milbank Quarterly* 67 (supp. 2, part 1):
59–91.
Cohen, Carl I. 1993. Poverty and the Course of Schizophrenia. *Hospital and Community Psychiatry* 44(10): 951–957.

Conrad, Peter. 1987. The Experience of Illness. *Research in the Sociology of Health Care* 6: 1–31.

Cook, Judith A. 1988. Who "Mothers" the Chronically Mentally Ill? *Family Relations* 37: 42–49.

Corbin, Juliet, and A. L. Strauss. 1987. Accompaniments of Chronic Illness: Changes in Body, Self, Biography, and Biographical Time. *Research in the Sociology of Health Care* 6: 249–281.

Dohrenwend, Barbara S., B. P. Dohrenwend, B. Link, and I. Levav. 1983. Social Functioning of Psychiatric Patients in Contrast with Community Cases in the General Population. *Archives of General Psychiatry* 40: 1174–1182.

Dohrenwend, Bruce P., I. Levav, and P. E. Shrout. 1983. Screening Scales from the Psychiatric Epidemiology Research Interview (PERI). In J. Myers, M. Weissman, and C. Ross, eds., *Community Surveys*. Rutgers, NJ: Rutgers University Press.

Dohrenwend, Bruce P., P. E. Shrout, G. Egri, and F. Mendelsohn. 1980. Nonspecific Psychological Distress and Other Dimensions of Psychopathology. *Archives of General Psychiatry* 37: 1129–1236.

Dozier, Mary, M. Harris, and H. Bergman. 1987. Social Network Density and Rehospitalization among Young Adult Patients. *Hospital and Community Psychiatry* 38(1): 61–65.

Dykacz, Janice M., and John C. Hennessey. 1989. Postrecovery Experience of Disabled-Worker Beneficiaries. *Social Security Bulletin* 52(9): 42–60.

Edgerton, Robert B. 1967. *The Cloak of Competence: Stigma in the Lives of the Mentally Retarded*. Berkeley and Los Angeles: University of California Press.

Estroff, Sue E. 1985. *Making It Crazy*. Berkeley and Los Angeles: University of California Press.

———. 1989. Self, Identity, and Schizophrenia: In Search of the Subject. *Schizophrenia Bulletin* 15(2): 189–196.

Estroff, Sue E. 1993. Identity, Disability, and Schizophrenia: The Problem of Chronicity. In S. Lindenbaum and M. Lock, eds., *Knowledge, Power, and Practice: The Anthropology of Medicine and Everyday Life*. Berkeley and Los Angeles: University of California Press, 247–286.

Estroff, Sue E., and Catherine Zimmer. 1994. Social Networks, Social Support, and the Risk for Violence among Persons with Severe, Persistent Mental Illness. In J. Monahan and H. Steadman, eds., *Violence and Mental Disorder: Advances in Risk Assessment*. Chicago: University of Chicago Press, 259–293.

Estroff, Sue E., with William S. Lachicotte, Linda Illingworth, Anna Johnston, and Bob Ruth. 1991. Everybody's Got a Little Mental Illness: Accounts of Illness and Self among Persons with Severe, Persistent Mental Illness. *Medical Anthropology Quarterly* 5: 331–369.

Fisher, G. A., and R. C. Tessler. 1986. Family Bonding of the Mentally Ill: An Analysis of Family Visits with Residents of Board and Care Homes. *Journal of Health and Social Behavior* 27: 236–249.

Frank, Jerome. 1973. *Persuasion and Healing*. Baltimore: Johns Hopkins University Press.

Friedland, Judith, and MaryAnn McColl. 1992. Disability and Depression: Some Etiological Considerations. *Social Science Medicine* 34(4): 395–403.

General Accounting Office. 1989. Social Security Disability: Denied Applicants' Health and Financial Status Compared with Beneficiaries. Report No. B-229289: Human Resources Division (November 1989).

———. 1992. Social Security: Racial Differences in Disability Decisions Warrants Further Investigation. Report No. HRD-92-56 (April 1992).

George, Linda K. 1989. Definition, Classification, and Measurement of Mental Health Services. In C. Taube, D. Mechanic, and A. Hohmann, eds., *The Future of Mental Health Services Research*. DSSH Pub No. (ADM)89-1600. Washington, DC: GPO, 303-319.

Goffman, Erving. 1961. *Stigma*. Englewood Cliffs, NJ: Prentice-Hall.

Goldman, Howard, and A. Gattozzi. 1988. Balance of Powers: Social Security and the Mentally Disabled, 1980-1985. *Milbank Quarterly* 66(3): 531-551.

Goldman, Howard, and R. W. Manderscheid. 1987. Chronic Mental Disorder in the United States. In R. W. Manderscheid and S. Barrett, eds., *Mental Health U.S.* DHHS Pub. No. (ADM)87-1518. Washington, DC: GPO, 1-12.

Grob, G. N. 1983. *Mental Illness and American Society: 1875-1940*. Princeton, NJ: Princeton University Press.

Gronfein, W. 1985. Incentives and Disincentives in Mental Health Policy: A Comparison of the Medicaid and Community Health Programs. *Journal of Health and Social Behavior* 26 (September): 192-206.

Harding, Courtenay. 1988. Course Types in Schizophrenia. *Schizophrenia Bulletin* 14(4): 633-644.

Harding, C., J. Zubin, and J. S. Strauss. 1987. Chronicity in Schizophrenia: Fact, Partial Fact, or Artifact? *Hospital and Community Psychiatry* 38(5): 477-486.

———. 1992. Chronicity in Schizophrenia: Revisited. *British Journal of Psychiatry* 161: 27-37.

Harding, C., J. S. Strauss, H. Hafez, and P. B. Lieberman. 1987. Work and Mental Illness. Part 1. Toward an Integration of the Rehabilitation Process *Journal of Nervous and Mental Disease* 175(6): 317-326.

Hatfield, Agnes. 1992. Leaving Home: Separation Issues in Psychiatric Illnesses. *Psychosocial Rehabilitation Journal* 15(4): 37-48.

Hatfield, Agnes, and H. Lefley, eds. 1987. *Families of the Mentally Ill*. New York: Guilford.

Hennessey, John C., and J. M. Dykacz. 1989. Projected Outcomes and Length of Time in the Disability Insurance Program. *Social Security Bulletin* 52(9): 2-38.

Hollingshead, A. B., and F. Redlich. 1958. *Social Class and Mental Illness*. New York: John Wiley and Sons.

Hopper, K., E. Susser, and S. Conover. 1985. Economies of Makeshift: Deindustrialization and Homelessness in New York City. *Urban Anthropology* 14(1-3): 183-236.

Institute of Medicine. 1990. *Chronic Disease and Disability: Beyond the Acute Care Model*. Institute of Medicine (The Pew Memorial Trust Health Policy Program).

Jacobs, H. E., D. Wissusik, R. Collier, D. Stackman, and D. Burkeman. 1992. Correlations between Psychiatric Disabilities and Vocational Outcome. *Hospital and Community Psychiatry* 43(4): 365-369.

Jacobson, David E. 1986. Types and Timing of Social Support. *Journal of Health and Social Behavior* 27: 250–264.

Kennedy, Cille, and R. W. Manderscheid. 1992. SSDI and SSI Disability Beneficiaries with Mental Disorders. In *Mental Health, United States, 1992*. DHHS. Washington, DC: GPO.

Kochhar, Satya. 1979. Blind and Disabled Persons Awarded Federally Administered SSI Payments, 1975. *Social Security Bulletin* 42(6): 13–23.

Koegel, P., M. A. Burnham, and R. K. Farr. 1988. The Prevalence of Specific Psychiatric Disorders among Homeless Individuals in Inner City Los Angeles. *Archives of General Psychiatry* 45: 1085–92.

Lamb, H. Richard, and A. S. Ragowski. 1978. Supplemental Security Income and the Sick Role. *American Journal of Psychiatry* 135(10: 1121–1224.

Lefley, Harriet. 1987. Aging Parents as Caregivers of Mentally Ill Adult Children: An Emerging Social Problem. *Hospital and Community Psychiatry* 38(10): 1063–1070.

———. 1990. Culture and Chronic Mental Illness. *Hospital and Community Psychiatry* 41(3): 277–286.

Lerman, P. 1985. Deinstitutionalization and Welfare Policies. *Annals of the American Acad. of Political and Social Science* 1985(479): 132–155.

Lindsey, Duncan, and M. Ozawa. 1979. Schizophrenia and SSI. *Social Work* (March): 120–126.

Link, Bruce G. 1982. Mental Patient Status, Work, and Income: An Examination of the Effects of a Psychiatric Label. *American Sociological Review* 47: 202–215.

———. 1987. Understanding Labeling Effects in the Area of Mental Disorders: An Assessment of the Effects of Expectations of Rejection. *American Sociological Review* 52: 96–112.

Luckoff, D., R. P. Liberman, and K. H. Neuchterlein. 1986. Symptom Monitoring in the Rehabilitation of Schizophrenic Patients. *Schizophrenia Bulletin* 12: 578–602.

Massel, H. Keith, R. P. Liberman, J. Mintz, H. E. Jacobs, T. V. Rush, C. A. Giannini, and R. Zarate. 1990. Evaluating the Capacity to Work of the Mentally Ill. *Psychiatry* 53: 31–43.

McCoy, John L., and K. Weems. 1989. Disabled-Worker Beneficiaries and Disabled SSI Recipients: A Profile of Demographic and Program Characteristics. *Social Security Bulletin* 52(5): 16–28.

McGuire, T. G. 1991. Measuring the Economic Costs of Schizophrenia. *Schizophrenia Bulletin* 17(3): 375–388.

Mechanic, D. 1987. Correcting Misconceptions in Mental Health Policy: Strategies for Improved Care of the Seriously Mentally Ill. *The Milbank Quarterly* 65(2): 203–230.

Mechanic, D., and D. A. Rochefort. 1992. A Policy of Inclusion for the Mentally Ill. *Health Affairs* (Spring): 128–150.

Moffitt, R., and B. Wolfe. 1993. Medicaid, Welfare Dependency, and Work: Is There a Causal Link? *Health Care Finance Review* 15(1): 123–133.

Murphy, Robert M., J. S. Scheer, Y. Murphy, and R. Mack. 1988. Physical Disability and Social Liminality: A Study in the Rituals of Adversity. *Social Science and Medicine* 26(2): 235–242.

Nagi, S. Z., and L. W. Hadley. 1972. Disability Behavior: Income Change and Motivation to Work. *Industrial and Labor Relations Review* 25(2): 223–233.

National Academy of Social Insurance. 1994. Rethinking Disability Policy: Preliminary Status Report of the Disability Policy Panel (March 1994).

Noble, J. H. 1984. Rehabilitating the SSI Recipient: Overcoming Disincentives to Employment of Severely Disabled Persons. In *The Supplemental Security Income Program: A Ten-Year Overview*. U.S. Senate Special Committee on Aging. Washington, DC: GPO, 55–102.

Noh, Samuel and R. J. Turner. 1987. Living with Psychiatric Patients: Implications for the Mental Health of Family Members. *Social Science and Medicine* 25(3): 263–271.

Okpaku, Samuel. 1985. A Profile of Clients Referred for Psychiatric Evaluation for SSDI and SSI: Implications for Psychiatry. *American Journal of Psychiatry* 142: 1037–1043.

———. 1988. The Psychiatrist and the Social Security Disability Insurance and Supplemental Security Income Programs. *Hospital and Community Psychiatry* 39(8): 879–883.

Overall, J., and D. Gorham. 1962. The Brief Psychiatric Rating Scale. *Psychological Reports* 10: 799–812.

Pary, Raymond, D. M. Turns, J. L. Stephenson, C. Tobias, and S. Lippman. 1992. Disability Status and Length of Stay at a VA Medical Center. *Hospital and Community Psychiatry* 43(8): 844—845.

Perl, Joseph L., and Marvin W. Kahn. 1983. The Effects of Compensation on Psychiatric Disability. *Social Science and Medicine* 17(7): 439–443.

Phillips, M. J. 1990. Damaged Goods: Oral Narratives of the Experience of Disability in American Culture. *Social Science and Medicine* 30(8): 849–857.

Rice, Dorothy P., S. Kelman, L. S. Miller, and S. Dunmeyer. 1990. The Economic Costs of Alcohol and Drug Abuse and Mental Illness: 1985. Report submitted to the Office of Financing and Coverage Policy, ADAMHA, U.S. Department of Health and Human Services. Washington, DC: GPO.

Scheffler, Richard, and R. Frank. 1989. The Economics of Mental Health. *Inquiry* 26(2).

Schmulowitz, Jack. 1973. Recovery and Benefit Termination: Program Experience of Disabled-Worker Beneficiaries. *Social Security Bulletin* (June): 3–15.

Scott, Charles G. 1989. A Study of Supplemental Security Income Awardees. *Social Security Bulletin* 52(2): 2–13.

Segal, Steven P., and Namkee Choi. 1991. Factors Affecting SSI Support for Sheltered Care Residents with Serious Mental Illness. *Hospital and Community Psychiatry* 42(11): 1132–1137.

Sherbourne, Cathy D., and R. D. Hays. 1990. Marital Status, Social Support, and Health Transitions in Chronic Disease Patients. *Journal of Health and Social Behaviour* 31 (December): 328–343.

Simmons, O. G. 1965. *Work and Mental Illness: Eight Case Studies*. New York: John Wiley and Sons.

Social Security Administrations. 1988–1991. *Social Security Bulletin Annual Statistical Supplements*. 1988: 198–99, 330–331; 1989: 2, 198, 330; 1990: 190–191, 309; 1991: 187–88, 300.

Steinwachs, Donald M., J. Kasper, and E. A. Skinner. 1991. Factors Affecting Unmet Needs for Care: Policy Implications. Paper presented at the annual meeting of the National Alliance for the Mentally Ill, San Francisco.

———. 1992. Family Perspectives on Meeting the Needs for Care of Severely Mentally Ill Relatives: Final Report. Unpublished ms.

Stone, Deborah A. 1979. Illness and the Dole: The Function of Illness in American Distributive Politics. *Journal of Health Politics, Policy, and Law* 4(3): 507–521.

———. 1984. *The Disabled State*. Philadelphia: Temple University Press.

Strauss, Anselm, and J. M. Corbin. 1988. *Shaping a New Health Care System: The Explosion of Chronic Illness as a Catalyst for Change*. San Francisco: Jossey-Bass.

Strauss, John S., H. Hafez, P. Lieberman, and C. M. Harding. 1985. The Course of Psychiatric Disorder. Part 3. Longitudinal Principles. *American Journal of Psychiatry* 142(3): 289–296.

Stubbins, J. The Politics of Disability. 1988. In H. E. Yuker, ed., *Attitudes towards Persons with Disabilities*. New York: Springer, 22–32.

Taube, Carl, and H. Goldman. 1989. State Strategies to Restructure Psychiatric Hospitals: A Selective Review. *Inquiry* 26 (Summer): 146–156.

Tessler, R. C., and H. H. Goldman. 1982. *Chronically Mentally Ill*. Cambridge, MA: Ballinger.

Test, M. A., W. A. Knoedler, D. J. Allness, and S. S. Burke. 1985. Characteristics of Young Adults with Schizophrenic Disorders Treated in the Community. *Hospital and Community Psychiatry* 36(8): 853–858.

Thoits, Peggy A. 1983. Multiple Identities and Psychological Well-Being: A Reformulation of the Social Isolation Hypothesis. *American Sociological Review* 48: 174–187.

Thoits, Peggy A., and M. Hannan. 1979. Income and Psychological Distress: The Impact of an Income-Maintenance Experiment. *Journal of Health and Social Behavior* 20 (June): 120–138.

Thompson, E. H. 1988. Variation in the Self-Concept of Young Adult Chronic Patients: Chronicity Reconsidered. *Hospital and Community Psychiatry* 39: 771–775.

Treitel, Ralph. 1979. Recovery of Disabled Beneficiaries: A 1975 Follow-up Study of 1972 Allowances. *Social Security Bulletin* 42(4): 3–23.

Trout, John, and D. R. Mattson. 1984. A Ten-Year Review of the Supplemental Security Income Program. *Social Security Bulletin* 47(1): 3–24.

U.S. Senate. 1983. Social Security Reviews of the Mentally Disabled. Special Committee on Aging, 95th Congress. S. HRG 98-170. Washington, DC: GPO.

Uttaro, Thomas, and David Mechanic. 1994. The NAMI Consumer Survey Analysis of Unmet Needs. *Hospital and Community Psychiatry* 45(4): 372–374.

Watt, D. L., K. Katz, and M. Shepherd. 1983. The Natural History of Schizophrenia. *Psychological Medicine* (13): 663–670.

Weber, A., and J. D. Orcutt. 1984. Employers' Reactions to Racial and Psychiatric Stigmata: A Field Experiment. *Deviant Behavior* 5: 327–336.

Williams, G. 1984. The Genesis of Chronic Illness: Narrative Reconstruction. *Sociology of Health and Illness* 6(2): 175–199.

Wolfe, Barbara, and R. Haveman. 1990. Trends in the Prevalence of Work Disability from 1962 to 1984, and Their Correlates. *The Milbank Quarterly* 68(1): 53–80.

Yelin, E. 1986. The Myth of Malingering: Why Individuals Withdraw from Work in the Presence of Illness. *The Milbank Quarterly* 6(4): 622–49.

———. 1989. Displaced Concern: The Social Context of the Work-Disability Problem. *The Milbank Quarterly* 67 (Suppl. 2, pt. 1): 114–65.

———. 1992. *Disability and the Displaced Worker*. New Brunswick, NJ: Rutgers University Press.

Zubin, Joseph, J. Magaziner, and S. R. Steinhauer. 1983. The Metamorphosis of Schizophrenia. *Psychological Medicine* 13: 551–571.

4 Mental Disorders, Work, and Choice

JOHN S. STRAUSS AND LARRY DAVIDSON

> Work was really crucial in making me feel like a valuable person. Now in this society, and maybe it's not right and maybe we shouldn't think this way, but as we know work defines you. I used to go to parties and people would say, "What do you do?" and I'd say, "Nothing." . . . It was hard, it was very hard. . . . To me, work is one of the most valuable things you can do to recover.
>
> —Woman with history of serious mental illness speaking to interviewer

For many people, it is work, rather than sleep, that "knits up the raveled sleeve of care." Work provides structure, purpose, and meaning in life, money for living, and esteem for self and from others (Neff 1977). Work also provides a way to make personal connections—to meet people and to be in society more generally—and work constitutes a major piece of one's development and personal identity (Berger 1964; Haan 1977). As noted by the woman quoted above, who has recovered from her own personal history of mental illness to hold a high-level job in a state department of mental health, the importance of work in people's lives, at least in this culture, is reflected in one of the first questions we often ask after meeting someone for the first time: "What do you do?"

Whether or not a person happens to have a severe mental disorder, work can, in fact, "define you." It is very likely to provide major threads of identity in a person's life. Work can be particularly crucial if a person has a severe mental disorder, since these disorders involve problems that eat at the heart of self-confidence, personal connection, life structure, and financial comfort. Work also appears to serve as a bridge across which a person can travel in leaving severe mental disorder and becoming an increasingly competent, intact, human being. Starting from this broad context, in this chapter we describe (1) the two major conceptual models for understanding the relationships between work and severe mental disorders, (2) how mental disorders affect work, (3) the impact of work on mental disorders, and (4) how the choice to work is facilitated or precluded. We then suggest briefly some implications of this discussion for mental health programming and policy, and some research directions that might help further resolve and clarify these issues.

Conceptual Models for the Relationship between Work and Mental Disorders

Where do people start when thinking about work and severe mental disorders? There are two particularly common ways to conceptualize the processes involved in the nature and course of severe mental disorders and their relationship to work (Strauss 1992). The most common views currently are the purely biological and the closely related diathesis-stress conception. From this perspective, mental disorders and their course are seen as determined primarily by biological factors, almost all of which remain either to be confirmed or discovered. Mental disorders are seen as impairing or even precluding work functioning, and work or other aspects of functioning such as social relationships are viewed either as helping to make the best of a bad situation or as being a source of or remedy for stress. In this view, the ideal is to find a balance between the need for a productive and meaningful social role and the need to avoid or minimize the detrimental effects of stress in one's life.

The notion of stress employed in most of these conceptions is greatly oversimplified, using, for instance, such constructs as "stimulus window" (Wing 1975). In this view, too much stimulus (i.e., stimulus that exceeds the "window") is stressful for a person with a disorder such as schizophrenia. Too little stimulus is also viewed as noxious. Such a mechanistic view implies that we know what a stimulus is (perhaps something like close relationships or responsibility). It also assumes that the differences between too much, too little, and just right are purely differences of quantity, and that the personal meaning of a situation is of no significance in drawing these distinctions.

A common observation in clinical practice, however, is that what should be extremely high levels of stimulus, such as a fire in a patient's hospital, often have an organizing effect on some people with severe mental disorder, just as a presumably only moderately stimulating experience, such as attending a concert or picnic, can exacerbate psychotic symptoms in others. In practice, it is extremely difficult to know *a priori* what is too much stimulus or too little stimulus for a particular person unless one knows the individual well and also knows the ways in which he perceives the meaning of and responds to various situations. Such complexity is difficult to incorporate for many causal views that otherwise appear to be elegant in their simplicity. On this and other scores, the relatively mechanistic approaches of both the purely biological and the diathesis-stress theories fall short of providing an adequate appreciation of the complex interplay between people, their activities, and their mental disorders.

The second approach to thinking about work and mental disorders uses a systems framework to conceptualize the nature of mental disorders, their etiologies, and their treatments. If we consider that a person and her disorder may have a complexity at least equal to, say, the endocrine system or even a single metabolic pathway, then, as with the endocrine system (or a metabolic pathway), we would see a variety of factors as influencing the processes connecting work and mental disorders at different points in their evolution. This influence has a recursive effect on the system itself, affecting its operation and subsequent course. If, beyond such a basic systems framework, we think that the person may have some influence over her own actions (Breier and Strauss 1983, Davidson and Strauss 1992), a belief not greatly emphasized currently in theories of severe mental disorders, then the system increases in complexity, since the person's intentionality and choice are influenced by and in turn influence the entire process. The tremendous difference between the two conceptual models clearly affects our understanding of the relationships between work and mental disorders and the kinds of programs, legislation, and research that we see as crucial.

The Impact of Mental Disorder on Work

We suggest throughout this chapter that in order to adopt a systems framework for conceptualizing the various relationships between mental disorders and work, it is best to begin with an effort to understand what the life of a person with severe mental disorder is like. Only by appreciating this life context, and situating all other efforts, both research and practice, within this framework, can we hope to achieve even an approximate fidelity to the richness and complexity of the phenomena we are attempting to study (Davidson and Strauss 1995). Taking the person and his overall life as our point of departure, we examine the needs of people with severe mental disorders who may wish to work and the ways in which they can be helped through treatment and rehabilitation efforts.

It is useful to highlight the importance of this life context because the mental health field in general, and its vocational rehabilitation arm in particular, have had a tendency to divorce the meaning of work for people with severe mental disorders from the various meanings that work has for the general public. In this more clinical context, work has been viewed primarily as adjunctive or as a support to treatment, with the expectation that recovery or cure will have to take place *before* work can return to playing a central role in the person's life. Such a view of mental disorder neglects the fact that the disabled person continues to live her life despite or in relation to her disorder, and that major dimensions of life such as work and social relationships may retain the meaning they had for the person prior to the onset of the disorder.

In fact, the life of a person with severe mental disorder is probably much more like the lives of the rest of us than we are inclined to recognize. Our theories of psychopathology and our diagnostic manuals may blind us to this fact. Those of us in the mental health field may be like the sightless person attempting to go down a complex stairway who needs to hold on to the bannister. For mental health professionals, the only bannister, the only faithful guide available, is an understanding of our own experiences as well as those of a variety of people without severe mental disorders. As soon as we turn our back on this body of first-person knowledge, this guide derived from our own lives, we start talking about "schizophrenics" or "manic depressives" or "borderlines" and begin to develop orientations for changing and fixing people in ways that we would never even consider if we were talking about our friends, our families, ourselves. Within such an orientation, work loses its fundamental meaning and importance in human existence and comes to be seen as an adjunct or support to a person's "real" treatment.

Although systematic empirical investigations of work have typically remained at a distance from the life contexts of the people studied, they have suggested certain important conclusions about the impact of mental disorders on work. In accordance with common sense, such studies have repeatedly shown that impairment in work functioning often occurs in persons with mental disorders (American Psychiatric Association 1987, Mintz et al. 1992, Carone et al. 1991, Anthony and Blanch 1987, Hamburger and Hess 1970). More specifically, it has been noted (Bell et al. 1992) that specific problems related to particular diagnostic groups tend to generate particular problems in the work setting. There appears, at least as demonstrated in the one study that focused on delineating trends over time (Andrews et al. 1992), to be a high likelihood that mental disorders have a continuing effect on work dysfunction. Certainly the definitiveness of these studies has yet to be established, given the complex but crucial questions that remain regarding such methodological issues as the characterization of the patients and work activities studied, and the nature of the evaluations conducted (Bond 1987).

More important, however, these apparently straightforward findings are challenged by qualitative, life-context inquiries that provide many examples of people with severe mental disorders using work in ways that do not fit the common, unidirectional stereotype that mental disorder "causes" inability to function. For example, a delusional man with paranoid schizophrenia, barely able to sit still for a research interview or deal with his family, but who had worked all his life, competently continues to work for thirty-seven hours a week as a machinist, except in the most extreme periods of symptomatology. A woman with schizophrenia sometimes looks under her bed to see where the voices are coming from but manages her household, care of her child, and an evening job as waitress, symptoms or no symptoms. Another woman who had been told she could not work returned to a teaching position while still psychotic and reported, ''I held it in all day, and then at night when I was home alone I would just go wild until I could settle down again.''

Longitudinal research provides a possible resolution of these apparently contradictory emphases regarding work impairment and work as a continuing strength in mental disorder. First, these studies have shown that in mental disorders work is a valuable predictor of outcome (Strauss and Carpenter 1977). Work is also an important outcome variable in its own right, correlated with but not identical to such other outcome variables as symptom severity, need for hospitalization, and social relations functioning (Strauss and Carpenter 1977). In fact, the moderate levels of correlation, the semi-independent relationship of work and mental disorder as both predictor and outcome variable, suggests that work is a longitudinal, relatively consistent area of functioning over time, and that it is both semi-independent of and related to other areas of functioning in mental disorders. These findings indicate that work is one system in an open-linked systems model of human functioning and development in people with mental disorders (Strauss and Carpenter 1977). Within that conceptual context, the role of work and people's ability to handle it in and out of severe psychopathology are closely tied to who those people are, where their values lie, their abilities to manage themselves in certain situations, and the specific ways in which their disorders, their coping mechanisms, and their vulnerabilities interact (Osipow 1983).

These studies seem to show that the impact of mental disorders on work functioning cannot be understood as a simple, linear, causal process, or in isolation from the life of the person with the disorder and his particular work history, goals, and resources. While this conclusion may leave us feeling that there is little that we can say definitively about the impact of mental disorders on work in general, it does leave a number of possible approaches for investigations of these relationships within the context of individual lives. Work functioning may be affected directly by the sequelae of the disorder, but it may also be affected indirectly by changes brought about by the disorder in a person's goals, desires, sense of personal identity, level of motivation, tolerance for stress and conflict, and ability to manage interpersonal relationships. It is also possible, however, that a person's interest in and ability to do certain kinds of work may not be at all affected, or only minimally affected, by the onset of a mental disorder. The systemic, life-context approach argued for here suggests that we can detect such relationships by a detailed and careful inspection of an individual's situation, guided by a general sense of the kinds of relationships that may be discovered.

The Impact of Work on Mental Disorders

We are driven to a similar conclusion regarding the impact of work on the course of mental disorder. A woman with a diagnosis of schizo-affective disorder pleaded to return to work while she was still hospitalized for her most recent episode and still hearing voices. Her clinician agreed that she could. Return to work? Undergo such stress? Well, maybe the work was simple and routine and thus of a low-stress nature. Not at all. She had a receptionist/secretarial job in a very busy office where people were coming from various directions and with various demands. When in a research interview one of us (JS) asked her how she was able to work in such a situation, she wondered, incredulous, how the interviewer could fail to understand. "Dr. Strauss, work keeps me organized. When I'm working, I have to hold myself together so that I can get things done."

Another subject at one interview smiled broadly at the interviewer as he told him, "Now I have five jobs." The interviewer was worried that the man was becoming manic again, but the subject said, "No, I have to keep myself together to manage all of them." And his wife, who also had a diagnosis of bipolar disorder, nodded, smiling, in assent. "It works too."

There has been concern for centuries about the many ways in which work plays a role in human life generally and the deleterious effects of certain kinds of work or work situations for certain people. Working can have many bad effects on human beings: stress (Cooper and Payne 1980, McLean 1974), conflicts set up by various job characteristics (Kahn 1973), and problems arising from the status of a particular worker (Kasl and French 1962) in the work context. But it has also been noted for centuries that work can have a salutory effect. In A.D. 172, Galen wrote, "Employment is nature's best physician and is essential to human happiness" (Strauss 1968). In the eighteenth century, Pussin and Pinel led the moral treatment movement, suggesting the useful role of work in even the most severe types of mental disorder (Weiner 1979). More recently, Kraepelin, his biological theory of dementia praecox (schizophrenia) notwithstanding, noted in 1902 that when people with dementia praecox worked, frequently the otherwise inevitable deterioration supposedly found in this disorder mysteriously ceased (Kraepelin 1902).

More recently still, a patient in an inpatient treatment setting for disturbed adolescents was heard, in returning from his work assignment, to say "Isn't it strange, when I'm shoveling snow I don't hear voices" (Strauss 1978). And in more systematic studies, work has actually appeared to bring about an improvement in even the most basic symptoms of severe mental disorders such as schizophrenia (Bell and Ryan 1984; Bell et al. 1993).

Thus, in considering the impact of work on mental disorders, as in considering the impact of mental disorder on work, the facts are more complex than any simple theory would suggest. Work can lead to a worsening of disorder, but it can also lead to improvement. And it appears that any simple notion of stress as some objective characteristic irrespective of a particular person's skills, needs, or meaning system is almost certainly inadequate. Work can have an impact on mental disorder, but the nature and direction of this impact appear to be interwoven in important ways with the specific characteristics of the work situation, of the person, and probably of the disorder as well.

Factors Affecting a Person's Choice to Work

Given the fundamental importance of work for people in general and its potential rehabilitative value in the recovery of people with severe mental disorders in particular, how are we to understand the various factors that influence a disabled person's choice of whether or not to work and the type of work to which she is attracted?

It has become progressively more commonplace in scientific circles to assume that such basic philosophical questions as the existence of free will are either irrelevant or trivial. Science, as an empirical discipline, has parted ways with such armchair pursuits as reflection on the basic assumptions framing our images of human nature and nature itself. However, the topic for this section refers back precisely to this level of basic uncertainty. The questions of whether or not a person with mental disorder chooses to work, and what affects this choice, at what point in the course of the disorder, under what circumstances, and to what end, must be at least as complicated as the age-old philosophical question of free will. The person with mental illness is, after all, still and fundamentally a *person,* with all of the dreams, virtues, frailties, and needs that all people possess. The question of the *choice* of work for a person with mental illness thus falls back to the question of any choice for any person. Do we in fact have such choices? If so, how are we to understand how choices are made and what impact they can have on our behavior, on the conduct of others, and on the world in general? We need to consider the unresolved philosophical issue of the nature and role of choice in what it means to be a person before we address what the particular choice of work means for the particular group of people with mental disorders.

The complexity of this question is reflected concretely in the vast literature accumulating in the field of industrial psychology describing the range of interactions between personal characteristics and job choices. While not focusing specifically on people with mental disorders, this literature encompasses the complex interactions between person and job (Dunnette 1976,

Posner and Randolph 1979), including the role of such characteristics as workplace pressures, types of tasks, types of remuneration, personality characteristics of the worker, life circumstances of the worker, and age and other demographic characteristics of the worker in the choice of work. The various relationships between worker and coworkers—supervisors, supervisees, and others—constitute another area for inquiry into the interface between the person and the job situation (Rosenthal 1978). These studies only begin to point to the possible roles and meanings of work for people in general. From Willie Loman to Shakespeare, we also know that work can mean drudgery and subsistence, it can provide a way to salvage one's self-esteem, to appear worthy in the eyes of others, to find a source of pride and feel useful. It can connote sacrifice and resentment, and it can provide a purpose and value for one's life in devotion to a higher cause.

Were this not enough uncertainty with which to begin considering the choice to work for people with mental disorders, we also suggest that in the field of severe mental disorder, especially in relation to schizophrenia, the question of free will becomes particularly crucial. Above and beyond the meaning of any choice for any person, in schizophrenia there appears to be a specific and essential question regarding the role of the person's will. The founding fathers of psychiatry, the very authors of the notion of schizophrenia in the late nineteenth and early twentieth centuries, Kraepelin and Bleuler, viewed the disintegration of the will as the central problem in schizophrenia. In the context of a disorder such as schizophrenia, such everyday processes as setting goals and actualizing them can become incredibly difficult. We need only consider some of the common experiences shared by people with schizophrenia to see why this is so. There is the person who feels that his mind has been invaded by voices over which he has no control, voices often telling him what to do or what he is thinking, as though some outside force had taken over his mind and deprived him of all privacy. Then there are the delusional thoughts that often amplify these experiences, together with what has been called "formal thought disorder," the various ways in which thoughts are chopped up, disorganized, and disconnected from each other. The combination of such experiences, along with other perceptual and cognitive distortions, often makes the person with schizophrenia feel as though he had no will (Davidson in press). As in Czechoslovakia under Soviet occupation, communication among people, values, and the ability to determine one's own fate are all profoundly threatened. How, within such an alienating and oppressive context, can choice continue to be meaningful for such a person?

In addition to these factors intrinsic to the disorder itself, a host of other, more "external," factors contribute to making choice or free will so difficult to actualize for people with schizophrenia (Davidson in press). For example, many people currently believe that schizophrenia is a neurobiological disease, even though, as is often the case, the belief extends well beyond its support by data. Some patients tell us, as they have themselves been told, that "it is a brain disease arising from a chemical imbalance." Some professionals, less diplomatic, have labeled it as arising from a "broken brain" (Andreasen 1985). These beliefs in pure biological causes for schizophrenia tend further to perpetuate the belief among patients, family members, and professionals that everything is out of the patient's control (Schizophrenia Bulletin 1989). Add to these beliefs generated by the mental health field itself the popular cultural stereotypes, stigma, and prejudice of the lay public surrounding mental disorder, and you have an overwhelming array of forces that almost preclude the existence of an environment supportive of the protection, cultivation, and recovery of a sense of will on the part of the person with schizophrenia.

What can be the meaning of choice within the network of beliefs built upon such a corrosive set of experiences that assault people with severe mental disorder both from within and without? Although one might conclude that choice can have no meaning at all, we contend exactly the opposite: that precisely for these same reasons the question of choice is crucial. In earlier work (Davidson and Strauss 1992), we have suggested that the process of recovery in schizophrenia involves the knitting back together of the will of the person afflicted. Almost by definition, this cannot be accomplished by an outside source, by treatment alone, or solely by the efforts of caring others; it must involve the efforts of the person with the disorder as well. As one subject in this research project taught us, a person cannot develop a sense of herself as an intentional, effective, and responsible agent by being solely the recipient of the actions of others. To develop a sense of self as having a will and being able to act successfully on desires, a person has to establish her own goals and act to achieve those goals herself (Davidson and Strauss 1992).

While not sufficient by itself for cure, perhaps, the reconstruction of a sense of self as an active, effective, and responsible agent certainly appears to be a necessary and essential part of the recovery process. Within this context, the role of work as a major source of a person's sense of self, as a primary, culturally sanctioned source of being a productive and useful individual, as a source for finding meaning and purpose in life, is a central arena for the exercise and development of this sense of agency.

Adopting such a framework for the integral role of personal choice in the development of a sense of agency changes how we view the role and importance of choice in a disabled person's return to work. The current psychiatric rehabilitation and community support literature emphasizes the need for client choice and self-determination in the rehabilitation and treatment enterprise (e.g., Anthony 1979, Salem 1990). From a narrow biological or diathesis-stress perspective, this appeal to the person's own wishes and control serves the function of humanizing psychiatric care. While this is a noble and admirable goal in itself, such a limited understanding of the importance of choice and self-determination in the lives of people with severe mental disorder falls well short of appreciating their central role in the recovery process. Within such a view both work and individual choice remain marginal to the causes and cures for schizophrenia. But we are reminded again of the example of Kraepelin, mentioned earlier, in which even the staunchest of biological theorists ran up against the limits of his own model in the face of clinical experiences that demonstrated that the choice to return to work could have a significant positive effect on this disease, which otherwise he believed would have an inexorable downward course.

Kraepelin's own experiences of actual people not fitting into his own conception of inevitable deterioration because they returned to work suggest that his own theory and its current derivatives miss an essential point about the role of the will and its recovery in improvement in schizophrenia. The alternative proposed here provides a better position from which to appreciate the importance of having a choice and making a choice in recapturing one's sense of agency and volition. Choice and self-determination in this view are not important solely as an exercise of the disabled person's civil rights—as important as that may be—but also as a necessary component of the improvement process itself. And, as noted earlier, recovery of a sense of agency and volition cannot happen solely through the actions of others, no matter how well intentioned and caring they may be. Following this train of thought leads to the conclusion that improvement in schizophrenia, beyond the most basic symptomatic improvement brought about by medications, also cannot happen solely through the treatment or rehabilitative efforts of others if those efforts are understood as happening *to* the person with the disorder. Improvement beyond symptom relief requires the efforts, choices, and actions of the person himself. While these actions can range from the most elemental level of turning on and off a radio to a more advanced level of returning to full-time employment as a mental health professional, they all have in common their origin in the person's own values, goals, and decisions.

In order to begin to examine the processes involved in redeveloping a sense of agency in the midst of mental disorder, we have in our earlier work (Davidson and Strauss 1992) delineated four basic aspects of the recovery of a sense of self: (1) discovering the possibility of a more active sense of self, (2) taking stock of the strengths and weaknesses of one's self and assessing possibilities for change, (3) putting into action some selected aspects of one's self and integrating the results of these actions into a revised sense of self, and (4) employing an enhanced sense of self in providing a refuge from the disorder and a resource for coping efforts. With regard to factors affecting a person's choice to work, the first two of these aspects are the most useful in bringing the notion of choice and self-determination into the forefront of understanding improvement in severe mental disorder.

The first aspect refers to a person's sense that there is at least the possibility of a more active sense of self than that associated solely with dysfunction and disability. This could be referred to as the rediscovery of hope for the future, or as the reawakening of desire for certain things in one's life. The wish to return to or to begin to work is one example of this aspect of improvement. The second aspect refers to the self-evaluation process that a person goes through prior to taking risks or tackling new projects. This process of taking stock may be conducted with various levels of conscious awareness and reflection, and with various degrees of input from an intuitive sense of one's abilities and the appraisals of others. Decisions about what one feels up to, when, and based on what information provide examples of this second aspect of improvement, which frames the decision-making process itself.

Taken together, these two aspects of desire and decision-making provide a useful framework for examining the various factors that influence the choices a person with severe mental disorder makes in relation to work. The desire to work and the particular type of work desired can be influenced by familial and social factors (e.g., what is valued by one's parents or by one's culture) as well as by personal talents, interests, and proclivities. Whether or not a person decides to attempt to work, and what kind of work the person attempts, can also be influenced by how that person views her own skills, abilities, deficits, limitations, and supports (Osipow 1983). This self-evaluation process is further influenced by messages received from others in the person's social context through personal interactions and mediated by the culture at large.

In order to illustrate the role of these factors and how their interactions influence the choice to work, we provide several examples that demonstrate the range of the combinations and permutations possible. In line with the systems and life-context approach outlined earlier, we experiment in these examples with ways to convey the various meanings that work can have for people and how their own life experiences contribute to their decisions regarding work. These examples thus differ from conventional clinical vignettes, in that we have tried to incorporate more of the person's life, as well as the perspective of the observer.

Examples

The first example illustrates the importance of the person's own hopes and desires in driving the improvement process. In this case, the person's own wishes conflicted with those of his treaters, who were part of a mental health system that has not often honored the client's own goals and self-evaluation, holding instead to the view that a person must be relatively cured or "stabilized," however defined, before returning to work.

> Bill, a middle-aged man with a twenty-year history of schizophrenia, left a day-treatment program against his treaters' wishes to take a part-time job washing dishes at a diner where he had frequently eaten his meals. The staff at the day program had repeatedly told Bill he was not ready to work because of his persistent auditory hallucinations and delusions regarding the influence of the devil in his everyday affairs. Despite staff input, Bill decided that he could use the extra money and that he could handle washing dishes a few hours a day, so he left treatment and pursued his own agenda. He quickly found part-time work more therapeutic than his stay at the day program had been, and gradually progressed to working several hours a day in addition to preparing at a local high school for his GED in the evenings, and spending his free time with his son and friends.

A second example is provided by another person with schizophrenia who had been told by a usually very sensitive rehabilitation counselor with whom he worked that his dream of working in the theater was totally unrealistic. As in the first example, the person's own wishes, dreams, and self-evaluation were not given much credence by the treatment system and its representatives. In this case, however, it is not the choice *to* work which is at issue, but the choice of the *kind* of work that the person wishes to pursue. As in the first example, this person left the rehabilitation program, which did not support his own goals, and initiated work outside of the treatment system. On his own, he applied for and obtained a job with a local theater company as a stage hand, failed and was fired, and then tried again a few months later with another theater group and succeeded. After several months he returned to the rehabilitation counselor and asked for help getting into more of the production and performance aspects of theater work. This time, impressed by the young man's persistence and success, the counselor agreed to try to help him accomplish his own goals as far as possible. In this case a collaboration arose that supported what the client wanted, what his own feelings and sense of meaning in work suggested, and what he realistically would be able to accomplish, given his own limitations and abilities.

Discouraging messages do not always come from the formal treatment system, of course, they can also come from other sources. A third example illustrates how the choice of work can be complicated by stigma and prejudice toward people with severe mental disorders in the general community and by the lack of a supportive work environment.

> Clyde is a funny-looking guy. Apparently he also was a funny-looking kid. He got lots of psychiatric treatment and was often picked on by other kids. But now he's twenty-eight and talks through his nose, is short and glances off here and there as we talk, and uses strange words like *merks* for psychiatrists and then laughs with a little giggle after he says it. And then he looks at me, and that tremendous sincerity, intelligence, and savvy about life come out: "You know it's hard working on a job looking the way I do, so people sometimes start making fun of me or picking on me. Hell, they don't have much else to do."
>
> He has gotten psychotic many times, and did so on three occasions during the two-year span of our ongoing research interviews. Not during the interviews particularly, although during hard times in his life he would get a little extra suspicious of the people at work, sometimes of the research ("Why are you doing this?"), but I would tell him again and he would settle right down. At other times when he seemed not to be doing so well, he would go into great detail regarding the chemical imbalance that was the basis of his problem (much like the language used by many of my professional colleagues), but, unlike them, he would then lapse into lengthy explanations of why vitamins and certain rare minerals were the obvious solution. After one of his relapses, however, he reasonably enough mostly gave up on these too.
>
> Clyde worked in a large mailroom. He was a letter-sorting machine operator. He made more money than some of my friends and had worked his way up over the years in the mail room. He had first gotten in, between periods of psychosis, by applying, then taking the test, then taking it again after they lost the result from the first one, passing the test, and starting work. He rarely missed work and often stayed on the job even during periods of mild psychosis, unless his suspiciousness, or his being picked on by coworkers, got so bad that he had to take off for a few days or a week or two.
>
> Clyde reminded me what it was like to get picked on. He described how his medications made him somewhat stiff and how he had always talked funny and began describing how the guys at the next machine would start to point at him, to make fun of his looks, his glasses, his funny gestures, and would imitate him. Mostly he'd just turn away and feel hurt. As he was describing this to me the first time, I thought, "of course", remembering the days in fifth grade at the private school where I was the only Jewish kid, the one who couldn't go to Sunset Camp, or dancing class with my classmates. And sometimes, I usually couldn't figure why, one of them,

usually Paul, a big kid who was pretty dumb, would start up. No
one would stand up to him, and there I'd be again, alone, isolated,
for a day or two, until one of the kids, often a girl, would start to
talk to me. I hated it. I remember it still. Poor Clyde, didn't he have
enough trouble just having schizophrenia?

Another example is provided by a young woman with schizophrenia whose
struggle embodies a conflict between her realistic self-evaluation and her
strong desire for a sense of identity rendered unavailable to her by the impact
of her disorder. Regardless of how supportive her environment and the others
in her life were, it was the discrepancy between her reach and her grasp that
kept this woman paralyzed and unable to take a step forward into part-time
employment.

Sheila had wanted to be a doctor. She had been a premed student
with a major in chemistry. She had only been a B–C student, but
she had wanted to go to medical school and had expected to get in.
She had no idea how such things worked: didn't know that she had
competition, didn't realize that just wanting it didn't make it so.
When she didn't get in and her life's dreams were shattered, she
took it personally. She figured that they must have meant for her to
suffer so. Not that she knew who "they" were, but that was a minor
matter, just a technicality. She believed that there was a "they" out
there operating globally, the same way that you or I believe that the
president can influence the course of world events, or that our boss
really has control over things at the office. It was just obvious.
Surely there must have been a "they" who kept her from getting
in, a "they" who, for whatever reason, wanted to bar her from their
exclusive club.
    And she could come up with several reasons. After all, the dean
of the medical school was Italian, and she was herself a devout
Catholic; surely the dean and the Admissions Committee didn't want
any more Catholics to get through medical school. That was it: she
was the object of virulent discrimination. Otherwise why would it
have hurt so bad? Otherwise, why would she have been denied the
only thing that ever mattered to her? So it seemed at the time.
    She had wanted to be a doctor. When I first met Sheila it was
already eight years after her rejection from medical school and her
first psychotic episode. She was not yet over this major disappoint-
ment. I know two other people, however—neither of whom has a
diagnosable mental disorder—who also did not get into medical
school. For both of them it had also been their life's dream. One,
after fifty-some rejections from medical schools here and in other
countries, became a chiropractor. The other became a dentist. But
Sheila was not able to switch gears like that, at least not yet. She
was still set on becoming a doctor, even though at moments of

lucidity she would tell me that it would be awfully hard for her to be a doctor with her schizophrenia. After all, her memory was shot, and her concentration was so poor that she had difficulty doing more than a one- or two-step task at the lab. Most mornings she had a hell of a time getting out of bed, and her Trilafon made her spacey during the day. She would worry over the simplest of everyday things and was quick to feel slighted by most people in her life. So becoming and being a doctor, she knew, would be a very difficult thing to do.

And yet she had wanted to be a doctor. She had spent these last eight years instead as a mental patient: in and out of hospitals, wandering from major university to major university trying to get a job in a medical field so that when she reapplied she would have a sure shot at admittance. Sheila's homeless meanderings only stopped in New Haven when a sympathetic mental health worker was able to get her a volunteer position in a chemistry lab at Yale Medical School. This, she was certain, would be the ticket back in. And at Yale there weren't any Italians heading the medical school or the Admissions Committee.

Ambivalence, Bleuler wrote, is a trademark feature of schizophrenia. I don't know if it comes from the illness or from eight plus years of wandering soullessly from university to university, from hospital to halfway house to supported apartment. But Sheila was offered a part-time job in the lab where she had been working as a volunteer. I had also tried to get her a job at the medical school library, and at U.S. Surgical. She allowed her indecisiveness to let all of these jobs pass her by. None of them would have looked good enough on her resume when it came time to reapply to medical schools, or so she said. But I keep trying to help Sheila find her niche. While getting by with her SSDI payments, she keeps hoping that she'll wake and it will be eight years ago, and she will be getting a letter of welcome from the University of South Carolina Medical School.

She had wanted to be a doctor. To become a dentist or a chiropractor is really to give up that dream. And it's been too hard a battle already to give up now, when things are finally starting to look up.

Another example comes from experience with a program designed to create an opportunity for people with severe mental disorder to offer something back to the treatment system that had helped them improve. This example suggests the importance of reawakening hope and desire in people who have become accustomed to a limited role in life, and the power that reawakened dreams can have in motivating people to return to work. It also attests to the power derived from support for those dreams and concrete opportunities to fulfill them.

It was striking from the start. From the first moment when the first
applicant showed up for the first interview, there was a striking
difference. A bit more attention was paid to clothing and presentation, more effort was made to hide or disguise what appeared to be
a bit more anxiety, a bit more thought was given to choosing words
and answering questions. These were people who wanted to impress—and who did.

And they didn't impress just me. After the first interview or two,
I looked at my colleagues and they looked at me. No one had to
say much. We were all thinking similar things. Even Midge, our
most skeptical colleague, the one who had at best tolerated the rest
of us all along, she too was smiling from ear to ear and beginning
to catch the excitement that was swirling around in the room. They
were different and we could tell; they were responding already to
having different demands placed on them. They were changing as
if before our eyes, and we had something to do with the transformation. It was indeed striking from the start.

We had expressly made having a history of severe mental disorder
an inclusion criterion for this project of training mental health consumers to provide peer education and support. We wanted to see if
our idea was applicable to true patients, not to people who weren't
really disabled, people who could or should be working in the real
world, people who didn't really know what it was like to be psychotic and struggling over long periods of time. But then we started
to get applicants who did have serious problems, who looked like
"chronic mental patients," who had just gotten out of the hospital,
who had no affect or blunted affect at best, who dressed funny or
poorly, who were known to be pains in the ass, who were de-
manding, or needy, or unstable. In short, we were getting patients
to apply who did know what mental illness was really like, but who
were still intimately acquainted with it—perhaps too much so. Or
so we worried.

But then on the first day of interviews, it began. There was
energy, and there was interest. People showed up early for their
interviews. The man who had been disheveled the week before
wore a coat and tie, and his pants almost reached the tops of
his shoes. The young woman who was known to have frequent
and impressive angry outbursts was poised, composed, and pol-
ished in her interactions. She presented her resumé gracefully, as
if there had never been a question that she had gone to school
and worked volunteer jobs at several hospitals in addition to being
a patient in them. Another woman caught herself when her speech
began to get pressured, telling us that we should ask her to slow
down whenever that happened, as she knew she could get hard
to understand when she became excited. And excited she was,
she said, for an opportunity to go back to school, and make

some money, and offer back some of the help she had been given when she had really needed it.

She may have impressed me the most, that woman, because she kept saying, "I only need a chance, you just give me a chance and you'll see. You put me to work, and I'll do the job." It was an odd mixture of self-confidence and desperation, one feeding the other. I don't know if she had ever felt that she had had an opportunity like this before to show her heart in the place where she felt that it had been returned to her. She brought it gently out for us to see and asked that we give it a chance to beat out in the open. We had to agree.

The program was not a complete success. Two people dropped out before graduation, and two who graduated never really completed their practica. We neither cured mental illness nor changed forever the face of the mental health system. And as sometimes happens in psychotherapy, we perhaps learned the most from the program that first day of the first interviews. A transformation did occur, both in them and in us. And we did have something to do with bringing it about. That is a powerful lesson, particularly in a setting where we have grown used to feeling that life holds little in the way of promise for a brighter future.

A final example illustrates one situation in which a person decides not to work, at least for a period of time. Not working can be a reasonable choice too.

"I'm going to go home and stay there. All I need is unconditional love, and my parents will give it to me." "My God," I thought, "she's going to be chronic for sure." We were finishing up a research interview. She was about to be discharged from the hospital after having been psychotic and gotten the diagnosis of schizophrenia. If I'd been her clinician, I would have tried to stop her from going home to regress when clearly she should have been headed for a halfway house and a part-time job. I knew her choice was a recipe for disaster and a sign of a severe lack of drive on her part. But I was only a research interviewer and had to hold my tongue, though she may have noticed something in my eyes. "It's all right. That's really what I need," she smiled. But I was not reassured, although I did feel a little guilty that she had read my mind, my expression.

We parted amicably and with my sincere wish for good luck. After all, we had done about five research interviews together over the two months she was in the hospital and had gotten to know each other a little. Two months later, at the time of the next research interview, she was still at home. "Damn it," I thought. "I knew this would happen."

At the time of the second follow-up research interview two months later she was working two jobs. Not jobs that were quite up to her previous level of responsibility as an office manager, but good, solid, paid work as a part-time receptionist and as a sales clerk. At both she was doing fine. And her symptoms had stayed minimal. And she felt good.

What happened? Well, for starters, she'd been right, and I'd been wrong. I guess she didn't need to go right to work and independent living, or semi-independent living. She'd needed unconditional love, just like she'd said. And rest. Later, when the research group figured this out better, we called it a woodshedding period, a time when, out of the everyday stresses of independent life, some people recovering from psychosis seem to do better "in the woodshed," a place where they can be by themselves a lot and just rest up, regaining their sense of self, their strength, at the very basic levels that are often required, apparently, after the horrendous disruption of a psychotic period. Her choice not to work, not to live in a halfway house, had apparently been just perfect for her. I'd learned a lesson.

We may conclude from these examples that rehabilitation, to be effective, must begin with each person's own wishes, desires, and sense of identity, facilitate a realistic and honest assessment of strengths and limitations and fit with job goals, and then provide the opportunities and supports that will allow the person to pursue the kind of work she has set as a goal, given the constraints of the job market, the persistent lack of adequate resources for mental health services, and the preponderance of stigma remaining in the larger community.

Program and Policy Implications

Efforts to provide work programs to assist people with mental disorders have been carried out over the centuries. Some of the better-documented programs go back at least to those of Pussin and Pinel, mentioned earlier. Since those efforts, a wide range of rehabilitation programs for persons with severe mental disorders has been suggested. The range of such recommendations goes all the way from the assumption that such people cannot work (and need to be supported) to the belief that they not only can but should take employment in competitive work situations. Between these extremes lie a variety of efforts. Sheltered workshops were an early effort, providing special protected employment settings for people with severe disorders. More recently it has been suggested, although not proved, that such workshops tend to be objectionable to people with mental disorders, and to freeze those people into second-class status. More active rehabilitation programs have also been developed. These include those described by Anthony and his coworkers at the

Boston University Center for Psychiatric Rehabilitation (Anthony 1979). These programs involve behaviorally oriented phased training to help people with mental disorders choose, get, and keep jobs, and have been widely used and taught. Another group of programs, transitional employment opportunities, provide protected but partially competitive work experiences (Malamud and McCrory 1988, Beard et al. 1982). Special programs combining partially protected and partially normal living and work situations for persons with mental disorder have also been developed (e.g., Fairweather 1969). These were essentially a logical extension of Pinel's programs for moral treatment in the eighteenth century. Reviews and an overview of these and related work rehabilitation approaches for mental disorders appear in Lamb et al. (1976), Ciardiello and Bell (1988), and Bond (1992).

More recently, work rehabilitation programs have emphasized support within normal settings rather than cloistered work settings, work-residential combinations, and protected transitional or training programs. "Supported employment," the provision of employment in regular work settings with various kinds of special support for the individual, has been espoused earlier by Wehman (1986), and most recently by Becker and Drake, who have studied the impact of normalization plus support and found apparently successful results (Becker and Drake 1992, Drake et al. 1994). There is now a growing body of evidence that such supported vocational programs can indeed be helpful for people with severe mental disorder (Bond and Boyer 1988, Bond and McDonel 1991, Bond 1992, Russert and Frey 1991). Drake et al. (1992, 1994), for example, provide data to suggest that such programs can help people with mental disorder to find employment and perhaps at the same time to improve their condition more generally. Such results suggest that legislation and funding to facilitate these programs might be particularly valuable.

But it is also important to reconsider the issues discussed in the preceding sections of this chapter, showing the value of a systems model for considering the relations between work and mental disorders, the complex nature of those relations, and the importance and individualized nature of work choice for people with mental disorders. The complexity of these features and relationships, while not conducive to hopes for stamped-out, production-line solutions, suggests that work opportunities can be extremely important and that flexibility in terms of setting, demand, support, and changes in work needs and capacities over time is a crucial factor that must be addressed in the development of any future mental health policy or the drafting of any future legislation in support of vocational programming for people with severe mental illness. Such an ideal of flexibility and responsiveness to each individual's needs based on his unique life history and the extent and nature of disability argues for the availability of an array of employment opportunities ranging from the most supported to the most independent and competitive. Given that an individual's needs and level of functioning also vary over time, it will be important for mental health programs to have permeable boundaries that permit clients to access services according to the extent and level of intensity needed at any particular time. Finally, the persistence of stigma concerning mental illness in the workplace will also be important to address in any future legislation (beyond the Americans with Disabilities Act of 1990, that is) that supports the rights of people with psychiatric disabilities, just as issues of discrimination based on race and gender have been in the past.

Some Research Directions

There has been considerable effort to study systematically some aspects and outcomes of work and work programs for people with mental disorders. There is, for example, a huge literature evaluating work settings for all kinds of disorders (e.g., Stout Rehabilitation Institute 1977). Studies evaluating rehabilitation programs have themselves been evaluated and reviewed by Bond (1992), Dellario (1982), Stein and Test (1980), and others. Both the effectiveness of programs and their cost-benefit ratios have been assessed. The work of Liberman et al. (1985), studying the use of specific behavioral learning modules, is an example of evaluative research applied to innovative programs.

As might be expected, given the complex roles and many facets of work in normal human life and in mental disorder, the conceptualization and value of the research conducted have varied widely. In fact, compared to many aspects of mental disorders, the role of work in these disorders has often been neglected, even though its importance has long been recognized. Research efforts in this area, for example, have lagged far behind research for other treatments. The double-blind control study now basic to studies of pharmacologic treatment, for instance, is just a will-o'-the-wisp in terms of what might be carried out in evaluating work programs. Even such relatively important concerns as studying not just job placement, but job retention (Solberg and Raschmann, 1980), is a relatively new and rare advance in the study of work and mental disorders. As Harding et al. (1987) have pointed out, the work needs of a particular person with mental disorder may vary over time. We can find no research on this topic. We found only one study on work choices, which suggests that the vast majority (71%) of people with severe mental disorders do have an active interest in working and finding jobs (Rogers et al. 1991). There are no studies on facilitating work choices for people with severe mental disorders.

Considering the complexity of the relationship between work and mental disorders, the fundamental research question may be, What kinds of work programs are valuable for what kinds of people with which disorders at what times in their disorder? It is also essential to study the flexibility of programs and their integration with other aspects of the person's life and treatment. Designing such studies could, of course, be a nightmare, especially if research methodology is restricted to the usual tightly controlled treatment formats.

While studies of work and work programs may not reach the elegance of more narrowly focused research in severe psychopathology, still they can have the considerable value of acknowledging the existence of and evaluating the impact of real-life situations. No matter what the preference of particular investigators might be, people with mental disorders are not merely isolated biological reaction systems. Given the complexity of the problems and the importance of life context and individual variation in these problems, it is essential to use whatever quantitative and qualitative research methods are available or could be developed for understanding these processes (Davidson and Strauss 1995).

One example of a promising research direction that will require this kind of methodologic creativity on the part of future investigators is presented by the Americans with Disabilities Act of 1990 (ADA). One of the most promising, but also most ambiguous, features of this legislation is its mandate that employers provide a disabled employee with "reasonable accommodations" in the workplace that make it possible for the employee to perform the essential functions of a job. Attempts to implement this legislation have run up immediately against the complex issue of how to provide reasonable accommodations for people with psychiatric, as opposed to physical, disabilities. It is obvious that cutting curbs into sidewalks and providing elevators that are wheelchair-accessible increase a person's access to the workplace if that person is wheelchair-bound. But what would be an equivalent environmental modification for a person with a severe psychiatric disability? What accommodations would be most useful in the domain of work for people with mental disorders? And how would one explore such possibilities and then demonstrate their efficacy in increasing access to employment?

These questions are complicated further by the fact that many of the accommodations suggested so far by and for people with psychiatric disabilities (e.g., Deegan 1991, Fabian et al. 1993, Howie the Harp 1993, Mental Health Law Project 1992, Parrish 1991) would be useful for the general public as well. Accommodations such as flexible scheduling, offering a private work space to decrease stress, assigning a supervisor who may be more patient and understanding, permitting a self-paced workload, and restructuring job duties to eliminate certain tasks may all prove to be effective in enhancing the work life and productivity of people with and without disabilities. Other accommodations that have been suggested, such as providing extra unpaid leave for psychiatric treatment, may be required particularly by a person with a psychiatric disability, but it is difficult to see how such an accommodation in and of itself would have a direct impact on a person's ability to obtain and function at a job. Indirect impact may be demonstrated, of course, by the fact that the person cannot be fired for having a disability, but this raises the issue of the impact of the ADA on discrimination in the workplace rather than on-the-job performance of persons with disabilities. Still other accommodations, such as providing a job coach, permitting phone calls to friends or other supportive individuals, and teaching supervisors how to give clear and detailed instructions regarding job duties, may be clearly required by and compensate for certain deficits associated with severe mental disorders. Despite these apparent distinctions, it is difficult, if not impossible, to separate the effects of the disorder from the influence of the person's life history and the contribution of the social milieu. The impact of discrimination and stigma on a person's job performance, for example, may be more deleterious than the effects of the illness itself. The interweaving of these various dimensions calls for naturalistic, descriptive studies to delineate the processes and variables involved in achieving favorable outcomes before turning to more controlled designs.

The recent focus on normalized work settings reveals the challenges faced by investigators attempting to measure the impact of the ADA or reasonable accommodations on the work performance of people with psychiatric disabilities. A common experience related by vocational program staff is their successful placement of clients with employers who run small and informal businesses, such as a filling station or wrought-iron workshop, where the work situation allows a considerable degree of flexibility in hours of work and unpredicted time off as well as warm supervision and training. While these features might be considered "reasonable accommodations" under the ADA, such work sites existed prior to the ADA and will most likely remain unaffected by this legislation. Contrast this situation with that of the mail room where the employee described earlier worked. This setting had been rendered more accessible to workers with disabilities by virtue of a certain bureaucratic "wheelchair ramp" equivalent (i.e., Clyde could not be denied a job based on his history of psychosis), but it remained a setting in which stigma and scapegoating by coworkers were preponderant. This setting, while altered somewhat by the ADA, continued to exert a negative impact which, when other things were going wrong in this person's life, contributed to a worsening of his condition. These examples raise the research question of how to identify changes brought about by the ADA, how to define reasonable accommodations, and how to assess their impact on job performance when a multitude of other factors continue to contribute to an individual's experience of the work setting.

To the extent that the ADA opens doors to employment opportunities for people with psychiatric disabilities, it is a significant step forward. To the extent that stigma and discrimination based on a history of psychiatric disability persist despite the ADA, people with psychiatric disabilities will continue to face significant obstacles to recovery in addition to the challenges posed by the disorders themselves. It remains for thoughtful and comprehensive investigations grounded in the context of individuals' actual lives to help us determine who can best benefit from these advances, in obtaining what kind of work, at what point in the course of which illnesses, through which kind of accommodations, and in what work sites.

Acknowledgments

This report was supported in part by NIMH Research Scientist Award MH00340, a grant from the National Alliance for Research on Schizophrenia and Depression (NARSAD), and by a grant from the Scottish Rite Foundation.

References

American Psychiatric Association. 1987. *Diagnostic and Statistical Manual of Mental Disorders*. 3d ed., revised. Washington, DC: APA Press.

Andreasen, N. 1985. *The Broken Brain*. New York: Harper & Row.

Andrews, H., J. Barker, J. Pittman, L. Mars, E. Struening, and N. LaRocca. 1992. National Trends in Vocational Rehabilitation: A Comparison of Individuals with Physical Disabilities and Individuals with Psychiatric Disabilities. *Journal of Rehabilitation* 58(1): 7–16.

Anthony, W. A. (1979). *Principles of Psychiatric Rehabilitation*. Baltimore, MD: University Park Press.

Anthony, W. A., and A. Blanch. 1987. Supported Employment for Persons Who Are Psychiatrically Disabled: An Historical and Conceptual Perspective. *Psychosocial Rehabilitation Journal* 11(2): 5–23.

Beard, J. H., R. N. Propst, and T. J. Malamud. 1982. The Fountain House Model of Psychiatric Rehabilitation. *Psychosocial Rehabilitation Journal* 5: 47–53.

Becker, D. R., and R. E. Drake. 1992. Individual Placement and Support: A Community Mental Health Center Approach to Vocational Rehabilitation. Paper presented at the forty-fourth Institute on Hospital and Community Psychiatry, Toronto, Canada (October).

Bell, M. D., R. M. Milstein, and P. H. Lysaker. 1993. Pay as an Incentive in Work Participation by Patients with Severe Mental Illness. *Hospital and Community Psychiatry* 44: 684–686.

Bell, M. D., R. M. Milstein, J. L. Goulet, P. H. Lysaker, and D. Cicchetti. 1992. The Positive and Negative Syndrome Scale and the Brief Psychiatric Rating Scale:

Reliability, Comparability and Predictive Validity. *Journal of Nervous and Mental Disorders* 180: 723–728.

Bell, M. D., and E. R. Ryan. 1984. Integrating Psychosocial Rehabilitation into Hospital Psychiatry. *Hospital and Community Psychiatry* 35: 1017–1022.

Berger, P. L., ed. 1964. *The Human Shape of Work*. South Bend, IN: Gateway.

Bond, G. R. 1987. Supported Work as a Modification of the Transitional Employment Model for Clients with Psychiatric Disabilities. *Psychosocial Rehabilitation Journal* 11: 55–73.

———. 1992. Vocational Rehabilitation. In R. P. Liberman, ed., *Handbook of Psychiatric Rehabilitation*. New York: Macmillan.

Bond, G. R., and S. Boyer. 1988. Rehabilitation Programs and Outcomes. In J. Ciardiello and M. Bell, eds., *Vocational Rehabilitation of Persons with Prolonged Psychiatric Disorders*. Baltimore, MD: Johns Hopkins University Press.

Bond, G. R., and E. C. McDonel. 1991. Vocational Rehabilitation Outcomes for Persons with Psychiatric Disabilities: An Update. *Journal of Vocational Rehabilitation* 1(3): 9–20.

Breier, A., and J. S. Strauss. 1983. Self-Control in Psychotic Disorders. *Archives of General Psychiatry* 40(10): 1141–1145.

Carone, B. J., M. Harrow, and J. F. Westermeyer. 1991. Posthospital Course and Outcome in Schizophrenia. *Archives of General Psychiatry* 48: 247–253.

Ciardiello, J., and M. Bell, eds. 1988. *Vocational Rehabilitation of Persons with Prolonged Psychiatric Disorders*. Baltimore, MD: Johns Hopkins University Press.

Community Support Network News. 1991, 8(2).

Cooper, C. C., and R. Payne, eds. 1980. *Current Concerns in Occupational Stress*. Chichester: John Wiley.

Davidson, L. In press. Intentionality and Identity in Schizophrenia: A Phenomenological Perspective. *Duquesne Studies in Phenomenological Psychology* 5.

Davidson, L., and J. S. Strauss. 1992. Sense of Self in Recovery from Severe Mental Illness. *British Journal of Medical Psychology* 65: 131–145.

———. (1995). Beyond the Biopsychosocial Model: Integrating Disorder, Health, and Recovery. *Psychiatry* 58: 44–55.

Deegan, P. 1991. Support and Accommodation Strategies in a Consumer-Run and Consumer-Controlled Program. *Community Support Network News* 8(2): 9.

Dellario, D. J. 1982. On the Evaluation of Community-Based Alternative Living Arrangements (ALAs) for the Psychiatrically Disabled. *Psychosocial Rehabilitation Journal* 5: 35–39.

Drake, R. E., D. R. Becker, T. Fox, and M. Lounsberry. 1992. Individual Placement and Support Model of Vocational Rehabilitation for People with Severe Mental Illness. Paper presented at the forty-fourth Institute on Hospital and Community Psychiatry, Toronto (October).

Drake, R. E., D. R. Becker, J. C. Biesanz, W. C. Torrey, J. G. McHugo, and P. F. Wyzik. 1994. Rehabilitative Day Treatment vs. Supported Employment. Part 1. Vocational Outcomes. *Community Mental Health Journal* 30: 519–32.

Dunnette, M. D., ed. 1976. *Handbook of Industrial and Organizational Psychology*. Chicago: Rand-McNally.

Fabian, E. S., et al. 1993. Reasonable Accommodations for Workers with Serious

Mental Illness: Type, Frequency, and Associated Outcomes. *Psychosocial Rehabilitation Journal* 17(2): 163–172.

Fairweather, G. W., et al. 1969. *Community Life for the Mentally Ill.* Chicago: Aldine.

Haan, N. 1977. *Coping and Defending.* New York: Academic Press.

Hamburger, M., and H. Hess. 1970. Work Performance and Emotional Disorders. In A. McLean, ed., *Mental Health and Work Organizations.* Chicago: Rand-McNally, 170–195.

Harding, C. M., J. S. Strauss, H. Hafez, and P. B. Lieberman. 1987. Work and Mental Illness. Part 1. Toward an Integration of the Rehabilitation Process. *The Journal of Nervous and Mental Disease* 175(6): 317–326.

Howie the Harp. 1993. A Crazy Folks' Guide to Reasonable Accommodation. Unpublished presentation given at the Connecticut Department of Mental Health, Middletown, CT.

Kahn, R. L. 1973. Conflict, Ambiguity, and Overload: Three Elements in Job Stress. *Occupation and Mental Health* 3(1): 2–9.

Kasl, S. V., and J. R. French, Jr. 1992. The Effects of Occupational Status on Physical and Mental Health. *Journal of Social Issues* 18(3): 67–89.

Kraepelin, E. 1902. *Clinical Psychiatry: A Textbook for Students and Physicians.* 6th ed., trans. A. R. Diefendorf. New York: Macmillan.

Lamb, H. R., et al. 1976. *Rehabilitation in Community Mental Health.* San Francisco: Jossey-Bass.

Liberman, R. P., H. K. Massel, M. D. Mosk, and S. E. Wong. 1985. Social Skills Training for Chronic Mental Patients. *Hospital and Community Psychiatry* 36(4): 396–403.

Malamud, T. J., and D. J. McCrory. 1988. Transitional Employment and Psychosocial Rehabilitation. In J. A. Ciardiello and M. D. Bell, eds., *Vocational Rehabilitation of Persons with Prolonged Mental Illness.* Baltimore, MD: Johns Hopkins University Press, 150–162.

McLean, A., ed. 1974. *Occupational Stress.* Springfield, IL: Charles C. Thomas.

Mental Health Law Project. 1992. *Mental Health Consumers in the Workplace.* Washington, DC: Mental Health Law Project.

Mintz, J., L. I. Mintz, M. J. Arruda, and M. S. Hwang. 1992. Treatments of Depression and Functional Capacity to Work. *Archives of General Psychiatry* 49: 761–768.

Neff, W. 1977. *Work and Human Behavior.* 2d ed. Chicago: Aldine.

Osipow, S. H. 1983. *Theories of Career Development.* Englewood Cliffs, NJ: Prentice-Hall.

Parrish, J. 1991. Reasonable Accommodation for People with Psychiatric Disabilities. *Community Support Network News* 8(2): 8.

Posner, B. Z., and W. A. Randolph. 1979. Perceived Situational Moderators of the Relationship between Role Ambiguity, Job Satisfaction, and Effectiveness. *Journal of Social Psychology* 109: 237–244.

Rogers, E. S., D. Walsh, L. Masotta, and K. Danley. 1991. *Massachusetts Survey of Client Preferences for Community Support Services.* (Final Report). Boston: Center for Psychiatric Rehabilitation.

Rosenthal, S. 1978. A Clinical Perspective of Work Organizations. *Psychiatric Opinion* 15: 19–28.

Russert, M. G., and J. L. Frey. 1991. The Pact Vocational Model: A Step into the Future. *Psychosocial Rehabilitation Journal* 14: 8–18.

Salem, D. A. 1990. Community-Based Services and Resources: The Significance of Choice and Diversity. *American Journal of Community Psychology* 18(6): 909–915.

Schizophrenia Bulletin. 1989. (Issue Theme: Subjective Experiences of Schizophrenia and Related Disorders.) 15(2).

Solberg, A., and J. K. Raschmann. 1980. The Effects of Vocational Services Provided to the Mentally Disabled. *Community Mental Heath Journal* 16: 112–120.

Stein, L., and M. A. Test. 1980. Alternative to Mental Hospital Treatment. Part 1. Conceptual Model Treatment Program and Clinical Evaluation. *Archives of General Psychiatry* 37: 392–397.

Stout Rehabilitation Institute. 1977. *Work Evaluation and Adjustment: An Annotated Bibliography 1947–1977.* Stout, WI: University of Wisconsin Press.

Strauss, J. S. 1978. Towards an Operational Systems Model for Psychopathology. Part 1. Basic Principles as Suggested in the Relationships between Work and Symptoms. Manuscript.

———. 1992. The Person: Key to Understanding Mental Illness: Towards a New Dynamic Psychiatry, III. *British Journal of Psychiatry* 161 (supp. 18): 19–26.

Strauss, J. S., and W. T. Carpenter, Jr. 1977. Prediction of Outcome in Schizophrenia. Part 3. Five-Year Outcome and Its Predictors. A Report from the International Pilot Study of Schizophrenia. *Archives of General Psychiatry* 34: 159–163.

Strauss, M. B. 1968. *Familiar Medical Quotations.* Boston: Little, Brown, 663.

Wehman, P. 1986. Supported Competitive Employment for Persons with Severe Disabilities. *Journal of Applied Rehabilitation Counseling* 17: 24–29.

Weiner, D. 1979. The Apprenticeship of Philippe Pinel. *American Journal of Psychiatry* 136: 1128–1134.

Wing, J. 1975. Impairments in Schizophrenia: A Rational Basis for Social Treatment. In R. D. Wirt, G. Winokur, and M. Roff, eds. *Life History Research in Psychopathology.* Vol. 4. Minneapolis: University of Minnesota Press.

5

Economic Opportunities and Disincentives for People with Mental Illness

RICHARD WARNER AND PAUL POLAK

Each day, people in our society, the mentally disabled among them, make decisions about how to earn and spend their money. A number of important considerations spurred the authors to conduct the pilot study, reported here, of these aspects of the day-to-day economic life of people with mental illness in the community.

In the first place, although work appears to have an important positive effect on the course of serious mental illness (Warner 1994) and many mentally disabled people have substantial work capacity, only 10%–20% of people with serious mental illness are employed in the United States (Anthony et al. 1988). Why is this so? Making the assumption that people with mental illness are a disadvantaged group whose members make rational economic decisions, we set out to establish whether they face disincentives to work.

Another major consideration focuses attention on the economic life of people with mental illness. Some European countries have been successful in establishing businesses which provide integrated work environments for a large proportion of people with mental illness. Is it possible to create similar employment opportunities in this country? Because of differences in the economic and political environment, we cannot assume that an approach which is successful in northern Italy will work in Colorado. What obstacles must be overcome? Can the purchasing power of people with mental illness as a group be used to create market opportunities for consumer-employing business enterprises? Based on the economic development experience of one of the authors (Polak), we conclude that the first step in exploring what initiatives might succeed is to gather basic economic data for members of the target group and to establish how they make their economic decisions.

Data Gathering

Detailed information on income and expenses, including both cash and non-cash exchanges, was collected in 1992 from a sample of fifty people with long-term serious mental illness living in the community in Boulder, Colorado. Subjects were selected nonrandomly as a stratified sample representing different income and employment groups from among the clients of the Mental Health Center of Boulder County. The subjects were predominantly male (62%), middle-aged (mean, 40 years; range, 22–65), well-educated (mean 13.8 years of education; range 9–19), and suffering from a psychotic disorder (96%). Eighty percent of the subjects were receiving one of the two government disability pensions, Supplemental Security Income (SSI; 40%) or Social Security Disability Insurance (SSDI; 40%). Changes in income and expenses of two of the subjects before and after taking employment were examined. We used both before and after data for these two cases when doing the aggregate analysis, resulting in averaged data for fifty-two cases.

The Mental Health Center of Boulder County serves a population of 225,000: most of the subjects live in the county's largest city, Boulder, which has a population of 89,000. The agency has a well-developed community support system with intensive case management available to clients who need such services. In consequence, virtually all enrolled mentally ill clients have an established source of income and housing: many live in subsidized (HUD Section 8) housing.

Subjects were assured of confidentiality and questioned by researchers, using a standardized interview format, about their cash and noncash income and expenses over the prior month. They were asked for details of their cash income from earnings, disability pension, food stamps, gifts, loans, illicit activities, and other sources, and for details of their noncash income from rent subsidy and donated items such as food, clothes, and services. The value of medication and health care purchased by health insurance agencies was calculated and included as noncash income. The actual cost of psychiatric care provided was determined from the center's financial records, and the amount not paid by the client was attributed to noncash income.

Subjects were also questioned about their cash expenses in a variety of areas, including housing, food, health care, transportation, entertainment, and illicit drugs. Substantial but occasional expenses, such as major purchases or vacations, were estimated on an annual basis, amortized over a suitable period, and the amount attributable to the month in question included. A similar procedure was followed for occasional cash income, such as tax rebates. Where a subject had a shared financial arrangement, as in a marital relationship, the income and expenses for the couple were divided evenly between the two. Subjects were questioned about goods and services they provided to others, such as meals, transportation, accommodation, and volunteer work, and the estimated cash value was recorded as a noncash expense. Sexual favors were included only if they were clearly provided in exchange for other goods, services, or cash. If a subject was receiving assistance with money management, the case manager/payee was also interviewed.

The data were organized by dividing the subjects into five reasonably homogeneous economic/employment categories: (1) those with no formal income ($n = 2$); (2) the unemployed (earning less than $50 a month) who received a disability pension or other financial support ($n = 18$); (3) those with limited (under thirty hours a week) employment, including sheltered employment who also, generally, received some support payments ($n = 18$); (4) full-time or nearly full-time workers ($n = 5$); and (5) those with relatively large sources of unearned income, for example, from a working spouse or a trust fund ($n = 9$).

Additional information was derived from a different questionnaire completed by eighty-four adult mental health center clients suffering from a functional psychosis. The survey included questions about the current employment, what work clients could do and would like to do, how many hours a week they wished to work, and how much they would need to earn to make work worthwhile.

The data gathered in these surveys are limited in value by the small sample size and nonrandom selection of subjects. They were collected as an exploratory measure to generate hypotheses for future research. The following discussion should be viewed in this light.

Economic Disincentives to Work

Mentally ill people in our sample balance several factors to optimize their income, as the following case illustrates.

> Floyd is an energetic thirty-two-year-old Hispanic man in outpatient treatment for long-standing schizophrenia. He lives in a group home which does not qualify for HUD Section 8 rent subsidy because it is owned by the mental health center, and he pays $280 a month for rent, utilities, and telephone. Meals at the group home, however, are cheap ($36 a month). He has Medicaid, which pays most of the cost of his medication ($40 a month).
>
> Floyd receives $329 a month from Social Security Disability Insurance (SSDI). The pension regulations allow him to keep all his earnings if they do not exceed $500 a month (see the appendix to this chapter), so he considers it worthwhile to take a minimum-wage job ($4.25 an hour). He works about half-time as a casual laborer for a recycling company, earning $45 to $75 a week. He also works

at a sheltered workshop for around five hours a week earning less than minimum wage on piecework: $5 to $15 a week. Floyd could quit the sheltered workshop and increase his hours at the recycling plant, but he chooses not to. The recycling work is harder and allows little time to socialize with friends as he can at the workshop. Furthermore, if he were to maximize his earned income, he would exceed the $500 monthly earnings allowance and lose his disability pension. He would need to work full-time, earn $5.20 an hour, and receive health insurance in order to match his maximum income on SSDI and part-time work—and then he would have no fallback income in low-earning months. Given the opportunities available, Floyd has chosen employment which provides security and optimum income while minimizing job stress.

Floyd has more incentive to work than do his friends who have a rent subsidy—their rent goes up by twenty-five cents for every dollar they earn—and more than those who receive Supplemental Security Income (SSI)—their pension checks decrease by fifty cents for every dollar earned after the first $65 or so (see appendix). Floyd told us that he would not work if the benefits were that low.

As Floyd's case illustrates, the decision to work is based on three counter-balancing factors: (1) the economic return, (2) the stress and effort involved, and (3) the satisfaction derived from the work. The extent to which work is fulfilling depends upon the job and on the individual's personal values. For the mentally ill, the effort of working is often particularly great because stress can exacerbate hallucinations or other symptoms. With the added risk of losing one's disability pension, the issue of economic return assumes major proportions.

Implicit Tax

The information we gathered suggests that the income differential between being unemployed and employed, in Boulder, does not offer much economic incentive for mentally ill people to work. Table 1 lists the major sources of cash income, and table 2 lists noncash income. Figure 1 displays the average income for the sample of interviewed subjects, excluding noncash income in the form of psychiatric treatment. (We exclude psychiatric treatment from this figure because the large value of these services obscures variations in other forms of noncash income which are of interest.) As figure 1 shows, the total cash and noncash income of subjects who work part-time is only a little more than for unemployed subjects. Part-time workers receive an average of $245 more a month in earned income than the unemployed but $156 less from Social Security, food stamps, and noncash sources of income. If unemployed subjects who start to work part-time encounter the same income

Table 1 Mean Monthly Cash Income in Boulder, 1992

	Whole Group (N = 52)	No Formal Income (N = 2)	Unemployed (N = 18)	Part-Time Employed (N = 18)	Full-Time Employed (N = 5)	High Income Support (N = 9)
Welfare/Soc. Sec.[a]	354	0	422	353	295	328
Wages (compet. emp.)	183	24	4	189	1129	41
Other sources[b]	156	0	23	59	2	739
Wages (sheltered emp.)	28	0	1	62	0	33
Food stamps	21	85	31	20	0	0
Miscellaneous[c]	31	91	40	15	77	13
Total cash income	773	200	521	698	1503	1154

[a]Includes SSI, SSDI, AND, AFDC
[b]Includes other pensions, trust funds, and spouse's income
[c]Includes cash gifts, tax rebates, loans, selling goods, and panhandling (in descending order)

Table 2 Mean Monthly Noncash Income in Boulder, 1992

	Whole Group (N = 52)	No Formal Income (N = 2)	Unemployed (N = 18)	Part-Time Employed (N = 18)	Full-Time Employed (N = 5)	High Income Support (N = 9)
Psych. treatment	1091	591	2064	1012	269	89
Rent subsidy	101	0	187	74	96	8
Medication	76	0	90	95	0	67
Meals	28	50	30	31	50	1
Shelter	22	200	2	27	40	0
Transportation	13	8	15	11	37	0
Other[a]	74	97	82	81	85	17
Total noncash income	1405	946	2470	1333	577	182

[a]Includes donated clothing, health care, gifts, alcohol, food, drugs, protection, entertainment, and laundry (in descending order)

loss, this would amount to what economists term an *implicit tax* of 64% on earned income. Thus, someone working part-time for minimum wage would actually keep, in real terms, $1.53 an hour.

The circumstances of another subject are illustrative.

Jennifer, a young single woman with a psychotic disorder, was receiving Supplemental Security Income (SSI) when she took a twenty-five-hour-a-week job as a teacher's aide for the developmentally disabled, earning $6.63 an hour. As a result, her SSI declined by $315 a month, she lost $17 a month in food stamps, and her rent subsidy went down by $143. Now that she was working, she could no longer stop and get lunch at her parents' house every day, and she was often too tired to go there to eat at night: as a result, the

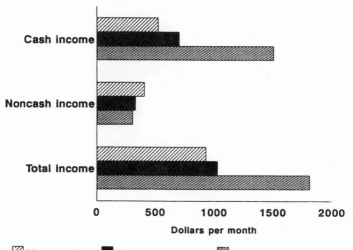

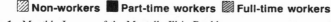
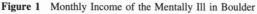

Figure 1   Monthly Income of the Mentally Ill in Boulder

cost of her meals went up by $110 a month. Overall, she found herself ahead by no more than $73 a month. The decision to continue in the job became based, therefore, not on economic gains, which were insignificant, but on such considerations as stress and self-esteem. Initially, because the disabled pupil to whom she was assigned was so difficult, she decided she would quit. When she was given an easier pupil to work with, however, she resolved to continue in the job. Without an analysis of her economic situation, her ambivalence about working would not have appeared as rational as it actually was, and might have been blamed on schizophrenic apathy, deficits in functioning, or just plain laziness.

The situation appears better for full-time workers. Full-time employed subjects in our sample earn an average of $1,125 a month more than the unemployed and receive $256 less from Social Security, food stamps, and noncash income sources. In moving from unemployment to full employment, therefore, these subjects meet an implicit tax of only 23%. One reason for their relative financial success is that full-time workers in our sample are in comparatively high-grade jobs (cabinetmaker, secretary, computer technician, post office worker, photo technician) and earning well above the minimum wage: their average wage, after payroll deductions, is $6.40 an hour. After deducting the implicit tax, therefore, these subjects are keeping about $5.00 an hour of their earnings.

Some of the subjects in our sample, moreover, had only recently begun working and were allowed to keep their SSDI (see appendix). This is an important factor in making work feasible: the implicit tax on these SSDI recipients (primarily loss of food stamps and rent subsidy) amounted to only 13%, which means they had net earnings of $5.25 an hour. Other researchers have found that mentally ill SSDI recipients are more likely to take a job than SSI recipients (Jacobs et al. 1992). This may be because SSI recipients tend to have an earlier age of onset of illness and a more severe form of illness, but it may also be a result of better work incentives for those who receive SSDI.

The Reservation Wage

How do mentally ill clients resolve the issue of economic incentives? Our interviews and survey results indicate that respondents identify a minimum earnings level—known to economists as the *reservation wage* (Berndt 1991)—which makes work an economically sensible choice. More than three-quarters of the clients we surveyed rule out the option of taking a minimum-wage job, but over 60% would be willing to work for $5.00 an hour, and 80% would work for $6.00 an hour. If these clients are to advance economically, it appears to be necessary to find or create jobs that pay $5.00 an hour or more.

Innovations in Social Policy for People with Mental Illness

The data presented in figure 2 support the possibility that the introduction of government disability benefits may have created disincentives to employment among people with mental illness. A time-series analysis of 269 long-term mentally ill patients discharged from Vermont State Hospital in the mid-1950s indicates the labor-force participation rate of the cohort declined steadily between 1960 and 1980 as the national participation in SSDI increased (Little, unpublished manuscript).

There is nothing novel about the observation that support payments produce disincentives to employment and engender welfare dependency. A single mother receiving Aid to Families with Dependent Children (AFDC), for example, may find that it does not pay her to return to work because of loss of dollar benefits, food stamps, and Medicaid and the additional cost of child care and payroll taxes (Sancton 1992). Recent congressional welfare reform efforts have sought solutions to the problems of work disincentives and welfare dependency (Haskins 1991) but the impact of this legislation has been modest (Sancton 1992), and more far-reaching recommendations to restructure welfare are gaining attention and support. President Clinton endorses many of the proposals of economist David Ellwood, who emphasizes that the primary problem underlying welfare dependency is that welfare recipients

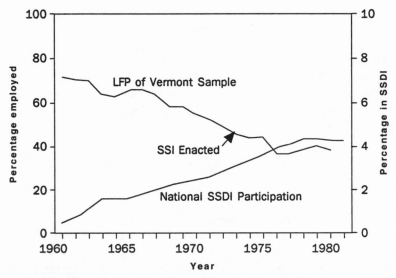

Figure 2 Labor Force Participation of Vermont Sample of Mentally Ill Patients and National SSDI Participation Rate, 1960–80. *Note:* SSDI participation is based on the national population of males 45 to 54 years old.

cannot earn enough to make work a viable economic choice. Ellwood (1988) proposes that welfare benefits be time-limited and that government ensure that welfare recipients have work that pays enough to prevent poverty. In a similar vein, Kaus (1986) argues for eliminating cash assistance altogether and replacing it with a program of guaranteed jobs.

Similar benefit reforms could be considered for the disabled. Innovations in SSI and SSDI to create work incentives would produce substantial savings if they reduced the number of people with mental illness on disability pension rolls. In 1991, the number of mentally disordered adults enrolled in these two programs totalled more than 1.3 million. The growth in SSDI beneficiaries with mental disorder between 1986 and 1991 exceeded 45%, and in adult SSI recipients, more than 75% (Scheffler 1992).

Among the ways to create economic incentives and a steeper income gradient for mentally ill clients entering the labor force are the following:

1. *Guaranteed work schemes.* Disability benefits could be restricted to the most disabled, and work opportunities guaranteed for others. The Italian cooperatives described below offer a model of a guaranteed work scheme, and we will discuss the viability of such enterprises on a local level in the United States. Providing guaranteed work *nationwide* for higher-functioning people with mental illness would be a massive task.

2. *Graduated benefit reduction.* Congress could establish a graduated benefit-reduction scheme for disability income for beginning workers which

would hold the implicit tax rate (the loss of prior income versus the increase in new income) to no more than 35%, even when loss of food stamps and rent subsidy are taken into account. We observed that the more liberal regulations for trial work periods under SSDI, compared to the rapid cutoff of SSI benefits (see appendix), were a major factor in maintaining the income of beginning workers in our sample and creating a work incentive; but the complete loss of SSDI when earnings exceed $500 a month during the extended eligibility period acts as a disincentive to increase work hours and earnings. Some researchers have noted that labor force participation rates for mentally disabled veterans, who are entitled to receive their VA pension in addition to earned income, is substantially greater than for the mentally disabled receiving SSDI or SSI (Rosenheck, personal communication).

An alternative plan (a modification of current SSDI regulations) might allow the beginning worker to earn up to $500 a month with no loss of SSI or SSDI; beyond that earning level, benefits would be reduced by thirty-five cents for every dollar earned. Disability payments would be reinstated immediately if employment were terminated. To test such a plan, econometric labor-supply models need to be developed for mentally ill recipients which can forecast the effects of policy change (Burtless and Hausman 1978; Moffit, 1990). Such models require the collection of a data set including (1) work and income information which allow the subject to be placed in a defined category of "budget constraint," (2) sufficient sample size to provide examples of each budget constraint, and (3) clinical measures of illness severity, functional capacity and diagnosis.

3. *Wage subsidy*. Clients whose reduced functioning requires a sheltered work setting need to be paid adequately if their work is to be financially rewarding. According to our pilot data, this would require a subsidy to raise the wage from actual productive earning capacity to around $5.00 an hour. Wage subsidies would make it possible to modify the traditional sheltered workshop. Full-wage workshops are not limited by the regulation requiring sheltered settings, if they are to receive preferential treatment for government contracts, to maintain a workforce of largely disabled people. The workforce could be expanded to include a greater proportion of fully productive, nondisabled people: new types of contracts could be sought to broaden the range of tasks. Such changes would make workshops more like mainstream employment, improve work satisfaction, reduce the stigma which clients associate with workshop employment, and encourage the enrollment of currently unemployed people.

How could wage subsidies be funded? Regulations governing SSI and SSDI might be waived to allow payments to be diverted into wage subsidies. Employers would be reimbursed the difference between the worker's rate of production and pay. The U.S. Department of Labor has established a time-study process which can be used to measure this difference (Roberts and Ward 1987).

If we could anticipate treatment-cost savings for patients who become employed, moreover, we might reasonably use the mental health treatment budget as a source for a wage subsidy. Psychiatric treatment costs are more than twice as high for the unemployed subjects in our sample than for the part-time employed. This could be explained in a number of ways: (1) unemployed subjects are more disturbed and require closer monitoring, (2) working patients do better because they are employed and need less treatment, or (3) workers have less time to be in treatment. One thing is clear: the cost of outpatient treatment of an unemployed patient is so high in Boulder (around $2,000 a month) that the expense of providing a half-time wage supplement for these clients could be met by a mere 10% reduction in treatment. Such a reduction seems possible, purely because the newly employed client would be in a work setting for half the week and less available for treatment. Being in a productive role, moreover, could enhance self-esteem and reduce alienation enough to improve the course of a client's illness.

Can Treatment Costs Be Reduced by Employing Patients?

A number of studies, while not addressing the issue of cost and service utilization directly, have been interpreted as indicating that work is associated with better outcome from mental illness. Several studies have shown that patients discharged from psychiatric hospitals who have a job are much less likely to be rehospitalized than those who are unemployed, regardless of the patient's level of pathology (Cohen 1955; Brown et al. 1958; Freeman and Simmons 1963; Fairweather et al. 1969; Jacobs et al. 1992). Although working patients fare better, it is not clear if work leads to the improvement in functioning or if higher-functioning patients are more able to hold employment.

Research that directly addresses the question of cost is extremely limited. A study conducted at the Mental Health Center of Boulder County (Ellis and Young 1983) found that psychiatric treatment costs were 34% lower for patients enrolled in the sheltered workshop ($n = 31$) than for those on the workshop waiting list ($n = 29$). It is possible, however, that the patients on the waiting list were less stable than those already enrolled. A more rigorously designed study conducted in Boulder demonstrated that treatment costs declined progressively over two years in a group of patients who were enrolled as members of a rehabilitation-oriented clubhouse, while these costs remained constant in a matched group of nonclubhouse members. The treatment-cost reduction in the clubhouse sample was restricted to those who were placed in work, suggesting that the savings may be a result of members' employment (Huxley and Warner, forthcoming).

The introduction of capitated mental health cost-reimbursement systems creates the opportunity for experimentation in this area. Agencies operating under a capitated Medicaid plan might reasonably offer a wage subsidy to clients with high outpatient treatment costs and track the subsequent cost of care.

Economic Opportunities

European Businesses Employing People with Mental Illness

Worker cooperatives employing people with mental illness began in Italy in the 1970s, and similar enterprises have subsequently been developed in Switzerland, Germany, the Netherlands, and elsewhere. Cooperatives in Trieste and Pordenone, Italy, and in Geneva, Switzerland, were studied by one of the authors (Warner) in 1991–95. Each business consortium employs a mixed workforce of mentally disabled and healthy workers in manufacturing and service enterprises. In Trieste, in northeastern Italy, the businesses include a hotel, a beauty shop, a café, a restaurant, a transportation business, a construction company, and a furniture workshop. In nearby Pordenone, the enterprises include an office-cleaning business, collecting money from public telephones, making park furniture, nursing-home aides, home help for the disabled, and a horticultural nursery business. In Geneva the cooperative ventures include a publishing house, cooperative housing, and a café.

Some small and some large, the enterprises compete successfully with local businesses, winning contracts by competitive bid. In Pordenone, about 90% of the work contracts are made with public agencies such as hospitals, schools, the post office, and the fire station. In Trieste, about 60% of contractual work is for public agencies, including the mental health service; but in Geneva, all the contracts are with the community at large.

The cooperatives use varying amounts of public subsidy. In Trieste, in 1994, the subsidy, in the form of direct grants, donated space, and staff time contributed by the mental health service amounted to about 20% of the total budget, and in Pordenone, about 1%.

The businesses are organized in large consortia employing substantial numbers of severely mentally disabled clients. In 1994, the production of the Trieste consortium totaled $5 million; in Pordenone, $7.1 million. In each consortium about half of the regular workers are mentally ill or otherwise disabled and earn a standard, full-time wage. Some mentally ill people work part-time as trainees and receive a modest rehabilitation income. Unlike most U.S. programs for people with mental illness, the cooperatives advertise

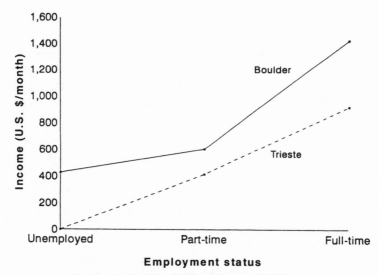

Figure 3   Income Gradient for the Mentally Ill in Trieste and Boulder

widely and have high community visibility. Thus, the scale and social impact of these enterprises exceed the usual achievements of vocational programs.

Income Gradient

An important reason for the success of the worker cooperatives in Italy is the greater incentive there for people with mental illness to participate in the work force. In Trieste, only the most disabled people with mental illness (80% disability) receive disability income (about $830 a month in 1991). Other mentally ill people must work for pay. Less productive patients work half-time as trainees in the cooperative and receive a stipend of about $290 a month with an incentive increment of $125 ($3.60 to $5.20 an hour). Fully productive workers are employed full-time for $920 a month ($5.75 an hour).

The difference in income gradient for people with mental illness in northern Italy and Colorado is shown in figure 3 (in which the Boulder figures are for mean cash income for our sample). The income gradient is more gradual for Boulder patients entering part-time employment because the economic incentive to begin part-time work is not as great as in Trieste.

American Cooperative Enterprises

Can U.S. mental health agencies develop nonprofit cooperative enterprises similar to the European models described above? Monadnock Family Services in Keene, New Hampshire, has successfully established a consumer-owned and managed cooperative with projects that began by buying, renovating, and selling houses (Boyles 1988) and has now moved on to building garden furniture (Silvestri, personal communication). Other U.S. ventures may be feasible. If they follow the Italian design, successful enterprises would employ an integrated workforce of mentally disabled and healthy workers, the proportion varying with the size and profitability of the enterprise.

To give a competitive advantage to consumer-employing businesses, contracts can be developed with mental health agencies and other public organizations. New York state agencies, for example, are obliged by a section of the state finance law introduced in 1987 to purchase new equipment from consumer-employing programs of the Office of Mental Health whenever possible. The products available for sale through the "Buy OMH" catalogue include furniture and equipment for offices and hospitals, curtains and shades, tee-shirt printing, and wheelchair repair (Surles et al. 1992). Similarly, a mental health center can shift services that are currently contracted to outside enterprises (property repair, courier services, secretarial help) to a consumer enterprise. As described below, higher-functioning consumers can also be employed in treatment-related roles as case manager aides and foster care providers.

The consumer economy can be improved by developing enterprises which exploit group purchasing power and recirculate money through the community to produce an economic multiplier effect. This is equivalent to establishing local ownership of the ghetto grocery store, so that capital is not drained from the neighborhood. Following this approach, enterprises would employ consumers where possible, aim to provide a valued service to the group, and return profits to the consumer group. The pilot data we gathered points to consumption markets that consumer businesses might exploit. Our subjects consume a large volume of services and goods, with an average value of over $2,000 per person each month. Table 3 lists subjects' out-of-pocket expenses and figure 4 illustrates their total consumption of various goods and services derived by combining the client's out-of-pocket expense with the value of donated goods or services. For example, the average cash expenditure on medication is $14 a month, but with the noncash contribution (from Medicaid or the mental health center), the total expenditure for each subject averages $90. The largest average monthly expenditures (cash expense plus noncash income) are (in descending order) psychiatric treatment, rent, food, medication, transportation, and meals out.

Considering these expenses, enterprises which could be developed to serve people with mental illness and benefit from their spending capacity include (1) treatment-related services for other clients, (2) a consumer-cooperative pharmacy, (3) housing cooperatives, (4) cafeterias, and (5) courier/transportation services. Some of these possibilities are discussed below.

Table 3 Mean Monthly Cash Expenses in Boulder, 1992

	Whole Group (N = 52)	No Formal Income (N = 2)	Unemployed (N = 18)	Part-Time Employed (N = 18)	Full-Time Employed (N = 5)	High Income Support (N = 9)
Rent	173	0	109	180	161	333
Food	102	86	108	103	94	97
Transportation	70	70	34	53	69	177
Meals out	43	10	22	43	92	63
Health care	33	0	17	17	81	77
Tobacco	28	15	30	35	29	12
Utilities	28	0	26	22	16	58
Psych. treatment	25	3	19	6	23	80
Alcohol	23	15	26	9	44	38
Other[a]	179	1	131	128	423	279
Total cash expense	704	201	522	596	1032	1214

[a]Includes clothing, entertainment, repaying loans, telephone, medication, house supplies, education, drugs, laundry, and theft loss (in descending order)

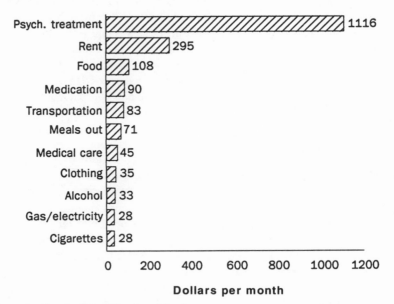

Figure 4 Consumption of Goods and Services

Consumers as Mental Health Staff

The consumption of psychiatric treatment, for the subjects we interviewed in Boulder, exceeds $13,000 a year per client on average. If consumers could participate in providing these services, the potential for improving their economic and vocational situation would be considerable. Such participation appears to be quite feasible.

An innovative program in Denver, Colorado, at the Regional Assessment and Training Center (RATC), has trained mental health consumers with long-term mental illness to work as case management aides within the state mental health system, as residential counselors, and as vocational rehabilitation staff (Sherman and Porter 1991). Trainees with well-controlled mental illness enter six weeks of classroom training and a fourteen-week field placement in a community mental health program. Following internship, trainees earn a college certificate and are guaranteed employment in the mental health system. As case manager aides, the graduates of the program help mentally ill clients with budgeting, applying for entitlements, and finding housing, and they counsel their clients on treatment, work, and other issues. By December 1995, the ninth year of the program's operation, over ninety consumers had been trained and placed in employment. At last count, 80% of the program graduates had completed a year or more of successful employment.

The program has continued successfully after initial demonstration grant funds were terminated, and has been replicated in other states. In Houston, Texas, a similar program has trained and placed fifty consumer case managers, and other replication projects have been established in Washington, Utah, and Oregon—all without demonstration grants. The consumer aides are relatively cheap ($6.00–$10.00 an hour). They perform tasks (for example, apartment hunting) which professionals are happy to see others take on, and they achieve some things which professionals cannot. In particular, they serve as role models for clients who are struggling to manage better, and they can reduce the antagonism which clients may show toward treatment.

Consumers as Peer Supports

Another innovative concept is proving successful on a smaller scale. Under this plan a higher-functioning mentally ill client lives with a lower-functioning client as a companion and live-in aide. Instead of being paid a salary, which would lead to loss of Social Security benefits and noncash income, the companion is reimbursed with free food and lodging. Thus the companion, who might, if unemployed, have a total cash plus noncash income of around $900 a month (excluding psychiatric treatment) could, with the addition of free board and lodging, increase total income to over $1,100—

more than the average part-time employed subject receives. Possible sources of the additional funding include (1) two-person HUD Section 8 rent subsidies which allow for live-in aides for the disabled, (2) contributions from the relatives of the lower-functioning client, or (3) home health aide funds.

A Consumer-Oriented Pharmacy for People with Mental Illness

In our Boulder sample, medication is one of the largest consumer markets which subjects do control—averaging $90 a month per person. A pharmacy which shares the profits from these medications with the consumer group would capture much of this business. The Mental Health Center of Boulder County has contracted with a pharmacy wholesale distributor to open an on-site consumer-cooperative pharmacy to supply clients of the agency. Pharmacy staff include two half-time consumer pharmacy technicians. Savings generated by the pharmacy (around $10,000 a year for an agency with two thousand open cases) are being used to establish other consumer-employing enterprises. Federal fraud and abuse statutes require that medical practitioners and agencies not profit from kickbacks by referring patients to other providers such as pharmacies. For this reason, the cooperation of a consumer organization (such as the Alliance for the Mentally Ill) in operating the pharmacy or receiving the profit share may be important.

Cooperative Housing

If consumers were able to become cooperative property owners instead of tenants, this would be a form of economic advancement. Housing cooperatives offer several advantages: long-term affordability, a feeling of community, and the opportunity to build leadership skills among members through the maintenance and managerial tasks required to operate the housing. On the down side, both mortgage lenders and potential residents may be put off by the cooperative governance structure. Several factors make cooperative housing more affordable. Each member owns a share of the cooperative corporation and leases a housing unit from the corporation. Since members are lessees, they qualify for rent subsidies, including Section 8 certificates. They retain ownership, however, and can profit from resale of the share. Operating costs are lower than for rental apartments because of resident involvement in management and the absence of a profit line in the budget (Davis and Thompson 1988).

The basic financing method for a cooperative is a blanket mortgage for which the cooperative corporation is liable. Members pay an initial membership price and a monthly assessment. They can obtain loans, backed by their cooperative shares, to allow them to meet the membership price. For example, poor families joining the Hillrise Mutual Housing Association in Lancaster, Pennsylvania, are required to pay a membership price of $1,500, but most pay $300 in cash and finance the rest through a share loan (Davis and Thompson 1988).

There are relatively few successful examples of cooperative homeownership for people with mental illness, however, because of a variety of problems. People with mental illness tend to be a fairly mobile group with little capital or monthly income. If hospitalized for a prolonged period, a person may lose benefits and be unable to pay the monthly assessment. SSI recipients, furthermore, cannot accumulate capital to purchase housing without adversely affecting their eligibility for SSI benefits.

Despite these difficulties, housing cooperatives for people with mental illness are viable. Some chapters of the National Alliance for the Mentally Ill (NAMI), including the Greater Chicago branch, have established nonprofit trusts. Residents are usually relatives of the investors: if a resident moves, the investor may dispose of his or her share to another family or claim a tax deduction. NAMI has proposed a low-cost revolving loan fund which, by building a large reservoir of capital, could access favorable loan rates (Flynn, personal communication).

Conclusion

The mentally disabled encounter significant disincentives to begin work or to increase their working hours. Research is required to evaluate (1) the effects of changes in the benefit structure, including graduated benefit-reduction schemes, on labor force participation by disabled workers; (2) the impact of subsidized wages on psychiatric treatment costs, and (3) the viability of guaranteed work programs for higher functioning clients.

Mixed-workforce business enterprises have been successful in expanding work opportunities for people with mental illness in many parts of Europe, but they have been little explored in the United States. Such ventures may be viable in this country, particularly if we use the consumption market of people with mental illness—including the provision of psychiatric treatment and related services—to create opportunities for consumer employment and economic betterment. The introduction of capitated health insurance schemes increases the viability of some of the innovations suggested in this chapter.

Appendix: Disability Benefits
Supplemental Security Income (SSI)

Definition. SSI is a federally administered disability program based on financial need and the presence of a disability expected to last twelve months or more. Medicaid coverage is included.

Earnings allowance. The exempt amount is $65 earned income plus $20 unearned (or a total of $85 earned, if there is no unearned income) per month. Over this allowance, $1 is deducted from the SSI check for every $2 earned.

Trial work period. None. The earnings allowance goes into effect immediately and continues indefinitely until the SSI check is reduced to zero. Eligibility continues as long as the recipient is disabled. Medicaid continues regardless of whether the check has been reduced to zero, as long as ongoing medical care for the disability is needed and the recipient cannot afford to purchase equivalent care (valued at over $15,000 a year) and is using Medicaid at least once every twelve months.

Social Security Disability Insurance (SSDI)

Definition. SSDI is a federal insurance program based on employer/employee contributions and the presence of a disability expected to last twelve months or more. Medicare coverage begins after twenty-four months of disability status.

Earnings allowance. None. The SSDI check is never reduced because of earnings. The recipient receives the whole amount or none at all.

Trial work period. The recipient may earn an unlimited amount of money initially. The trial work period ends after nine (not necessarily consecutive) months in which earnings exceed $200.

Extended period of eligibility. After the trial work period, the SSDI check is issued for any month in which earnings fall below $500 for a period of thirty-six consecutive months. Each month's check is based on the previous months' earnings. The first month after the thirty-six-month extended eligibility period in which earnings exceed $500 triggers the termination of SSDI. Medicare benefits continue for twenty-four months after termination.

References

Anthony, W. A., M. R. Cohen, and K. S. Danley. 1988. The Psychiatric Rehabilitation Model as Applied to Vocational Rehabilitation. In J. A. Cardiello, and M. D. Bell, eds., *Vocational Rehabilitation of Persons with Prolonged Psychiatric Disorders*. Baltimore: Johns Hopkins University Press, 59–80.

Berndt, E. R. 1991. *The Practice of Econometrics: Classic and Contemporary*. Reading, MA: Addison-Wesley.

Boyles, P. 1988. Mentally Ill Gain a Foothold in Working World, *Boston Sunday Globe*, 5 June.

Brown, G. W., G. M. Carstairs, and G. Topping. 1958. Post-Hospital Adjustment of Chronic Mental Patients. *Lancet* 2: 685–689.

Burtless, G., and J. Hausman. 1978. The Effects of Taxation on Labor Supply:

Evaluating the Gary Income Maintenance Experiments. *Journal of Political Economy* 86: 1103–1130.

Cohen, L. 1955. Vocational Planning and Mental Illness. *Personnel and Guidance Journal* 34: 28–32.

Davis, M., and B. Thompson. 1988. *Cooperative Housing: A Development Primer.* Washington, DC: National Cooperative Business Association.

Ellis, R. H., and C. Young. 1983. Cost Savings Associated with Sheltered Workshop Employment. Brief Report, no. 2. Denver: Colorado Division of Mental Health.

Ellwood, D. 1988. *Poor Support.* New York: Basic Books.

Fairweather, G. W., D. H. Sanders, H. Maynard, et al. 1969. *Community Life of the Mentally Ill.* Chicago: Aldine.

Freeman, H. E., and O. G. Simmons. 1963. The Mental Patient Comes Home. New York: Wiley.

Haskins, R. 1991. Congress Writes a Law: Research and Welfare Reform. *Journal of Policy Analysis and Management* 10: 616–632.

Huxley, P., and R. Warner. Forthcoming. *A Controlled Evaluation of Clubhouse Membership on Quality of Life and Treatment Utilization.*

Jacobs, H. E., D. Wissusik, R. Collier, et al. 1992. Correlations between Psychiatric Disabilities and Vocational Outcome. *Hospital and Community Psychiatry* 43: 365–369.

Kaus, M. 1986. The Work Ethic State. *The New Republic* 7 July, 22–33.

Little, J. 1994. Chronic Mental Illness, Labor Force Participation and Disability Income. University of Colorado, Boulder, Colorado. Manuscript.

Moffit, R. 1990. The Econometrics of Kinked Budget Constraints. *Journal of Economic Perspectives* 20: 119–139.

Roberts, J. D., and I. M. Ward. 1987. *Commensurate Wage Determination for Service Contracts.* Columbus, OH: Ohio Industries for the Handicapped.

Sancton, T. 1992. How to Get America off the Dole. *Time,* 25 May, 44–47.

Scheffler, R. 1992. Financing Mental Health Services. Paper presented at NIMH workshop on Organizing and Financing Services for People with Severe Mental Disorders, Park City, Utah, December 9–11.

Sherman, P. S., and R. Porter. 1991. Mental Health Consumers as Case Management Aides, *Hospital and Community Psychiatry* 42: 494–498.

Surles, R. C., B. J. Morrison, J. L. Sheets, and G. E. Shaheen. 1992. *Buy OMH Directory of Products and Services.* Albany, NY: New York State Office of Mental Health Bureau of Psychiatric Rehabilitation Services.

Warner, R. 1994. *Recovery from Schizophrenia.* 2d ed. London: Routledge.

PART 3

Mental Disorders and Disability Entitlement Programs

Two separate bodies of law bear on work disability, and both establish legal entitlements. One body of law entitles covered persons to benefits because they are unable to work. The other body of law, epitomized by the ADA, provides legal protection (enforceable nondiscrimination rights) to persons with disabilities precisely because they *are* able to work, notwithstanding their disabilities. Thus, in the first case, a finding of "disability" represents a legal judgment that the person with a disability "cannot" (i.e., is not expected to) work, and in the second case, protection is predicated on a legal judgment that the person with a disability *is* able to work and is entitled to any reasonable accommodation that would enable him to do so. This part focuses on the fabric of disability benefit laws, while part 4 covers the ADA. In the following chapter, Professor Ellen Smith Pryor reviews disability entitlement programs and highlights common themes and problems relating to persons with mental disorders.

6

Mental Disabilities and the Disability Fabric

ELLEN SMITH PRYOR

The patchwork quilt of American disability policy does not lie evenly over both mental and physical work disabilities. For mental rather than physical work disabilities, workers' compensation programs afford far less coverage; private disability insurance generally is more restricted; vocational rehabilitation appears to be less accessible in a number of ways; and methods for calculating benefits are often dramatically different. What explains these and other features of the disability fabric as it bears on mental impairments? Are these features defensible, and if so why?

These questions deserve closer examination than they have received. Although extensive data and analyses exist regarding certain parts of the disability structure, and to a lesser extent regarding the structure as a whole, less attention has been focused on disability policy as it relates to work disabilities arising from mental disorders. About many crucial issues relating to this topic, we know very little. For example, no analysis has examined the ways in which impairment-rating guidelines used in many workers' compensation programs, such as the American Medical Association's *Guides to the Evaluation of Permanent Impairment,* apply to the evaluation of mental impairments. And very little scholarly or research attention has been directed to the private disability insurance market as it relates to mental impairments (save possibly internal studies performed by insurers).

These gaps, in turn, create others. Information on the questions just noted, for example, is necessary to evaluate the adequacy of vocational rehabilitation services provided to individuals with mental impairments (because these services often are tied to workers' compensation benefit decisions or to coverage under private insurance disability), and whether the combination of workers' compensation and social security disability forms a coherent and defensible means of providing benefits to individuals with mental disabilities.

Recent developments have only heightened the need for a closer look at these issues. The Americans with Disabilities Act (ADA) is one such development, of course, but others of significance have received little attention: numerous recently enacted statutes limiting coverage of mental impairments in workers' compensation; changes during the past ten years in the private disability insurance market; and increased interest in integrated disability management and in dissolving the distinction between occupational and nonoccupational impairments.

This chapter aims to cast light on the still-underexamined topic of U.S. disability policy as it relates to work disabilities that stem from mental disorders. Because a single chapter cannot analyze all the important features of and issues relating to each disability program, the strategy here is to focus on three crucial topics: (1) the considerations that might justify differential treatment of mental as distinct from physical impairments and disabilities; (2) the ways in which current disability policy affects employers' incentives with respect to prevention, accommodation, and rehabilitation of mental impairments and work disabilities; and (3) the criteria that state workers' compensation programs use in delivering benefits to persons with mental impairments.

The chapter begins with a brief descriptive overview of the U.S. disability fabric as it relates to mental impairments and work disabilities. This discussion includes state workers' compensation programs, Social Security Disability Insurance (SSDI), social security Supplemental Security Income (SSI) for individuals with disabilities, vocational rehabilitation (VR) under the federal-state VR program, VR under state workers' compensation programs, private disability insurance, and emerging proposals for integrating workers' compensation with private health or disability insurance.

After a general look at these programs, the next section, "General Policy Concerns," addresses the most obvious question that this general look raises: What considerations, if any, justify the differential treatment of mental and physical disabilities? The section evaluates four possible considerations: adverse selection, moral hazard, difficulties in ascertaining the relevant loss, and decisional fairness and accuracy. As the section makes clear, these factors may explain and partially support some differential treatment of mental impairments/disabilities, but they are hardly satisfying reasons for much of the differential treatment that does in fact exist.

The next section examines how the disability fabric affects the incentives of employers to play a role in preventing and accommodating mental impairments. In exploring this topic, the section looks at the roles of voluntary incentives, private insurance, workers' compensation, and the ADA. The section concludes with some recommendations and observations about how to increase the prevention/accommodation effect of this web of influences.

Our focus then shifts from the subject of prevention/accommodation to the issue of delivering benefits to those who are partially or totally disabled.

Specifically, the section focuses on how workers' compensation programs define and measure compensable mental disabilities. This has been the subject of much legislative and insurer interest in recent years, and yet enormous problems remain in this part of the disability fabric.

A note about terminology is necessary. When using the terms *impairment* and *disability,* this paper refers, respectively, (1) to organ-level abnormalities or restrictions (such as episodes of panic in an anxiety disorder), and (2) to restricted ability to perform a social role within the expected range, due to an impairment, the history of an impairment, or the perception of an impairment. The shorthand phrase *arising from an impairment* refers to each of these three causes (impairment, history of, perception). The paper will use the term *work disability,* not just *disability,* when referring to the limited ability to work. This is consistent with the Institute of Medicine's approach (Institute of Medicine 1991), but should not pose problems when discussing the ADA or other programs. When using the terms *disability* and *impairment* in any other way (such as the specific terms of the ADA, Social Security disability, or workers' compensation), the paper will make this clear.

Several other definitions also should be useful. As to mental health, each of the public or private threads of the disability fabric bears on one or more of the following aims: (1) preventing mental impairments in the first instance; (2) accommodating (both at the hiring stage and later) individuals with work disabilities arising from mental impairments; (3) delivering benefits, particularly cash benefits for income replacement or for subsistence when a mental disability reduces the individual's ability to work; and (4) rehabilitating individuals with work disabilities arising from mental impairments. As used here, *prevention* refers to reducing the incidence or severity of mental impairment (as distinct from reducing disability), and *rehabilitation* refers to training, education, or services (by an employer or third party) beyond what we would normally view as required by reasonable accommodation.

The boundaries between prevention, accommodation, and rehabilitation are not impermeable or definitely fixed, but the categories are still helpful in exploring the aims and effects of various programs, and the connections between them. For example, although workers' compensation programs have traditionally been "about" prevention, compensation, and (sometimes) rehabilitation, they also have an important effect on accommodation by the employer. And, although the ADA is viewed as "about" accommodation rather than prevention, it may influence the latter as well.

An Overview of the Disability Structure as It Relates to Mental Impairments and Disabilities

The disability structure in the United States includes benefits programs (such as SSDI); programs aimed primarily at rehabilitation, such as the federal-state vocational rehabilitation scheme; tort law; private insurance mechanisms; and "rights" legislation, such as the ADA and the many state antidiscrimination statutes. The following discussion gives an overview of these (with the exception of tort law and the ADA and other antidiscrimination statutes) as they relate to persons with mental impairments and disabilities.[1]

Employer-Provided Private Insurance Benefits

Many private employers offer group health and possibly disability policies (short-term, long-term, or both) for the benefit of their employees. Disability protection provides replacement of some percentage of lost income, such as 60%, capped by a maximum monthly amount (Unum Life Insurance 1991b, 6). Disability insurance, unlike workers' compensation insurance, is not limited to disabilities caused by work-related injuries. Rather, "disability" under disability insurance is more broadly defined as inability to perform an occupation. Some disability insurance covers for at least some period of time the individual's inability to perform her own occupation; other forms of disability insurance cover only the inability to perform any occupation (Unum 1991b, 6–9). Policies also vary in whether they cover only total disability or whether they also afford income replacement for reductions in the individual's ability to work.

How frequently are employees covered by disability insurance, either short-term or long-term? According to the most recent study by the Department of Labor, larger employers (those with 100 employees or more) provide some sort of short-term disability protection (through sick leave, sickness and accident insurance, or both) to 89% of full-time employees (U.S. Department of Labor 1989, 18). Employer-provided long-term disability benefits cover 45% of full-time employees. The degree of employee participation among types of employee groups varies widely; white-collar workers are more than twice as likely to have long-term disability insurance than are blue-collar workers. Usually, benefits from group long-term disability insurance are coordinated with those from other sources, so that the combined benefits received are set to a level that does not exceed 60% of the individual's previous wage rate (Health Insurance Association of America 1993, 16).

Smaller establishments (100 or fewer employees) provide short-term disability protection of some sort to 60% of all full-time workers, and to 10% or less of the part-time employees (U.S. Department of Labor 1991, 17, 89). Long-term disability insurance is provided to only 19% of the full-time employees, and virtually never to part-time workers (U.S. Department of Labor 1990, 18, 90).

Notably, 94% of the long-term disability participants have plans that include some coverage for disabilities caused by mental impairments (U.S.

Department of Labor 1989, 20–21, 38), but both short-term and long-term disability policies usually restrict coverage for mental disabilities. Some policies may exclude any coverage for disabilities due to mental illness, although such exclusions are not permissible in some states. Other policies provide coverage for mental disabilities, but limit the benefits to a relatively short period, such as two years and thereafter only for the duration of any institutionalization (U.S. Department of Labor 1990; Unum Life Insurance Company 1991b).

Are such restrictions consistent with the ADA? The Equal Employment Opportunity Commission (EEOC) has issued an "interpretive guidance" on the question of disability-based distinctions in employer-provided insurance. Under the EEOC's reasoning, limitations aimed at broad categories of disability, such as "mental and nervous impairments," are not "disability-based" distinctions that trigger application of the ADA. Even if a particular restriction does constitute a disability-based distinction, the employer may justify it on various grounds of actuarial necessity (U.S. EEOC 1993).

Workers' Compensation

Workers' compensation programs exist in every state and also at the federal level. The programs require employers to provide insurance to cover the medical expenses and disability costs resulting from injuries or diseases that arise out of and occur in the course of employment. These insurance benefits do not require a showing of fault, and contributory fault by the worker—with only a few exceptions—does not bar or reduce recovery. In exchange for these no-fault benefits, workers' compensation programs immunize employers against tort suits by employees. Only a handful of states allow employers not to participate in the workers' compensation system and take their chances with tort liability; in almost all states, participation in the workers' compensation system is compulsory.

The states administer workers' compensation programs though an administrative process that usually includes hearing officers and appeals procedures that culminate in judicial review. In most states, however, the insurance itself is primarily provided through private carriers or by self-insured employers. Many states administer a workers' compensation fund for employers that are unable to obtain workers' compensation insurance in the private market. In only a small handful of states is a state fund the exclusive means of providing workers' compensation insurance (Alliance of American Insurers 1994, 53).

Disability benefits are available for both partial and total disability, and for both temporary and permanent disabilities. Temporary disability benefits—both total and partial—are paid weekly, in an amount equal to some percentage of the employee's lost wages (subject to a cap based on average weekly wages in the state) during the temporary period of disability. Permanent total disability benefits are paid for the worker's lifetime, for the duration of disability, or for some large number of weeks, such as 500 or 401 (Alliance of American Insurers 1994, 18–20).

Permanent partial disability benefits have long proved the most troublesome category. They often provoke lengthy and costly adjudication, and though they make up a minority of claims, they represent a majority of the payments made in workers' compensation (Berkowitz and Burton 1987, vii). States vary widely in their methods for assessing permanent partial disability, and in recent years many legislative reforms have included revision of these methods. One increasingly common method is the use of an "impairment schedule"—very often the American Medical Association's *Guides to the Evaluation of Permanent Impairment*—to obtain a percentage of "whole-person impairment." This percentage then is often used to determine the duration of permanent partial disability benefits. For example, in Texas a worker receives three weeks of compensation for each percentage of whole-person impairment.

Another common approach to permanent partial benefits is to use a schedule for certain specified types of injuries—such as the loss of a toe, foot, or eye—and for all other injuries to base compensation on the degree to which the injury or illness has diminished the worker's wage-earning capacity.

Workers with mental impairments, then, usually face two hurdles that may prove especially imposing. First, the worker must prove that the impairment occurred in the course and scope of, and arose out of, the employment. The purpose, effect, and defensibility of this work-relation test is discussed later in this chapter. Second, in an increasing number of states, permanent benefits (both partial and total) are not available simply on a showing that the impairment has reduced the worker's ability to earn a wage. Instead, the worker must show that the impairment constitutes an impairment under the terms of the state's impairment schedule. Frequently, this schedule is the AMA *Guides*. Later discussion will consider in more detail this measurement issue as it relates to mental impairments.

SSDI and SSI

THE DEFINITION AND EVALUATION OF DISABILITY

Social Security Disability Insurance (SSDI), added to the Social Security program in 1956, pays benefits to workers (and to their eligible spouses, children, and survivors) who have gained insured status and are found to be disabled. *Disability* is defined as "inability to engage in any substantial gainful activity by reason of any medically determinable physical or mental impairment which can be expected to result in death or has lasted or can be expected to last for a continuous period of not less than 12 months'' (42 U.S.C. §423(d)(1)). To obtain insured status, the individual must have worked in covered employment for the requisite number of quarters, and must have the necessary amount of recent covered work. The program is not means-tested. Monthly benefits are based on the worker's annual taxable earnings, averaged over most of the worker's adult years; the payment is subject to a maximum family benefit amount.

Supplemental Security Income (SSI), added to the Social Security program in 1972, is a social welfare program that differs from SSDI in several ways: it is means-tested (generally, the individual can earn no more than $500 monthly); it does not require insured status or, for that matter, any previous attachment to the work force; and its benefits reflect a flat-rate, subsistence payment that is lower than average SSDI payments: the average payment for SSI disability in December 1992 was $409; and the average payment for SSDI in November 1993 was $625.70 (Social Security Administration 1993, 65, 110). The definition of *disability* under SSI and SSDI is the same, and an individual can be eligible for benefits under both SSDI and SSI.

Both programs link up to other support and compensation systems in a number of ways. After a two-year waiting period, recipients of SSDI benefits who are disabled and under the age of sixty-five are eligible for Medicare; in most states, disabled SSI recipients are automatically eligible for Medicaid. Social Security disability benefits are offset by workers' compensation benefits, to the extent that the sum of the payments under both programs exceeds 80% of the individual's average earnings (20 C.F.R. §404.408 (1993)). Many workers' compensation statutes also contain offset provisions relating to the receipt of SSDI and SSI benefits (U.S. Chamber of Commerce 1993, 20–23).

Procedurally, the disability determination process is now marked by four possible stages of administrative decision making (initial decision, reconsideration, hearing, and Appeals Council Review). The initial and reconsideration decisions are made by state agencies designated to make disability determinations; the agencies must follow regulations and performance standards issued by the Social Security Administration (20 C.F.R. §404.1503 (1993)).

Substantively, the disability determination process is marked by a five-step "sequential evaluation" process: (1) Is the claimant currently engaging in substantial gainful activity? (If so, a finding of not disabled); (2) Does the claimant have a severe impairment? (If not, a finding of not disabled); (3) Does the claimant meet or equal a "listed" impairment? (If so, a finding of disabled); (4) Does the claimant's impairment prevent her from doing past relevant work? (If not, a finding of not disabled); (5) Does the claimant's impairment prevent him from doing any other work, taking into account the claimant's residual functional capacity (RFC), age, education, and past work experience? (If so, a finding of disabled.)

This sequential evaluation applies to both mental and physical impairments. Yet, during the 1980s, the Social Security Administration (SSA) used an inappropriately truncated version of the sequential evaluation process when considering mental impairments: If the claimant's mental impairment was not severe enough to satisfy the listed impairments, then the SSA did not go on, as it was required to do, to engage in a specific determination of the individual's ability to perform substantial gainful activity. Instead, the SSA simply presumed that claimants who lacked listed mental impairments retained the capacity to engage in unskilled work (Goldman and Gattozzi 1988; Levy 1991).

Eventually, court challenges and greater awareness of these practices prompted reforms in this and other features of the decisional process. Among the reforms enacted by Congress was a mandate, in 1984, that the SSA develop new rules for determining mental disability (42 U.S.C. §421 (1988)). The resulting regulation added to the sequential evaluation process a specific procedure for evaluating the severity of mental impairments (20 C.F.R. §404.1520a (1993)).

This mental evaluation procedure is perhaps most notable in requiring the completion of a standardized functional assessment as to any mental impairment. The assessment must consider four areas of functioning and must rate the claimant's functioning according to a five point scale:

Area of Function	Degree of Limitation				
Activities of daily living	None ( )	Slight ( )	Moderate ( )	Marked ( )	Extreme ( )
Social functioning	None ( )	Slight ( )	Moderate ( )	Marked ( )	Extreme ( )
Concentration, persistence, and pace	Never ( )	Seldom ( )	Often ( )	Frequent ( )	Constant ( )
Deterioration or decompensation in work or worklike settings	Never ( )	Seldom ( )	Often ( )	Frequent ( )	Constant ( )

This standard assessment, which is contained in a form called the "Psychiatric Technique Review Form," must be completed at each of the four stages of administrative decision (initial, reconsideration, hearing, and appeals council review), and must be completed and signed by a medical consultant at the first two of these stages.

This process differs markedly from that used with physical impairments. In theory, any impairment, physical or mental, that reaches steps 4 or 5 of the sequential evaluation process requires some sort of functional assessment, but the SSA has not yet adopted standardized functional assessment measures for physical impairments.

DISABILITY RECEIPT BY PERSONS WITH MENTAL DISABILITIES

Recent analyses of SSA data show a "steady and substantial" rise since at least 1985 in the rate at which both SSDI and SSI are awarded for mental disabilities (Kennedy and Manderscheid 1992, Figure 5.2). From 1985 to 1991, the number of SSDI recipients with mental disabilities increased by 50.5%. When SSI is added, the increase is 62.8% (Kennedy and Manderscheid 1992, 222). Mental disorders (excluding mental retardation) constitute one of the two largest categories of new disability awards in the SSDI program for each year since 1987; the other category is musculoskeletal conditions (Kennedy and Manderscheid 1992, 221). Age is also a notable factor: nearly twice as many individuals under the age of thirty receive disability awards because of mental disorder than the overall number of awards for this age group (Kennedy and Manderscheid 1992, 221).

Two major differences between SSDI/SSI payments and workers' compensation payments bear emphasis. First, the former requires only a yes/no decision about total disability; all workers' compensation programs also provide payment for partial disabilities. Second, the duration of workers' compensation benefits is usually limited to a fixed period, such as a number of weeks that is tied to the percentage of impairment or disability rating. SSDI and SSI are not so limited. Perhaps in light of these fixed periods, workers' compensation programs do not contain formalized "continuing disability review" procedures, as does the SSA (20 C.F.R. §404.1590 (1993)).

Vocational Rehabilitation

Two major public sources of vocational rehabilitation (VR) exist: (1) the federal-state vocational rehabilitation program, and (2) vocational rehabilitation provisions under state workers' compensation laws. In theory, both are available to individuals with mental disabilities. As the following discussion will make clear, however, the federal-state VR program is the more important source of services for individuals with mental disabilities.

THE FEDERAL-STATE VR PROGRAM

The federal-state VR program has evolved and expanded significantly since its inception in 1920. In its early years, it primarily provided funding for individuals who were likely to find employment (Haveman, Halberstadt, and Burkhauser 1984, 138). Now the federal rehabilitation statute (the Rehabilitation Act of 1973, as amended, 29 U.S.C. §701–797b (1994)) authorizes funding for a far broader range of services. To receive funding under the program, a state must submit a plan that complies with detailed federal regulations, and must pass legislation authorizing a state entity to administer the program in accordance with these requirements.

In theory, individuals with mental disabilities have long been eligible for vocational rehabilitation. Yet significant acceptance of vocational rehabilitation aimed at persons with severe and persistent mental illness has occurred only within the past decade (Reznicek and Baron 1991, 21). Recent studies of the VR system, moreover, have revealed numerous trouble spots with respect to VR and mental disabilities. First, supported employment services for individuals with mental disabilities are, in the main, hard to access and coordinate (Andrews et al. 1992; Office of Technology Assessment 1994; Reznicek and Baron 1991, 2–5). Second, improvements are necessary in the measures used to assess VR outcomes of individuals with mental disabilities (Anthony, Cohen and Nemec 1987; Farkas and Anthony 1987; Office of Technology Assessment 1994, 57–58).

A third crucial problem area is the need for increased cooperation and coordination between the mental health service systems and the VR systems within individual states. Such cooperation could and should take place with regard to many issues, including the development of referral guidelines for VR, service development planning, and evaluating program effectiveness (Reznicek and Baron 1991, 2–5). The absence of such cooperation has produced many gaps in service delivery: many VR counselors have been reluctant to support transitional employment or supported employment services; mental health professionals and VR counselors remain unclear about the importance of and the financial responsibility for supportive services; and the systems have not agreed on long-term goals or on the nature of their own responsibilities for providing long-term services (Reznicek and Baron 1991, 2–14). Yet, although the federal-state VR statute specifies a need for intersystem and interagency collaboration, some studies estimate that little or no such collaboration takes place in nearly one-half of all local settings.

Recent amendments to the federal VR statute may help address some of these concerns. First, the 1992 amendments will probably broaden the eligibility for VR services of those with serious mental disabilities. Until 1992, vocational rehabilitation services were available to those who could "reasonably be expected to benefit in terms of employability'' (29 U.S.C. §706(7)(A)(1985)). Studies have shown that this criterion—as applied by many state and local VR units—was often a stumbling block for individuals with mental disabilities. One extensive study, conducted shortly before the 1992 amendments, found that 68% of the responding local VR administrators and 80% of the responding state mental health administrators felt strongly that a broader standard of VR eligibility was necessary for individuals with mental impairments (Reznicek and Baron 1991, 11).

Under the 1992 amendments, the individual must be one who "can benefit in terms of an employment outcome" (29 U.S.C. §706(8)(A)(1994)). Yet this ability to benefit will be *presumed* unless the state unit can demonstrate by clear and convincing evidence that the criterion is not satisfied (29 U.S.C. §722(a)(4)(A)(1994)). Although no substantial data yet show whether this change has addressed the concerns about the VR eligibility of persons with mental disabilities, it should have the effect of increasing eligibility.

A second important change reflected in recent amendments is the emphasis on service strategies other than the traditional VR model. That model, whose conceptual core is a notion of physical and not mental disability, emphasizes an intervention (training, education) that is defined in duration and that does not need revisiting after the completion of this VR service delivery. Individuals with serious and persistent mental disabilities, however, often require ongoing medical, rehabilitative, psychosocial, and other supportive services to seek and to retain employment (Reznicek and Baron 1991, 4, 21). Studies of these strategies, though still sparse, suggest the efficacy of and need for this approach.

Recent amendments to the VR statute specifically endorse these sorts of delivery strategies. The statute now authorizes funding for a wide range of transition services (defined as a coordinated set of activities that will promote movement from school to postschool activities, including postsecondary education, vocational training, supported employment, independent living, or community participation), and for supported employment services (ongoing support services needed to support and maintain individuals with the most severe disabilities in supported employment).

VOCATIONAL REHABILITATION UNDER WORKERS' COMPENSATION

The workers' compensation statutes of many states include some type and degree of VR services. In some states the services are mandatory for eligible workers; sometimes they are only voluntary. Of course, a worker is entitled to such services—even in the states that mandate such benefits—only if he has established a work-related disability. It thus seems plausible to suppose that workers' compensation VR is infrequently available to individuals with primarily mental disabilities.

Aside from this surmise, we know little about the operation of workers' compensation VR with regard to individuals with mental disabilities. A number of states have begun or recently completed studies of workers' compensation VR (California Workers' Compensation Research Institute 1989a, 1989b; State of Washington 1991; Texas Workers' Compensation Research Center 1993), and some other entities, such as the Workers' Compensation Institute, have performed others (Gardner 1986, 1988a, 1988b). But these studies do not address, except in the most general sense, the topic of VR for individuals with mental disorders.

There are also no studies or analyses exploring how mandatory versus voluntary VR might affect the availability and type of VR offered to individuals with mental disabilities. For example, in systems with mandatory rehabilitation, with what frequency do workers with mental impairments meet the eligibility formula? In systems with less than mandatory rehabilitation, what determines whether workers with mental impairments receive VR, and which services do they receive? Some data suggest that VR represents a smaller percentage of the total cost per claim when the claim is for a mental disability arising out of job-related conditions or stresses. In California, where rehabilitation is mandatory, a study of mental stress claims showed that VR expenditures in mental-mental claims is less than one-third that of other claims (California Workers' Compensation Research Institute 1990). It seems plausible to suppose that a voluntary scheme is more likely to underrefer and underserve persons with mental impairments than those with physical impairments. As Betram Black has noted, mental health practitioners often lack interest in referring their patients for VR, for a variety of reasons (Black 1988, 17).

More general changes in the climate of workers' compensation suggest that the availability of VR will only narrow in years to come. Recent years have seen cutbacks in the VR benefits of many state workers' compensation programs. These have stemmed from doubts about the efficacy of VR and concerns that VR may lengthen the dispute process and intensify the contentiousness of the claim (National Council on Compensation Insurance 1993b, 9; State of Washington 1991, 8).

General Policy Concerns

Even a cursory look at the disability fabric reveals many differences in how it addresses mental and physical impairments. At the outset, then, it should be useful to identify some of the policy concerns that might explain (even if they do not wholly justify) many of these differences. Key among these concerns are adverse selection; moral hazard; lack of determinability to a degree that undermines insurability; and decisional accuracy and consistency.

Adverse Selection

Adverse selection refers to a problem that private insurers often encounter in the voluntary market, and which certainly plagues the private disability insurance market. The problem occurs when individuals who seek coverage know more about their expected losses than the insurer (even after the insurer obtains information during the underwriting process). Inevitably, individuals who know that they pose above-average risks will disproportionately choose insurance coverage—if offered—that is priced according to the average risk posed by a pool of insureds. The collected premiums are then insufficient to cover the losses incurred by the pool, which in turn will require a premium increase. Yet a premium increase drives out of the pool some individuals who pose lower-than-average risks, thus driving up the average expected loss yet more and requiring yet a further premium increase. This process continues until only the high-risk individuals remain in the pool, at which point the insurance mechanism generally will fail (Abraham 1986, 15; Hanson and Logue 1990, 140; Rejda 1992, 27–28).

To illustrate the problem as it affects disability insurance, suppose an insurer proposes to offer an individual long-term disability policy. When offering this product to a prospective insured, the insurer will price the policy according to the average expected losses posed by the entire pool of insureds into which the insurer has placed the prospective insured (for example, the pool of physicians in a certain type of practice, of a certain age, and with a certain type of medical history).

Suppose, however, that one or more prospective insureds knows more than the insurer about the insured's likely disability loss—that, for example, the insured has suffered intermittent balance and vision problems that might be the early signs of a neurological disease. These insureds will be attracted to the offered policy in numbers disproportionate to the numbers of higher-risk individuals that the insurer assumed when setting the rate. Thus, the premiums collected will eventually prove inadequate to pay the losses that will be incurred.

Insurers respond to this problem in a number of ways, primarily by being more selective in their underwriting practices (the process of selecting whom the insurer will insure and on what conditions) and by inserting into the insurance contract preexisting condition clauses. The inevitable result, then, is incomplete insurance coverage: those with poorer health histories or other disfavored indicia will be unable to purchase coverage or will be limited to more restrictive coverage.

How does the fear of adverse selection relate to mental impairments? Because adverse selection is not a concern when coverage is mandatory—as it is under workers' compensation, social security, and public vocational rehabilitation programs—the phenomenon cannot be used to justify any restrictions on mental impairments in these programs. Private disability insurers, of course, have reason for adverse selection concerns. But is adverse selection a greater problem with mental than with physical impairments?

There is no evidence of this, although we can make a few conjectures. Prospective insureds who have reason to know of a potentially disabling mental disorder may be better able to conceal this fact from the insurer during the application process. For example, if individuals are less likely to seek professional treatment for mental than for physical disorders, then application queries directed to past medical treatment would not level the informational playing field. Or perhaps it would be harder, in a later coverage dispute, for an insurer to prove that an applicant with an incipient mental disorder "misrepresented a material fact" during the application process. Yet no evidence exists to support these surmises, and even intuitively they are not especially persuasive.

To the contrary, perhaps individuals with potential mental disorders are *less* likely to engage in adverse selection than individuals with possible physical disorders. Adverse selection requires a certain thought process on the part of the prospective insured: "I know or have a good reason to suspect that I have a condition, and that the condition will prove to be disabling." Individuals may be more likely to reach this conclusion about physical conditions whose disability outcomes are well-known, such as multiple sclerosis, than about mental disorders, about which far less is usually known or understood. Again, however, no evidence exists that suggests a conclusion on the point.

In sum, concerns about adverse selection might explain why private disability coverage for both mental and physical disabilities is not more widely available than it currently is. But concerns about adverse selection do not seem to justify differences in the coverage of mental and physical impairments. Reasons for differential coverage must therefore be found somewhere other than in concerns about adverse selection.

Moral Hazard

It is a commonplace that the existence of insurance itself may affect the incidence or the severity of losses and claims. The possibility of benefits might induce an individual consciously to incur a loss in the first instance;

consciously to feign a loss; or, less consciously, to be careless about preventing or minimizing losses. The term "morale hazard" is often applied to the less conscious types of conduct, and "moral hazard" to the more conscious (Rejda 1992, 7–8).

Both problems exist in all insurance, public or private. Yet, for several reasons, both are thought to be especially troublesome with respect to disability benefits. First, the size of the moral hazard concern depends on how successfully the insurer can control or monitor the insured's conduct with respect to a loss. These hazards would not pose a problem if the insurer could always document when the insured herself caused a loss intentionally or faked a loss, or if the insurer could precisely measure the degree to which the insured's lack of vigilance or effort increased the resulting loss (Abraham 1995, 4). But of course this is not possible, especially when the existence and extent of the relevant loss are subjective and difficult to verify—which is the case with all definitions of disability.

Second, these hazards are greater when individuals are more likely to cause, to feign, or to fail to minimize the type of losses that the insurance policy covers. Individuals are not thought likely, for example, to incur or feign injury so that they can receive benefits under a medical payments policy. But, as both theory and empirical evidence suggest, individuals might rationally choose to accept disability benefits rather than remaining at or returning to work (Worrall and Butler 1985).

Third, disability researchers and rehabilitation professionals have long been concerned about the "sick role" phenomenon: that the receipt of disability benefits results in self-labeling that exacerbates or reinforces the initial disability and thus renders rehabilitation even less likely. Many studies have aimed to explain and document this in one setting or another, but most agree on the central notion that disability benefits can produce a reinforcement effect distinct from the economically motivated "malingering" effect (see Estroff et al., chapter 3 in this volume).

How do these concerns relate specifically to mental disabilities? They are sometimes *thought* to apply with greater force to mental disabilities (Weber 1991). Yet, of the problems just noted—monitoring, economic incentives, and the sick role—only monitoring seems more troublesome with regard to mental rather than to physical disabilities. There is no evidence that either the economic incentive or the sick role problem is a greater concern for mental than for physical disabilities.

To say that the monitoring problem may be greater for mental impairments, however, does not justify any and all coverage restrictions on mental impairments. Thus, we look closely later at the many differential standards relating to mental impairments, and evaluate whether the monitoring problem justifies them.

Difficulty in Ascertaining the Loss, to a Degree That Undermines Insurability

When a loss is, to a substantial degree, difficult to identify and to measure, this undermines the availability of private insurance. Private insurers in the voluntary market may decline to enter or may withdraw from a line of coverage when the measurement difficulties prevent actuarily acceptable predictions about the average risks posed by a given pool of insureds, and perceived measurement difficulties may impede the creation of social insurance for the loss or may result in substantial limitations on the available coverage. Indeed, this measurement concern was a major reason why enactment of the SSDI program was delayed until 1956, some twenty years after the rest of the social security program (Derthick 1979, 295–315). Measurement concerns have continued to play a dominant role in legislative and administrative alterations of the SSDI and SSI programs.

The serious measurement challenges posed by disability, then, could be expected to result in a more limited private market and in more restricted social insurance coverage. The differences that exist in the measurement problems posed by mental rather than physical disabilities might explain and justify particular distinctions in coverage or proof standards for mental and physical disabilities. As we will see later, however, workers' compensation programs apply to mental disabilities a number of coverage restrictions and proof requirements that may be prompted—but ultimately are not justified—by measurement concerns.

Decisional Fairness and Accuracy

Difficulties of measurement pose, *ex ante,* problems of insurability, and, *ex post,* problems of decisional accuracy and consistency—decisional qualities that are important from both efficiency and justice perspectives. Again, therefore, the different measurement problems posed by mental disabilities might explain and justify particular decisional standards. Some such standards, however, even if prompted by aims of fairness and accuracy, remain indefensible. This, as will be shown, is often the case with workers' compensation programs.

Prevention and Accommodation by the Employer
Introduction: What We Should Examine; What We Don't Know

Since the ADA's passage, a growing literature has begun to address the accommodation of mental disabilities in the workplace. Yet no analysis has yet examined the entire web of influences that may bear on an employer's accommodation and prevention of mental disabilities and impairments. The ADA is one such influence, of course, but others include private health and disability insurance, workers' compensation, and incentives provided by the marketplace itself. This section explores this larger web of influences, identifies many of the crucial pieces of information that we still lack about the subject, and offers some recommendations for increasing prevention and accommodation by employers with respect to mental impairments and disabilities.

Employers can take actions that relate both to prevention and to accommodation of mental impairments and disabilities. We know that, even when employment factors cannot reduce the incidence or severity of mental impairment, employer action can accommodate (and thus reduce) work disability arising from mental impairment. But employer action can also relate to prevention (reducing the incidence or severity) of mental impairments. By preventing physical injury, employers also prevent the frequent and substantial mental impairments resulting from or exacerbated by the physical injury. By effecting general changes in the workplace or features of employment, employers might be able to reduce the incidence or severity of stress-related mental impairments. And by accommodating the specific needs of individuals with mental disabilities, employers also might affect the incidence or severity of the impairment itself. Consider, for example, Strauss and Davidson's examples of individuals for whom the activity of working actually reduced impairment in chapter 4 in this volume.

When addressing the possible incentives for prevention/accommodation, the discussion includes references to the empirical data or theoretical "proofs" available about certain topics. Ultimately, however, an examination of these influences must rest heavily on analysis and hypothesis, not on confirming empirical data or economic proofs.

Here are some of the major questions, still unanswered, that are important to an understanding of prevention and accommodation by employers of mental impairments and disabilities. (1) What types of general changes in features of employment (if any) are linked to reductions in the incidence or severity of stress-related impairments? (2) What is the effectiveness of specific accommodations for individuals with mental disabilities? (3) As to the private disability insurance market, how do insurers' underwriting processes look for potential mental disability in the individual private market, and does any kind of underwriting aimed at mental illness take place in the group market? (4) In what ways, how commonly, and with what level of effectiveness do insurers exert influence on employers to engage in prevention/accommodation with respect to mental disabilities?

As to workers' compensation, an extensive economic and empirical literature exists on the safety-related effects of the system, but most of it casts little light on the topic of prevention or reduction of mental impairments. And no studies yet address the extent to which workers' compensation promotes accommodation, either generally or with respect to mental impairments. There is little available information about the extent to which insurers influence employers to undertake prevention or accommodation as to mental impairments. No studies tell us whether and how employers are integrating the incentives and provisions of workers' compensation with the antidiscrimination mandates of the ADA, either generally or as to mental impairments.

Voluntary Steps

Employers might take prevention or accommodation steps on their own, even if the ADA did not apply and even if these steps would produce no change in the employers' costs for workers' compensation or other benefits. For example, an employer might institute a "healthy company" program or expressly follow a policy of accommodation for disability, including those related to mental health. Some employers have instituted "employee assistance plans" to increase the health of workers and to offer assistance in resolving emotional, financial, and other problems (Barge and Carlson 1993). As of 1989, these plans covered 49% of full-time workers in private business establishments with more than 100 employees and 15% of the full-time employees of smaller business (Office of Technology Assessment 1994, 71). These steps might be viewed as likely to attract or keep good workers, as enhancing productivity, as possibly reducing the "compensating wage" that the employer must pay to the employee, or as reflecting humanitarian principles that the employer considers important.

Both theory and empirical evidence show that market incentives do operate to enhance safety in the workforce (Moore and Viscusi 1990), but such incentives have their limitations. Chief among these limits is employee knowledge; optimum workplace safety requires full employee knowledge of risk (Danzon 1987). The extent of this and other limits, and thus the degree to which market incentives do or can produce optimal workplace safety, is the subject of a still-developing empirical and theoretical literature.

Neither theoretical nor empirical attention, however, has been directed to whether and how these market incentives apply to the prevention or accommodation of mental impairments. Surveys have shown that service providers under employee assistance plans are sometimes trained in mental health issues, but that on the whole, these providers have not taken on the role of educating employers and employees about mental health issues (Office of Technology Assessment 1994, 71). And one can plausibly posit that both employers and employees generally give less consideration to mental than to physical impairments when making calculations about workplace hazards, partly because conceptions of workplace safety probably are dominated by physical hazards. And, even if workers and employers recognize a general link between the workplace and mental health, they might not take prevention/accommodation steps because they are unaware of such steps or overestimate their financial or practical costs.

Employer-Provided Insurance Benefits

As described earlier, employer-provided group health and group disability insurance (both short-term and, less frequently, long-term) covers many employees. In addition to the obvious effect of providing income support for disability, employer-provided disability insurance can influence prevention/ accommodation. An employer might take prevention or accommodation steps to the extent that these are linked to reductions in premiums (or, under a self-insured plan, costs) or to the ability to obtain attractive coverage.

The disability insurer might play a direct role in initiating such steps. For example, the disability coverage offered by one major disability insurer now includes an "accommodation assistance program," which includes attention to mental disorders (Unum Corporation 1993). Or a disability insurer might undertake a "health-disability" analysis of the worksite, suggesting changes that the employer can make to reduce the incidence and severity of claims, including those related to mental health (Barge and Carlson 1993).

Whether or not such steps are taken with respect to mental impairments, however, depends on the degree to which the employer perceives that prevention or accommodation will result in reduced premium costs or increased availability of attractive insurance coverage. These effects, in turn, are linked to whether the insurer finds that the costs of various sorts of feature rating, experience rating, and prevention programs are sufficiently outweighed by the benefits of such steps, which might include reduced insurance payouts and increased actuarial precision.

Do disability and health insurers, in practice, rely on feature rating, experience rating, or prevention programs with respect to potential mental impairments? And, once a worker files a claim for disability arising from mental impairment, do disability insurers commonly encourage employers to accommodate the workers' disability? Information on these questions is hard to obtain. Intuition suggests that insurers would find feature rating not particularly helpful with respect to mental impairment claims. Experience rating, which is possible mainly with large employers, seems more likely: an employer who experiences significant increases in claims relating to mental impairments might well be subject to a premium increase or even to cancellation (Soule 1989, 208–210). Some disability insurers do offer prevention analyses and programs that appear to include attention to mental as well as physical impairments (Unum Corporation 1993).

Yet several factors seriously limit the potential of employer-provided insurance to prevent or to promote accommodation of mental impairments. First, and most obviously, many employees do not have disability insurance as an employee benefit. Long-term disability does not cover even half of employees in firms with over 100 employees, and even fewer in smaller establishments. Second, some disability policies limit or exclude coverage for disabilities due to mental illness, although outright exclusions are not permissible in some states. Limitations on coverage, as explained earlier, can pass scrutiny under the ADA, according to the EEOC's current interpretive guidance.

Third, health insurance, which is more commonly provided than disability insurance, is not likely to be more available or less costly to employers who accommodate than to those who do not. Thus, health insurance does not give employers an accommodation incentive. Fourth, even if disability insurance were universally provided and universally covered mental disabilities, insurers and employers would take steps toward prevention/accommodation only if they perceived these steps to be linked to lower benefits payouts. This requires, at a minimum, a judgment that certain worksite changes and accommodations can help reduce mental impairments and disabilities, and this judgment seems less likely as to mental than as to physical impairments, for several reasons.

Historically, safety and prevention concerns on the worksite focused on physical and not mental-emotional hazards; only in relatively recent years has attention begun to focus on the latter (Barge and Carlson 1993). Even when employers and insurers perceive the importance of the worksite in mental health issues, they may doubt that prevention/accommodation with respect to mental disabilities will produce benefits significant enough to justify the costs. Far less evidence is available about "mental health safety" than about, for example, the safety benefits of handguards, boiler inspections, and keyboard-terminal design. But this doubt also is rooted in invalid assumptions: that mental impairment is "in" the individual and thus cannot be much affected by the workplace, and that mental disability cannot be accommodated or rehabilitated.

Notably, there are many signs of change in these views. One sees increasing attention to overall disability management on the worksite, and the wide-lens perspective of such programs often includes attention to mental health as well (Barge and Carlson 1993, 267–289). In recent years, the risk-management dialogue among insurers has included more intense interest in mental impairments and disabilities, including accommodation and rehabilitation (Barge and Carlson 1993, 267–289). But another development cuts in the opposite direction: an upsurge of attention to risk management relating to workplace violence. One recent risk-management article, for example, listed the common signs of "beserkers," and stated that "many workplace violence incidents can be prevented if employees are properly trained to spot dangerous co-workers" (Manigan 1994, 9).

Workers' Compensation

Workers' compensation programs also carry the potential for influencing employers' actions relating to prevention and accommodation of mental impairments and disabilities. Because all workers' compensation programs impose some sort of work-relation test, workers' compensation will be less significant for those with severe and persistent mental impairments. Nonetheless, workers' compensation has much potential importance for less severe and persistent mental impairments, and its ripple effects (on hiring decisions and accommodation) can affect those with more severe and persistent mental impairments. To understand and evaluate all these effects, we must first explore the theory behind the work-relation requirement of workers' compensation.

THE WORK-RELATION TEST: GENERAL THEORY

Coverage under workers' compensation does not require a showing of employer fault, but the claimant must satisfy a work-relation test. For claims categorized as injuries, the work-relation test requires that the injury arise out of and occur in the course and scope of employment. For claims classified as occupational disease claims, the work-relation test assumes several forms, such as proving that the disease was not an "ordinary disease of life."

The work-relation requirement finds a powerful potential justification in the aim of prevention. From an economic standpoint, if employers are the "least-cost avoiders" of certain injuries and impairments, and if employees incompletely understand workplace hazards, then the marketplace will fail to produce optimal safety investments. Instead, a liability rule is necessary to internalize to the employer the costs of untaken precautions, thus inducing the employer to take cost-justified preventative steps (Danzon 1987, 268–269).[2] An extensive literature supports the conclusion that workers' compensation results in significant safety advantages not produced by the private market or regulatory structures (Moore and Viscusi 1990). But this literature has not focused on mental disabilities.

THE EFFECT ON THE HIRING DECISION

Workers' compensation can affect an employer's incentive to hire an individual with a disability, as well as the prevention/accommodation incentives with respect to workers already hired. As to the hiring incentive, the ADA does not permit an employer to base a hiring decision on the fear that the applicant will increase the employer's workers' compensation costs (U.S. EEOC 1992, ix-1). But such fears have often played a role in hiring discrimination regarding individuals with disabilities (e.g., *E. E. Black, Ltd. v. Marshall*, 497 F. Supp. 1988 (1990)), and it would be naive to suppose that the ADA's mandate will eliminate such decisions; thus, any other factors that bear on the shape and force of this fear are important to note.

Individuals with mental disabilities might face a special problem in this respect. First, the classic work-relation test—whether an injury arises out of and in the course and scope of employment—requires causal assessments that may be especially difficult to make with precision for mental disabilities. Employers, then, might fear that this "fuzziness" will cut in favor of coverage. In reality, the work-relation test for mental disabilities (discussed below) has grown increasingly restrictive; still, the fear may be present.

Second, the disability benefits paid by workers' compensation programs usually have a defined duration (depending on the degree of disability), but medical costs traditionally have not been limited in duration or by coinsurance or deductibles. The rapidly rising component of health care costs has prompted more and more state workers' compensation programs to experiment with controls on such expenditures, including managed care plans (Kaddatz and Farley 1994). Concerns about health care costs might be especially acute with respect to mental health treatments: the necessity (or nonnecessity) of such care might be harder to document, and it might be especially difficult to decide when the treatment needs have ended for the work-related disability. For example, the state of Washington recently completed a managed care feasibility study for its workers' compensation system, which noted that mental health treatment decisions represent a hard call for claims managers, especially with respect to duration (State of Washington, Department of Labor and Industries, 5). Third, mental disability claims in many states are contested more frequently than other categories of claims (Helvacian 1993, 5; Victor 1985, 16), more frequently involve attorneys (Helvacian 1993, 7), and thus generate claims-management costs that are perceived to be high (California Workers' Compensation Institute 1985, 4; Schachner 1994).

Most workers' compensation programs contain a "second-injury fund," a feature that in theory should allay many financial fears about hiring workers with disabilities. Under the general approach of such funds, when a worker with a preexisting disability suffers a compensable work-related injury, the employer is charged only with the costs of the second injury, while the fund picks up the difference (Ellenberger 1992, 55). But many of these claims relate only to certain degrees of aggravation or to certain types of resulting disabilities, such as permanent total disabilities or disabilities involving an eye or a member of the body (Alliance of American Insurers 1994, 44–49), and usually the second injury fund does not assist with medical costs (Alliance of American Insurers 1994, 44–49).

PREVENTION/ACCOMMODATION OF MENTAL IMPAIRMENTS

Workers' compensation programs cover far more employees than private disability insurance, and some coverage of mental impairments exists in all the programs. Thus, for several reasons, workers' compensation in theory could promote employer action aimed at prevention/accommodation of mental as well as physical impairments. First, self-funded employers must pay workers' compensation benefits and thus have an incentive to reduce the cost and severity of losses. Second, for larger employers that are not self-insured, workers' compensation premiums usually are experience-rated (Victor 1985). The experience modifier is based on a formula that takes into account both the number and the severity of claims, with the number being more heavily weighted. (This is based on the assumption that the employer can do more to affect the incidence than the severity of injury—an assumption that might bear reexamining in the wake of the ADA.) Third, even if an insured employer does not expect that certain types of safety-related actions will affect its premium, it has an incentive to avoid becoming an unattractive candidate for purchasing insurance. So, for example, if workers' compensation insurers require safety inspections or cooperation with rehabilitation managers, the employer's failure to cooperate will limit its insurance options.

Yet several factors limit these potential incentives for prevention, accommodation, and rehabilitation as they apply to mental impairments and disabilities. The first, similar to that discussed in the section on private disability insurance, is that employers and insurers might doubt the connection between employment and mental health. Or, more likely, they might not see how any particular changes in workplace conditions or job requirements will decrease the incidence or severity of claims containing a mental impairment component.

Second, although workers' compensation should and probably does produce some incentive to accommodate workers with job-related disabilities, the incentive is perhaps less forceful than it should be—both generally and perhaps even less so for mental impairments. *If* accommodation can be expected to lower the employer's overall costs, then in theory employers who are self-insured or experience-rated will have reason to make the accommodation. And accommodation might indeed produce lower claims costs, especially under workers' compensation programs that cut off or reduce an employee's disability benefits when the employee does not accept a "reasonable" job offer from the employer.

But—leaving aside for now the influence of the ADA and considering only workers' compensation—employers might well fail to see accommodation as an overall cost-reducer. Instead, they might view a claimant-employee as less productive or as more likely than other employees to file claims in the future. Although workers' compensation statutes usually prohibit retaliation against the employee for filing of a claim, they do not usually require (much less enforce) accommodation. Thus, if given the choice between (1) retaining, via accommodation, an unproductive, future claim-filing worker; and (2) discharging the employee and incurring the possible additional claims costs, an employer might find the second more attractive.

How this calculation comes out also depends on other aspects of the specific workers' compensation plan. Incentives to return the employee to work may be higher when the program provides a different and more limited tier of disability benefits for workers who are reemployed (National Council on Compensation Insurance 1993a, 7). Or specific provisions that penalize the worker for rejecting reasonable job offers might give the employer an incentive to make an accommodation. But even these might not offset the perceived undesirability of retaining the worker. Another factor linked to nonaccommodation is the air of mutual suspicion that often surrounds the filing of a workers' compensation claim (Bell 1993b).

What do we know about the real-world accommodation effects of workers' compensation, either generally or with respect to mental impairments? There is no literature, either of an empirical nature or along the lines of economic modeling, that speaks to this issue. Nor does evidence exist relating to the effects of provisions that cut off or reduce the employee's benefits when the employer makes a reasonable job offer. Thus, we are left with the hypotheses just outlined. If, indeed, workers' compensation often produces no incentive (and maybe even a disincentive) to accommodate, this may be even more likely with regard to mental impairments.

A third limit on the incentives for prevention, accommodation, and rehabilitation produced by workers' compensation is probably the most significant: Many mental impairment claims face severe coverage obstacles. As a very general rule, an injury usually is covered if it arises out of and occurs in the course and scope of employment. But, when a claimant asserts what usually is called a *mental-mental* claim (that is, the source of the injury is mental, and the nature of the injury is mental), most programs translate the "arising out of" test into more specific and restrictive requirements. Because these standards so substantially limit coverage of some mental impairments, they require close examination.

LIMITATIONS ON COVERAGE FOR MENTAL-MENTAL CLAIMS

The history of mental-mental claims can be divided into two stages. First, before the 1980s, states developed several different standards for the coverage of mental-mental claims: no coverage at all; coverage only if the source of the mental impairment is a sudden or shocking event; coverage only if the stress of the employment exceeds that of ordinary life or employment; and, as to the latter standard, variations on whether the worker's own judgment of "ordinary stress" would govern, or whether an "objective" standard would prevail.

In the 1980s, most states perceived an increase in the rise of mental-mental claims. A 1985 study of the National Council on Compensation Insurance, the authorized rating organization for workers' compensation in over two dozen states—reported the following:

> [T]here is no question that an increasing number of our workers are claiming that mental stress in the workplace has caused a mental disability.
>
> In the past, little data were available to confirm suspicions that claims of mental stress and mental disability were increasing. . . .
>
> A recent statistical study of information received in an NCCI detailed claim call confirmed that in recent years, claims involving mental disorders, sufficiently severe to prevent the worker from performing the normal duties of employment, but not arising from a single traumatic incident, or related to a physical condition developed through the cumulative effects of work, are a significant percentage [about 11%] of all occupational disease claims. (National Council on Compensation Insurance 1985, 5)

Other studies reached similar conclusions (California Workers' Compensation Institute 1985).

This growth of claims led to the second stage: Many legislatures added to or strengthened the restrictions on mental impairment claims. Probably the most common changes were (1) to require claimants to show that the employment contributed to the impairment by at least a certain percentage, ranging from 10% in some states to 75% in another; and (2) to exclude coverage for claims arising from bona fide personnel actions, such as layoffs, demotions, discharges. In every state, then, a mental-mental claim is either not covered at all, or must satisfy one or more of the standards devised during either stage and described above.

Currently, the sense among the insurer-employer workers' compensation community seems to be that mental-mental claims do not pose the cost and insurability threat that they once appeared to present. A recent study, based on data from the National Council of Compensation Insurance from 1979 through 1990, shows that the incidence of mental stress claims in ten states increased through the mid-eighties, peaked in 1987, and has since abated (Helvacian 1993, 4). California insurers and employers, for example, appear satisfied with the recent shift from a 10% to a 51% causal relation requirement (Schachner 1994). A recent nationwide poll of risk managers found that stress-related workers' compensation claims had dropped off the list of major concerns (Marley 1994).

But does this reduced sense of crisis mean that the coverage standards for mental impairments are now appropriate? Answering this requires an analysis of what coverage standards would be appropriate for mental impairments and disabilities, given the goal of prevention/accommodation.

DEVISING A BETTER WORK-RELATION TEST FOR MENTAL IMPAIRMENTS AND DISABILITIES, FROM THE STANDPOINT OF PREVENTION/ ACCOMMODATION

From a prevention/accommodation perspective, what is the most desirable work-relation test? A coverage standard, from this perspective, is overly restrictive if it results in noncoverage for mental impairments and disabilities that the employer could fairly or efficiently prevent or accommodate. Granted, factors other than workers' compensation may prompt the employer to internalize the costs of unprevented or unaccommodated mental impairments. For example, the accommodation mandate of the ADA, in theory, could force employers to see that some costs of certain nonprevented impairments will ultimately be theirs in any event, regardless of whether the impairments are covered under workers' compensation. The point, then, is not that workers' compensation is the only method of internalizing costs. But we will come closer to the optimum level of prevention/accommodation if workers' compensation provides coverage at least for the impairments that the employer is optimally suited to prevent or to accommodate.

In deciding which (if any) version of a work-relation test would be most desirable from a prevention/accommodation standpoint, two standards can be rejected altogether. The first is the requirement that the mental stimulus which caused the mental injury be sudden as distinct from gradual. Perhaps gradually produced mental impairments are less preventable or minimized by changes in the workplace, but this surmise is not very convincing. More likely, the requirement stems from a concern about the filing of fraudulent mental impairment claims; the requirement has received support on this basis (Staten and Umbeck 1983, 107). Yet the requirement does little to guarantee the authenticity of the degree of the impairment, and unquestionably will leave uncovered many nonfraudulent claims.

A second troublesome set of limitations consists of requirements that the mental stimulus causing the mental injury be different from the ordinary stresses of this employment, or from the ordinary stresses of employment generally. We would not consider seriously a similar restriction with respect to physical hazards; increased safety is often desirable even as to ordinary physical hazards.

This restriction must therefore rest on a different justification. Perhaps it is seen as a check on the genuineness of the claim—but this explanation falls short because the "greater than typical employment stress" inquiry has little to do with the genuineness of the mental impairment claim. More likely, the restriction simply reflects a policy choice that employees should bear the risk and loss of ordinary nonphysical features of the worksite. This policy choice, in turn, probably stems from concerns about the financial and decisional strains that mental-mental claims will place on the system.

These concerns are legitimate, but there are less drastic ways of responding to them. Other causation standards can be devised, and disability assessment standards can reduce concerns about excessive benefits, inaccuracy, and inconsistency. The National Council on Compensation Insurance, the largest workers' compensation insurers organization and the authorized rating organization in over two dozen states, has taken the position that approaches less drastic than exclusion can allay concerns about the cost and insurability of such claims (National Council on Compensation Insurance 1985, 28).

Is there a desirable alternative to these two common restrictions? Two possibilities deserve attention. The first is simply to treat mental claims in the same way as physical claims. For the basic physical impairment scenarios, the claimant must show that the employment caused the impairment in a "but for" sense; that is, but for the employment, the injury would not have occurred. When the employee has a preexisting physical injury that is aggravated by the employment, the general rule is that the employer "takes the employee as he finds him." Thus, the worker usually receives full compensation (the employer's part might be minimized by a contribution from the "second injury fund" that exists in almost every state).

So why not use the same rule for mental impairments and disabilities? The major problem is that the minimum causal test would so often lead to a coverage conclusion. In part this is because employment, to some degree, probably does aggravate or contribute to many mental impairments in ways that employers cannot prevent. Even when the employment has not so contributed, policymakers justifiably could worry that the proof uncertainties surrounding cause and mental impairments would lead to false positives on this minimum causal inquiry.

But why would the high positive rate under the minimum causal inquiry be undesirable? One key problem is that the approach almost surely will place on employers the costs of some impairments that are unpreventable or which the employer is not in the best position to prevent. If some of these are more appropriately preventable by the employee, then the approach may place the prevention incentive on the wrong person. Or if, as is more likely, some degree of the covered impairment is not preventable by anyone, then this approach would essentially be a type of "employer mandate" to provide disability insurance to all mental impairments that have some quite minimum link to the workplace.

If *this* is the functional effect of the approach, then the approach needs to be justified on these terms, that is, on the basis of a loss-spreading aim. But the loss-spreading justification runs into big difficulties. The first is historical and descriptive: workers' compensation has never been viewed as a system for spreading losses that are not primarily attributable to the workplace. A second flaw is that, if loss-spreading were virtually the only justification of the approach, then there would be no need for even the minimum, "but for" causal test. Indeed, the test would simply reflect an additional decisional step (along with often sizable administrative and decisional error costs) that serves no purpose. If we use an employer mandate to fund this disability insurance program, then employers will still have an incentive—even absent the "but for" test—to prevent or accommodate those impairments and disabilities that are efficiently preventable. So the minimum causal test is unnecessary for even the prevention/accommodation that we would like to retain.

A third problem is fairness among classes of disabilities: Why fund a mandatory disability system for mental disabilities and not for other types? A partial answer might be that other disabilities are more likely to result from a causal agent from whom tort law will demand compensation. But, although mental disabilities do in some ways receive disfavored status from the tort system, tort "coverage" for other disabilities (especially for many diseases) hardly amounts to a meaningful and reliable level of insurance.

A fourth problem is that the way workers' compensation actually goes about paying benefits for mental impairments and disabilities is riddled with problems from a loss-spreading perspective. These will be detailed later, but they include the virtual absence in some jurisdictions of standards for deciding how to determine mental disabilities. So, at a minimum, this "mandatory disability insurance" justification would require reworking almost the entire measurement fabric in some jurisdictions. (This last criticism, though, is not just a criticism of the mandatory insurance justification; whatever our view of workers' compensation coverage, many programs contain serious flaws relating to measuring mental disabilities.)

The next possible option is to strengthen the minimum causal test by requiring that the employment cause some specified degree of the resulting impairment, such as a "substantial" degree or, as under recently amended California standards, over 50% of the impairment. In theory, these standards match the prevention/accommodation aim better than does the minimum causal test. Of course, when the employment is deemed a substantial cause of a mental impairment or disability, this does not mean that employer action, in fact, can prevent the impairment or accommodate the disability. It does mean that the employer is likely to be in the best position to take any prevention or accommodation steps that are feasible.

The obvious question raised by these standards is how workable they are in practice. In this respect, though, all the possible causal tests—save perhaps the most minimum test of "contributed to"—raise concern. If the tests call for more causal precision than is possible given current diagnostic and evaluative knowledge, or if the standards prove especially subject to forensic manipulation, then decisional cost, accuracy, and fairness all suffer. And these flaws lead to others: moral hazard; reduced attractiveness to insurers of participating in the workers' compensation market; and the creation of uncertainty on the part of employers and insurers about the costs they will bear under workers' compensation—uncertainty that, among other problems, reduces the prevention/accommodation potential of the system.

What evidence do we have about the decisional adequacy of these standards? No studies have appeared relating to their accuracy or consistency. Insurers and employers generally seem to approve of these standards, which at least suggests that the standards do not produce uncertainties so significant as to undermine actuarial predictions about workers' compensation costs. Perhaps this is because, in practice, these causal thresholds prove too high even for claimants with mental disabilities that, to a substantial degree, could have been minimized by employer prevention or accommodation. But this is just a surmise, and it is somewhat undercut by the continued attention being given to mental health issues in the workers' compensation and business health literature.

On the whole, then, this second alternative—heightening the causal threshold—seems capable of producing prevention/accommodation without converting the workers' compensation system into an employer-mandated disability insurance system for mental disabilities. Research on the validity and reliability of such standards would be both possible and highly valuable.

TWENTY-FOUR HOUR COVERAGE?

This look at the difficulties posed by the work-relation test leads us naturally to reflect on the recent upsurge of interest in *twenty-four hour* coverage. This label has actually been applied to several quite different proposals that, to a greater or less extent, would do away with the distinction between occupational and nonoccupational impairments and disabilities. At one end of the spectrum, the term could refer to "integrated" disability or health insurance plans, which coordinate claims management of workers' compensation (for work-related injuries) and private insurance benefits. At the other end of the spectrum are proposals, none yet adopted, for replacing the disability or medical cost component of workers' compensation, along with the employer-provided health and disability policies, with coverage not linked to the work-site-nonworksite distinction. A number of states are conducting feasibility or pilot studies of plans that fit somewhere along this spectrum (Bateman and Veldman 1991).

A shift in the direction of some form of twenty-four hour disability coverage would represent a significant expansion in coverage for mental disabilities. Because the work-relation test proves such a substantial hurdle for individuals with mental disabilities, and because private disability insurance does not cover most employees, some forms of twenty-four hour coverage would provide far greater coverage than currently exists. Even if the duration of payments for mental disabilities were limited to several years, as it commonly is now under group policies, this coverage could provide a partial or temporary level of income protection that currently does not exist for most workers with mental disabilities. This large shift, in turn, would have implications for accommodation, rehabilitation, and the workings of SSI and SSDI.

SUMMING UP: HOW TO INCREASE THE PREVENTION/ACCOMMODATION INFLUENCE OF PRIVATE DISABILITY INSURANCE AND WORKERS' COMPENSATION

Several factors limit the degree to which private disability insurance or workers' compensation can induce greater prevention/accommodation of mental impairments and disabilities by employers. First, and most obviously, changes within employers' control, such as healthy company programs, employee assistance plans, and disability accommodation, will simply not prevent many mental impairments. And some disability accommodations will not reduce work disability.

Second, even if particular changes could produce some prevention of impairments or some reductions of work disability, knowledge of this is crucial. If employers or insurers remain unaware of or unconvinced about the link between certain prevention/accommodation steps and the reduction of mental impairment or mental disability, they will not take action, even if workers' compensation or private disability insurance does place on employers the costs of a particular unprevented impairment or disability. This underlines the need for more research about the efficacy and costs of prevention and accommodation directed at mental impairments and disabilities (Office of Technology Assessment 1994).

Third, suppose employers knew that a certain feature or accommodation of the employment could prevent or reduce mental impairment or disability. Even then, private disability insurance or workers' compensation would not give them an incentive to take prevention/accommodation steps unless these programs placed on employers the costs of unprevented impairments and disabilities. Both programs have gaps in this respect. For private disability insurance, the gaps are that most workers are not covered by long-term disability insurance, that short-term disability insurance probably does not produce prevention/accommodation incentives, and that underwriting and limits on benefits reduce the coverage of mental disabilities. Some of these gaps (less-than-universal coverage of workers, underwriting-selecting that rejects individuals with mental treatment histories) cannot be eliminated within the voluntary market.

For workers' compensation, the major gap is the work-relation require-ment. In theory, the requirement is no gap, because it places on employers at least some of the costs of work-related mental impairments and disabilities. In practice, however, the requirement has been translated into standards that are underinclusive with respect to the prevention/accommodation aim, and that are not justified by other concerns, such as decisional integrity. Chief among these are the requirements that the workplace stress or precipitating event be sudden and not gradual, and that it be something different from the ordinary hazards of the employment. As I have argued, these should be replaced with causal standards requiring that the employment be the substan-tial cause, or the cause of more than some specific percentage, of the im-pairment-disability.

Fourth, even when private disability insurance and workers' compensation apply and thus theoretically impose the costs of unprevented impairments/ disabilities on employers, these systems may themselves generate other incen-tives against accommodation or prevention. The fear of increased workers' compensation costs might discourage the initial hiring of individuals with disabilities, including mental disabilities. The ADA, of course, proscribes actions based on this concern, but the point here is that the incentives created by workers' compensation may operate at times in the opposite direction. In addition to nonhiring or nonaccommodation at the outset, the adversarial and suspicious tone that often characterizes the insurer-employer-claimant relationship may discourage accommodation. This problem is explored in more detail in the next section, which discusses the interplay between the ADA on the one hand, and private disability insurance and workers' compensation on the other.

THE RELATIONSHIP OF THE ADA TO PRIVATE DISABILITY INSURANCE AND WORKERS' COMPENSATION

Other chapters in this book concentrate in detail on how the ADA applies to mental disabilities and employment. This section focuses on the interplay between the ADA, private disability insurance, and workers' compensation as they bear on prevention and accommodation of mental impairments and disabilities.

First, the good news. At least in theory, the ADA, workers' compensation, and private disability insurance march in the same direction in many respects. Depending on the details of funding, rate-setting, and insurer practices, workers' compensation can create incentives for the employer to accommodate a worker who becomes temporarily or partially disabled as a result of either mental or physical impairments. The ADA can strengthen the preventative impact of workers' compensation, by instructing employers that the costs of unprevented disabilities will be theirs in any event, at least to the extent of the costs of accommodation. In addition, the ADA, by prompting more accommodation, will magnify substantially the database for forming judgments about the real-world efficacy and costs of various accommodations. This increased knowledge should spill over into the workers' compensation and private insurance markets, resulting in greater incentives for accommodation (such as reduced rates, greater awareness by self-funded employers of the advantages of accommodation, or the availablity of disability-managment services by insurers).

There are many signs that this theoretical coincidence of aims is bearing out in practice. Prominent insurance trade journals include dozens of ads from workers' compensation insurers and private disability insurers extolling the benefits of (and their services for) overall disability management—that is, providing prevention analysis, return-to-work analyses, rehabilitation services, and consultation about possible accommodations (*Business Insurance* 1994, 15, 31, 33). Many states are rethinking their workers' compensation schemes or conducting research in light of these same goals (Hunt et al. 1993; State of Washington 1994, 2–3). Numerous articles, books, and seminars devoted to the same topic have appeared in recent years (Akabas et al. 1992; Barge and Carlson 1993; Woijik 1994). To quote from one,

> From now on, managing risk will start before a contract is signed, and continue through the length of the policy.

> In a seamless disability environment, risk management will help to prevent disabilities. Time and again, research shows that workplace disabilities are directly related to environment. Wellness programs, on-site day care, accommodations for the handicapped, employee assistance programs, mentor programs, informal management forums, and employee participation in performance reviews have been proven to reduce the rate of disabilities.
>
> Disability insurance carriers will insist that workplaces be conducive to preventing disabilities, and some carriers will foot the bill to provide solutions upfront in the form of predisability risk management. (Rosen 1991, 55)

A number of factors have enhanced the interest in active and integrated disability management. The ADA unquestionably has been one. Some insurers explicitly tout the added benefit of assisting with ADA compliance (Prudential Insurance Company 1994). For example, some insurer literature notes that a return-to-work emphasis requires a full understanding of what modified jobs might be available, and that a jobs analysis done for this purpose also can be helpful for ADA purposes (Unum Corporation 1993).

But the incentives created by the ADA and by workers' compensation do not always coincide. First, as noted earlier, employers might view applicants or workers with disabilities as more likely to raise workers' compensation rates. The second-injury funds that exist in most states were created—years before the ADA—to dampen this reaction. These funds apply only to certain (often quite limited) categories of impairments, however, and thus do not altogether allay employers' fears and prejudices.

Second, despite its classification as a no-fault system, workers' compensation often results in contention, protracted adjudication, and mutual suspicion. This may lessen the inclination of employers to accommodate and of employees to return to work or press for modified job positions. Again, the insurer-employer community seems increasingly receptive to altering this culture. They stress, for example, the benefits of keeping in touch with employees who are at home with a disability and of involving the employee with the management of the disability. But we do not know how common such steps are, or whether they promote meaningful accommodation and rehabilitation.

This "culture clash" may be especially pronounced with respect to mental disabilities or to physical disabilities with a substantial mental component. The mutual suspicion may be higher in the first instance, and insurers-employers could well be less inclined to believe in the benefits of any accommodation.

The third point of conflict is the tension between compensation and rehabilitation: Does the receipt or prospect of disability benefits enhance or prolong (whether more or less consciously) the disability, and thus reduce the chances for accomodation/rehabilitation? The question has generated a wealth of studies in many contexts. Despite the criticisms that apply to much of the research, both the empirical and narrative literature suggest that the receipt of disability benefits does in some way cut against medical or vocational improvement (see above, chapter 3).

Disability Benefits: The Workers' Compensation System

The preceding section explored how the disability fabric influences prevention and accommodation by employers. This section turns to perhaps the more obvious role of disability programs: the delivery of benefits to those deemed disabled within the meaning of particular programs. As the earlier descriptive discussion made clear, virtually every disability program applies different standards to the coverage, identification, and measurement of mental as distinct from physical disabilities. Deciding whether these differences are defensible requires a specific inquiry into each program.

Few such inquiries have appeared except regarding the social security disability system. No literature or accessible data explores how disability determinations are made under private disability schemes, and so we are left with only the basic inferences available from policy language and general insurance principles. In the workers' compensation realm, much analysis and some empirical research have focused on whether or not certain mental disability claims are compensable at all. So, for example, we have some data about the rates of increase during the 1980s of mental disability claims, and much analysis of various work-relation tests. But virtually no research or analysis has explored how mental disabilities are evaluated once the work-relation test has been satisfied.

This section focuses on this underexamined subject: how workers' compensation programs identify and measure mental disabilities once the work-relation test has been satisfied. The discussion first exposes some critical problems with the current workers' compensation approach, and then suggests directions for reform.

The Problem

Surveying the vast and varied canvas of workers' compensation benefits structures, one has good reason to conclude that the evaluation of what usually is termed *permanent partial disability* (PPD) is to a large extent a disaster when the disability is a mental one or has a significant mental component. To locate the subject of this criticism, one needs to understand that workers' compensation programs usually provide four types of disability payments:

temporary total, temporary partial, permanent partial, and permanent total. The calculation of permanent partial disability for all disabilities has been the most enduring and confounding problem of the benefit structure, so criticism of PPD evaluation is nothing new. But the criticism thus far has focused on the evaluation of physical and not mental disabilities, and as we shall see, reforms aimed at physical disabilities have skipped over—and may even have intensified—the problems with mental evaluation.

Here is the problem in brief. In many states, the benefit determination for most mental and physical disabilities turns, entirely or to some extent, on a specific percentage of impairment as determined according to some set of guidelines, most commonly the American Medical Association's *Guides to the Evaluation of Permanent Impairment*. (A small handful of states promulgate their own guidelines.) Yet the AMA's guidelines do not contain a method for generating a specific percentage of impairment—the very item that is necessary to make the benefit determination!

How did this happen? The explanation begins with the shift in many states, over the past 15–20 years, away from the classic two-part approach to calculating benefits. That approach applied a "schedule" of compensation to certain anatomical losses, such as a finger, eye, hand, or leg. The schedule specified the total sum of weekly benefits payable for each loss; say, 50 weeks for a finger, 120 weeks for a leg. All other losses, including any mental disabilities, were deemed "general" injuries and usually were compensated according to the degree to which the claimant suffered lost wage-earning capacity.

Dismayed by the continued contention and high administrative costs associated with the PPD system, many states sought reform by standardizing the process of assessment. At this writing, dozens of states now require that the claimant be evaluated according to the AMA *Guides*. This requirement takes several forms. At its mildest, it does not represent a shift away from a lost earning-capacity approach or general injuries, but instead just adds a particular method of assessment to the decisional steps, presumably to help guide decisions and promote consistency. In its stronger versions, however, these reforms eliminate or greatly limit the basic use of lost wage-earning capacity, replacing this with an "impairment-based" method of determining compensation. That is, compensation no longer depends on the measure of lost wage-earning capacity, but on the measure of one's functional assessment relative to some measure of "normal" functioning of the body as a whole.

To illustrate, a worker with a serious back impairment and affective disorder, under the milder version of these reforms, would have to produce a rating according to the *Guides*. But her compensation award would still be based on the decision maker's assessment of lost wage-earning capacity, and the decision could take into account other assessment methods and factors such as age, education, and work experience. Under the stronger version, her compensation would be linked directly to her percentage of impairment as determined by the *Guides*. Under the recently revised Texas scheme, for example, she would receive three weeks of compensation for each percentage point of impairment, as measured under the *Guides*.

This shift to use of the *Guides* can be criticized for many reasons, some relating to the way in which the states use the *Guides*, and some relating the flaws in the *Guides* that affect measurements of all impairments, physical and mental (Pryor 1991). Use of the *Guides* poses special problems for mental impairments, especially when benefit decisions require a specific percentage impairment rating. The source of the problems is partly the *Guides*, and partly in the way that programs use the *Guides*.

First, let us see the problem with the *Guides* as it relates to mental impairments. The basic point of the *Guides* is to provide evaluation protocols for each of over a dozen bodily systems (e.g., musculoskeletal, cardiovascular, skin) which, once applied, will generate a single "percentage of impairment" figure that reflects the individual's "whole-person" impairment. Impairment, the *Guides* appropriately makes clear, is not the same as work disability (AMA 1988, 5–6). Indeed, the *Guides* stresses that its impairment-rating scheme cannot solve, for workers' compensation or other programs, the riddle of determining disability (AMA 1988, 5–6).

Yet, despite these caveats, until the publication of the fourth edition, in 1993, the *Guides'* introductory "concepts" chapter made broad and unsupportable claims about the purely "medical" nature of the impairment determination, and the objectivity, validity, and reliability of its measurement protocols. So the states' eager embrace of the *Guides* has been partly the result of these promising claims (Pryor 1991). Consider just a few excerpts from the third edition, published in 1988:

> [The *Guides'* value] arises from the precise application of fundamental medical and scientific concepts; the systematic analysis that introduces each of the clinical chapters; the detail of the medical evaluation protocols; and the thorough state-of-the-art analysis that underlies the rating tables. (AMA 1988, 1)

> If the protocols and tables have been followed, the clinical findings may be compared directly to the criteria and related as a percentage of impairment with confidence in the validity and acceptability of the determination. (AMA 1988, 4).

> [When disagreements over impairment ratings arise, these should not be resolved] by asking a nonmedical third party to adjudicate an issue of medical fact! Such differences are best handled through the ordinary process of everyday patient management. . . . [After physicians and nonphysicians verify that the information required

by the *Guides* has been obtained,] it is a straightforward matter to verify whether or not a numerical rating of impairment is substantiated in accordance with the criteria contained in the *Guides*. (AMA 1988, 4–5)

What chapter 1 gave, chapter 14 (on mental and behavioral disorders) took away. "[T]here is no available empirical evidence," the chapter acknowledged, "to support any method or assigning percentage of impairment of the whole person" when the impairment is mental (AMA 1988, 232). Indeed, the chapter gave no method for arriving at either a precise percentage impairment or an impairment range (such as 50–70%).

The problem is not the absence of a method for arriving at percentages ratings. Rather, the flaw is the discrepancy between the absence of such a method and the first chapter's promises of a valid, comprehensive, and objective rating scheme. Granted, states should not have adopted the *Guides* in such wholesale fashion without themselves first inspecting its contents and its range. But the *Guides*' own broad promises also played a role in this.

The recently published fourth edition is a major step in the right direction. Its introductory chapter contains an entirely different tone and content with regard to the issues of validity, reliability, objectivity, the purely medical nature of impairment, and the comprehensiveness of the *Guides*. For example, "[i]t should be understood that the *Guides* does not and cannot provide answers about every type and degree of impairment. . . ."; an "impairment percentage" is "an informed estimate"; " 'normal' is not a fine point or an absolute in terms of physical and mental functioning." (AMA 1993, 1/2 and 1/3). But these modifications do not solve the problem posed by legislative or administrative requirements that the individual produce a specific percentage rating of impairment. Reform of these requirements themselves is necessary.

Reform Approaches

What direction should reform take? Specifically, given that the main compensatory aim of workers' compensation is to replace some meaningful degree (typically two-thirds) of lost earning capacity (Berkowitz and Burton 1987, 20–24), what measurement approach or mental disabilities is most appropriate? Two possibilities can be rejected; another is far more plausible, but much more attention must be devoted to constructing it.

To start with the less desirable options, programs could create a mental impairment schedule that purports to generate a specific number among 100 possible choices on a 100-point scale, as is the case with physical disabilities under the *AMA Guides*. But most experts in the psychiatric and psychosocial rehabilitation community would reject such an artificially nuanced approach. Indeed, even the Veterans Administration's (VA) schedule for psychiatric disabilities, which uses percentage findings, does so only in rougher grada- tions, corresponding to one of five degrees of severity in the resulting "social and industrial inadaptability": total (100%); severe (70%); considerable (50%); definite (30%); and mild (10%) (38 C.F.R. §4.132 (1993)).

Another approach that should be rejected is to *retain* the use of an *ex ante* schedule for physical disabilities and *eliminate* the use of an *ex ante* schedule for mental impairments (even one with more general increments, such as the schedule used in the veterans' benefits program), replacing the mental impairment schedule with an individualized assessment of lost earning capac- ity. No program currently uses such an approach.

At first glance, the method seems promising. The fundamental aim of workers' compensation benefits is to compensate for lost wage-earning capac- ity—not to compensate for impairment in and of itself (although the latter is a proper subsidiary goal). Thus, the major justification for impairment-based measures has been as a proxy for this (Pryor 1990, 811). And the attrac- tiveness of the proxy depends on the trade-off between (1) gaining the pre- sumably greater efficiency and consistency of the proxy, and (2) sacrificing some nuances of individually assessing lost earning capacity. So, when we run into a type of work disability—mental—for which the impairment proxy provides virtually no benefits of efficiency and consistency, the case for using the proxy largely vanishes.

But rejecting the *ex ante* schedule approach *only* for mental disorders will not work, after all. A program could not, for example, use the AMA *Guides* for all physical disorders and then use lost earnings or lost earning capacity for mental disorders. Many claimants will present disabilities arising from both mental and physical impairments. Measuring the lost earnings or lost earning capacity caused only by the mental impairment would be impossible.

The remaining option is to use a schedule for both mental and physical impairments, but to include in the mental impairment schedule only several gradations. So stated, the option is skeletal indeed; many more tasks remain before the approach is fleshed out, and there is little to guide us. One crucial step is to identify what the conceptual heart of the mental schedule would be. Would the schedule aim to measure the degree to which the disorder has limited the person's ability to function with respect to some standard set of both work-related and non-work-related activities? (This concept underlies the *Guides'* measures of *physical* impairment.) Or would it simply set out a certain procedure, and evaluative labels, for assessing how a particular individual's mental disorder has affected that individual's ability to work? This seems basically the conceptual underpinning of the VA schedule. If this latter approach is used, then the schedule is not much like the *Guides* or other impairment schedules. Instead, it is really a protocol for measuring lost earning capacity, not an impairment-based proxy for lost earning capacity.

This "protocol" rather than "proxy" approach should be chosen for any mental schedule. As argued above, the hunt for proxy measures of *physical* disability is not doomed at the outset; the reliability and consistency of some measures might justify the loss of individual nuance. But no proxy measure for mental disability could ever produce any such advantages, and so the proxy approach just clouds the process and interferes with the aim of replacing lost earning capacity.

In sum, to say that workers' compensation programs have room for improvement is to speak too mildly. The programs have not even found the trail. First, in the minority of programs that do not use the *Guides* in some fashion, benefits are based on judgments of lost earning capacity, but no standard protocols seem to be in use. Second, in programs that use the *Guides* in the strong fashion—that is, where the *Guides* are determinative of some or all benefits—claimants with mental or mental-physical disabilities are left at the mercy of the programs' incoherent mandate to produce a specific percentage. One can only speculate about what, indeed, happens in such cases.

Third, problems exist even in programs that use the *Guides* in a milder fashion, such as those in states that recommend a *Guides*-based measurement but do not base benefits entirely on that measure. The program might continue to subscribe to the view of impairment that the *Guides* espouses at least generally—that something termed *impairment* exists that is meaningfully distinct, from a measurement perspective, from the notion of disability. This would simply reduce the chances that the program will initiate reform efforts aimed at devising better measurement protocols.

Finally, and most depressingly, the use of the *Guides* seems locked into place in most jurisdictions. No great interest seems to exist among legislatures or insurers to investigate empirically the functioning of the *Guides*. A handful of validity and reliability studies have been performed by the medical community in clinical settings detached from any programmatic influence, and only a few studies have appeared about the use of the *Guides* in an actual programmatic setting (Boden 1992). None of these, moreover, related to the *Guides'* application to mental impairments.

Conclusion

Examination of the disability fabric as it relates to mental disabilities reveals some defensible differential strands and some hopeful signs of features that may improve the fabric with regard to both mental and physical disabilities: the possible synergistic relation between private disability insurance, workers' compensation, and the ADA; the increased emphasis on devising better functional assessment devices; the intense interest in coordinating the disparate strands of the disability fabric into overall disability management both on and off the worksite; recent and proposed reforms to the Social Security disability program; and increased interest in vocational rehabilitation approaches aimed at providing the type of training and support necessary for individuals with severe mental disabilities, including supported employment.

But significant systemic flaws and limitations also exist, often with special force, for individuals with mental disabilities. Both workers' compensation and private insurance provide more limited coverage of mental disabilities; employers and insurers lack the information that might prompt them to take prevention/accommodation steps with respect to mental disabilities; the adversary and suspicious tone that often characterizes workers' compensation claims is heightened with respect to mental disabilities, thus making return to work less likely; employers' fears about higher workers' compensation costs could discourage hiring; the methods for determining benefits for mental disabilities in many workers' compensation programs are a disaster; and incentive measures in SSDI and SSI have not seemed to make much difference in removing the disincentive to return to work. This chapter has examined many of these trouble spots and suggested some reforms.

Only by continuing to examine, question, and study each strand of the disability fabric, as it relates to mental disability and as it fits into the overall disability structure, will we be able to improve the prevention, accommodation, compensation, and rehabilitation of mental impairments and disabilities.

Notes

1. In addition to the programs discussed in the main text, another important disability program consists of the disability benefits and rehabilitative services provided through the veterans' benefits program (Veterans Administration 1994, xv). Disability benefits are payable for both service-connected and non-service-connected disabilities. In 1991, approximately 2.7 million individuals received disability benefits under the veterans' program (Social Security Administration 1992, 318). In addition, the federal Black Lung program, established by the Federal Coal Mine Health and Safety Act of 1969, provides disability and death benefits to miners, widows, and dependents.

2. One possible criticism of this argument is immediately apparent. Surely the optimal prevention strategy for many impairments would require preventative steps by both the employer and the employee. In such cases, some type of apportioned liability would seem necessary. Yet workers' compensation does not contain any sort of comparative or contributory negligence rule, save the frequent coverage exceptions for willfully inflicted injury, horseplay, and intoxication.

This criticism, however, loses much force when one appreciates that workers' compensation benefits often fall far short of compensating for the worker's true loss.

Given this, the absence of a comparative responsibility provision has less potential for reducing the employee's existing incentives to take care. The empirical and theoretical debate over whether workers' compensation produces the right incentives for employees is still in flux.

References

Abraham, K. S. 1986. *Distributing Risk: Insurance, Legal Theory, and Public Policy*. New Haven: Yale University Press.

———. 1995. *Insurance Law and Regulation: Cases and Materials*. 2d ed. Westbury, NY: The Foundation Press.

Akabas, S. H., L. B. Gates, and D. E. Galvin. 1992. *Disability Management*. New York: Amacom.

Alliance of American Insurers. 1994. *Survey of Workers' Compensation Laws*. Schaumburg, IL: Alliance of American Insurers.

American Medical Association. 1988. *Guides to the Evaluation of Permanent Impairment*. 3d ed. Chicago: American Medical Association.

———. 1993. *Guides to the Evaluation of Permanent Impairment*. 4th ed. Chicago: American Medical Association.

Andrews, H., J. Barker, J. Pittman, L. Mars, E. Struening, and N. LaRocca. 1992. National Trends in Vocational Rehabilitation: A Comparison of Individuals with Physical Disabilities and Individuals with Psychiatric Disabilities. *Journal of Rehabilitation* (January/February/March): 7–16.

Anthony, W. A., M. R. Cohen, and K. S. Danley. 1988. The Psychiatric Rehabilitation Model as Applied to Vocational Rehabilitation. In J. A. Ciardiello and M. D. Bell, eds., *Vocational Rehabilitation of Persons with Prolonged Psychiatric Disorders*. Baltimore: Johns Hopkins University Press, 59–80.

Anthony, W. A., M. Cohen, and P. Nemec. 1987. Assessment in Psychiatric Rehabilitation. In B. Bolton, ed., *Handbook of Measurement and Evaluation in Rehabilitation*. Baltimore: Paul H. Brookes, 299–312.

Barge, B. N., and J. G. Carlson. 1993. *The Executive's Guide to Controlling Health Care and Disability Costs*. New York: John Wiley.

Barth, P. S. 1980. *Workers' Compensation and Work-Related Illnesses and Diseases*. Cambridge, MA: MIT Press.

Bateman, K. T., and C. J. Veldman. 1991. *Twenty-Four Hour Coverage: An Analysis and Report about Current Developments*. Schaumburg, IL: Alliance of American Insurers.

Bell, C. G. 1992. Workers' Compensation and Work-Related Injury. In *The Americans with Disabilities Act*. Cambridge: Workers Compensation Research Institute, 39–47.

———. 1993a. (Attorney: Jackson, Lewis, Schnitzler and Krupman, Washington, DC) Remarks at Conference on Mental Health and Work Disability, sponsored by the John D. and Catherine T. MacArthur Foundation, Washington, D.C., December 2–3.

———. 1993b. Draft of Proposed Ammendment to the California Workers' Compensation Act.

———. 1995. The Americans with Disabilities Act, Mental Disability, and Work. Chapter 7 in this volume.

Berkowitz, E. D. 1987. *Disabled Policy*. Cambridge: Cambridge University Press.

Berkowitz, M., and J. F. Burton. 1987. *Permanent Disability Benefits in Workers' Compensation*. Kalamazoo, MI: W. E. Upjohn Institute for Employment Research.

Berkowitz, M., M. Horning, S. McConnell, J. Rubin, and J. Worrall. 1982. An Economic Evaluation of the Beneficiary Rehabilitation Program. In J. Rubin, ed., *Alternatives in Rehabilitating the Handicapped*. New York: Human Sciences Press, 1–87.

Black, B. J. 1988. *Work and Mental Illness*. Baltimore: Johns Hopkins University Press.

Boden, L. I. 1992. *The AMA Guides in Maryland*. Cambridge: Workers Compensation Research Institute.

Bond, G., and S. Boyer. 1988. Rehabilitation Programs and Outcomes. In J. A. Ciardiello and M. D. Bell, eds., *Vocational Rehabilitation of Persons with Prolonged Psychiatric Disorders*. Baltimore: Johns Hopkins University Press, 231–263.

Business Insurance. 1994. 25 April 1994.

Calabresi, G. 1970. *The Costs of Accidents*. New Haven: Yale University Press.

California Workers' Compensation Institute. 1985. *Mental Stress Claims in California Workers' Compensation: Incidence, Costs and Trends*. San Francisco: California Workers' Compensation Institute.

California Workers' Compensation Research Institute. 1989a. *The Employee's View of Vocational Rehabilitation: Outcomes and Attitudes*. San Francisco: California Workers' Compensation Research Institute.

California Workers' Compensation Research Institute. 1989b. *Vocational Rehabilitation Effectiveness in California*. San Francisco: California Workers' Compensation Research Institute.

California Workers' Compensation Research Institute. 1990. *Mental Stress Claims in California Workers' Compensation: Incidence, Costs, and Trends*. San Francisco: California Workers' Compensation Research Institute.

Danzon, P. M. 1987. Compensation for Occupational Disease: Evaluating the Options. *Journal of Risk and Insurance* 54: 263–281.

Derthick, M. 1979. *Policymaking for Social Security*. Washington, DC: Brookings Institution.

Eccleston, S. M., and P. S. Gray. 1992. The Americans with Disabilities Act: Impact on Workers' Compensation Systems. In *The Americans with Disabilities Act*. Cambridge: Workers Compensation Research Institute, 7–38.

Ellenberger, J. N. 1992. Implications of the Americans with Disabilities Act or Workers' Compensation Systems: A View From Labor. In *The Americans with Disabilities Act*. Cambridge: Workers Compensation Research Institute, 48–59.

Farkas, M., and W. A. Anthony. 1987. Outcome Analysis in Psychiatric Rehabilitation. In M. J. Fuhrer, ed., *Rehabilitation Outcomes: Analysis and Measurement*. Baltimore: Paul H. Brookes, 43–56.

Gardner, J. A. 1986. *Vocational Rehabilitation Outcomes*. Cambridge: Workers Compensation Research Institute.

———. 1988a. Appropriateness and Effectiveness of Vocational Rehabilitation in Florida. Cambridge: Workers Compensation Research Institute.

———. 1988b. *Vocational Rehabilitation in Florida Workers' Compensation*. Cambridge: Workers Compensation Research Institute.

Goldman, H. H., and A. A. Gattozzi. 1988. Balance of Powers: Social Security and the Mentally Disabled, 1980–1985. *Milbank Quarterly* 66: 531–551.

Griswold, P. P. 1985. The Relationship of Private Sector Rehabilitation to Traditional Rehabilitation Systems. In L. Taylor, M. Golter, G. Golter, and T. Backer, eds., *Handbook of Private Sector Rehabilitation*. New York: Springer, 15–26.

Hanson, J. D., and K. D. Logue. 1990. The First-Party Insurance Externality: An Economic Justification for Enterprise Liability. *Cornell Law Review* 76: 129–96.

Haveman, R. H., V. Halberstadt, and R. V. Burkhauser. 1984. *Public Policy toward Disabled Workers*. Ithaca: Cornell University Press.

Health Insurance Association of America. 1993. *Source Book of Health Insurance Data*. Washington, DC: Health Insurance Association of America.

Helvacian, N. M. 1993. Workers Compensation Paranoia: Mental Stress Claims. Manuscript.

Henderson, R. 1969. Should Workmen's Compensation Be Extended to Nonoccupational Injuries? *Texas Law Review* 48: 117–57.

Hunt, H. A., R. V. Habeck, B. VanTol, and S. M. Scully. 1993. *Disability Prevention among Michigan Employers*. Final Report Submitted to the Michigan Department of Labor. Kalamazoo, MI: W. E. Upjohn Institute.

Institute of Medicine. 1991. *Disability Policy in America: Toward a National Agenda for Prevention*. Washington, DC: National Academy Press.

Johnson, W. G. 1983. Work Disincentives of Benefit Payments. In J. D. Worrall, ed., *Safety and the Work Force*. Ithaca: Cornell University Press, 138–153.

Joseph, L. 1983. The Causation Issue in Workers' Compensation Mental Disability Cases: An Analysis, Solutions, and a Perspective. *Vanderbilt Law Review* 36: 263–321.

Kaddatz, M. M., and T. P. Farley. 1994. Reform on the Western Front. *Public Risk* (February): 8–11.

Kennedy, C., and R. W. Manderscheid. 1992. SSDI and SSI Disability Beneficiaries with Mental Disorders. In United States Department of Health and Human Services, *Mental Health, United States, 1992*. Washington, DC: GPO. 219–230.

Larson, A. 1989. *Workers' Compensation Law*. New York: Matthew Bender.

Levitan, S., and R. Taggart. 1982. Rehabilitation, Employment, and the Disabled. In J. Rubin, ed., *Alternatives in Rehabilitating the Handicapped*. New York: Human Sciences Press, 89–149.

Levy, R. E. 1991. Social Security Claimants with Developmental Disabilities: Problems of Policy and Practice. *Kansas Law Review* 39: 529–584.

Manigan, C. 1994. The Graveyard Shift. 1994. *Public Risk* (January): 6–10.

Marley, S. 1994. Tort Reform Tops Concerns. *Business Insurance* 18 April 1994.

Mashaw, J. L. 1983. *Bureaucratic Justice*. New Haven: Yale Univ. Press.

———. 1988. Disability Insurance in an Age of Retrenchment: The Politics of Implementing Rights. In T. Marmor and J. Mashaw, eds., *Social Security and the Rhetoric of Crisis*. Princeton: Princeton Univ.

McGough, P. J. 1983. Commentary on U.S. General Accounting Office Report: Social Security Administration and Mental Disability Claims. Social Security Reporting Service 1: 1115. St. Paul: West.

Moore, M. J., and W. K. Viscusi. 1990. *Compensation Mechanisms for Job Risks*. Princeton: Princeton University Press.

Muller, L. S. 1992. Disability Beneficiaries Who Work and Their Experience under Program Work Incentives. *Social Security Bulletin* 55: 2–19.

———. 1994. (Researcher, Office of Research and Statistics, Social Security Administration.) Personal communication.

National Council on Compensation Insurance. 1985. *Emotional Stress in the Workplace: New Legal Rights in the Eighties*. Boca Raton, FL: National Council on Compensation Insurance.

National Council on Compensation Insurance. 1993a. *Wisconsin Closed Claim Study*. Boca Raton, FL: National Council on Compensation Insurance.

———. 1993b. *1993 Issues Report*. Boca Raton, FL: National Council on Compensation Insurance.

Office of Technology Assessment, U.S. Congress. 1994. *Psychiatric Disabilities, Employment, and the Americans with Disabilities Act*. Washington, DC: GPO.

Pincus, H. A., C. Kennedy, and S. J. Simmens, et al. 1991. Determining Disability Due to Mental Impairment: APA's Evaluation of Social Security Administration Guidelines. *American Journal of Psychiatry* 148: 1037–1043.

Prero, A. J. 1993. Shifting the Cost of Self-Pay for SSI Workers in Supported Employment. *Social Security Bulletin* 56: 44–51.

Prudential Insurance Company. 1994. Advertisement. In *Business Insurance* 25 April 1994: 31.

Pryor, E. S. 1990a. Compensation and a Consequential Model of Loss. *Tulane Law Review* 64: 783–856.

———. 1990b. Flawed Promises: A Critical Evaluation of the American Medical Association's Guides to the Evaluation of Permanent Impairment. *Harvard Law Review* 103: 964–76.

———. 1991. Compensation and the Ineradicable Problems of Pain. *George Washington Law Review* 59: 239–306.

Rejda, G. E. 1992. *Principles of Risk Management and Insurance*. 4th ed. New York: Harper Collins.

Reznicek, I., and R. C. Baron. 1991. *An Assessment of Vocational Rehabilitation/ Mental Health Collaboration on Behalf of Persons With Long-Term Mental Illness*. (Final report). Philadelphia: Matrix Research Institute.

Rosen, E. 1991. Mending the Gaps in DI Coverage. *Best's Review* (February): 52.

Schachner, M. 1994. California Stress Claims Fall. *Business Insurance* 25 April 1994: 17.

Social Security Administration. 1992. *Annual Statistical Supplement*. Washington, DC: GPO.

Social Security Administration, Office of Research and Statistics. 1993. *Social Security Bulletin*. Washington, DC: GPO.

Soule, C. E. 1989. *Disability Income Insurance: The Unique Risk.* 2d ed. Homewood: Dow Jones-Irwin.

State of Washington, Department of Labor and Industries, Industrial Insurance Division, Health and Rehabilitation Services Research. 1991. *Vocational Rehabilitation in Washington's Industrial Insurance System, 1985 to 1990.* Olympia: State of Washington.

State of Washington, Department of Labor and Industries, Industrial Insurance Division. 1993. *Managed Care Feasibility Study.* (Study prepared by Wyatt Company, consultants.) Olympia: State of Washington.

State of Washington, Joint Labor Management Task Force for the Prevention of Long-Term Disability. 1994. *Final Report to the Legislature.* Olympia: State of Washington.

Staten, M., and J. Umbeck. 1983. Compensating Stress-Induced Disability: Incentive Problems. In J. D. Worrall, ed., *Safety and the Work Force.* Ithaca: Cornell University Press.

Texas Workers' Compensation Research Center. 1993. *Return-to-Work Patterns and Programs for Injured Workers Covered by Texas Workers' Compensation Insurance (Summary Report).* Austin: Texas Workers' Compensation Research Center.

United States Chamber of Commerce. 1993. Analysis of Workers' Compensation Laws. District of Columbia: United States Chamber of Commerce.

United States Department of Labor, Bureau of Labor Statistics. 1989. *Employee Benefits in Medium and Large Firms, 1989.* Washington, DC: GPO.

United States Department of Labor, Bureau of Labor Statistics. 1990. *Employee Benefits in Small Private Establishments, 1990.* Washington, DC: GPO.

United States Equal Employment Opportunity Commission. 1992. *Technical Assistance Manual on the Employment Provisions (Title I) of the Americans with Disabilities Act.* Washington, DC: GPO.

———. 1993. Notice: Interim Enforcement Guidance on the Application of the Americans with Disabilities Act of 1990 to Disability-Based Distinctions in Employer-Provided Health Insurance. 8 June 1993.

United States General Accounting Office. 1993. *Vocational Rehabilitation: Evidence for Federal Program's Effectiveness Is Mixed.* Report to the Chairman, Subcommittee on Select Education and Civil Rights Committee on Education and Labor, House of Representatives. Washington, DC: GPO.

———. 1993b. *Social Security: Sustained Effort Needed to Improve Management and Prepare for the Future.* Report to the Commissioner, Social Security Administration. Washington, DC: GPO.

Unum Life Insurance Company. 1991a. *Sample Policy: Comprehensive Disability Protection, Long-Term Income Protection, Two-Year Own Occupation* with Residual. Portland: Unum Life Insurance Company.

———. 1991b. *Sample Policy: Long-Term Own Occupation.* Portland: Unum Life Insurance Company.

Unum Corporation. 1993. *Accommodation Assistance Program: Managing Disability to Advantage.* Portland: Unum Corporation.

Veterans Administration. 1994. *Annual Report.* Washington, DC: GPO.

Victor, R. B. 1985. Experience Rating and Workplace Safety. In J. D. Worrall and David Appel, eds., Workers' Compensation Benefits: Adequacy, Equity, and Efficiency. Ithaca: ILR Press, 71–88.

Victor, R. B., ed. 1988. *Liability for Employee Grievances*. Cambridge: Workers Compensation Research Institute.

Weber, D. O. 1991. Shrinking the Head Cases. *Insurance Review* (July): 35–38.

Woijik, J. Managing Work Comp, Group Health Costs. *Business Insurance* (April): 22.

Worrall, J. D., and R. J. Butler. 1985. Benefits and Claim Duration. In J. D. Worrall and David Appel, eds., Workers' Compensation Benefits: Adequacy, Equity, and Efficiency. Ithaca: ILR Press, 57–70.

PART 4

Mental Disorder and Employment under the Americans with Disabilities Act

A central aim of the Americans with Disabilities Act (ADA) is to facilitate access to the labor market for people with disabilities. The most visible beneficiaries of the ADA are people with motor impairments due to neurological disorders or loss of limbs and people with impaired hearing or vision. The goal envisioned by the drafters of the Act is to remove the substantial barriers to employment of persons with disabilities by requiring employers to focus on their abilities rather than their limitations.

For people with serious mental illnesses, achieving this goal is a daunting challenge. As shown in earlier chapters, the employment rate among people with serious mental disorders is very low, and many people with severe psychiatric disabilities experience significant functional impairments that reduce their ability to retain competitive employment. As a result, when the ADA was enacted, most observers did not expect it to play a significant role in increasing employment among individuals with serious mental disorders. Instead, they expected the ADA to be of assistance primarily to people with less severe mental disorders who were already in the workforce.

Early data on the first few years of experience under the ADA tend to bear out these predictions. According to Russell Redenbaugh, a member of the United States Commission on Civil Rights, who is blind, "the goal of increasing employment opportunities for those of us who are seriously disabled has not been met at all" (Mathews 1995, A1). Most complaints under the ADA have been filed by people with much less serious impairments. According to a survey conducted for the National Organization on Disabilities, the proportion of people with disabilities who have entered the workforce has hardly changed (Holmes 1994). Only 31% of people with disabilities, aged 16–64, were working full- or part-time at the time of the survey, down from 33%

found to be working in a similar survey in 1986. The employment rate of people with mental disabilities has also remained unchanged.

Many explanations can be offered for this continuing futility. One factor repeatedly mentioned by disability rights activists in explaining the continuing low job rate among people with disabilities is the fear of losing disability benefits (Holmes 1994). For example, disability rights activists explained that "many disabled people are too fearful of losing the benefits that they have or are uncomfortable about taking the kind of aggressive action that is often necessary to overcome barriers to employment." (Holmes 1994, 1) This concern is said to be especially high among people with severe disabilities who would be able to work only at or near the minimum wage.

It would be a mistake to conclude that the ADA is a failure because people with the most serious impairments have not benefited. People with less severe disorders may have had an easier time remaining in the labor force under the ADA than previously. The legislation may also have empowered people with mental disorders to be less self-conscious about requesting accommodations or seeking job redefinition in order to minimize the impact of their symptoms. Unfortunately, the experience of people *in the labor force* under the ADA has not yet been studied in any systematic way.

The impact of the ADA on persons already in the labor force calls attention to one of the most contested issues in the field—the outer boundary of the definition of disability under the ADA. Critics claim that a large proportion of the complainants who invoke the ADA in disputes with employers do not have the kinds of serious disorders that Congress meant to include in the class of persons protected by the Act. In support of this contention, critics point to the profile of people who have complained to the Equal Employment Opportunity Commission during the first three years of experience under the ADA (West 1994, Holmes 1994, American Psychiatric Association 1995). Of the 45,000 complaints filed under Title 1 through 31 March 1995, the largest proportion (19%) referred to back problems. Neurological impairments were claimed in 11.9% of the cases. Another 11.6% involved emotional/psychiatric impairments. Half of the complaints allege unwarranted discharges, and another quarter allege a failure to provide reasonable accommodation. The EEOC had closed slightly more than half of the compaints as of mid-1995.

These data are difficult to interpret. To what extent do these complaints represent legitimate grievances by people who have significant "activity limitations," or functional impairments, within the meaning of the ADA? Conversely, to what extent do they represent opportunistic complaints and clever lawyering on behalf of disgruntled employees who are trying to take advantage of ambiguous statutory language?

As might be expected, there seems to be tension within the disability rights community regarding the proper coverage of the ADA. On the one hand, some say the Act should be construed narrowly to cover only persons with significant impairments who have been most subject to exclusion and discrimination. Under this view, the noble inclusionary purpose of the ADA should not be trivialized by including people with less serious impairments. Instead, disability should be defined to focus exclusively on the more severe conditions that merit the remedial interventions of the ADA. On the other hand, some disability advocates and consumer groups argue that the important idea under the ADA is that differences among people should not matter unless they are relevant to essential job functions. From this standpoint, the employer's legal obligation under the Act can be reduced to a single fundamental norm—to treat all people fairly as individual human beings—and the concept of disability should be given a broad reach to cover all perceived differences.

We are left then with an ambiguous blending of contradictory assumptions regarding the nature of disability and the moral underpinning of the ADA. Does *disability* refer to an objectively defined category of major impairments in functioning, perhaps rooted in biological factors over which the individual has no control? Alternatively, is disability best understood as a politically constructed category of individual characteristics that employers should not be permitted to take into account? Although resolution of controversies about the boundaries of the ADA will have little bearing on the ultimate social impact of the Act, it has much to say about the evolving attitudes of our society regarding norms of fair treatment in the workforce.

The four chapters that follow reflect four complementary views of the ADA. In chapter 7, Christopher Bell offers an overview of the specific provisions of the Act, emphasizing the unique issues raised by mental disabilities and the legal obstacles encountered by people with mental disabilities, especially severe ones, who seek protection under the ADA. In chapter 8, Jean Campbell and Caroline Kaufmann highlight some of the reasons why people with mental disorders may be reluctant to invoke the supposed protections of the ADA. Next, in chapter 9, Laura Lee Hall focuses on issues of implementation, highlighting the interpretive and educational tasks that will be required to "make the ADA work for people with psychiatric disabilities." Finally, in chapter 10, philosopher Norman Daniels explores the ethical foundations of the ADA from the perspective of the principle of fair equality of opportunity. He argues that the ADA is a reasonably good legislative approximation to what is required to implement such a principle. He also explores several issues of particular concern in the context of mental disorders, including the boundaries of protection under the ADA and the relation between the ADA and disability entitlement programs, an issue also addressed by Christopher Bell in chapter 7.

References

American Psychiatric Association. 1995. Definition of Disability under ADA Clarified in Guidelines from EEOC. *Psychiatric Services* 46: 843.

Holmes, S. A. 1994. In four years, Disabilities Act Hasn't Improved Jobs Rate. *New York Times,* 23 October 1994, 1.

Mathews, J. 1995. Landmark Law Failing to Achieve Workplace Goals. *Washington Post,* 16 April 1995, A1.

West, J. 1994. *Federal Implementations of The Americans with Disabilities Act, 1991–94.* New York: Milbank Memorial Fund.

7 The Americans with Disabilities Act, Mental Disability, and Work

CHRISTOPHER G. BELL

The Americans with Disabilities Act is landmark civil rights legislation that holds much promise for persons with disabilities who seek to enter or remain in the labor force. The ADA's employment provisions prohibit discrimination against persons with disabilities in all aspects of the employment process including hiring, training, compensation and benefits. The law also requires employers to provide a reasonable accommodation to enable a qualified individual with a disability to perform essential job functions. An accommodation is not required if it would impose an undue hardship on the operation of the employer's business. The ADA promotes competitive employment of persons with disabilities. With or without reasonable accommodation, a person with a disability must be able to satisfy an employer's uniformly applied quality and quantity of work standards. An employer is not required to employ an individual who would pose a direct threat to the health or safety of the individual or others in the workplace. The ADA's protection is limited to individuals with a "disability." A "disability" exists if an individual has

1. a physical or mental impairment that substantially limits one or more of the individual's major life activities;
2. a "record of" an impairment that substantially limited the individual in the performance of major life activities in the past from which the individual has recovered in full or in part; or has
3. been "regarded as" having an impairment that substantially limits major life activities.

Violations of the ADA can be costly for employers. A successful ADA plaintiff can recover up to $300,000 in compensatory and punitive damages plus back pay, reasonable accommodation, reinstatement, and attorneys' fees. While most ADA plaintiffs lose their cases in court, the occasional large jury award is a reminder that disability discrimination can be costly. *The Wall Street Journal* recently reported that an employer who failed to accommodate an attorney with depression was ordered to pay him $1.1 million under a state disability discrimination law with provisions similar to the ADA (Stevens 1995).

Nonetheless, concern has been raised about the ADA's efficacy in protecting the equal employment opportunity of persons with psychiatric disabilities. Surprisingly, however, persons claiming to have a mental illness account for 11% of the 49,974 ADA charges filed with the Equal Employment Opportunity Commission (EEOC) through 30 June 1995.

Advocates for persons with psychiatric disabilities were highly critical of aspects of the EEOC's ADA regulations and Technical Assistance Manual that were designed to help employers comply with the Act. Concerns were raised about the EEOC's interpretation of disability, the direct threat to health or safety standard, and reasonable accommodation. According to many, the agency's interpretation of the ADA narrowed its benefits for persons with psychiatric disabilities.

In addition to problems raised in the regulatory process, the law itself creates many obstacles for persons with psychiatric disabilities who seek its protections. This chapter briefly explores the nature and scope of some of these obstacles. It suggests that the ADA may not help persons with severe psychiatric disabilities to find or retain employment.

Why the ADA Will Not Be Fully Effective for People with Psychiatric Disabilities

The ADA's Paradigm of Disability and Work

The ADA's provisions are based on certain beliefs about the nature of disability discrimination, the abilities of persons with disabilities, the nature of the workplace, and the nature of civil rights enforcement. In many ways, the ADA was crafted in the image of many of the disability rights advocates who pushed for its passage. These were, by and large, highly educated and disciplined professionals with good self-esteem and assertiveness skills. They were people who had risen above the societal and medical obstacles presented by their disabilities. Most advocates had physical rather than mental disabilities. They were wheelchair users, or had prosthetic limbs, walked with a white cane or guide dog, used a hearing aid or sign-language interpreter. They helped to write and enact a law providing employment protection only for those capable of competitive employment. To be protected, an individual must be able to compete with other applicants and employees in spite of having a disability. The all-important reasonable accommodation entitlement, needed to overcome barriers created by the interaction of functional limitations and workplace demands, requires an individual both to disclose her disability and to request differential treatment. The EEOC's implementing regulations suggest that an employer and an applicant or employee with a disability work together to identify the most appropriate form of reasonable accommodation, on the assumption that the person with the disability has the self-awareness, knowledge, and communication skills required to guide an unenlightened employer through the accommodation process.

The ADA's enforcement process also creates obstacles for persons with psychiatric disabilities. The ADA is largely self-administering. It depends upon the goodwill of employers as they make decisions concerning the hiring and employment of a person with a disability. Should discrimination occur, a person with a disability must be sufficiently assertive to file a charge of discrimination with the EEOC or a local or state fair employment practices agency. If, as is usually the case, the government declines to prosecute the complaint, then the aggrieved individual must retain an attorney and begin the arduous course of litigating the discrimination claim. And, even though there are now compensatory and punitive damages available for victims of intentional disability discrimination, these remedies may be awarded by a jury, whose action may be based upon societal prejudice and stereotypes about persons with psychiatric disabilities.

It is easy to see how persons with severe physical or mental disabilities will not be aided by the ADA's employment provisions. The law does not address the needs of those who cannot succeed in competitive employment. The law's focus on empowerment and opposition to paternalism is a boon to some segments of the disability community but an obstacle to others. Persons with severely impaired interpersonal, cognitive, or communication skills will find the ADA to be of significantly less benefit.

The Disabled-but-Qualified Trap

The ADA requires that one be simultaneously disabled yet qualified. These twin standards are not always contradictory. For example, an individual is protected from discrimination based on a past record of a disability, such as a history of psychiatric hospitalization as well as from being perceived as more disabled than one actually is. Stigma and bias that block the path to employment of a qualified person can be readily addressed by the ADA without being caught in the law's catch-22. Reasonable accommodation also can turn an unqualified person with a disability into a qualified person with a disability by reducing or eliminating the effects of the functional limitation without affecting disability status. However, where a person cannot be effectively accommodated and the job's essential functions require the use of physical or mental functions that are impaired, the person is not likely to be qualified and protected by the ADA or its federal-law progenitor, the Rehabilitation Act of 1973.

Several courts have used plaintiffs' sworn statements on applications for disability insurance benefits that they are totally and permanently disabled as a basis for indicating that they are not qualified, resulting in dismissal of their discrimination claims: *August v. Offices Unlimited, Inc.*, 981 F.2d 576 (1st Cir. 1992); *Beauford v. Father Flanagan's Boys' Home*, 831 F.2d 768, 770–771 (8th Cir. 1987), *cert. denied*, 485 U.S. 938 (1988); *Reigel v. Kaiser Foundation Health Plan of North Carolina*, 859 F. Supp. 963 (E.D.N.C. 1994). To avoid this problem, some individuals with disabilities have asserted that their only disability stems from an employer's perception that they are not qualified for a position because of an impairment that is not truly a disability. This emphasis on being qualified rather than disabled also has doomed some claims, as some courts have concluded that such individuals are not protected by the ADA because they are not disabled; see, for example, *Wooten v. Farmland Foods*, 58 F.3d 382, 386 (8th Cir. 1995); *Milton v. Scrivner, Inc.*, 53 F.3d 1118, 1123 (10th Cir. 1995).

In addition to the dilemmas created by the paradox of having to be both disabled and qualified, the definitions of *disability* and *qualified individual with a disability* present special problems for persons with psychiatric disabilities.

Definition of a Disability

IMPAIRMENT

Impairment is the first part of the ADA's definition of *disability*. An individual must have, have a record of, or be regarded as having, an impairment. EEOC regulations make plain that impairment includes "any mental or psychological disorder such as mental retardation, organic brain syndrome, emotional or mental illness, and specific learning disabilities" (29 C.F.R. §1630.2(h)). The ADA expressly excludes certain categories of mental illness, including compulsive gambling, kleptomania, pyromania, psychoactive substance-use disorders resulting from current illegal use of drugs, voyeurism, certain gender-identity disorders and other sexual behavior disorders (42 U.S.C. §12211). The latter exclusions were offered by Senator Armstrong of Colorado on the floor of the Senate. Senator Armstrong's initial proposed amendment would have excluded all conditions covered by the DSM-III-R.

While the EEOC's definition of impairment remains quite broad, several issues remain. One is the extent to which the ADA would apply to persons with stress disorders. The EEOC's Technical Assistance Manual indicates that only recognized stress disorders would be considered to be impairments. An individual struggling with common family or workplace stressful situations would not have an impairment and therefore not have a disability (*Weiler v. Household Finance Corp.*, 3 AD Cas. 1337 (N.D. Ill. 1994)). Likewise, poor judgment or impulse control can be character traits rather than an impairment (*Hindmann v. GTE Data Services*, 3 AD Cas. 641 (M.D. Fla. 1994)). The very breadth of the definition of impairment led the EEOC to narrowly interpret the two other aspects of the definition of disability. An impairment must "substantially limit" a "major life activity."

SUBSTANTIAL LIMITATION

It is not clear to what extent a mental impairment must affect major life activities in order to constitute a disability under the ADA. The EEOC regulations state that an impairment is substantially limiting if it prevents performance of major life activities or if it significantly restricts the condition, manner, or duration under which major life activities are performed as compared to the ability of the average person in the general population. Other factors include the nature and severity of the impairment, the duration or expected duration of the impairment, and its long-term or permanent impact (29 C.F.R. §1630.2(j)). These standards are difficult to apply when, for example, a person's mental impairment is episodic in nature. When an impairment manifests itself in an acute but brief flare-up, is this an impairment of short duration with little permanent or residual impact? If the courts utilize this standard, the individual is likely not to be covered.

Moreover, two courts have held that the effects of medication to control mental illness can affect disability status. A former employee who had been successfully treated for paranoid schizophrenia with medication which controlled the disorder was found not to have a disability under the Rehabilitation Act: *Castorena v. Runyon*, No. 92-1456-PFK (D. Kan. May 23, 1994). Similarly, an employee with a bipolar disorder was found not to be disabled, as medication stabilized his condition and no major life activity was substantially limited: *Mackie v. Runyon*, 804 F. Supp. 1508 (M.D. Fla. 1992). On the other hand, an employee whose medication for a psychiatric illness resulted in significant side effects affecting his work could have a disability: *Fehr v. McLean Packing Corp.*, 860 F. Supp. 198 (E.D. Pa. 1994).

MAJOR LIFE ACTIVITIES

Advocates of persons with psychiatric disabilities express concern that the EEOC's ADA regulations do not include activities relating to persons with mental or emotional illness. The regulations provide a nonexclusive listing of major life activities but mention only caring for oneself, performing manual tasks, walking, seeing, hearing, speaking, breathing, learning, and working: 29 C.F.R. §1630.2(i). During the rulemaking process, advocates sought to have the list expanded to include activities such as interpersonal skills, socialization, concentration, and cognitive processing. These requests were rejected because EEOC commissioners expressed alarm over how easy it would be for an employee to claim disability discrimination in challenging discipline for disability-caused poor judgment or inappropriate behavior. Such claims were not infrequently raised to the EEOC by federal employees appealing cases of disability discrimination under the Rehabilitation Act. The commissioners believed that persons with genuine psychiatric illnesses would be able to demonstrate disability status without providing other employees who had performance or behavior problems a basis for claiming disability discrimination. The EEOC took a major step to address these concerns when it issued subregulatory guidance on the ADA's definition of disability in March 1995. The EEOC indicated that mental and emotional processes such as thinking, concentrating, and interacting with others also constituted major life activities (*EEOC Compliance Manual,* vol. 2, no. 915.002, §902.3).

Qualified Individual with a Disability

As noted above, the regulatory definition of a "qualified individual with a disability" requires that an individual satisfy an employer's legitimate, uniformly applied qualifications standards and be able to perform the essential functions of a job with or without reasonable accommodation (29 C.F.R. §1630.2(m)). The concept of qualification standards is quite broad under the ADA. It can include behavioral and interpersonal norms and safety and medical criteria, as well as education, work experience, and licensing requirements (29 C.F.R. §1630.2(q)). Some employers also utilize preemployment tests as part of a multifaceted selection process. Many such qualification standards pose barriers to persons with psychiatric disabilities. A qualification standard, selection criterion, or employment test which screens out, or tends to screen out an individual or class of individuals with disabilities can be challenged under the ADA, and the employer must show that the challenged practice is both job-related and necessary for the business. The employer must also show that no form of reasonable accommodation that could be provided would enable the individual with a disability to satisfy the qualification standard (42 U.S.C. §12113(a)).

Notwithstanding this exacting provision, persons with psychiatric disabilities are likely to find the ADA of little assistance in many contexts. For example, many psychiatric conditions affect self-awareness and interpersonal skills. In an era when teamwork is becoming the corporate norm, ability to interact effectively with coworkers becomes ever more important. Likewise, some employers are using personality tests to select candidates for entry-level sales positions who are upbeat, warm, friendly, outgoing and energetic. Some studies show significantly increased sales and productivity arising from persons with those personality traits in sales positions. Persons with some forms of mental illness may be screened out from such jobs either because of an episodic manifestation of the mental impairment, or because of side effects from medications used to treat such impairments. Even so, it seems unlikely that the ADA will prohibit the use of such qualification standards for such common entry-level jobs, and there appears to be no way to accommodate an individual with such deficits.

Safety-related qualification standards may also create problems for some persons with psychiatric disabilities. As interpreted by the EEOC, the ADA permits employers to exclude a worker who would pose a significant risk of substantial harm to his own health or safety or the health or safety of others in the workplace (29 C.F.R. §1630.2(r)). Advocates for persons with psychiatric disabilities have been very concerned about these standards. The common belief that persons with psychiatric disabilities pose a risk of violence in the workplace remains a significant barrier to employment. At least two factors will make this stereotype more difficult to resolve in the workplace. First, recent studies have demonstrated that there is a link between mental disability and violence, although it is quite limited (Monahan 1992; see also Campbell and Kaufmann, chapter 8 in this volume). Second, workplace fatalities are on the rise. According to a census of fatal occupational injuries recently issued by the Bureau of Labor Statistics, homicide accounted for 17% of all workplace deaths in 1992. Many of these deaths befall convenience store clerks and taxi drivers who are victims of robbery attempts. Still others reflect domestic violence spilling over into the workplace. However, the number of professionals, managers, and supervisors killed by disgruntled employees is on the rise. Layoffs, terminations, and discipline for inappropriate behavior such as sexual or racial harassment often trigger violent events in the workplace.

The number of violent perpetrators who have psychiatric impairments probably is not known. Nonetheless, the growing awareness of violence in the workplace is causing many employers to rethink selection criteria, facility security, and response mechanisms. Forensic psychiatrists are advising employers to monitor and compile examples of odd or "bizarre" behavior by employees. Violent behavior is not easily predictable, yet some observers say with hindsight that there are many warning signs before a coworker commits a violent act against another employee.

Some employer reactions to forestall workplace violence may run afoul of the ADA. Monitoring the behavior of an employee with a psychiatric disability or requiring a person to undergo a psychiatric evaluation as a condition of employment will no doubt be challenged under the ADA. The ADA's "direct threat to health and safety" standard is a stringent one. The employer must identify the specific behavior which poses the risk of substantial harm; the actions must be based on the most current medical knowledge or best objective facts as to a number of factors, including the imminence of the harm, the probability of the harm, the duration of the risk, and the nature of the harm. Speculation or conjecture is not adequate to exclude an individual with a disability from the workplace (29 C.F.R. §1630.2(r)).

An administrative decision by the EEOC under Section 501 of the Rehabilitation Act illustrates just how the ADA's "direct threat to others" standard might be applied in the context of a potential for psychiatrically based violence in the workplace. In *Whitmoyer v. U.S. Postal Service,* Request No. 05870390 (EEOC April 27, 1987), the EEOC was asked to review the actions of the Postal Service which required an employee to undergo monthly psychiatric evaluations at his own expense before being allowed to return to work. The issue arose when a coworker allegedly heard the employee say that he had a gun at home and that he was going to get the Postmaster if he were ever disciplined or suspended again. The coworker informed the Postmaster. The Postmaster reviewed the employee's medical records and discovered that the employee had been discharged from the military service because of homicidal tendencies. The Postmaster ordered the employee off the facility and told him not to return without a psychiatric evaluation indicating that he did not pose a risk of harm to others. As directed, the employee underwent a rigorous psychiatric examination, and the psychiatrist reported that, in his view, the employee did not pose a danger to himself or others, although he did have a very obstructive personality. The employee was permitted to return to work but was under orders to return for monthly psychiatric evaluations at his own expense. The EEOC, on appeal from a determination by the Postal Service finding no discrimination, reversed in part. The EEOC determined that there was adequate evidence to support the Postal Service's initial requirement of a psychiatric fitness-for-duty examination in light of the statement allegedly made to the coworker and the employee's history of psychiatric discharge from the military service. However, the EEOC also found that once the psychiatrist had cleared the individual to return to work, the Postal Service lacked the basis to order a continuing monthly psychiatric evaluation absent any subsequent behavior providing the basis for such a requirement.

Under the EEOC's interpretation, an employer is also permitted to exclude from the workplace an individual who poses a direct threat to her own health or safety. The statute itself does not mention exclusion for threat to self, only threat to others. The EEOC, however, added threat to self on the basis of case law that had developed under the Rehabilitation Act as well as the legislative history of the ADA. While that legislative history makes plain the intent of Congress not to permit exclusion based upon paternalism, portions of it also address an employer's legitimate concern about liability for workplace injuries. The EEOC was concerned that an employer not be required to bear workers' compensation liability when it had evidence that a worker would pose a high probability of substantial harm to herself in the workplace. Nonetheless, some psychiatric disorders pose a heightened risk of suicide. The question remains whether an employer would use the threat-to-self standard in the ADA to justify the exclusion of employees with suicidal tendencies. For example in *Doe v. Region 13*, 704 F.2d 1402 (5th Cir. 1983), the court of appeals upheld the dismissal of a mental health therapist with suicidal tendencies because the court was concerned that the therapist who accepted suicide as a legitimate choice could pass this view along to patients. The court was also concerned about the effect the therapist's suicide might have upon her patients. In *Pesterfield v. Tennessee Valley Authority*, 941 F.2d 437 (6th Cir. 1991), another court of appeals found unqualified an employee who threatened to kill himself and who otherwise exhibited extreme anxiety and could not accept criticisms.

Reasonable Accommodation

Reasonable accommodation was the most feared aspect of the ADA from the standpoint of employers and its most popular aspect from the standpoint of the disability community. Reasonable accommodation can transform an "unqualified" individual with a disability into a "qualified" individual with a disability. Reasonable accommodation requires that an employer view every applicant or employee with a disability on an individualized, case-by-case basis, responding to that individual's disability-based workplace needs so long as the accommodation would not impose an undue hardship on the employer's operations. The ADA provides a list of examples of accommodations, including making facilities accessible to and usable by persons with disabilities; job restructuring; part-time or modified work schedules; reassignment to a vacant position; modifying policies or training materials; and providing qualified readers and interpreters (42 U.S.C. §12111(9)). The list is not intended to be exclusive.

An employer is obligated to provide a reasonable accommodation only if it knows of the "physical or mental limitations" of an "otherwise qualified" individual (42 U.S.C. §12112(b) (5) (A)). The EEOC has also indicated that, generally, an individual must request an accommodation.

For persons with psychiatric disabilities, there are two basic ADA accommodation issues.

DISCLOSURE

In order to be provided with a needed reasonable accommodation, a person with a psychiatric disability must request an accommodation and disclose the nature of the mental limitation(s) to be accommodated. The widespread stigma and fear about mental disorders make such disclosure risky both objectively and from the perspective of the individual with a disability. There appears to be no consensus as to how, when, to whom, or what information should be disclosed in the accommodation process. Poor self-awareness or self-denial may also make disclosure difficult. This frequently means that an individual with a disability does not request an appropriate accommodation until discharge has been proposed by the employer for poor performance or attendance. For example, in *Landefeld v. Marion General Hospital*, 994 F.2d 1178 (6th Cir. 1993), a court of appeals upheld the termination of staff privileges of an internist who tampered with fellow physicians' mailboxes. The court of appeals noted that the board of directors had no knowledge of the internist's bipolar disorder and was merely reacting to the misconduct. Lacking knowledge of a disability or a request for accommodation supported by medical documentation, an employer has no obligation to provide an accommodation to an employee. This is so even when a relative of an employee informs the employer that the employee is falling apart and will be hospitalized (*Miller v. National Casualty Co.*, 61 F.3d 67 (8th Cir. 1995)).

PARTICIPATION IN THE REASONABLE ACCOMMODATION PROCESS

Case law under the Rehabilitation Act places a burden on the person with a disability to produce some evidence of a plausible reasonable accommodation that would enable him to perform the essential functions of the job satisfactorily. In general, this is not a difficult burden to meet. The EEOC's ADA regulations indicate that the employer and applicant or employee should consult about appropriate reasonable accommodations. This consultation process can be critically important where the accommodation is not obvious. If an employer and a person with a disability cannot identify a possible reasonable accommodation, the employer has some duty to seek the assistance of outside experts to come up with a possible form of accommodation, according to the EEOC. However, if neither party, after reasonable effort, identifies an accommodation, the employer has fulfilled its duty, and the employee or applicant has no claim. For example, an abusive, belligerent employee with a bipolar disorder cannot simply assert that accommodation is possible by pointing to the statutory list of examples of accommodation without explaining how a specific accommodation will enable her to meet her employer's legitimate expectations for performance and conduct (*Carrozza v.*

Howard County, Maryland, 847 F. Supp. 365 (D. Md. 1994), *aff'd,* 4 AD Cas. 512 (4th Cir. 1995)). Accordingly, full participation in the accommodation process can be critical for persons with disabilities. In many instances, this requires the individual with a disability to have good self-awareness, self-esteem, and communication skills. If these abilities are impaired by a psychiatric disability, the individual's participation in the accommodation process will also be limited, which reduces the chances for successful accommodation. For this reason, some persons with psychiatric disabilities may prefer to use a third party such as a job developer or job coach to assist with any necessary disability disclosure and identification of possible accommodations.

TYPES OF ACCOMMODATION

The reasonable accommodation requirement is a broad one. It encompasses many types of accommodation that are useful to persons with psychiatric disabilities.

Leave. Leave and flexibility in scheduling are the most frequently cited forms of accommodation for a person with a psychiatric disability. This may include taking time off for therapy, adjustment of medications, or hospitalization. It also can include a part-time work schedule on a temporary or permanent basis. Additional unpaid leave may also be a form of reasonable accommodation (29 C.F.R. §1630.2(o) app.). However, the courts have not been very accepting of leave requests as a form of reasonable accommodation; see, for example, *Myers v. Hose,* 50 F.3d 278 (4th Cir. 1995) (indefinite leave not required); *Tyndall v. National Education Centers,* 31 F.3d 209 (4th Cir. 1994) (presence at the school is an essential function of a teacher position); *Jackson v. Veterans Admin.,* 22 F.3d 277, 280 (11th Cir. 1994) (Rehabilitation Act does not require federal agency to accommodate periodic, unanticipated absences of probationary employee).

The Family and Medical Leave Act of 1993 is another federal law which may provide important leave rights to employees with psychiatric impairments. It requires an employer to provide at least twelve weeks of unpaid leave for a variety of family and medical leave issues, including treatment of a "serious health condition." The Family and Medical Leave Act provides significant aid to persons with psychiatric disabilities by requiring employers to provide leave flexibility to all employees. Nevertheless, as with the ADA, a person with a psychiatric disability must disclose his mental health status in order to obtain the leave. This presents problems similar to the disclosure issues raised by the ADA.

Job restructuring. Job restructuring is expressly mentioned by the ADA as an example of reasonable accommodation (42 U.S.C. §12111(9)). However, the EEOC has made clear that an employer is not required to eliminate or have another employee perform an essential job function (29 C.F.R. §1630.2(n) app.). The courts have agreed. For example, an employer was not required to reduce the amount of time a customer-service representative spent handling customer phone calls, even though such telephone work caused the employee to have panic attacks (*Larkins v. CIBA Vision Corp.*, 858 F. Supp. 1572 (N.D. Ga. 1994)). Nor was an employer required to hire another person to reduce a disabled employee's workload (*Michell v. Lydall, Inc.*, 16 F.3d 410 (4th Cir. 1994)).

Part-time work. Like job restructuring, part-time work is expressly mentioned as an example of reasonable accommodation in the ADA. However, working part-time may result in eliminating an essential job function. For example, an employee with a stress disorder was denied her request to work part-time because of the significant amount of contact her job required with coworkers and the amount of on-site training she was expected to provide to others (*Daniels-Merritt v. Johnson*, 2 AD Cas. 1719 (D. Mo. 1993)).

Working at home. The courts are split over whether working at home can be a form of reasonable accommodation. Compare *Langon v. HHS*, 959 F.2d 1053 (D.C. Cir. 1992) (Rehabilitation Act may require federal agency to consider accommodating a computer programmer with multiple sclerosis by allowing her to work at home) with *Vande Zande v. Wisconsin Dept. of Admin.*, 44 F.3d 538 (7th Cir. 1995) (working at home is rarely required by ADA).

Reassignment to a vacant position. Reassigning an employee who can no longer do a job because of a disability is a form of reasonable accommodation specifically mentioned in the statute as a way of overruling earlier Rehabilitation Act case law; see 42 U.S.C. §12111(9) (B), but see also *Reigel v. Kaiser Foundation Health Plan of North Carolina, supra* (ADA does not require reassignment citing pre-ADA Rehabilitation Act case law). Where courts have found a duty to consider reassignment, they have differed over the scope of the duty. One court has indicated that an employer only has a duty to reassign an employee within the facility where the employee works (*Emrick v. Libbey-Owens Ford Co.*, 875 F. Supp. 393 (E.D. Tex. 1995)). On the other hand, the Ninth Circuit ruled that under the Rehabilitation Act, it might be a reasonable accommodation to reassign a postal worker with HIV from Mississippi to California for better medical treatment (*Buckingham v. U.S. Postal Service*, 998 F.2d 735 (9th Cir. 1993)). The Fifth Circuit has also determined that reassignment does not require preferential placement of a disabled employee. Only if a disabled employee can prove that reassignment was denied for a discriminatory reason will a violation of the ADA be found (*Daugherty v. City of El Paso*, 56 F.3d 695, 700 (5th Cir. 1995)). It logically follows that an employer can pick the most qualified person for a vacancy without preferring an employee with a disability unless the employer provides such preferential placement as a matter of its own policy. In addition, there must be a vacant position to which the employee can be reassigned, and the employee must be qualified to perform the position. An employer is not required to create a new job or to provide "light duty" (*Magel v. Federal Reserve Bank of Philadelphia,* 776 F. Supp. 200, 204 (E.D. Pa. 1991), *aff'd,* 5 F.3d 1490 (3d Cir. 1993) ("[h]owever reasonable accommodation is defined, it does not include creating a new job."); see also the *EEOC Technical Assistance Manual* §9.4).

A change in supervisors has also been suggested as a form of reasonable accommodation. This may be possible if an individual can be reassigned to a vacant position for which she is qualified that is under another supervisor. On the other hand, the ADA is not likely to sanction a concept of reasonable accommodation that includes a change in supervisor whenever a dispute develops with an employee. While the literature recognizes the importance of having a sensitive, flexible supervisor for many persons with psychiatric disabilities, it is doubtful that the law is violated if one's supervisor has an authoritarian, inflexible management style. It is difficult to imagine that the EEOC or the courts will require employers to move supervisors around in an effort to find the best "fit" between a person with a psychiatric disability and the boss; this would simply be too disruptive of the workplace, and of the relationships established between other employees and supervisors. It would also be subject to great abuse by employees with poor performance or conduct records when the causal link to a disability is unclear.

Supported employment. Another frequently cited form of reasonable accommodation for persons with psychiatric disabilities is supported employment. The EEOC has taken the position that supported employment is not synonymous with reasonable accommodation (Interpretive Appendix to 29 C.F.R. §1630.2(o)). Under some circumstances the ADA may require an employer to provide a job coach to assist a person with a psychiatric disability to obtain and be trained for employment with a particular employer. The possibility that an employer would be required to pay for a job coach on a permanent basis is subject to the ADA's undue hardship limitation. On the other hand, many forms of supported employment would not be required as reasonable accommodations, including job restructuring to the point of eliminating essential job functions and reduction of the quantity and quality of work standards.

Providing or monitoring medication. Some advocates have also suggested that paying for, providing, or requiring medications can also be a form of reasonable accommodation. The EEOC has already indicated in its interpretive guidance on the ADA that an employer is not required to provide an accommodation for the personal use of an individual with a disability on or off the job. This would appear to exclude any requirement that an employer pay for or provide medications for the treatment or control of psychiatric conditions. Less clear, but just as problematic, is the issue of whether the ADA would require an employer to establish procedures to monitor and ensure that an individual with a psychiatric disability is taking his necessary medications. It can be argued that such a requirement would assist many persons with psychiatric disabilities who have problems in maintaining the appropriate use of their medications. This could be critical for the employment of some individuals where the failure to take medication would result in their posing a direct threat or being otherwise unqualified. Advocates can point to the ADA's provision that expressly permits employers to perform drug testing to ensure that the current illegal use of drugs is not occurring in the workplace as a basis for requiring that an employer establish drug testing to ensure that an individual is taking necessary medications. This approach, however, has many detractors. Many advocates feel that this is equivalent to coercive treatment of persons with psychiatric disabilities, an issue about which there is great sensitivity in the disability community. Employers, too, frequently do not wish to be involved in the medical management of an employee's well-being, believing that this level of responsibility for the employee should not rest upon the employer. It is unclear how this issue will be resolved. In *Hogarth v. Thornburgh*, 833 F. Supp. 1077 (S.D.N.Y. 1993), a district court concluded that the government had failed to prove it would be an undue hardship to monitor an FBI clerk's compliance with his medication regime to control his bipolar disorder. However, the court concluded that effective monitoring was not possible, as it would require both observing the employee take his medication and checking the medication level in his blood twelve hours later, long after the employee's work day had ended.

A case involving a postal worker with paranoid schizophrenia illustrates some of the difficulties inherent in the issue of medication as reasonable accommodation. In *Franklin v. U.S. Postal Service*, 687 F. Supp. 1214 (S.D. Ohio 1988), a district court upheld the discharge of a postal worker whose refusal to take psychotropic medicine resulted in attempted aggression against public officials. The employee resisted taking her medication because of its deleterious side effects. When on the medication, she had been able to function with the Postal Service for ten years. However, after not taking the medication for several weeks, she developed psychotic episodes. One such episode involved her attempt to gain forcible entry into the office of the Ohio governor. She was discharged by the Postal Service but later reinstated on the condition that she take her medication. Subsequently, she again failed to take her medication and again tried to gain forcible entry into the governor's office. She was again discharged but was reinstated under a last-chance agreement specifying that she would be dismissed if there were any further incidents. When she attempted to enter the White House, she was arrested, committed to St. Elizabeth's Hospital, and discharged from the Postal Service. The court upheld her discharge, indicating that her aggressive behavior and unwillingness to take her medication rendered her "unqualified."

Modifying discipline to forgive misconduct. The EEOC has taken the position that an employer is not required to modify its uniformly applied discipline policy or to alter discipline as a reasonable accommodation. Misconduct due to disability has not been excused by the courts under either the ADA or the Rehabilitation Act; see *Adams v. Alderson,* 723 F. Supp. 1531 (D.D.C. 1989), *aff'd,* 1990 WL 45737 (D.C. Cir. April 10, 1990) ("One who is unable to refrain from doing physical violence to the person of a supervisor, no matter how unfair he believes the supervision to be or how provocative its manner, is simply not otherwise qualified for employment"); *Mazzarella v. U.S. Postal Service,* 849 F. Supp. 89 (D. Mass. 1994) ("[T]o qualify for employment of any nature, the employee must have the ability to refrain from willfully destroying his employer's property"); and *Misek-Falkoff v. International Business Machines Corp.,* 854 F. Supp. 215 (S.D.N.Y. 1994) ("It is certainly a 'job-related requirement' that an employee, handicapped or not, be able to get along with coworkers and supervisors. Thus, conduct associated with a handicap, as distinct from the handicap itself, may be relevant to the determination of whether a person is qualified").

Training. To forestall coworkers' resentment over accommodations provided to employees whose disabilities are not obvious, or to allay employee fears regarding persons with mental illness or other disabilities, an employer may wish to provide education to employees on the ADA and on the needs of persons with particular types of disabilities. While such education is not expressly required by the ADA, it may be necessary to forestall harassment or workplace disruption because of the provision of a reasonable accommodation. Provision of such education, however, also presents difficult issues. In addition to being accurate, the information must be presented in such a way as to avoid disclosure of a particular employee's disability and the creation of prejudice or stereotypes.

Undue hardship. Many of the accommodations described above that were rejected by the courts pertained to requests that the courts determined to be unduly burdensome or not reasonable.

The ADA and Disability Benefits Programs

The ADA is likely to have a profound impact on our nation's disability benefit programs, including SSDI, SSI, and workers' compensation. Current eligibility criteria do not take into account either the ADA's focus on performance of "essential job functions" or the required provision of "reasonable accommodation'' applicable to employers of fifteen or more employees. The ADA stresses ability in spite of disability, while benefit programs reward inability due to disability. Some may see benefit programs and the ADA as complementary because the ADA enables those who can to work, and benefit programs enable those who cannot work to receive income maintenance payments; however, the perceived harmony is illusory.

As the costs of disability benefit programs increase with the aging of the American workforce, pressure is likely to mount to tighten eligibility criteria based upon the ADA. The increasing cost of disability benefits is not the only reason why this is likely to occur. Employers are already beginning to experience how the ADA provides injured workers with an additional avenue of compensation over and above what they are entitled to receive under workers' compensation. The traditional employer practice of terminating workers who become injured and unable to perform their full range of duties without accommodation is creating substantial ADA liability.

As ADA litigation increases and the costs of disability benefit programs mount, pressures will increase to incorporate ADA provisions into eligibility programs and otherwise tighten eligibility for disability benefits. Yet, if society's image of disability is transformed even slightly from one of inability to one of some ability, there will be increasing expectations that persons with disabilities should be working in spite of their disabilities.

The end result of these political forces may be that individuals with severe disabilities, including psychiatric disabilities, may find it more difficult to receive benefits. There is a risk that the disability rights model may replace the benefits model not only with respect to those who are capable of working in spite of disability, but also with respect to those who are not. As so often happens, the pendulum may swing too far, from a benefits model to a disability rights model, with catastrophic results for many individuals. The ADA presupposes a level of ability, knowledge, training, and rehabilitation that simply does not exist for many persons with disabilities. To the extent that the disability rights model embodied in the ADA ignores this fact, many persons with disabilities will suffer.

Conclusion

The ADA provides people with disabilities with significantly expanded civil rights protection. Its promoters assumed that its enactment would open up employment opportunities for people with disabilities who are not now in the labor force. It is too early to say whether this will actually occur.

Significant barriers continue to impede the entry into the workforce of persons with psychiatric disabilities. The ADA's advantages for persons with severe psychiatric disabilities are limited by its focus on protecting persons seeking competitive employment, its restrictive definition of disability, and its limitations on the duty to provide a reasonable accommodation. These limitations reflect general features of the civil rights approach to disability rather than particular defects in the ADA itself. Most of the barriers faced by people with *severe* psychiatric disabilities do not result from societal actions, either intentional or unintentional. In a society which places an increasing emphasis on cognitive and mental abilities, education, training, and interpersonal skills, people who have impairments affecting those life functions will be disadvantaged. The civil rights model is inherently limited in its ability to provide equal employment opportunity in this context. The civil rights model requires society to change in order to augment employment opportunities on the supposition that society has created the barriers to opportunity. Because this is only partly true with respect to psychiatric disability, society's willingness and ability to overcome barriers caused by impairments rather than by social prejudice will be distinctly limited. Rather than change the ADA in an attempt to meet the needs of people with severe psychiatric and other disabilities, the better course is to provide complementary benefits and supportive services that promote independence, integration, and self-sufficiency to the maximum extent possible without compromising the ADA's focus on equal opportunity for competitive employment.

References

Monahan, J. 1992. Mental Disorder and Violent Behavior: Perceptions and Evidence. *American Psychologist* 47: 511–21.
Stevens, A. 1995. Boss's Brain Teaser: Accommodating Depressed Worker. *Wall Street Journal* 11 September 1995, B1.

8

Equality and Difference in the ADA: Unintended Consequences for Employment of People with Mental Health Disabilities

JEAN CAMPBELL AND CAROLINE L. KAUFMANN

Employers already are required to make reasonable accommodations for physically handicapped workers. Broadening the definition of a handicapped employee to include individuals with mental and emotional disorders would make one wonder just what further accommodation would be required. Would every business be obliged to install padded cells for the convenience of the mentally unbalanced?

(*Gardena Valley News,* 19 Oct. 1983)

When work provides opportunities for control, creativity, and challenge—when it is self-expressive and enhances an individual's unique potentialities—then it contributes to the worker's sense of self-respect and dignity and at least partially overcomes the stigma of low status. Alienated work—without control, freedom, or responsibility—on the other hand simply confirms and deepens the feeling that societal estimates of low status and little worth are valid.

(Blauner 1964, 31)

This chapter explores the consequences of claiming protection from discrimination under Title I of the Americans with Disabilities Act (ADA) for people with psychiatric diagnoses. It may seem ironic that legislation designed to promote social good, in this case to protect and promote the civil rights of people with disabilities,[1] may have negative effects on people with one particular type of disability. However, unintended consequences are likely given the heterogeneity within the class of people regarded as members of the disability community.

Unintended Consequences of Reforms: The Oregon Health Plan

As the nation faces dramatic changes in the delivery of health and human services, it is particularly important to consider the role of unintended consequences as social policies are implemented to redress inequality and accommodate the needs of society's most vulnerable citizens (Campbell 1994). To that end, an exploration of the impact of the Americans with Disabilities Act on the 1992 Oregon Medicaid decision is instructive. In August, 1992, Oregon Governor Barbara Roberts was surprised to receive a letter from Health and Human Services Secretary Louis W. Sullivan sending back for revision Oregon's health care rationing plan. Public officials in Oregon felt that the plan struck a precarious balance between the needs of 120,000 people— primarily women and children—who lived below the poverty line but earned too much to qualify for Medicaid, and the extraordinary needs of some of its sickest citizens.

Sullivan argued, however, that the statewide proposal to provide universal health care coverage by restricting the number of conditions and procedures that would be paid for was biased against persons with disabilities and violated the ADA. While Oregon officials felt they were serving the needs of people with disabilities, Sullivan's argument was based on the belief that this proposal promoted the "premise that the value of the life of a person with a disability is less than the value of the life of a person without a disability." In particular, Sullivan's letter questioned the manner in which rankings of medical conditions were derived. Oregon had attempted to determine democratically the rankings of treatments and conditions through telephone surveys of residents. However, findings tended to quantify stereotypic assumptions about persons with disabilities; therefore, subsequent rankings discriminated against disability (U.S. Department of Health and Human Services 1992, 2).

The reasoning supporting the HHS decision illustrates how the best of intentions can produce unintended consequences for people with disabilities. The ADA specified that those with disabilities must enjoy the same treatment under the law as other Americans. This principle transformed a debate on where to draw the line on public subsidies for health care to an ethical conundrum about the inequitable consequences of a rationed health care plan for people with disabilities. In determining which medical procedures to fund under the Oregon plan, policy makers adjusted the rankings on the basis of certain community values, including quality of life and ability to function, which are based on the concepts of restored health and functional independence as the best outcomes. Persons without disabilities were favored because treatments for severe or exacerbated conditions were removed from coverage (U.S. Department of Health and Human Services 1992, 2). The original plan to ration health care in Oregon did violence to the value of equality as embodied in the ADA. At the same time, this application of the ADA resulted in the denial of basic health care coverage for many poor and disadvantaged persons, *including many who were disabled*. Therefore, the legislation had inadvertently replicated inequalities of race, gender, and class both within and outside protected disability status.

Justin Dart, chairman of the President's Committee on Employment of People with Disabilities, wrote that the day that the ADA was signed into law was "a landmark date in the evolution of human culture." He went on to relate that until recent decades people with disabilities have been treated as "sub-human" (Dart 1990, 1). Their history is a chronicle of isolation and segregation. "In virtually every aspect of society—housing, employment, education, recreation, transportation, public accommodations, communication, health services, and even voting—persons with disabilities have been shunned" (West 1991, xix). People with disabilities constitute the largest, poorest, and least educated minority in America (Harris 1987, 194). A recent Harris survey conducted by the National Organization on Disability found that 59% of adults with disabilities live in households with total income of less than $25,000, compared to only 37% of those without disabilities. In addition, 25% of people with disabilities have less than a high school education, compared to only 12% of individuals without disabilities (National Organization on Disability 1994).

The fallacy of this seemingly paradoxical situation is in thinking of people who are disabled as a homogeneous group with common needs and equal social power. Such thinking is in itself stereotypic. Because civil rights legislation such as the ADA exists within the context of a stratified society, it necessarily reproduces profound social contradictions in the politics of equality and difference. To meet the call of former President Bush to "let the shameful wall of exclusion finally come tumbling down," requires a case-by-case, as well as class, analysis of how inequality is manifested and sustained in the communities in which heterogenous people work and live.

Disability and Difference

In the simplest view of disability, membership in the community of "the disabled" is both involuntary and obvious. The ideal type of disability envisioned by the ADA is physical in nature and manifest through functional limitations that are commonly assumed to be beyond the control of the disabled person. For example, a casual observer seeing someone in a wheelchair assumes that the person would prefer to walk if he were able. A person does not choose to be disabled, and is in many ways obligated to do everything he can do to maintain a functional status as close as possible to that of an "able-bodied" person. People with physical disabilities who are able to perform major social roles, such as parent or worker, are usually admired. At the same time, they are regarded with an ambivalent mixture of sympathy and disgust (Bogdan 1988; Fiedler 1978).

Psychiatric disabilities are different because they usually manifest themselves through behavior that may appear to be voluntary. Thus a person experiencing major depression may demonstrate poor productivity at work. Since adults in this society generally are held responsible for their behavior, the person may be scorned for misbehavior over which she has little control. The problem is that symptoms of a mental disorder are easily interpreted as defects of character. The depressed worker may be chastised for being lazy rather than disabled. Public views of mental disabilities are ambivalent because, among other things, the person with a mental illness appears to be making poor choices. The assumption that human beings can exercise rational control over their behavior makes poor choices in behavior more likely to be the subject of punishment than empathy.

The second common feature of the ideal type of disability is immediate recognition. Disability is frequently an obvious physical characteristic. Assistive devices make this more obvious. A wheelchair or white-tipped cane indicate inability to walk or visual impairment. Psychiatric disabilities are different because they are not necessarily visible. They do not usually require the use of assistive devices. A person with a mental illness may look like a person without a disability; therefore, there is no immediate social recognition of his status as a disabled individual. To be so recognized, the person must disclose the disability through some type of verbal explanation or have the disability revealed through third-party reports.

Ambivalence and Discrimination within the Disability Community

By legal definition, serious mental illness constitutes a disabling condition because it substantially limits the person's ability to participate actively in one or more major life activities. The disability community, however, is not immune to the same stereotypical attitudes that affect the nondisabled community. People with mental illnesses are generally among the most stigmatized of those with disabilities. Because the ADA exists in a stratified society, even within the disability community, the ADA may facilitate discrimination by actually limiting equal opportunity. Key provisions of the ADA allow employers to abridge rights in ways that disproportionately affect people with mental disorders.

For example, the ADA exempts employers from the requirement to provide reasonable accommodation to a person with disabilities if that person poses a significant risk to the safety of others. While the direct-threat standard understandably places public safety before individual rights, such value choices in the ADA compromise protection against prejudice and discrimination for person diagnosed with mental illness. Because of widespread acceptance of the cultural stereotype of the violent mental patient, the ADA inevitably subsumes issues of psychiatric stigma and discrimination. While employers should not be compelled to expose their employees to danger, the following section describes how the direct-threat standard undermines the benefits of reasonable accommodations provided under the ADA for persons with psychiatric disabilities and mediates the ability of such persons to receive equal protection under the disabilities rights law.

Exemptions for Dangerousness and Nondisclosure

The drafters of the ADA included persons with psychiatric disabilities within the protected class but provided caveats that limited the scope of their protections. The first limiting provision allows employers to claim that the person poses a significant risk to the safety of others. The second limiting condition is the provision that employers must only accommodate the known disabilities of an employee. While both these exemptions apply in cases of physical as well as mental disabilities, people with mental disabilities are more vulnerable to their misuse. We examine each of these exemptions and provide illustrations of unintended consequences in the following discussion.

The direct-threat standard in the ADA attempts to balance the rights of persons who have disabilities against the needs of a society to protect itself from harm. Yet, there is "no escaping value choices in constructing a working definition of harm for the public welfare domain" (La Fond 1992, 2). According to interviews with mental health opinion leaders in a national study of public attitudes toward persons with chronic mental illness, the public is "very much afraid of people with mental illness" because they believe that "people who suffer from a mental disorder are prone to commit violent acts" (Yankelovich 1990, 90, 94). This fear permeates all levels of social interaction and provides implicit justification for discrimination. The result of such public attitudes is well understood by people with psychiatric diagnoses, and persons with mental illness must often learn to live with other people's fear of them (Campbell et al. 1994, 633). According to one study of mental health clients in California, clients reported that when their psychiatric history is known, people treat them "all" or "most" of the time like children (21%), as unpredictable (26%), as dangerous (17%), as incapable of caring for children (19%), as incapable of holding a job (33%), and as unable to know their own best interests (31%) (Campbell and Schraiber 1989, 90–91).

The "inclusion of mental illnesses in the ADA was challenged by opponents seeking to derail the bill. Ugly reminders of the stigma unfairly attached to mental illnesses were circulated," reported Jim Havel of the Mental Health Policy Resource Center in Washington, D.C. (Havel 1990, 18). One salient example was the effort of Rep. Chuck Douglas to characterize persons diagnosed with mental illness as gun-toting maniacs out to kill coworkers. In a memo to fellow members of the House of Representatives, Douglas claimed that the ADA would open the door for "Berserkers: Time Bombs in the

Work Place.'' Under an illustration of a man taking aim at the reader with a rifle, he asked, ''How can we protect ourselves from an apparently growing menace? He then answered, ''Certainly by not passing the Americans with Disabilities Act in its present form that protects people who do not have physical disabilities'' (Tirrell-Wysocki 1990, 11).

While Douglas's memo was inflammatory, he was responding to the legitimate fears of employers that they would be forced to hire dangerous people or be subject to charges of discrimination under the ADA. In such circumstances, the threat to public safety in the workplace could exacerbate prejudicial attitudes against persons with a psychiatric diagnosis. Further, an employer could be liable for harm to employees due to violent acts of a ''psychotic worker.''

Despite the stigmatizing characterizations and employer concerns, there was intense lobbying by persons with psychiatric disabilities and their families and united resolve by the entire disability community to include psychiatric disabilities among those covered by the ADA (Havel 1990, 18). Congress remained steadfast in its support of persons with psychiatric disabilities but yielded to the concerns of employers by seeking a compromise between the rights of persons with psychiatric disabilities and the need to preserve community health and safety.[2] In congressional conference, a direct-threat standard which allowed employers to fire or not hire a person who posed a significant risk of danger to other employees was added to the legislation. The direct-threat standard as applied to persons with psychiatric disabilities protects the employer from charges of civil rights violation in the rare case where violence is threatened.

Cultural beliefs regarding the dangerousness of people with mental illness have a long historical precedent (Monahan 1992a). The belief that persons with psychiatric diagnoses are prone to violence has informed public policy. As Monahan notes,

> there can be little doubt that this assumption has played an animating role in the prominence of ''dangerous to others'' as a criterion for civil commitment and the commitment of persons acquitted of crime by reason of insanity, in the creation of special statutes for extended detention of mentally disordered prisoners, and in the imposition of tort liability on psychologists who fail to anticipate the violence of their patients. (Monahan 1992b, 511)

Under the ADA, a selective policy of preventive discrimination exists against people with psychiatric diagnoses, similar to the policy of preventive detention for ''dangerousness'' under civil commitment laws. The direct-threat standard may perpetuate psychiatric stigma and discrimination by reinforcing the perception of a strong correlation between mental illness and violence. It is important to carefully examine evidence related to mental illness and the risk of violence in order to probe how the assessment of the risk of violence and the presumption of violence interact. Our point here is that the problem with the direct-threat standard is not its inclusion per se. Rather, the combined effects of limited scientific knowledge supplemented by entrenched social stereotypes combine to make it very difficult to assess the potential for violent behavior among persons with psychiatric diagnoses.

The popular conception of people with mental illness as violent has found some empirical support. A review of results from several recent studies demonstrates modest but statistically significant relationships between mental disorder and violence (Mulvey 1994). As Monahan concluded, the convergence of findings using a variety of methods, instruments, and diverse samples makes the denial of such an association difficult (Monahan 1992b). For example, in a comparison of mental patients and never-treated community residents, Link and his colleagues found that mental patients experiencing psychotic symptoms had higher rates on all measures of violent/illegal behaviors (Link et al. 1992, 283). Swanson and others analyzed ten thousand responses collected in a federal door-to-door survey to determine the rate of people with symptoms of mental disorder in the general population. They found a slightly greater tendency toward violent behavior among those who reported symptoms of major psychiatric disorders. Those with symptoms of serious mental illness were more likely to engage in assaultive behavior than those who were free of mental illness and substance abuse (Swanson et al. 1990, 768). However, the rate of violence was still very low, and the number of violent acts committed by a person with a psychiatric diagnosis was a small percentage of total violence. Further "substance abuse by itself [was] associated with a very high relative risk for violent behavior, whether or not it occurs along with other psychopathology" (Swanson and Holzer 1991, 955). These findings imply that public fear of people with a psychiatric diagnosis is "largely unwarranted though not totally groundless" (Swanson et al. 1990, 769).

The context in which violence occurs has also warranted examination. Link makes clear that higher rates of violence among those with psychiatric diagnoses are modest and confined to people who are actively experiencing psychotic symptoms. A history of psychotic symptoms in the past bears no direct relationship to current violence. He qualifies the relationship further by offering the following caveat:

> Even for persons with psychotic symptoms, we cannot conclude that the symptoms per se cause violent behavior. It may be that psychotic

symptoms are incomprehensible to others and produce annoyance or fear that lead to attempts to coerce or control the psychotic person. These attempts to coerce may anger the psychotic person, thereby leading to a spiral that turns into violence. (Link et al 1992, 290)

In a study of social networks, social support, and violence among persons diagnosed with severe, persistent mental illness, Estroff and Zimmer found that violence by this population appears to occur most frequently within a family dynamic in which the person with a psychiatric diagnosis feels threatened (Estroff and Zimmer 1994; Estroff et al. 1994). The empirical association between violence and mental illness is not only modest, but appears to be context-dependent. Risks are real but dependent on setting and acuteness of illness.

Even though research suggests only a modest relationship between mental illness and violent behavior, such findings still appear to reinforce the dominant cultural stereotype of "the violent mentally ill" and often overwhelm interpretations that mitigate against such a bald conclusion (Hiday 1995). Because the stereotyping of people with mental illness is ubiquitous and empirical evidence equivocal, it is not surprising that many studies demonstrate that employers have strong negative perceptions of persons known or thought to have a mental illness (Colbert et al. 1973; Combs and Omvig 1986; Kirszner 1990). One study reported that employers who had never worked with persons with psychiatric disabilities rated "the fears of danger/ violence and strange behavior highest among possible concerns in hiring people with mental illness" (Kirszner 1990). Another revealed that employment acceptance showed a decreasing preference on a continuum from ethnic background, physical disability, and prison affiliation to mental instability (Colbert et al. 1973). The following case illustrates a personal attempt to evaluate the relative biases of employers.

A man in his late twenties who has been paroled from state prison, having served ten months of a two-year sentence for assault, had been diagnosed as having a personality disorder with psychotic features. By his own report, he is verbally confrontational with psychiatric hospital staff and deeply resents their attempts to "turn everything I say around" and interpret his statements as a sign of mental illness. In a support group meeting, this man asked whether it was harder to get a job if you tell someone that you have been in prison or that you have been in a psychiatric hospital. After receiving no clear answer from the group, he mused that it was probably worse to tell an employer that you had been in the hospital because people generally assume that mental patients are violent. Several members of the group agreed with him and said that they would more likely hide the fact that they receive psychiatric treatment than anything else in their background. In this case, the individual felt that even though he had been convicted of a crime of violence, he would stand a better chance in getting a job if he hid his psychiatric background rather than his criminal record. (Kaufmann, private communication).

The paramount questions for use of the direct-threat standard are (1) What is the standard of proof of significant risk of violence for a person with a psychiatric disability? and, (2) Who bears the burden of proof? The great costs of underprediction of violence for employers could pressure psychiatrists to err on the safe side. This conservative tendency has already been documented among psychiatrists and other mental health professionals (Coleman 1984). Lawrence Gostin argues that the ADA "will unleash a powerful review mechanism that will set effective boundaries on the historic exercise of public health powers" (Gostin 1991, 269). However, when applied to people with mental illness, these powers may actually be expanded.

Disclosure as Disabling

Because psychiatric disabilities are not necessarily apparent by visual cues, the person with such a disability has the option to disclose or not disclose his situation. Therefore, claiming to be a disabled person is a matter of personal choice. On the other hand, the ADA can only provide protection from discrimination and the benefits of reasonable accommodation for someone who discloses his status to an employer (Crist and Stoffel 1992, 437). Yet, the consequences of claiming such a status are at best ambiguous in terms of specific legal protections and more general social reactions to psychiatric disclosure.

Claiming status as a person with a mental illness poses significant risks. The fear of loss of freedom is key to understanding the issues of disclosure faced by persons diagnosed with mental illness. Almost half of the mental health clients in the statewide study of well-being in California reported that they had avoided seeking mental health treatment for fear of involuntary commitment (Campbell and Schraiber 1989). Because the direct-threat standard may increase the possibility of civil commitment for someone who is known to have a mental illness, it could produce a "chilling effect" on disclosure.

As employers join other gatekeepers of the mental health system in monitoring the behavior of persons known to have psychiatric diagnoses, internalized oppression due to psychiatric stigma may be perpetuated by the very legislation that seeks to overcome its public expression. This clearly illustrates the dilemma faced by people diagnosed with mental illness under the ADA. It is not surprising that in vocational rehabilitation it has been a common practice for counselors "to encourage their clients to withhold information about prior hospitalizations from potential employers," and they may even assist them "in devising strategies for masking gaps in their employment resumes" (Kaufmann 1993). Some agencies require that the functions of employment-assistance specialists be performed discretely and totally off site. While understandable from the perspective of employee confidentiality, this is another reflection of the pressure to keep psychiatric disabilities hidden (Anthony and Blanch 1987, 12).

In addition, the dominant feature among the entire disabled community is the fact that membership is frequently unwanted and unclaimed. People with disabilities of any sort do not see disability as a strength. Socially, the term does not evoke images of success; therefore, some choose to avoid the label. Others refuse to acknowledge the presence of a disability if they are employed, competent, attractive, or have other valued social characteristics. One full-time employed person who is blind remarked, "People frequently say, 'I don't consider you disabled.' That's because I make accommodations to my disability. . . . I'm accommodating all the time, but they don't know or realize it." In the context of work, the person who successfully accommodates to a disability renders the disability invisible, even when the disability is blindness. For a person with mental illness, the disability is even less apparent than blindness. The person's accommodations are likely to go unnoticed because they involve successful management of a class of mental events. The following account is from a young man with atypical psychosis who works as a part-time courier.

> The voices are talking to me almost all the time at work. The medicine only makes them softer, but they never go away completely. . . . And when I try to ignore them, they get softer, and I can hear them whispering, 'He's not listening to us. . . . He pretends he can't hear us.' If I pay attention, they get louder, and start callin' me names. . . . saying I'm bad and that God's gonna punish me for what I did. . . . I have to concentrate all the time so they don't get loud so I can't hear." (Kaufmann, private communication)

This man exerts a considerable effort to block out the voices and notes that he is often exhausted after two or three hours on the job. His disability and resultant accommodation are not apparent to his employer, and he does not mention the voices to either his supervisor or his coworkers. He presents himself as able-bodied and feels ashamed about what the voices say to him and the fact that he keeps this experience secret. For an invisible disability, one gets neither credit for successfully managing limitations nor presumptive protection from discrimination.

Further, the nature of psychiatric disability and its treatment are so shrouded in myth that even those directly involved in care and advocacy for people with mental illness act on stereotypes. The following example reported by a researcher illustrates the subtle negative consequences of disclosure in the work setting.

> Some time ago, I was involved in a collaborative research project with a local mental health service agency. In this case, I had a dual role as both the director of the research project and a consumer who facilitated one of the support groups in the project. In this dual capacity, my diagnosis and treatment status were well known to both staff and clients. The project required a great deal of negotiation and compromise on the part of both the researcher and the agency staff. On one occasion, a staff member and I disagreed about revisions to a form that was to be used for data collection. The staff member insisted that the form be revised according to his specifications. I was equally insistent about the final version of the form and felt my view should take precedence. We argued briefly about the merits of both our positions, and the staff member reluctantly agreed to follow my lead in revising the form. Later, he called me to say that he had spoken to my supervisor about the confrontation and had told him that, in his opinion, I had argued with him because I was not taking medication. This was a fact I had mentioned off-handedly several days before. He acknowledged that his remark was a mistake and wanted me to know what he had done. I asked him, "Do you really believe that I argued with you because I hadn't taken meds?" He did not reply. (Kaufmann, private communication)

The point of this anecdote is that the vulnerability of a person with a disability is resurrected each time a person discloses that difference publicly, because disability is socially constructed to allow the stigmatization of difference. The ability of the law to influence basic social processes is a matter of considerable debate, but the ADA is designed to force changes in behavior that may not be immediately reconcilable with existing social norms (Kaufmann 1993). Once a person admits to psychiatric disability in a work setting, she risks being scrutinized for potential bizarre behavior. As a result, private behaviors are likely to come to the attention of others more often—even if there is no threat of harm. In fact, mental health professionals are encouraging employers to watch their employees for signs and symptoms of psychiatric disorders. Reporting on a seminar hosted by the Washington Foundation for Psychiatry and attended by labor attorneys, business representatives, and human resource and employee-assistance plan directors, *Psychiatric News* wrote as follows:

> Norman Tamarkin, M.D., a psychiatrist in private practice in Washington, D.C., told employers at the seminar to be aware of the most

common psychiatric complaints as well as be on the lookout for less common but also treatable disorders like schizophrenia. "Failure to treat lowers productivity and increases absenteeism," he added. (Cody 1992, 5)

The problem with such seemingly innocuous and even potentially helpful advice is that once people are diagnosed with mental illness, their behaviors and emotional reactions to situations are often seen as expressions of illness rather than as authentic responses to the environment and relationships. This situation also occurs frequently when people with physical disabilities, who may be angry at discrimination, are assumed to be angry at their disabilities, even when they feel pressured by expectations to perform above the standards expected of nondisabled employees.

Mary Lee Stocks, a person with a psychiatric disability who works as a licensed social worker, related that in order to be looked upon as "normal" or "functioning," she had to maintain an evenness of mood or she wouldn't be accepted by her colleagues. She writes in *Yes I Can,*

> Were I not labeled "manic depressive," [this] would, in itself, be considered almost pathological. . . . Although everyone has "bad days," the person with a mental illness cannot afford the luxury of them. For many of the mental health professionals with whom I work, I will never have a "normal mood"; because of the label and the stereotypes attached to my illness, any deviation is viewed as "exacerbation" or "decompensation." (Stocks 1990, 8–9)

These experiences show what can happen if psychiatric disability is known: persons cannot show grief, joy, anger, or ambivalence without risking scrutiny of their mental status and, subsequently, their competence and ability to perform. In other words, it is the disabled person's task to learn how to live with other people's fears. As one man confided,

> After I got out of the hospital I found out I wasn't allowed to show any anger. Other people could do that, but if I did it, it freaked everybody out. I got in a fight with my brother once, and they put me back in the hospital. After that I just held it in. (Campbell and Schraiber, private communication).

Problems of social awkwardness, demoralization, and unemployment induced by stigma cannot always be overcome by persons with psychiatric disabilities through individual coping mechanisms such as keeping their history of treatment a secret, educating others about their situation, or avoiding situations in which rejection might occur. Quite the contrary, research reaffirms that stigma is "powerfully reinforced by culture, and not easily overcome at the individual level" (Link et al. 1991, 302). None of these coping orientations are effective in diminishing negative labeling effects on unemployment. Whether a person discloses or not, he must contend with stereotypes in the process of maintaining an acceptable identity for himself or others. History teaches that discrimination readily assumes different forms or aspects. As with racism and sexism, for people with psychiatric disabilities overt discrimination may become more subtle even as institutionalized discrimination is obscured. Whenever a film or television program features grisly crimes or destruction of property attributed to a "psychotic," or news reports link a history of mental illness with a violent act, or casual conversation includes the use of epithets such as "lunatic," "crazy," or "schizo" to describe socially undesirable behavior, the personhood of someone diagnosed with a mental illness is diminished. As Leonard Kaplan told interviewers in a California study of consumer well-being,

> some clients are dangerous, but few of them. Fewer than society would think, because most mental health clients have exactly the opposite problem—they're too passive. They wouldn't hurt a fly. I know I wouldn't hurt a fly. . . . As far as my ego is concerned, I've been humbled; I feel I have to take things and not speak out, and I've gotten used to it. I don't think it's my fault, but I feel less capable, less competent, less worthwhile than the so-called normal person. (Campbell and Schraiber 1989, 45)

The Benefits of the ADA

The ADA requires employers to make reasonable accommodations to the known physical or mental limitations of a qualified applicant or employee, unless such accommodations would impose an undue hardship on the employer. The impact of the ADA on employment of disabled persons could be substantial, but again the benefits of the Act may not be as great for persons with psychiatric disabilities because the meaning of reasonable accommodation as applied to people with mental illness has seldom been explored. Examples of workplace accommodations in government and industry are rare. Reasonable accommodations that are physical in nature and are a direct response to physical disabilities are relatively easy to interpret under the ADA. Mental health disabilities are more problematic because they are frequently manifested in behaviors and therefore require behavioral accommodations. A review of the literature on reasonable accommodation found that "textbooks, government publications, and journal articles generally neglect to mention psychiatric disability, focusing instead on accommodations for people with physical disabilities" (Mancuso 1990, 5). In the private sector, the Job Accommodation Network reported that since October 1988, mental illness has been identified in only about 1% of 8,270 accommodations

(p. 6) provided under Section 504 of the Rehabilitation Act of 1973. Since passage of the ADA, this pattern of omission has not abated. Most sources mention that provisions of reasonable accommodation apply both to persons with physical disabilities and persons with psychiatric disabilities, but examples are generally limited to discussions of accommodations for physical disabilities.

Further, the confounding conditions of disclosure due to psychiatric stereotyping vitiate the protections and benefits the Act affords: How is someone with a psychiatric disability to be protected from discrimination if the person does not invoke the law by claiming to be covered by the Act, that is, claiming to be mentally ill? One attorney pointed out that

> despite its limitations, the ADA constitutes a cultural as well as legal mandate to include people with disabilities in the social and economic mainstream. While the act is no more likely to completely eliminate the myths, fears, and discrimination faced by people with disabilities than earlier civil rights laws eliminated discrimination based on race, the new legislation will nonetheless contribute to the enormous educational effort needed to combat widespread misinformation and stereotypes about disabilities. (Haimowitz 1991, p. 23)

Therefore, the ADA supports public education to eliminate disability stereotypes. While educational efforts to change attitudes are necessary, they are not sufficient to end social inequality. The following conclusion was drawn from a national cross section of disabled persons conducted by Louis Harris and Associates in 1985: "The story of the disabled is this: If you are shut in, you are likely to be shut out" (Harris 1987, 194–195). Since civil equity is realized through community integration, the ADA can only succeed by opening "doors of opportunity for millions of isolated, dependent Americans to become employees, taxpayers, and welcome participants in the life of their communities" (Dart 1990, 1). For persons with psychiatric disabilities, the ADA may not be able to push open the factory door due to the weight of public prejudice and fear.

Engaging Questions of Justice

There is no way to deny the legacy of hidden tragedy that psychiatric disability provokes in the drama of human relationships. Policy makers can only offer the possibility of help by confronting the totality of what difference encompasses. If the intent of the ADA is to support equality of opportunity for each individual, then the state must stipulate the rights and entitlements of people with widely different needs. In laying the foundation for social change, public policy must channel attention and resources in the direction of improving the quality of living for all people within the context of a society fraught with tensions between equality and difference.

The preceding analysis of the ADA has revealed an essential tension in the politics of difference and equality based on the dynamics of stereotypy. Concurrently, it explored the difficulty in anticipating the changes the ADA will engender. The results of research conducted on policies implemented to redress racial inequalities in American society illustrate that the problems of researching both intended and unintended consequences of social legislation are not new (Coleman et al. 1975; Olzak et al. 1992).

Public research has often demonstrated that human interactions cannot be legislated, nor changes predicted accurately in any social reality. This suggests the value of evaluating public policies in open dialogue where all constituencies can participate in the looking, the finding, and the understanding of the multilayered meanings of social reality. Common ground can only be reached through a deep respect for what differences can teach. The progressive enterprise of civil rights legislation can legitimate critical discourse and create openings in public and private spaces where engagement of questions of justice can take place. That engagement begins with the courage to risk the comforts of an unexamined conscience. Rather than shrink from passion and the energy that passion represents, policy research has the capacity to engage people at a profound personal level and, therefore, represents a potentially dynamic force in the struggle to reshape and reweave the social fabric.

Bob Kafka, a national disability activist, wrote on the day of the signing of the ADA of a question that lingered with him as he traveled back from Washington, D.C. to his home in Texas. Was the ADA the end or beginning? Would the enthusiasm and battles that made the bill possible continue once people went back to their own communities? He concluded as follows:

> I realized that the ADA could be the beginning of a new era in equality for persons with disabilities if we used it aggressively and in concert with other strategies like direct action organizing. If we believe that ADA is the power and we are the recipients of its strength, rather than we are the power and ADA is a tool for us to use, I fear we may still have a long way to go. (Kafka 1990, p. 22)

The reason the ADA is embraced, however ambivalently, by people with psychiatric disabilities is that it provides legal grounds for testing commonsense prejudgments about mental illness. Once we begin to learn about people with mental illnesses, we find that awareness of the type of mental illness has limited value in day-to-day interactions. It may be useful in an everyday situation, to know that, for example, a person experiencing a hypomanic episode may be easily aroused sexually. It may be useful to know that someone with a diagnosis of schizophrenia has had in the past some psychotic experiences. But the simple label ("manic depression" or "schizophrenia") leaves a great deal out of the picture. While differences in diagnosis are important at the level of psychiatric treatment, they may mean little when dealing with a person as a coworker.

Conclusion

While the ADA attempts to repair the historical damage caused by discrimination against people with psychiatric disabilities, it also promotes every person's ability to embrace diversity and feel more comfortable with personal uniqueness. Mental health is evident through the formation of a social identity that is acceptable to oneself and others.

The stereotype of the violent, unpredictable mental patient fulfills the social need to control disturbing thoughts and behaviors by situating violence outside normal human agency. Acknowledging the capacity to perform violent acts in one's "right mind" would demand a fundamental reassessment of normality and human capacity for evil. Human beings have the capacity for a wide range of behaviors, both rational and irrational. In drawing distinctions between people with psychiatric disorders and those without them, we may risk denying the implicit connectedness among people that is based on both difference and commonality.

Employers will be lulled into a false sense of security if they focus their efforts on "keeping the crazies out" and ignore fundamental environmental factors that provoke workplace violence, such as low pay, long hours, high stress at work and home, little chance for advancement, and layoffs. On the other hand, application of the ADA could bring a fuller realization of the commonalities that bind all people and thus improve the workplace environment for everyone. The problems and triumphs of persons with disabilities are universal. Our hope is that the issues raised by this legislation will encourage us all to examine our own lives and arrive at some conclusions about relationships of equality, social well-being, and the law.

Acknowledgments

The final draft of this article is enriched by the comments and editing of earlier manuscripts by Sara Watson, Virginia Hiday, and Sue Estroff. We wish to give special acknowledgment to Sara Watson for her overall collaboration on the organization of the ideas presented. Further, her insights about potential barriers to a true understanding of workplace violence are crucial to our concluding remarks.

Notes

1. For purposes of this chapter, we use the definition of *disability* currently listed in the ADA. Thus any person with a physical or mental impairment that substantially limits her ability to perform essential daily activities, or a person who regards herself or is regarded by others as such, falls within the class of persons to be protected from discrimination.

2. The Senate bill had limited the direct-threat standard to persons with contagious diseases, following the Supreme Court decision in *School Board of Nassau County Florida v Arline*. There the court had held that persons with infectious disease are "otherwise" qualified for employment if they do not pose a "significant risk" of communicating the disease. The decision recognized that "few aspects of handicap give rise to the same level of public fear and misapprehension as contagiousness," and that the law is carefully structured to replace reflexive reactions to actual or perceived handicaps with actions based on reasoned and medically sound judgment (Cole 1990, 2086).

References

Anthony, W., and A. Blanch. 1987. Supported Employment for Persons Who are Psychiatrically Disabled: An Historical and Conceptual Perspective. *Psychosocial Rehabilitation Journal* 11(2): 5–23.

Blauner, R. 1964. *Alienation and Freedom: The Factory Worker and His Industry.* Chicago: University of Chicago Press.

Bogdan, R. 1988. *Freak Show: Presenting Human Oddities for Amusement and Profit.* Chicago: University of Chicago Press.

Campbell, J. 1994. Unintended Consequences in Public Policy: Persons with Psychiatric Disabilities and the Americans with Disabilities Act. *Policy Studies Journal* 22(1): 133–145.

Campbell, J., and R. Schraiber. 1989. *The Well-Being Project: Mental Health Clients Speak for Themselves.* Sacramento: California Department of Mental Health.

Campbell, J., S. Stephan, and A. Loder. 1994. Taking Issue: Putting Violence in Context. Hospital and Community Psychiatry 45(7): 633.

Caras, S. 1994. Disabled: One More Label. *Hospital and Community Psychiatry* 45(4): 323–324.

Cody, P. 1992. Mentally Disabled to Benefit from New Law: Psychiatrists May Play Major Role. *Psychiatric News* 5, 17.

Colbert, N., A. Kalish, and P. Chang. 1973. Two Psychological Portals of Entry for Disadvantaged Groups. *Rehabilitation Literature* 34: 194–202.

Cole, H. 1990. The AIDS Litigation Project: A National Review of Court and Human Rights Commission Decisions. Part 2: Discrimination. *Journal of the American Medical Association* 263(15): 2086–2093.

Coleman, J., S. Kelly, and J. Moore. 1975. *Trends in School Segregation, 1968–1973.* Washington DC: Urban Institute.

Coleman, L. 1984. *The Reign of Error: Psychiatry, Authority, and Law.* Boston:

Beacon Press. I. Combs, and C. Omvig. 1986. Accommodation of Disabled People into Employment: Perceptions of Employers. *Journal of Rehabilitation* 52: 42–45.

Crist, P. A., and V. Stoffel. 1992. The Americans with Disabilities Act of 1990 and Employees with Mental Impairments: Personal Efficacy and the Environment. *The American Journal of Occupational Therapy* 46(5): 434–43.

Dart, J. 1990. ADA: Landmark Declaration of Equality. *Worklife* 3(3): 1.

Estroff, S., and C. Zimmer. 1994. Social Networks, Social Support, and Violence among Persons with Severe, Persistent Mental Illness. In J. Monahan and H. Steadman, eds., Violence and Mental Disorder: *Developments in Risk Assessment.* Chicago: University of Chicago Press.

Estroff, S., C. Zimmer, W. Lachicotte, and J. Benoit. 1994b. The Influence of Social Networks and Social Support on Violence by Persons with Serious Mental Illness. *Hospital and Community Psychiatry* 45(7): 669–678.

Fiedler, L. 1978. *Freaks: Myths and Images of the Secret Self.* New York: Simon and Schuster.

Gardena Valley News. 19 October 1983. An Insane Piece of Legislation. Gardena, CA.

Gostin, L. 1991. Public Health Powers: The Imminence of Radical Change. In Jane West, ed., *The Americans with Disabilities Act: From Policy to Practice.* New York: Milbank Memorial Fund, 268–290.

Haimowitz, S. 1991. Americans With Disabilities Act of 1990: Its Significance for Persons With Mental Illness. *Hospital and Community Psychiatry* 41(1): 23–24.

Harris, L. 1987. *Inside America.* New York: Vintage Books.

Havel, J. 1990. The Struggle to Include Mental Illness. *Worklife* 3(3): 18.

Hiday, V. 1995. The Social Context of Mental Illness and Violence. *The Journal of Health and Social Behavior* 36(2): 122–37.

Kafka, R. 1990. The End or Beginning? *Worklife* 3(3): 22.

Kaufmann, C. 1993. Reasonable Accommodation to Mental Health Disabilities at Work: Legal Constructs and Practical Applications. *International Journal of Psychiatry and Law* 21(2): 153–174.

Kirszner, M. 1990. Employer Participation in Supported and Transitional Employment for Persons with Long-Term Mental Illness. Paper presented at the First Case Management Conference, Cincinnati, OH.

La Fond, J. 1992. *Toward a Working Model of Outcome Measures for The Public Welfare Domain.* Washington DC: National Institute on Mental Health/U.S. Department of Health and Human Services.

Link, B., H. Andrews, and F. Cullen. 1992. The Violent and Illegal Behavior of Mental Patients Reconsidered. *American Sociological Review* 57 June: 275–292.

Link, B., J. Mirotznik, and F. Cullen. 1991. The Effectiveness of Stigma Coping Orientations: Can Negative Consequences of Mental Illness Labeling Be Avoided? *The Journal of Health and Social Behavior* 32(3): 302–320.

Mancuso, L. 1990. Reasonable Accommodation for Workers with Psychiatric Disabilities. *Psychosocial Rehabilitation Journal* 14(2): 5–19.

Monahan, J. 1992a. "A Terror to Their Neighbors": Beliefs about Mental Disorder and Violence in Historical and Cultural Perspective. *Bulletin of the American Academy of Psychiatry and Law* 20: 191–195.

————. 1992b. Mental Disorder and Violent Behavior: Perceptions and Evidence. *American Psychologist* 47(4): 511–521.

Mulvey, E. 1994. Assessing the Evidence of a Link between Mental Illness and Violence. *Hospital and Community* 45(7): 663–668.

National Organization on Disability. 1994. *NOD Survey of Americans with Disabilities.* (910 16th St. NW, Washington, DC 20006.)

Olzak, S., E. West, and S. Shanahan. 1992. Did Desegregation Provoke Racial Conflict in America? Paper presented at the 1992 annual meeting of the American Sociological Association, Pittsburgh, PA.

Stocks, M. 1990. Mary Lee Stocks, M.S.W., L.S.W. In N. Nide, ed., *Yes I Can!* Columbus, OH: AMI of Franklin County.

Swanson, J., and C. Holzer. 1991. Violence and ECA Data. *Hospital and Community Psychiatry* 42(9): 954–955.

Swanson, J., C. Holzer, V. Ganju, and R. Jono Tsutomu. 1990. Violence and Psychiatric Disorder in the Community: Evidence from the Epidemiologic Catchment Area Surveys. *Hospital and Community Psychiatry* 41(7): 761–770.

Tirrell-Wysocki, D. 1990. Douglas Blasted for Stand on Bill He Calls 'Flawed.' Manchester, N.H. *The Union Leader* 4 April: 11.

U.S. Department of Health and Human Services. 1992. Analysis Under the Americans with Disabilities Act (ADA) of the Oregon Reform Demonstration, *HHS News,* 3 August.

West, Jane, ed. 1991. *The Americans with Disabilities Act: From Policy to Practice.* New York: Milbank Memorial Fund.

Yankelovich, Daniel. 1990. *Public Attitudes toward People with Chronic Mental Illness.* Princeton, NJ: Robert Wood Johnson Foundation.

9 Making the ADA Work for People with Psychiatric Disabilities

LAURA LEE HALL

The Americans with Disabilities Act (ADA) outlaws discrimination against people with disabilities in nearly every domain of public life: employment, transportation, communication, recreational activities, and other services. The ADA enjoyed bipartisan support during its sinuous legislative sojourn, winning the president's signature on 26 July 1990. Disability rights advocates celebrated its passage, hailing it as the most sweeping mandate ever invoked against discrimination directed at people with disabilities. In contrast to their coverage of previous disability rights legislation, the news media showered attention on the ADA's passage and milestones during its early implementation. Executive branch agencies lumbered into action, preparing regulations in the prescribed time frame and launching other requisite activities. Businesses geared up for compliance and voiced concerns about the lack of specific guidance, costs, and the risk of litigation associated with this new law. And a new industry emerged, marketing ADA expertise and technical assistance.

Undoubtedly, the ADA is a watershed event in the history of disability rights. The ADA also has captured the attention of mental health advocates, especially in terms of its employment provisions (e.g., Koyanagi and Goldman 1991; Mancuso 1990; Milstein et al. 1991; O'Keefe 1993; Parry 1993; Scallet and Rohrer 1990). The law extends its reach explicitly to many people with psychiatric disabilities. Furthermore, jobs are a matter of particular concern to many people with mental disorders. Employment remains an elusive goal for most people with severe mental disorders, and many employees with a current or past mental health problem apparently guard this as a secret, for fear of the stigma and discrimination attached to these conditions. Reflecting the misperceptions, fears, and lack of information about mental disorders as well as the difficult issues sometimes raised by these conditions—subjectivity of claims, impact on behavior and social interactions at

241

work—some employers have expressed concerns about the ADA's provisions for employing people with psychiatric disabilities (Lechner 1993).

The ADA's ultimate success in helping to end employment discrimination depends upon the effective implementation and enforcement of the law. Among other factors, accurate and relevant information about psychiatric disabilities, employment, and the ADA is prerequisite for this success. What do we know about the nature of psychiatric disabilities? How does this dovetail with the definition of disability in the ADA? What barriers to employment do people with psychiatric disabilities face? How can the ADA help in removing these barriers? How can psychiatric disabilities be accommodated in the work place? The answers to these questions and others, disseminated to employees, employers, advocates, care providers, implementors of the law, and policy makers, will help make the ADA work for people with psychiatric disabilities.

Ongoing congressional interest in the ADA and mental health issues led to a study by the Office of Technology Assessment (U.S. Congress 1994). The OTA report examined current knowledge about psychiatric disabilities and employment in the context of the ADA's requirements, and reviewed federal activities directly or indirectly aimed at promoting the ADA's employment provisions for people with psychiatric disabilities. This chapter highlights three topics discussed in the OTA report: (1) the ADA's definition of disability as it relates to the nature of psychiatric disability; (2) disclosure of psychiatric disability; and (3) useful accommodations for people with psychiatric disabilities.

Defining Disability

Drawing from the Rehabilitation Act, the ADA offers a three-pronged definition of disability with respect to an individual (42 U.S.C. §12102(2)):

1. A physical or mental impairment that substantially limits one or more of the major life activities of such individual

2. A record of such an impairment

3. Being regarded as having such an impairment

After iterating the ADA's disability definition, the EEOC expands on the first prong by defining physical or mental impairment. Mental disorders explicitly are included: "Physical or mental impairment means . . . [a]ny mental or psychological disorder, such as . . . emotional or mental illness" (56 F.R. 35735). Note that the EEOC does not equate mental impairments with a particular diagnostic framework (e.g., the *Diagnostic and Statistical Manual,* third edition, revised). However, many experts contend that it is difficult to envision a mental or emotional impairment that is not coverd by a DSM-III-R diagnosis. "As a practical matter . . . a diagnosis is necessary but not sufficient to cross the impairment threshold in the first prong of the ADA definition" (Bonnie 1993). The EEOC further delimits the notion of impairment in its guidelines, which specify, notably, that an impairment exists even when the condition is completely controlled by medications or other devices. Distinguishing between "impairments and physical, psychological, environmental, cultural, and economic characteristics that are not impairments" is, however, considered paramount. For example, "normal" traits, such as poor judgment or a quick temper, are deemed distinct from impairments (56 F.R. 35741).

Simply having an impairment—any impairment—does not equal having a disability under the first prong of the definition. The ADA further circumscribes the concept of disability by adding that the impairment must "substantially limit one or more of the major life activities." By spelling out "substantially limit" and "major life activities," the EEOC upholds the basic principle that a disability reflects both impairment and functional result. In line with the spirit of the law and the opinion of many advocates, the EEOC's interpretation also asserts that the ADA's protection is for those with "significant," or nontrivial, impairments. However, the guidance offered by the EEOC on these two points is not without critics, including mental health advocates.

The EEOC's regulations state as follows (56 F.R. 35735).

> The term substantially limits means:
>
> (i) Unable to perform a major life activity that the average person in the general population can perform; or
>
> (ii) Significantly restricted as to the condition, manner or duration under which an individual can perform a particular major life activity as compared to the condition, manner, or duration under which the average person in the general population can perform that same major life activity. . . .
>
> The following factors should be considered in determining whether an individual is substantially limited in a major life activity:
>
> (i) The nature and severity of the impairment;
>
> (ii) The duration or expected duration of the impairment; and
>
> (iii) The permanent or long-term impact, or the expected permanent or long-term impact of or resulting from the impairment.

As noted above, this explanation connotes significant impairment. Certain mental disorders, by their very nature, could be considered disabilities under the ADA. The EEOC guidelines state as follows:

> The determination of whether an individual has a disability is not
> necessarily based on the name or diagnosis of the impairment the
> person has, but rather on the effect of that impairment on the life
> of the individual. Some impairments may be disabling for particular
> individuals but not for others, depending on the stage of the disease
> or disorder, the presence of other impairments that combine to make
> the impairment disabling, or any number of other factors. Other
> impairments, however, . . . are inherently substantially limiting. (56
> F.R. 35741)

While not listed, certain mental disorders are, by their nature and definition,
chronic and quite disabling. For example, the DSM-III-R diagnostic criteria
for schizophrenia include severe symptoms (e.g., hallucinations and catatonic
behavior); marked functional impairment, and a duration of at least six
months (APA 1987). People with schizophrenia often suffer a chronic (indeed, lifelong) degenerating course. Certainly the determination of a work
accommodation normally requires more information than a diagnosis, for
mental disorders or other conditions, and some advocates and experts note
that classifying a particular disorder as "severe" or "chronic" can be stigmatizing. However, it is clear that the diagnostic criteria for certain mental
disorders make them, by definition, "inherently substantially limiting." Advice to the EEOC on this point, from experts and advocates, could assist in
delineating diagnoses that fall in this category.

Another point to consider with regard to the definition of "substantially
limiting" is the duration of an impairment. The EEOC, in both its regulations
and guidelines, asserts that the duration of an impairment is an important
consideration in determining whether it is substantially limiting. The guidelines elaborate as follows: "[T]emporary, nonchronic impairments of short
duration, with little or no long-term or permanent impact, are usually not
disabilities" (56 F.R. 35741). The U.S. Department of Justice regulations
for Title II also indicate, in slightly different language, that "short-term or
transitory illnesses are not disabilities if they do not place a substantial limitation on a person's major life activities." Some advocates and experts object
to defining "substantial limitation" in terms of duration or temporal limits
(Jones 1993). While the guidelines do not list a psychiatric impairment as an
example, ("[S]uch impairments may include, but are not limited to, broken
limbs, sprained joints, concussions, appendicitis, and influenza"), conditions
such as short-term depression following the loss of a spouse (a temporally
delimited mental disorder included in the DSM-III-R) will probably not be
considered disabilities under this rationale.

Experts have expressed concern over how impairments that episodically
remit and then intensify fit into the ADA's definition of disability (e.g., Parry
1993). While many major mental disorders are chronic conditions, like other

types of impairments (e.g., multiple sclerosis), symptoms may wax and wane over time. A new chapter for the ADA's *Compliance Manual* on the topic of "Disability" will expressly address this issue. EEOC staff members have indicated that:

> Episodic disorders, which remit and then intensify, may be ADA disabilities. They may be substantially limiting when active or may have a high likelihood of reoccurrence in substantially limiting forms. In addition, such conditions may require a substantial limitation of a major life activity to prevent or to lessen the likelihood or severity of recurrence. Finally, side-effects of medications may be substantially limiting in themselves." (U.S. EEOC 1993)

"Major life activities" is the other defining phrase discussed by the EEOC: An impairment rises to the level of disability if it limits a major life activity. The EEOC defines major life activities in its regulations as "functions such as caring for oneself, performing manual tasks, walking, seeing, hearing, speaking, breathing, learning, and working." The interpretive guidelines provide further comment: "Major life activities are those basic activities that the average person in the general population can perform with little or no difficulty."

Even though the list of major life activities provided by the EEOC is not meant to be exhaustive, many mental health advocates and experts have criticized it, asserting that none of the examples are especially relevant to psychiatric disabilities (e.g., Parry 1993; Haggard 1993). The American Psychological Association's comment on the regulations follows:

> In the listing of "major life activities," the only activity listed which is likely to pertain to people with mental disabilities is "working." "Working" is a very general term and so persons with mental disabilities will be put in the difficult and possibly untenable position of having to prove they are qualified to work at the same time that they have to demonstrate that they are substantially limited in their ability to work in order to be covered by the ADA (APA 1991)

It is important to note that neither the EEOC nor all experts concur with this viewpoint (Liberman 1993). As noted by the EEOC, "In our view, the major life activities of learning, caring for oneself, and performing manual tasks all may be substantially limited by psychiatric disorders or by the side-effects of psychotropic medications" (U.S. EEOC 1993). Advocates' concerns reflect, in part, the fact the people do not generally appreciate how mental disorders can impair a person's functioning. More explicit guidance in terms of mental disorders and related disabilities would undoubtedly be very useful to employers and employees attempting to implement the ADA.

It is widely held that the final two prongs of the ADA's disability definition

are critical for people with psychiatric conditions. It is here that a record
of past impairment or the perception of it is included in the law's definition
of disability. The EEOC defines these concepts in its regulations (56 F.R.
35735):

> "Has a record of such impairment" means has a history of, or has
> been misclassified as having, a mental or physical impairment that
> substantially limits one or more major life activities.
>
> "Is regarded as having such an impairment" means:
>
> (1) Has a physical or mental impairment that does not substan-
> tially limit major life activities but is treated . . . as constituting
> such limitation;
>
> (2) Has a physical or mental impairment that substantially limits
> major life activities only as a result of the attitudes of others toward
> such impairment; or
>
> (3) Has none of the impairments defined (above) . . . but is treated
> by a covered entity as having a substantially limiting impairment.

The law itself, and these regulations and guidelines from the EEOC, reflect
an attitude of zero tolerance for employment decisions based on stereotypes or
discriminatory beliefs. The recognition that the attitudes of others are important contributors to disability was expressed in the often-cited decision of the
Supreme Court in *School Board of Nassau v. Arline* (1987):

> [S]ociety's accumulated myths and fears about ability and diseases
> are as handicapping as are the physical limitations that flow from
> the actual impairment.

The stigma attached to psychiatric disabilities epitomize the problem described by the U.S. Supreme Court. Indeed, the negative attitudes surrounding mental disorders are so strong that job application forms commonly
ask, "Have you had a nervous breakdown?" "Have you ever been hospitalized in a mental institution?" or "Have you ever received treatment for a
nervous or emotional condition?" These questions evince the firmly entrenched belief in our society that mental illness, present or past, is incompati-
ble with work. Research and experience reflected in the subsequent discussions show that this simplistic belief is false.

The ADA should make such questions a thing of the past. Title I of the
ADA prohibits employers from asking applicants about their disabilities, an
important protection for such "invisible" conditions as psychiatric disabilities. Employers are barred from using any source of information about disability status—voluntary medical examinations, educational records, prior

employment records, billing information from health insurance, psychological tests, and others—under the ADA. In addition to prohibiting pre-job-offer medical exams and prescribing a specific mechanism for conducting post-offer exams, the Act also places the burden of proof on employers. While the burden of proving that one is disabled under the ADA's definition lies with the individual alleging discrimination, the EEOC's guidelines indicate that the second prong ''of the definition is satisfied if a record relied on by an employer indicates that the individual has or has had a substantially limiting impairment.'' In terms of the third prong of the definition, the EEOC guidelines require employers to ''articulate a nondiscriminatory reason for the employment action . . . [or else] an inference that the employer is acting on the basis of 'myth, fear or stereotype' can be drawn'' (56 F.R. 35743).

The above discussion reveals several questions about psychiatric disability that are relevant under the ADA. How do mental disorders affect life activities? Which impairments are most limiting? What temporal course of symptoms and functional limitations do various mental disorders run? Many of the legal issues await further governmental guidance and adjudication. However, knowledge from research on the past experience with mental disorders can help inform ongoing ADA implementation.

Mental disorders and their functional sequelae are important to society at large and in the workplace. They are prevalent and costly, if not always appreciated as such.

- People with mental disorders account for 9.7% of the charges filed by individuals with the EEOC between 26 July 1992 and 31 August 1993, representing the second largest population of disabilities. (U.S. EEOC 1993)

- Decreased productivity and lost work days result in the largest cost imposed by mental disorders on society. Of the total estimated cost of $136.1 billion in 1991, $60.0 billion, or nearly 50%, accrues from lost output, exceeding the cost of hospitalization, care-provider consultation, and medication combined. (Rice et al. 1990; NFBR, 1992)

- Data from a recent survey of white-collar workers confirm the high toll of depression on business: 9% of the men and 17% of the women surveyed experienced an episode of major depression during the previous year. More than 50% of employees with depressive symptoms reported work impairments. (Bromet et al. 1990)

- Data from several studies link depression to disability at work (Wells et al. 1989; Broadhead et al. 1990; Johnson et al. 1992). Individuals with depression were shown to experience four times

as many disability days when compared to asymptomatic individuals. In fact, depressive symptoms lead to levels of disability comparable to major heart conditions and exceeding other major medical disorders such as diabetes. Furthermore, simply the presence
of depressive symptoms—far below the threshold for a diagnosis
of major depression—significantly impairs functioning.

Mental disorders encompass a broad range of conditions, classified on the
basis of expressed thought processes or emotions, observed behaviors, physical symptoms, and functional impairments (U.S. Congress 1992). Like physical conditions, mental disorders can range from temporary, relatively minor
conditions to chronic and severely incapacitating disorders. The more common and serious conditions, such as major depression, typically have a
chronic course, with symptoms remitting and relapsing (table 1). While the
causes of many mental disorders have not been determined, ongoing research
is providing more clues about the biological and psychological substrates and
contributors, and in many cases effective treatments, including medication
and psychotherapy, are available.

Just how prevalent are mental disorders? The most recently reported findings from the National Institute of Mental Health's (NIMH's) Epidemiologic
Catchment Area (ECA) program show that more than one in five American
adults has a diagnosable mental disorder in a given year (Regier et al. 1993;
see table 2). Conditions range from the less common disorders of schizophrenia, with a one-year prevalence rate of $1.1 + 0.1\%$, and bipolar disorder,
or manic depression $(1.2 + 0.1\%)$ to exceedingly prevalent mood disorders
involving a major depressive episode $(5.0 + 0.2\%)$ and chronic depressive
symptoms in dysthymia $(5.4 + 0.2\%)$. The ECA data provide another handle
on psychiatric impairments in the United States: service utilization. In one
year 14.7% of American adults—more than 23 million people—sought treatment for mental health problems from mental health specialists, primary care
providers, other human service personnel (such as pastoral counselors), and
peers, families, and friends (table 3).

The ECA data reveal the broad spectrum of diagnoses and service needs
that typify mental health problems in the United States. This diversity will
undoubtedly surface in the workplace, as indicated by requests received by
the Job Accommodation Network, (JAN)[1] which is funded by the President's
Committee on the Employment of People with Disabilities. While 47% of
the inquiries received by JAN related to mood disorders, calls sought information on a wide variety of mental disorders (Judy 1993; see table 4). What
these data on diagnoses, symptoms, and service use do not relate is the notion
of associated disabilities. Data from other research characterize the nature
and prevalence of psychiatric disabilities.

The most recent data concerning the prevalence of psychiatric disabilities and associated limitations in activity are derived from a random survey of adults living in the community (Barker et al. 1992). The results of the 1989 supplement to the Natonal Health Interview Survey indicate that approximately 5 million adults, 3.3 million of them currently in the community—1.8% of the total population—have a serious mental illness, that is, a mental disorder during the past year that seriously interfered with daily life. Nearly 80% of individuals with a psychiatric impairment were limited in taking care of personal needs such as eating, dressing, and bathing (activities of daily living); managing money, doing everyday household chores, and getting around outside the home (instrumental activities of daily living); and in cognitive and social functioning. Impaired functioning translated into employment problems for many. Nearly 50% of the people with serious mental illnesses between the ages of 18 and 69 were either completely unable to work (28.9%) or limited in work (18.4%). A significant fraction of these individuals—23.2%—receive disability payments from the government because of their mental conditions. Clearly, serious psychiatric disability hinders employment, at least full-time work, for many people. No doubt, this reflects both the barriers to employment inherent in society as well as the functional limitations of the conditions themselves.

This study also characterizes specific functional limitations associated with mental disorders and especially relevant to employment. More than 90% of those restricted in work (1) experience problems in social functioning; (2) find it difficult to concentrate long enough to complete tasks; and (3) have problems coping with day-to-day stress (table 5). These data mirror guidelines for assessing disability (e.g., SSA disability determinations), experience in service delivery, and a large body of research. Preliminary data and analyis related to the ADA also echo these findings. Telephone requests handled by the JAN since the ADA's implementation identify stress intolerance as an important functional limitation in mental illness (Judy 1993). Other limitations related by callers include behavioral issues that may contribute to problems in interpersonal relationships and the reduced ability to concentrate. Similarly, in a report on several employed individuals with serious mental disorders, common functional limitations included difficulty concentrating, handling stress, initiating personal contact, and responding to negative feedback (Mancuso 1993).

While conceptual models of psychiatric disabilities embrace the notion of impairment and functional limitation, the relative role of each factor in work and how they act is less clear, indeed controversial. On the one hand, there is a strong current of thought in the psychosocial rehabilitation community, based on research reviews, experiences, and values, which disavows a high correlation between symptoms or diagnosis and employment outcome (Anthony et al. 1990; Anthony and Jansen 1984; NIDRR 1992).

Table 1 Some Serious Mental Disorders

Disorder	Some Common Symptoms	Common Treatment Approaches
Schizophrenia	Delusions, hallucinations; impaired ability to integrate information, to reason, to concentrate, or to focus attention; usually marked by incoherence, bizarre behavior, suspicion, paranoia (psychotic, or "positive," symptoms); dulling of emotions or inappropriateness of emotional response (e.g., a "wooden" personality), apathy, social withdrawal (nonpsychotic, or "negative," symptoms). Symptoms vary widely among patients, combine in different ways, and may change over time.	Treatment usually integrates antipsychotic medications to manage psychosis and supportive psychotherapy aimed at helping individuals understand illness, reduce stress, and enhance coping skills; may involve hospitalization.
Major depression	Complete loss of interest or pleasure in activities; weight gain or loss; insomnia or hypersomnia; slowed or agitated movement; fatigue; intense feelings of guilt or worthlessness; diminished ability to think or concentrate; recurrent thoughts of death or suicide.	Treatment often consists of antidepressant medications and/or various forms of psychotherapy; short-term hospitalization and/or electroconvulsive therapy (ECT) may be required in severe cases.
Bipolar disorder (manic-depression)	Symptoms of depression are described above. Mania is characterized by an extremely elevated, expansive, or irritable mood; inflated self-esteem or grandiosity; decreased need for sleep; extremely talkative and distractible; agitated motion; excessive involvement in pleasurable activities (e.g., buying sprees, sexual indiscretions); psychotic symptoms (delusions and hallucinations) may also occur.	Depressive episodes are treated as above. Manic episodes are usually treated with lithium carbonate. Psychosis may be treated with antipsychotic drugs; hospitalization may be required.

Obsessive-compulsive disorder	Obsessions are recurrent and persistent ideas, thoughts, impulses, or images (e.g., the feeling of being dirty, the desire for symmetry) that although irrational and unwanted, cannot be resisted. Compulsions are repetitive, purposeful, and intentional behaviors (e.g., hand-washing, checking if stove is on or door is locked). The obsessions or compulsions cause marked distress, are time-consuming, or significantly interfere with the person's normal routine.	Treatment currently consists of medication and/or behavioral therapy.
Panic disorder	Hallmark symptom includes sudden, inexplicable attacks of intense fear that is associated with powerful physical symptoms, including shortness of breath, dizziness or faintness, trembling, sweating, choking, nausea, numbness, flushes, chest pain, fear of dying, fear of going crazy, or of doing something uncontrolled. May be associated with agoraphobia—fear of being in public places.	Treatment may include medication (antidepressant and/or antianxiety drugs) or psychotherapy (especially behavioral and cognitive therapies as well as relaxation techniques), or both.

Source: U.S. Congress, Office of Technology Assessment, *The Biology of Mental Disorders*, OTA-BA-538 (Washington, DC: U.S. Government Printing Office, September 1992).

Table 2   One-Year Prevalence of Some Mental Disorders among American Adults

Type of Disorder	One-Year Prevalence Rate (percent ± standard error)	Estimated Number of Persons
Schizophrenic disorders	1.1 ± 0.1	1,749,000
Mood disorders	9.5 ± 0.3	15,143,000
Bipolar disorder	1.2 ± 0.1	1,908,000
Major depression	5.0 ± 0.2	7,950,000
Dysthymia	5.4 ± 0.2	8,586,000
Anxiety Disorders	12.6 ± 0.3	20,034,000
Phobic disorders	10.9 ± 0.3	17,331,000
Panic disorders	1.3 ± 0.1	2,067,000
Obsessive-compulsive disorder	2.1 ± 0.1	3,339,000
Antisocial personality disorder	1.5 ± 0.1	2,385,000
Any mental disorder	22.1 ± 0.4	35,139,000
Any mental/substance-abuse disorder	28.1 ± 0.5	44,679,000

Source: D. A. Regier, W. E. Narrow, D. S. Rae et al., "The de Facto U.S. Mental and Addictive Disorders Service System: Epidemiologic Catchment Area Prospective 1-Year Prevalence Rates of Disorders and Services," *Archives of General Psychiatry* 50: 85–94.

Table 3   American Adults Accessing Mental or Addictive Disorder Services in One Year

Service Setting	Population (%)	Estimated Number of Persons
Specialty mental health/addictive	5.9	9,381,000
General medical	6.4	10,043,000
Other human services	12.5	19,734,000
Voluntary supports	4.1	6,535,000
Total[a]	14.7	23,107,000

Source: D. A. Regier, W. W. Narrow, D. S. Rae et al., "The de Facto U.S. Mental and Addictive Disorders Service System: Epidemiologic Catchment Area Prospective 1-Year Prevalence Rates of Disorders and Services," *Archives of General Psychiatry* 50: 85–94.
[a]Total is less than sum of service in each setting since individuals often access more than one type of provider.

> A number of studies illustrate the lack of relationship between a variety of assessments of psychiatric symptomatology and future ability to live and work independently. . . . Although occasional studies do report a relationship between a type of symptom and rehabilitative outcome . . . the evidence is overwhelming that little or no relationship exists. (Anthony et al. 1990)

On the other hand, some researchers offer evidence of a significant correlation between psychopathology and work performance. For example, data from a recently completed study of nearly five-hundred individuals with various mental and addictive disorders reveal a close correlation between the type and severity of symptoms and work performance and employment (Liberman et al. 1993; Liberman 1989):

> [A]ssessments of psychiatric symptoms and vocational performance on the work capacity evaluation and longitudinal, predictive evaluations of employment status documented that severity of psychiatric symptoms was significantly related to the functional capacity for work in a wide variety of mental disorders. Persons with psychotic disorders performed much more poorly on work performance than those with nonpsychotic disorders. . . . The impairments . . . and negative symptoms . . . [such as] motor retardation, affective flattening, and emotional withdrawal. (Liberman et al. 1993).

These seemingly antithetical results reflect distinct measures of psychiatric symptomatology, measures of work performance, and vocational outcomes. Furthermore, treatment status and individual ability are almost always ignored in these studies as are traditional labor force predictors (e.g., age, gender, ethnicity, and social class), the type or amount of any vocational services that the individual may have received, and prior job history (Cook et al. 1993). Complete resolution of how impairment, functional limitation, and work disability related to one another awaits further research, although we can draw certain conclusions. Data and experience permit the assertions that follow.

Psychiatric symptomatology has practical relevance for employment. As indicated above, some research data suggest an important link between certain psychiatric impairments and work outcomes. Indeed, several scholars, upon review of the research literature, have acknowledged data supporting the link between symptoms and functioning, commenting on the association between severe and chronic conditions, psychotic features, and subsets of symptoms and work (see Cook and Rosenberg, in press; Anthony et al. 1990; Wallace 1993). What does this mean right now, in practical terms? People with psychiatric disabilities as well as care providers, advocates, and other experts

Table 4 Inquiries Received by the Job Accommodation Network on Specific Mental Disorders

Specific Disorder (as specified by caller)	Total Inquiries on Mental Disorders (%)
Bipolar disorder (manic-depression)	30
Depression	17
Schizophrenia	15
Stress/anxiety	11
Phobias	7
Other (personality disorder, post-traumatic stress disorder, obsessive-compulsive disorder)	20

Source: Job Accommodation Network, 1993.

Table 5 Serious Mental Illness, Functional Limitations, and Work

Work limitation status among people 18–69 years of age	Total with serious mental illness (in thousands)	Limited in personal care activities such as eating, dressing, and bathing (% of total)	Limited in instrumental activities of daily living such as managing money, household chores (% of total)	Limited in social functioning (% of total)	Limited in coping with day-to-day stress (% of total)	Limited in concentrating enough to complete tasks (% of total)
Unable to work	829	7.7	48.8	70.4	86.5	72.9
Limited in work	529	2.6	30.2	61.2	80.1	67.2
No current work limitation	1,032	—	4.6	26.8	52.6	21.4
Does not work for other reasons or work-limitation status unknown	485	—	9.8	30.7	54.3	32.0
Total	2,875	2.7	22.9	46.3	67.7	46.5

Source: P. R. Barker, R. W. Manderscheid, G. E. Hendershot et al., "Serious Mental Illness and Disability in the Adult Household Population: United States, 1989," Advance Data From Vital and Health Statistics of the Center for Disease Control/National Center for Health Statistics, 16 Sept. 1992.

note that exacerbation of symptoms may require brief time away from work for treatment. In fact, access to treatment may become paramount.

Many people with psychiatric disabilities will find access to appropriate treatment necessary for maintaining employment. Even experts who highlight the importance of functional and environmental interventions admit that medication, psychotherapy, and/or other clinical interventions are necessary components of care. "Psychiatric treatment and psychiatric rehabilitation procedures ideally occur in close sequence or simultaneously" (Anthony et al. 1990). Results from a recent study of depression reinforce this point. Data from ten major studies of depression treatment revealed that symptom relief significantly improved work function and outcome (Mintz et al. 1992). The authors of the study concluded that "behavioral impairments, including missed time, decreased performance, and significant interpersonal problems are common features of depression that appear to be highly responsive to symptomatically effective treatment given adequate time" (Mintz et al. 1992).

That effective treatment may positively influence work disability must be considered in terms of access. The good news is that there are many effective treatments available for various mental disorders. Recent reviews of the literature confirm the effectiveness of medications, psychotherapeutic interventions, and other approaches. On the downside, access to effective treatment is far from universal. Research and policy analyses point to several barriers to treatment, including limitations on insurance coverage, underrecognition of symptoms by care providers, and inadequate or inappropriate treatment offered by some care providers. No matter how important treatment is for symptom relief and work functioning, without access to it the protections and requirements of the ADA become a moot point.

While important, the relevance of psychiatric symptoms and treatment to employment remains limited and not clearly understood. The precise relationship among impairments, functional limitations, and work is obscure and complex. For example, the course of symptoms over time does not tightly parallel that of functional limitations. An author of one recent review of the data concluded that "diagnoses do not predict rehabilitation outcomes except in the broadest terms, and there are wide variations in outcomes within diagnostic groups" (Wallace 1993). Also, while research data increasingly characterize the nature of cognitive impairments in schizophrenia—including problems with attention, memory, information processing, and other aspects of learning—very little is known about how these specific deficits relate to job performance (Penn et al. 1993; Nuechterlein and Dawson 1984; Wallace 1993). Certainly the presence of even unusual symptoms does not necessarily hamper work performance. A real-world example, shared by a rehabilitation specialist, conveys this last point. A computer programmer, who suffered hallucinations that could be distracting, found that audibly responding to the voices allowed him to continue successfully with his work (Bell 1993). No doubt, the young man's talking to himself appeared unusual to his coworkers, but his work did not suffer.

Clinical treatment can have a paradoxical effect on disability and employment. While effective treatments are available for many mental disorders, they are not a panacea. Medications are not effective for everyone, and some of the most disabling symptoms of mental disorders may resist their effects. In fact, medication has little direct impact that has been measured on such functional issues as interpersonal relationships (Wallace 1993; Armstrong 1993). Furthermore, the side effects of psychotropic medications can prove quite annoying if not outright disabling. Some common side effects of psychoactive medications include dry mouth, constipation, blurred vision, memory difficulties, restlessness, tremor, and sedation. Data from a recent survey of employed individuals with psychiatric disabilities confirm this observation: medication side-effects commonly led to functional difficulties on the job (Mancuso 1993). Similarly, a reviewer of the research literature concluded that while standard or minimal medication dose in schizophrenia was associated with positive work outcomes, a "surprising number of studies [suggested] that higher dose or more consistent neuroleptic treatment might be associated with poorer work outcomes" (Mintz, Mintz, and Phipps 1992).

To focus too exclusively on impairments and their treatment would fail to provide other relevant information on future performance and useful accommodations. As described above, much is known about the functional limitations associated with mental disorders. It is also well known that the way in which affected individuals and others respond to mental disorders can be quite debilitating (Wallace 1993; Bachrach 1992). Individuals with mental disorders can be severely hampered by the demoralization, stigma, and discrimination they so frequently endure. The very degenerative course attributed to severe mental disorders such as schizophrenia is posited to reflect not just the nature of the condition but environmental and social factors as well. And while some symptoms and diagnoses may be statistically related to employment outcome, they do not predict future work performance on an individual basis (Liberman, personal communication; Anthony 1990). Research data consistently show that prior work experience and history are the most reliable indicators of future work performance. As noted in a review of prior research on vocational outcomes among persons with mental disorders,

> one of the most reliable predictors of whether and how well the mentally ill can work is their level of occupational attainment and performance before the onset of their illness . . . Notably, every study that investigated the link between prior work history and future

vocational performance has found a significant, positive relationship between these two variables. (Cook and Rosenberg, in press)

Given the importance of previous work experience and training, it is relevant to note that some of the most severe mental disorders interrupt key aspects of vocational development. For most people, late adolescence and early adulthood are critical periods for building vocational skills and gaining knowledge, via education or early work experience. This is just the time that symptoms of disorders such as schizophrenia first erupt. The resulting disruption of educational achievement is borne out by ECA data. While the educational achievement of people with schizophrenia is comparable to that of others at the start of college, it diverges by the end of college: only 4.8% of individuals with schizophrenia obtain a degree, compared to 17% in the total population (Keith et al. 1991).

What do these data imply for the ADA? Quite bluntly, people with the most severe mental disorders, and often with less education and a checkered work history, are unlikely to achieve competitive employment by virtue of the ADA's passage alone. Individuals with severe psychiatric disabilities will require a broad range of educational, psychosocial, and vocational services to prepare them for the workplace and to help maintain employment. While the ADA is an important tool for fighting the discrimination all too commonly attached to psychiatric disabilities, it is only one piece of the puzzle for people with the most severe conditions.

Several experts have commented that the ADA's impact will be most strongly felt by people with less severe mental disorders:

> There are many people, probably a much larger number, in the work force with less severe conditions or less pronounced functional limitations, who have much to gain from the ADA. It is particularly for their vocational needs that the provisions of the ADA provide a good fit. (Bonnie 1993)

Indeed, data described throughout this section demonstrate the prevalence of diagnosable mental disorders and symptoms among working-age adults. However, much less is known about this population's functional limitations, their employment characteristics, accommodation needs, or even who among this group would be covered under the first prong of the ADA's definition of disability, which refers to individuals with serious or nontrivial disabilities. While courts have been expansive in defining mental impairment per se under the Rehabilitation Act, substantially limiting psychiatric impairments have sometimes been defined more restrictively. Unless questions are answered concerning these less severe conditions (e.g., Which ones are covered? How can such determinations be made?), the ADA is open to excessive subjectivity in claims of psychiatric disability.

Disclosing a Psychiatric Disability

Before an employer provides an accommodation, indeed before the ADA requires one, an applicant or employee must disclose his need. As indicated in the EEOC guidelines,

> employers are obligated to make reasonable accommodation only to the physical or mental limitatons resulting from the disability of a qualified individual with a disability that is known to the employer. Thus, an employer would not be expected to accommodate disabilities of which it is unaware. If an employee with a known disability is having difficulty performing his or her job, an employer may inquire whether the employee is in need of a reasonable accommodation. In general, however, it is the responsibility of the individual with a disability to inform the employer that an accommodation is needed. (56 F.R. 35748)

For many individuals, revealing the presence of a disability is not a voluntary decision. Although the specific impairment and needed accommodations may not be apparent, a person in a wheelchair visibly discloses a disability. This is not the case for many people with psychiatric disabilities, whose impairments are not physically obvious. Thus, disclosure is a deliberate—and often wrenching—decision. Many factors influence the decision to disclose, including awareness of the ADA, perceived pros and cons of disclosure, and practical decisions as to when, how much, and to whom. Almost no empirical data speak to the issue of disclosing psychiatric disabilities to employers, and the EEOC is largely mute on the subject. The following discussion is based on data from preliminary studies and the published or verbally conveyed testimony of various individuals, including consumer/survivors, rehabilitation experts, other mental health advocates, and business representatives.

Employee awareness of the ADA is the gateway to disclosure. Considerable media attention was focused on the passage and early implementation of the ADA, and other facors suggest that at least some individuals with psychiatric disabilities are aware of the ADA. National consumer-run technical assistance centers as well as the national offices of mental health advocacy organizations have advertised and prepared information on the ADA; federal monies have been granted to two private organizations for technical assistance that focuses on the ADA and psychiatric disabilities; and a sizeable proportion of information requests and charges with the Job Accommodation Network and the EEOC, respectively, relate to psychiatric disabilities. In fact, mental

Total charges = 17,377

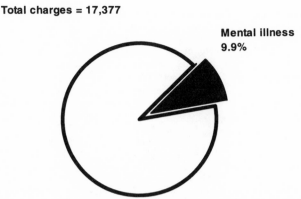

**Mental illness
9.9%**

Figure 1 United States Equal Employment Opportunity Commission ADA Charges, 26 July 1992–31 October 1993. *Note*: Of 17,355 total ADA-related charges filed with the EEOC between 26 July 1992 and 31 October 1993, the second highest percentage—1,710 charges—was related to mental illness. *Source*: U.S. Equal Opportunity Commission, 1 December 1993.

illness accounted for the second highest percentage of charges of discrimination filed with the EEOC in 1992 (figure 1). Some data do suggest, however, that the majority of people with psychiatric disabilities are unaware of the ADA. Informal surveys of ADA and rehabilitation experts as well as representatives of business indicate that many employers and employees have no knowledge of the ADA or its coverage of people with psychiatric disabilities, and data from a recent survey of people with all disabilities showed that less than 30% of them had heard of the ADA (Harris 1993). Given that ADA awareness is a critical prerequisite for disclosing and invoking the protection of the Act, efforts to insure their awareness seem critical. Various entities, including advocacy and consumer groups and business organizations, can work to increase ADA awareness. Information from interviews of attorneys, federal officials, rehabilitation professionals, and people with disabilities indicates that service providers can be critically important for educating people with psychiatric disabilities about the ADA (Solomon 1993).

People with psychiatric disabilities and other experts and advocates testify that the greatest obstacle to disclosure appears to be, ironically, the ADA's intended prey: stigma and discrimination. By disclosing, an individual with a psychiatric disability risks discrimination, teasing or harassment, isolation, stigmatizing assumptions about her ability, and the labeling of all of her behaviors and emotions as pathological (Mancuso 1993; U.S. Congress 1992; Solomon 1993). Charge data from the EEOC seem to confirm the problem that people with psychiatric disabilities have with harassment. While mental illness accounted for less than 10% of all ADA-related charges received by the EEOC by the end of 1992, these conditions made up 12.5% of all ADA-

Table 6   Issues Raised by ADA/Mental Illness Charges with the U.S. Equal Employment
Opportunity Commission: 26 July 1992–31 December 1992

Issues	No. of charges related to mental illness (% of total mental illness charges)	Total number of charges (% of total ADA charges)	Percentage of total ADA charges due to mental illness
Discharge	140 (52.8%)	1,548 (46.1%)	9.0%
Reasonable accommodation	44 (16.6%)	684 (20.4%)	6.4
Harassment	38 (14.3%)	303 (9%)	12.5
Benefits	11 (4%)	114 (3.4%)	9.6
Hiring	36 (13.5%)	516 (15.4%)	7.0
Total	269	3,165	7.9

Source: U.S. Equal Employment Opportunity Commission, 1993.

charges having to do with harassment (U.S. EEOC 1993; see table 6). A
leader in the consumer/survivor movement describes the difficulties and implications of disclosure as follows:

> Disclosure of one's psychiatric history is a very personal matter
> which can aid in one's recovery, allow reasonable accommodation
> under the ADA, and yet can lead to discrimination. . . . Though I
> am presently open about being a mental health consumer/survivor,
> I only arrived at this position through a gradual process. At first I
> did not appreciate the stigma involved in having a psychiatric label.
> This quickly changed. While strolling down a corridor on pass dur-
> ing my first hospitalization, I met a surgeon who was a colleague
> of my father's and whom I had known since childhood. He asked
> me what brought me to the hospital. When I told him I was a
> patient on the psychiatric unit, a look of horror gripped his face
> momentarily. This expression was too quickly replaced by forced
> humor. "That's a good one, Danny," he laughed too loudly and
> briskly walked on. I knew from that time on I was branded and
> should not lightly share information about my hospitalization.
> (Fisher 1993)

As indicated in the above passage, disclosure also may bring benefits.
Experts, advocates, and people with psychiatric disabilities have noted that
openly admitting the diagnosis of a mental disorder may enhance self-esteem,
diminish shame, permit coworkers and others to offer support, and even
empower another individual's revelation (Fisher 1993; Parrish 1989; Mancuso
1993; Link 1993). Data from one retrospective study of people with psychiatric disabilities participating in a vocational rehabilitation program suggested
that refusal to disclose was linked to a shorter job tenure (Fabian et al.
1993). Data from another study indicate that employers who knowingly hire

individuals with mental disorders have a more positive attitude about accommodations and the abilities of such individuals than employers who hire without such knowledge (Cook et al. in press). Evidence also suggests that actual experience with workers who have psychiatric disabilities decreases the perception that mental illness is linked to violence or hostility (Cook et al. in press). An important point for this discussion is that disclosure invokes the protection of the ADA. We can draw at least one conclusion about the decision to disclose or not, with its well known negative consequences and potential positive effects: Research into the impact of disclosure, of which there is a dearth, undoubtedly would inform and improve this process.

The decision to disclose, while exceedingly difficult and important, is only the first of several considerations. What exactly should one disclose, and to whom, and when? The EEOC suggests that "an employee needs to disclose enough information about his disability-related work limitations to support his need for accommodation" (U.S. EEOC 1993). Such goals would rarely necessitate a complete medical/treatment history; indeed, "[b]ecause of the flexible nature of this process, the EEOC does not necessarily require employees to disclose specific diagnoses (psychiatric or otherwise) as a prerequisite for reasonable accommodation" (U.S. EEOC 1993). Employer confirmation of a psychiatric disability, however, as well as EEOC investigation of a charge of discrimination may require more information, including a diagnosis. It is interesting to note that a recent case study found that managers of people with serious psychiatric disabilities, many of whom were referred by rehabilitation services, seem to know surprisingly little about the nature of their employees' impairment (Mancuso 1993). This finding confirms the experience of vocational and psychosocial rehabilitation service providers in general.

In addition to the issue of what to disclose, employees must consider when and how to do so. Should one reveal a psychiatric disability or history of one at the time of application, when hired, when an accommodation is needed, or after perceiving that one has been discriminated against? Again, few research data shed light on this issue. Some people with psychiatric disabilities interviewed in a recent case study recommend waiting to disclose, first establishing oneself as a good employee (Mancuso 1993). While there may be little reason to disclose prior to the need for an accommodation (and no legal requirement) and ample reason not to disclose too soon, waiting too long also may be problematic. As noted at an OTA meeting (Bell 1993),

> from the employer perspective the big concern is that these issues tend to arise when there is some kind of performance problem or conduct problem. Somebody isn't coming to work on Mondays and Fridays or is missing a lot of work, and the employer doesn't know why and begins progressive discipline. And, typically, what happens is the person doesn't say anything relating to a medical condition,

and then when the axe is about to fall and termination is proposed
and is imminent, all of a sudden the person says, "Wait a minute.
All of my problems are due to my medical condition, my disability,
and you can't discharge me."

At that point the employer's emotional reaction typically is,
"Well, you never said anything about this before and it's too late."
Whether or not it's too late is an interesting legal issue for the
EEOC, but that's where it arises and that may be the only reason
why someone may wish to disclose in advance of problems to deal
partly with the legal requirement and partly with the interpersonal
relationship with the employer.

An employee may be uncertain as to who should be told about a psychiatric
disability. The EEOC regulations and guidelines make clear that information
about a disability may be distributed to various individuals, including one's
direct supervisor, who may be responsible for providing the accommodation;
medical or emergency personnel, who may be called on during a crisis;
and government officials investigating compliance with this and other laws.
Guidance about who to contact, initially, in the organization is lacking, as
is research data on who employees approach and what happens as a consequence. Establishing a procedure for disclosure may indeed ease employee
disclosure and assist employers in implementing the ADA. A mental health
advocate and expert explained at a recent meeting (Rubenstein 1993) that

procedure is very important. . . . what the EEOC and others can do
is work on making it possible for people to disclose by designating
an office or individual for an employer who is the reasonable accommodation person, whose job it is to make it comfortable to disclose,
to be a mediating force with supervisors and other employees so
that if disclosure has to occur under the ADA there's a way to make
it easier.

The assumption of this discussion so far, that revealing a psychiatric disability is a voluntary and premeditated action, is not always correct. As noted
in the ADA and relevant regulations and guidelines, information about an
impairment or history of impairment may arise from a variety of sources, such
as medical examinations after an offer of employment or medical insurance or
workers' compensation records. Also, some people with serious psychiatric
disabilities have gaps in employment history or arrest or criminal records that
reflect the course of their condition. The EEOC stresses that "an employer
may not make pre-offer inquiries about disability, and that this prohibition
extends to requests for workers' compensation records, health insurance records, references, or other relevant materials. In terms of criminal records or
gaps in employment or educational history, an employer may inquire about

the employment gaps and criminal records but may not ask whether they reflect the course of disability'' (EEOC 1993). People with psychiatric disabilities who have an arrest or criminal record or employment history gap stemming from their disability may face the dilemma of either not gaining employment because of these factors or having to disclose their disability in order to explain their record. Data on the prevalence of this occurrence and the results would undoubtedly assist people with psychiatric disabilities in making this decision.

Employers may face another difficult situation related to the disclosure of a psychiatric disability. A change in behavior or performance may suggest to a coworker or employer that an employee is suffering from a psychiatric impairment. However, the employee may not recognize such symptoms or may not be willing to admit to having a problem. Indeed, a psychiatric impairment may not exist. Under the ADA, employers are generally forbidden from inquiring about a possible impairment or disability. These limitations on medical inquiries offer important protection to employees with psychiatric disabilities, given the stigma attached to mental disorders, the ease in which our society equates poor job performance or unusual behavior with a mental illness, and the cultural diversity that exists in our society, which makes inferences about individual behavior difficult. However, medical inquiries may be made during employment if they are job-related and consistent with business necessity. This means, according to the EEOC, ''that inquiries must be related to the specific job at issue and must concern performance of an essential function of that job. Under this standard, medical inquiries are allowed . . . if an employee is having difficulty performing essential job functions effectively, an employer may inquire about the difficulties and whether they may have a medical cause without violating the ADA'' (U.S. EEOC 1993).

Providing a Reasonable Accommodation

The ADA charges employers with providing ''reasonable accommodations'' for qualified individuals with disabilities.[2] In fact, the law equates discrimination with not making such accommodations. As the linchpin of the ADA's antidiscrimination requirement, the identification of effective accommodations for people with psychiatric disabilities becomes critical. Unfortunately, it appears that because many people construe a disability as a physical disability, such as being in a wheelchair, accommodations are often viewed in physical terms, such as building a ramp. Many experts and advocates note that employers are unfamiliar with the measures that may assist people with psychiatric disabilities in the workplace (e.g., Edwards 1992–93; Mancuso 1993; Mancuso 1990).

A variey of workplace modifications may assist people with psychiatric disabilities (table 7). Changes to the physical environment, such as a private office or secluded work space, may be useful, but measures such as restructuring job tasks or schedules may often be required. That such "nonphysical" interventions may form "reasonable accommodations" under the ADA is made clear in the law itself, as well as in EEOC regulations and guidelines and reviews of case law interpretations of the Rehabilitation Act. The EEOC regulations include the following:

> Reasonable accommodation may include but is not limited to . . . (j)ob restructuring . . . (or) part-time or modified work schedules. (56 F.R. 35736)

The guidelines go on further to explain:

> (O)ther accommodations could include permitting the use of accrued paid leave or providing additional unpaid leave for necessary treatment. . . . An employer . . . may restructure a job by reallocating or redistributing nonessential, marginal job functions. . . . An employer . . . may also restructure a job by altering when and/or how an essential function is performed. For example, an essential function customarily performed in the early morning hours may be rescheduled until later in the day as a reasonable accommodation to a disability that precludes performance of the function at the customary hour. . . . The reasonable accommodation requirement is best under-

Table 7 Accommodations Enumerated by the President's Committee on Employment of People with Psychiatric Disabilities, 1993

Flexibility
  Providing flexible leave for mental health problems
  Providing self-paced workload and flexible hours
  Allowing people to work at home and providing necessary equipment
  Providing more job-sharing opportunities
  Modifying job responsibilities
  Providing supported employment opportunities
  Keeping the job open and providing a liberal leave policy (e.g., granting up to two months
    of unpaid leave, if it does not cause undue hardship on the employer)
  Providing backup coverage when the employee needs a special or extended leave
  Providing the ability to move laterally, change jobs, or change supervisors within the same
    organization so that the person can find a job that is a good fit
  Providing time off for professional counseling
  Allowing exchange of work duties
  Providing conflict-resolution mechanisms

Supervision
  Providing written job instructions
  Providing significant levels of structure, one-to-one supervision that deals with content and
    interpersonal skills

Table 7 *continued*

Providing easy access to supervisor

Providing guidelines for feedback on problem areas and developing strategies to anticipate and deal with problems before they arise

Arranging for an individual to work under a supportive and understanding supervisor

Providing individualized agreements

Emotional supports

Providing ongoing on-the-job peer counseling

Providing praise and positive reinforcement

Being tolerant of different behaviors

Making counseling/employee assistance programs available for all employees

Allowing telephone calls during work hours to friends or others for needed support

Providing substance-abuse recovery support groups and one-to-one counseling

Providing support for people in the hospital (e.g., visits, cards, telephone calls)

Providing an advocate to advise and support the employee

Identifying employees who are willing to help the employee with a psychiatric disability (mentors)

Providing on-site crisis intervention services

Providing a twenty-four-hour hot-line for problems

Providing natural supports

Physical accommodations at the workplace

Modifying work area to minimize distractions

Modifying work area for privacy

Providing an environment that is smoke-free, has reduced noise, has natural light, easy access to the outside, well-ventilated, and so on

Providing accommodations for any additional impairment (e.g., if employees with psychiatric disabilities have a visual or mobility impairment, they may need such accommodations as large print for written materials, three-wheel scooter, etc.)

Wages and benefits

Providing adequate wages and benefits

Providing health insurance coverage that does not exclude preexisting conditions, including psychiatric disabilities, HIV, cancer, and so on

Permitting sick leave for emotional well-being, in addition to physical well-being

Providing assistance with child care, transportation, care for aging parents, housing, and so on

Providing (specialized) training opportunities

Dealing with coworkers' attitudes

Providing sensitivity training for coworkers

Facilitating open discussions with workers with and without disabilities, to articulate feelings and to develop strategies to deal with these issues

Developing a system of rewards for coworkers without disabilities, based on their acceptance and support for their coworkers with disabilities

Source: President's Committee on Employment of People with Disabilities, 1993.
Note: The items on this list do not necessarily reflect ''reasonable accommodations'' as defined by the ADA.

stood as a means by which barriers to the equal employment opportunity of an individual with a disability are removed or alleviated.
These barriers may . . . be rigid work schedules that permit no
flexibility as to when work is performed or when breaks may be
taken, or inflexible job procedures that unduly limit the modes of
communication that are used on the job, or the way in which particular tasks are accomplished. (56 F.R. 35744)

The legal definition of accommodation thus makes explicit reference to
adjustments that are useful to people with psychiatric disabilities. The question then becomes, What measures could be enacted for a specific individual
with a psychiatric disability in a specific workplace? This question cannot be
answered in the abstract, it must be addressed on an individual basis, taking
into account a particular employee's limitations, abilities, and preferences,
as well as the nature of the job and workplace and the employer's resources.
Enumeration of potentially useful measures, however, could inform this decision-making process. While few data address the impact of such measures
in a competitive work setting, several experts and consumer groups have
begun compiling lists of potentially useful accommodations, based on surveys, experience in vocational rehabilitation, and preliminary studies (Mancuso 1990; Crist and Stoffel 1992; Carling 1993; Fabian et al. 1993; Mancuso
1993; U.S. Department of Health and Human Services 1991; President's
Committee 1993; Haggard 1993; U.S. Department of Labor 1982; Tashjian
et al. 1989).

All of these sources strike similar chords. In general, many accommodations considered useful address the functional limitations commonly associated with psychiatric disabilities: difficulties in concentrating, dealing with
stress, and interpersonal interactions. In order to help an individual concentrate on work tasks, employers may provide a private office or space for
work, so as to limit interruptions and noise; maintain structure through well-
defined daily task schedules; eliminate nonessential or secondary tasks that
may be distracting; and minimize supervisor/coworker interruption of an
employee. Accommodations that may help an employee deal with stress
include increased positive feedback and sensitivity on the part of supervisors
and coworkers; making time or other resources (e.g., support from supervisor
or willing coworker; counseling services at the office) available for contacting
a support network; permitting a self-paced workload, flexible hours, and
work at home (with provision of necessary technical equipment such as a
computer). Orienting supervisors and coworkers may also help ease the difficulties that people with psychiatric disabilities may have with interpersonal
interactions.

Among the most common accommodations listed by experts and people with psychiatric disabilities are those which address symptoms or treatment side effects. All lists compiled include providing leave when short-term hospitalization may be required to control symptoms. Other relevant accommodations include use of part-time work schedules, job-sharing or more frequent breaks (for those who do not have the stamina for full-time work); flexible hours (that take into account medication side effects, such as early morning drowsiness); time off each week for clinical services; and limited night/shift work when contraindicated by symptoms/medication protocol.

Some advocates have suggested that decreased work standards may be a useful accommodation for people with psychiatric disabilities (U.S. Congress 1994; see previous discussion). In fact, evidence from the preliminary study of people with psychiatric disabilities participating in a vocational rehabilitation program show that "accommodations" often involved modifying performance expectations (Fabian et al. 1993). However, case law under the Rehabilitation Act indicates that employers are not required to modify legitimate performance standards to accommodate individuals with psychiatric disabilities (Edwards 1992–93), and the EEOC's statements regarding essential functions of the job indicate that the ADA does not bar legitimate productivity requirements, so long as they are enforced in a nondiscriminatory manner. More directly, "employees with disabilities should not be evaluated on a lower standard or disciplined less severely than any other employee. This is not equal employment opportunity" (U.S. EEOC 1992).

Lists of commonly desired or used accommodations, while they inform the decision-making process, do not supplant the need for case-by-case assessment. Workplaces and jobs vary, as do people with psychiatric disabilities, who include a broad range of talent, ability, and functional limitations. Some individuals with psychiatric disabilities may even be insulted by the suggestion that they cannot work full-time or need very detailed supervision or should be secluded. "I have seen lists of accommodations, and some seem highly unnecessary for most people, such as an accommodation which arranges for a person having difficulty with people to work in isolation" (Schmidt 1993).

The education of supervisors and coworkers as a commonly cited accommodation. People often do not understand psychiatric disabilities, fear them, may feel uncomfortable around people with such a disability, or may simply not know how to act. At least two studies have shown that in-service education in higher educational settings decreases fear of disruption by people with mental disorders (Cook et al. 1993; Wolf and Dipietro 1992). Worksite training or orientation, however, requires careful consideration of methods. For example, coworker training may have a variety of purposes, such as dispelling the ignorance and harmful myths attached to mental disorders or providing information on how best to manage an employee with a psychiatric disability. Obviously, the target audience and information provided in these situations would differ according to its purpose. Another concern involves educating coworkers in a way that is nonstigmatizing for people with psychiatric disabilities. Focusing a training course around an individual employee identified as having a psychiatric disability may be exceedingly stigmatizing (and illegal). Experience with AIDS workplace education programs shows that while effective education need not be costly, more than a pamphlet is required. Data indicate that simply distributing pamphlets or literature on AIDS increased employee anxiety rather than diminishing it (Herold 1989, 1991). Also, a workplace policy defining the company's position and practices as they relate to an employee with a disability appears critical. It guides employee attitudes and behavior, establishes a framework for communication; instructs supervisors on how to address the issue, and lets all employees know where to go for confidential information and assistance.

The EEOC is undecided on the issue of coworker training as a reasonable accommodation. The agency has stated that

> "[o]n the one hand, coworker training would be a requirement imposed on other employees in the workplace, and we have concluded in some instances that requirements imposed on other workers are not reasonable accommodations for the qualified individual with a disability. For example, we do not think that an appropriate accommodation for a qualified individual with a chemical sensitivity disability is to prohibit all other employees from wearing perfume in the office. On the other hand, coworker training could help a qualified individual with a psychiatric disability to interact more effectively with coworkers and therefore to perform his or her essential job functions more effectively. On this basis, an argument could be made that it is a reasonable accommodation. We will continue to consider this issue." (U.S. EEOC 1993)

Many mental health advocates and experts note the parallel between useful accommodations for people with psychiatric disabilities, such as workplace flexibility and an individualized approach to management, and good management practices that would benefit any worker. They assert that adjustments of job demands to the temperament, sensitivities, strengths, weaknesses, and preferences of a valued employee occur frequently. Data from a recent preliminary study support this observation (Mancuso 1993). Several supervisors responded that they made accommodations to employees with psychiatric disabilities "because it made good business sense and because they made such modifications for any employee who needed them.'' Data from another recent study indicate that those who already employ persons with psychiatric disabilities are quite knowledgeable about the needs of these workers for accommodation, have more positive attitudes, and may be quite open to accommodating these workers if need be: exposure is a critical element (Cook et al. in press). The apparent routine nature of such management practices is paradoxical and potentially problematic. Employers who are familiar with accommodations that may be useful for people with psychiatric disabilities do not equate the concept with common management practices. Also, some accommodations, such as working at home or flexible hours, which may be necessary for a person with a psychiatric disability to perform his job are desired by many employees. Coworkers may resent such special treatment, especially if the employee with an invisible disability has disclosed it to his supervisor alone, and not to fellow coworkers. Data from a preliminary study have suggested that people with psychiatric disabilities can suffer negative social and/or personal consequences from receiving accommodations in the workplace, in part because of the general desirability of such accommodations. Perhaps the most troublesome legal issue emerges when an accommodation conflicts with a collective bargaining agreement. Shift work, office space, and leave time, all issues that may arise when accommodating people with psychiatric disabilities, are often dealt with in collective bargaining agreements. The law and EEOC regulations and guidelines have not fully addressed the overlap between collective bargaining agreements and reasonable accommodations. Clearly, further guidance is needed in managing such complexities and conflicts. The EEOC is now developing policy about reasonable accommodations and undue hardship in the context of collective bargaining agreements.

While the accommodations described so far form an important resource for employers and employees, as emphasized in this chapter, the information was not derived from carefully controlled research. Questions about applicability, effectiveness, preference, and impact on the workplace are largely unaddressed. For example, many of the listed accommodations stem from the experience of people with the most severe conditions, who receive a high density of services and support; whether such accommodations generalize to others with psychiatric disabilities in the competitive work environment is unknown.

The ADA does not require businesses to enact every accommodation that an employee requests. An employer need only accommodate qualified employees with disabilities, and even this requirement is overridden if the accommodation imposes an undue hardship. As stated in the EEOC regulations,

it is unlawful for a covered entity not to make reasonable accommodation to the known physical or mental limitations of an otherwise
qualified applicant or employee with a disability, unless such covered entity can demonstrate that the accommodation would impose
an undue hardship on the operation of its business. (56 F.R. 35737)

An "undue hardship" refers to significant difficulty or expense incurred
by a covered entity. Factors to be considered in determining an undue hardship include the following:

- The nature and net cost of the accommodation needed under this
  part, taking into consideration the availability of tax credits and deductions, and/or outside funding;
- The overall financial resources of the facility or facilities involved
  in the provision of the reasonable accommodation, the number of
  persons employed at such facility, and the effect on expenses and
  resources;
- The overall financial resources of the covered entity, the overall
  size of the business . . . with respect to the number of its employees, and the number, type, and location of its facilities;
- The type of operation or operations of the covered entity, including the composition, structure, and functions of the work force of
  such entity, and the geographic separateness and administrative or
  fiscal relationship of the facility or facilities in question to the covered entity; and
- The impact of the accommodation upon the operation of the facility, including the impact on the ability of other employees to perform their duties and the impact on the facility's ability to conduct
  business. (56 F.R. 35736)

Many claim that the cost of accommodating people with psychiatric disabilities is negligible. The source of this often-stated assertion is a study of the
practices of two thousand Federal contractors under the Rehabilitation Act
(U.S. Department of Labor 1982). In fact, the survey data indicated that half
of the accommodations made for all types of disabilities were cost-free; another 30% cost less than $500. Notably, the cost-free accommodations (e.g.,
changes in management practices) were among those most frequently used
for people with psychiatric disabilities. These cost data, however, are not
comprehensive. Estimates did not include the cost of extended leaves of
absence,[3] increased supervision, or worksite training. Certainly, these accommodations can represent a significant expenditure, especially for smaller companies without extensive management resources or a large workforce to ab-
sorb demands. Advocates and other experts increasingly recognize the more
elusive nature of costs for accommodating people with psychiatric disabili-

ties. As recently acknowledged by the Job Accommodation Network (Judy 1993): "Costs usually are $0 in terms of purchasing equipment. Costs come in terms of training, absenteeism, and lost productivity." And Mancuso (1990) notes that costs may be sustained over time: "[S]uch accommodations have the disadvantage of requiring sustained changes in practice over time. This stands in contrast to one-time, physical adaptations such as raising the height of a desk to accommodate a worker using a wheelchair." Research is needed to ascertain the costs of accommodating people with psychiatric disabilities.

The EEOC's guidance on undue hardship goes beyond dollars, as indicated above: " 'Undue hardship' refers to any accommodation that would be unduly costly, extensive, substantial, or disruptive." This does not translate into accommodating misperceptions and ignorance, however.

> It should be noted . . . that the employer would not be able to show undue hardship if the disruption to its employees were the result of those employees' fears or prejudices toward the individual's disability and not the result of the provision of the accommodation. Nor would the employer be able to demonstrate undue hardship by showing that the provision of the accommodation has a negative impact on the morale of its other employees but not on the ability of these employees to perform their jobs. (56 F.R. 35752)

While outright stigma and prejudice are not valid excuses for discrimination, accommodating aberrant or unusual behavior raises some difficult issues. Most lists of accommodations cited in this chapter recognize that increased tolerance of unusual behavior is desirable. Some of the sources include conflict-resolution counseling as a useful accommodation. The EEOC provides no explicit guidance on this issue. Case law under the Rehabilitation Act generally limits the employer's responsibility to accommodate disruptive behavior. Review of court decisions under the Rehabilitation Act led one legal scholar to the conclusion that "when the employee's mental disability leads to episodes of disruptive behavior, most decisions require little accommodation on the part of the employer under the Rehabilitation Act. . . . The holdings in these cases reflect that inappropriate behavior justifies adverse action, if the same action would have been taken in the absence of disability" (Edwards 1992–93).

How the ADA deals with supported employment services may be critical for people with severe psychiatric disabilities. Research data and experience suggest that supported employment can assist many individuals to maintain competitive employment (e.g., Tashjian et al. 1989). However, preliminary data indicate that neither employers nor people with psychiatric disabilities view supported employment as a required accommodation (Mancuso 1993). And the EEOC draws a careful distinction between the two:

The term ''supported employment,'' which has been applied to a wide variety of programs to assist individuals with severe disabilities in both competitive and noncompetitive employment, is not synonymous with reasonable accommodation. Examples of supported employment include modified training materials, restructuring essential functions to enable an individual to perform a job, or hiring an outside profession (''job coach'') to assist in job training. Whether a particular form of assistance would be required as a reasonable accommodation must be determined on an individualized, case-by-case basis.

While the ADA may require some large employers to provide a job coach or other supported employment service as an accommodation, undoubtedly many employers, especially smaller businesses, will not be so mandated, given the cost. Alternate sources of funding for supported employment services may prove critical for some people with severe psychiatric disabilities. The EEOC, in its guidance, explicitly permits alternative funding streams:

If the employer or other covered entity can show that the cost of the accommodation would impose an undue hardship, it would still be required to provide the accommodation if the funding is available from another source, e.g., a State vocational rehabilitation agency, or if Federal, State, or local tax deductions or tax credits are available to offset the cost of the accommodation.

These guidelines specify two potential sources for funding: the Vocational Rehabilitation program and tax incentives offered to businesses. The U.S. Congress has mandated the Federal-State Vocational Rehabilitation program to gear supported employment services to people with the most severe disabilities and to dovetail these efforts with the requirements of the ADA. In fiscal year 1993, the federal government provided nearly $2 billion in grants to the states for vocational rehabilitation programs; another $32 million was aimed at the development of collaborative programs to provide supported employment programs. Although forty-two state VR agencies have funded supported employment programs since 1985, people with psychiatric disabilities can find it difficult to obtain those services (Tashjian et al. 1989; Reznicek and Baron 1991). The challenge remains to gear supported employment services to people with psychiatric disabilities and for employers to tap into such services, through state VR programs, mental health agencies, and other providers.

Three types of federal tax assistance are available to businesses to reduce the costs of accommodating people with disabilities in the workplace. Under section 51 of the Federal Internal Revenue Tax Code, businesses may be eligible for a Targeted Jobs Tax Credit of 40% of up to $6,000 of an employee's first year of wages when hiring people with disabilities and others with special employment needs. Under section 190 of the Internal Revenue Tax Code, businesses may be eligible for a tax deduction of up to $15,000 for costs incurred to remove architectural and transportation barriers from the workplace. And, a few months after the ADA was passed, Congress created a new tax credit, specifically aimed at small businesses. The Omnibus Reconciliation Act of 1990 (P.L. 101-508) added section 44 to the Federal Internal Revenue Tax Code, allowing eligible small businesses a tax credit equal to one-half of expenditures in excess of $250 but not greater than $10,250 to reduce the costs of providing access to people with disabilities in the workplace. In general, these methods of tax assistance have rarely if ever been applied to the accommodation of people with psychiatric disabilities.

Summary and Conclusions

The ADA represents a significant advance in the history of disability rights. The language of the law, the regulations and guidelines offered by the EEOC, experience with the Rehabilitation Act of 1973, the activities of employers and employees in implementing the ADA, and technical assistance efforts all guide the ADA's implementation. Nonetheless, employers and people with psychiatric disabilities have concerns about the law and its implementation. Employers fear the costs of implementation and liability under the law and want more specific guidance as to their responsibilities. People with psychiatric disabilities fear that the language of the law and relevant guidelines often do not speak to their needs. Indeed, inadequate knowledge of the relationships between psychiatric disabilities and employment coupled with few efforts to apply available knowledge of the requirements of the ADA are major impediments to the law's implementation. In the absence of further research and guidance, employers and people with psychiatric disabilities are handicapped in exercising their rights and responsibilities under the law.

Given that the current levels of guidance, technical assistance, and research activities are unlikely to optimally assist employers and people with psychiatric disabilities in implementing the ADA, there is an ongoing need to gather and distribute information on psychiatric disabilities. This need reflects several factors: Psychiatric disabilities are still poorly understood and greatly stigmatized in our society. These conditions can be complex; they can be difficult to assess in an objective fashion, and, with their impact on behavior and social interactions, they sometimes raise difficult issues for employers. Limited federal resources and the low priority historically assigned to the topic of employment and mental disorders have also constrained research and technical assistance efforts.

People with psychiatric disabilities and employers are the ultimate targets of guidance, technical assistance, and education. How can these audiences be reached? Organizations already providing technical assistance to businesses and people with disabilities, including the EEOC, the National Institute on Disability and Rehabilitation Research (NIDRR), and the National Council on Disabilities, can better incorporate information on psychiatric disabilities. There are other targets that would help as well:

- Mental health advocacy organizations: All mental health advocacy organizations assert the importance of employment or meaningful activity for people with psychiatric disabilities. Expanding on current ties with consumer groups, the Community Support Program funded by the Center for Mental Health Services (CMHS), the two Rehabilitation Research and Training Centers supported jointly by NIDRR and the CMHS, the two national consumer self-help centers funded by the CMHS, and the DEPRESSION Awareness, Recognition, and Treatment (D/ART) program funded by the National Institute of Mental Health (NIMH) could provide information on the ADA in the form of materials and training sessions.

- Employee assistance programs (EAPs) and other human resources professionals: Many mid- and large-sized companies have EAPs and/or other human resource offices, whose responsibilities include health education, the provision of or referral for counseling services, disability management, and ADA implementation. These managers and service providers clearly need and are prime targets for information on psychiatric disabilities. The NIDRR, with its grant to the Washington Business Group on Health, the NIMH's D/ART program have already begun targeting these groups. Continued and expanded efforts could build on this foundation.

- Private and state-affiliated care providers: Mental health care providers and advocates in the private sector and state mental health and protection and advocacy agencies interact with individuals with psychiatric disabilities, and they are a potentially useful conduit for information about the ADA. Care providers generally lack knowledge about the ADA. Federal mental health agencies could develop professional training materials and disseminate them at national and regional meetings sponsored by the federal government and professional societies. Also, materials and information could be disseminated in cooperation with state mental health and protection and advocacy agencies through the granting mechanism of the CMHS.

There is another critical target requiring information on psychiatric disabilities: the EEOC field offices, which are responsible for investigating charges of discrimination. Many lack any information on psychiatric disabilities. Federal mental health agencies, especially the CMHS, could assist the EEOC by providing baseline information and by linking field offices with resources in state and community mental health centers and advocacy groups. These local resources could then provide seminars for the field offices in their communities and, perhaps more important, form a network of local experts to which EEOC investigators could turn when specific cases arise.

Several topics (not all discussed here) require further guidance from the EEOC as well as experts, representatives of businesses, and people with psychiatric disabilities:

- The impact of and mechanisms for disclosing a psychiatric disability
- How psychiatric disabilities limit life activities and how such limitations can be assessed
- The identification of behavioral and social requirements on the job
- Accommodating difficult or threatening behavior
- Issues surrounding access to and potential requirement of psychotropic medication or other treatment.

Workshops focused on such topics would be a useful first step. A fair and full exploration of these specific topics would include the perspective and expertise of legal experts and the EEOC, experts in psychiatric disabilities, people with psychiatric disabilities, and employers. The workshop discussions could inform ongoing technical assistance activities as well as official EEOC guidance.

Finally, this analysis identifies many research questions (see table 7). These questions require different types of research approaches, including the following:

- Descriptive research, aimed at ascertaining current issues and practices (e.g., typical approaches to disclosure; the prevalence of violence and mental disorders in the workplace)
- Evaluation studies, which would assess the effectiveness and costs of interventions or procedures (e.g., the impact of coworker education or disclosure; the net costs of accommodating psychiatric disabilities; the effectiveness of stress-reduction techniques in accommodating people with psychiatric disabilities)
- Hypothesis-driven research aimed at clarifying such issues as the confluence of factors involved in the path from impairment to work disability, and the validity of functional assessment techniques.

Clearly, this research agenda falls under the jurisdiction of NIDRR, NIMH, and CMHS. Workable communication among agencies is required to avoid overlap, to assist in collaboration, and to ensure that new information flows among the research agencies as well as to those enforcing the law and providing technical assistance.

Notes

1. The Job Accommodation Network is a government-funded technical assistance program aimed at offering employers and employees practical advice on how to accommodate disabilities in the workplace.

2. The ADA calls for accommodation in three contexts: during employee selection, on-the-job, and in terms of benefits and privileges of employment. This section focuses on the accommodation of employees on-the-job.

3. Employer provision of unpaid medical leave, which may be a reasonable accommodation under the ADA, also may be required of employers with fifty employees or more by the Family and Medical Leave Act. Thus, even if unpaid medical leave is deemed too costly to be reasonable under the ADA, it may be required by the Family and Medical Leave Act.

References

American Psychiatric Association. 1987. *Diagnostic and Statistical Manual of Mental Disorders*. 3d ed., (DSM-III-R). Washington, DC: APA.

American Psychological Association. 1991. Letter to U.S. Equal Employment Opportunity Commission, 29 April.

Anthony, W. A., and M. A. Jansen. 1984. Predicting the Vocational Capacity of the Chronically Mentally Ill: Research and Policy Implications. *American Psychologist* 39: 537–44.

Anthony, W., M. Cohen, and M. Farkas. 1990. *Psychiatric Rehabilitation*. Boston, MA: Center for Psychiatric Rehabilitation.

Armstrong, H. E. 1993. Review of Psychosocial Treatment for Schizophrenia. In D. L. Dunner, ed., *Current Psychiatric Therapy*. Philadelphia, PA: W. B. Saunders.

Bachrach, L. L. 1992. Psychosocial Rehabilitation and Psychiatry in the Care of Long-Term Patients. *American Journal of Psychiatry* 149: 1455–1463.

Barker, P. R., R. W. Manderscheid, G. E. Hendershot et al. 1992. Serious Mental Illness and Disability in the Adult Household Population: United States, 1989. *Advance Data from Vital and Health Statistics of the Centers for Disease Control/National Center for Health Statistics* no. 218 (16 September).

Bell, C. G. 1993. Attorney, Jackson, Lewis, Schnitzler and Krupman, Washington, DC. Remarks at Americans with Disabilities Act, Mental Illness, and Employment, a workshop sponsored by the Office of Technology Assessment, U.S. Congress, 21 April.

Bonnie, R. J. 1993. Visiting Professor of Law, Cornell Law School, Ithaca, NY, personal communication, 1 October.

Broadhead, W. E., D. G. Blazer, L. K. George et al. 1990. Depression, Disability Days, and Days Lost from Work in a Prospective Epidemiologic Survey. *Journal of the American Medical Association* 264: 2524–2528.

Bromet, E. J., D. K. Parkinson, E. C. Curtis et al. 1990. Epidemiology of Depression and Alcohol Abuse/Dependence in a Managerial and Professional Work Force. *Journal of Occupational Medicine* 32: 989–995.

Carling, P. J. 1993. Reasonable Accommodations in the Work Place for Individuals with Psychiatric Disabilities.'' *Consulting Psychology Journal,* Research and Practice, Special Issue (April): Implications of the Americans with Disabilities Act of 1990 for Psychologists, ed. J. O'Keeffe.

Cook, J. A., and H. Rosenberg. In press. Predicting Community Employment among Persons with Psychiatric Disability: A Logistic Regression Analysis. *Journal of Rehabilitation Administration.*

Cook, J. A., L. Razzano, M. Straiton et al. In press. Cultivation and Maintenance of Relationships with Employers of Persons with Psychiatric Disabilities. *Psychosocial Rehabilitation Journal.*

Cook, J. A., J. Yamaguchi, and M. L. Solomon. 1993. Field-Testing a Post-Secondary Faculty In-Service Training for Working with Students Who Have Psychiatric Disabilities. *Psychosocial Rehabilitation Journal* 17: 157–169.

Crist, P. A. H., and V. C. Stoffel. 1992. The Americans with Disabilities Act of 1990 and Employees with Mental Impairments: Personal Efficacy and the Environment. *American Journal of Occupational Therapy* 46: 434–443.

Edwards, M. H. 1992–93. The ADA and the Employment of Individuals with Mental Disabilities. *Employee Relations Labor Journal* 18: 347–389.

Fabian, E. S., A. Waterworth, and B. Ripke. 1993. Reasonable Accommodations for Workers with Serious Mental Illness: Type, Frequency, and Associated Outcomes. *Psychosocial Rehabilitation Journal* 17: 163–172.

Fisher, D. B. 1993. Disclosure, Discrimination, and the ADA. Paper presented at conference: Rehabilitation of Children, Youth, and Adults with Psychiatric Disabilities, Tampa, FL, January 1993.

Haggard, L. K. 1993. "Reasonable Accommodation of Individuals with Mental Disabilities and Psychoactive Substance Use Disorders Under Title I of the Americans with Disabilities Act." *Journal of Urban and Contemporary Law* 43: 343–390.

Harris, Louis and Associates. 1993. Attitudes of Disabled People on Politics and Other Issues. New York: Louis Harris and Associates.

Herold, D. M. 1989. AIDS in the Workplace: What Georgia Workers Are Thinking. Paper presented at conference: Managing AIDS in the Work Place, sponsored by Georgia Institute of Technology, Atlanta, GA, January 1989.

———. 1991. Worksite AIDS Education and Attitudes towards People With the Disease. Manuscript.

Johnson, J., M. M. Weissman, and G. L. Klerman. 1992. Service Utilization and Social Morbidity Associated with Depressive Symptoms in the Community. *Journal of the American Medical Association* 267: 1478–1483.

Jones, N. L. 1993. Legislative Attorney, American Law Division, Congressional Research Service, Library of Congress, Washington, DC. Personal communication.

Judy, B. 1993. Executive Director, Job Accommodation Network. Remarks at Americans with Disabilities Act, Mental Illness, and Employment, a workshop sponsored by the Office of Technology Assessment, U.S. Congress, 21 April.

Keith, S. J., D. A. Regier, and D. S. Rae. 1991. Schizophrenic Disorders. In L. N. Robins, and D. A. Regier, eds., *Psychiatric Disorders in America: The Epidemiologic Catchment Area Study.* New York: The Free Press.

Koyanagi, C., and H. Goldman. 1991. *Inching Forward: A Report on Progress Made in Federal Mental Health Policy in the 1980s.* Alexandria, VA: National Mental Health Association.

Lechner, W. 1993. Manager, Research and Policy, National Federation of Independent Business, Washington, DC. Personal communication.

Liberman, R. P. 1989. *Psychiatric Symptoms and the Functional Capacity for Work: Provisional Final Report.* Research Grant No. 10-p-98193-9004 from the Social Security Administration (23 March).

Liberman, R. P. 1993. Professor of Psychiatry, UCLA School of Medicine and Director, Clinical Research Center for Schizophrenia and Psychiatric Rehabilitation, Camarillo, CA. Personal communication.

Liberman, R. P., J. Mintz, H. K. Massel et al. 1993. Psychopathology and the Functional Capacity for Work. Abstract provided to OTA.

Ling, B. G. 1987. Understanding Labelling Effects in the Area of Mental Disorders: An Assessment of the Effects of Expectations of Rejection. *American Sociological Reviews* 52: 96–112.

———. Associate Professor of Public Health, Division of Epidemiology, Columbia University, New York. Personal communication.

Link, B. G., F. T. Cullen, J. Mirotznik et al. 1992. The Consequences of Stigma for Persons with Mental Illness: Evidence from the Social Sciences. In P. J. Fink and A. Tasman, eds., *Stigma and Mental Illness.* Washington, DC: American Psychiatric Press.

Mancuso, L. L. 1990. Reasonable Accommodation for Workers with Psychiatric Disabilities. *Psychosocial Rehabilitation Journal* 14 (2): 3–19.

———. 1993. *Case Studies on Reasonable Accommodations for Workers with Psychiatric Disabilities.* Sacramento, CA: California Department of Mental Health.

Milstein, B., L. Rubenstein, and R. Cyr. 1991. The Americans with Disabilities Act: A Breathtaking Promise for People with Mental Disabilities. *Clearinghouse Review* (March): 1240–1249.

Mintz, J., L. I. Mintz, M. J. Arruda et al. 1992. Treatments of Depression and the Functional Capacity to Work. *Archives of General Psychiatry* 49: 761–768.

Mintz, J., L. I. Mintz, and C. C. Phipps. 1992. Treatments of Mental Disorders and the Functional Capacity to Work. In R. P. Liberman, ed., *Handbook of Psychiatric Rehabilitation.* New York: Macmillan.

National Foundation for Brain Research. 1992. *The Costs of Disorders of the Brain.* Washington, DC: NFBR.

National Institute on Disability and Rehabilitation Research. 1992. Strategies to Secure and Maintain Employment for Persons with Long-Term Mental Illness. Consensus Validation Conference, Washington, DC, September.

Nuechterlein, K. H., and M. E. Dawson. 1984. Information Processing and Attentional Functioning in the Developmental Course of Schizophrenic Disorders. *Schizophrenia Bulletin* 10: 160–203.

O'Keeffe, J. 1993. Disability, Discrimination, and the Americans with Disabilities Act. *Consulting Psychology Journal: Practice and Research* 45: 3–9.

Parrish, J. 1989. The Long Journey Home: Accomplishing the Mission of the Community Support Movement. *Psychosocial Rehabilitation Journal* 12: 107–124.

Parry, J. W. 1993. Mental Disabilities under the ADA: A Difficult Path to Follow. *Mental and Physical Disability Law Reporter* 17: 100–112.

Penn, D. L., A. J. Willem Van Der Does, W. D. Spaulding et al. 1993. Information Processing and Social Cognitive Problem Solving in Schizophrenia: Assessment of Interrelationships and Changes Over Time. *Journal of Nervous and Mental Disease* 181: 13–20.

President's Committee on Employment of People with Disabilities. 1993. Personal communication.

Regier, D. A., W. E. Narrow, D. S. Rae et al. 1993. The de Facto U.S. Mental and Addictive Disorders Service System: Epidemiologic Catchment Area Prospective One-Year Prevalence Rates of Disorders and Services. *Archives of General Psychiatry* 5: 85–94.

Reznicek, I., and R. C. Baron. 1991. *Vocational Rehabilitation and Mental Health Systems in Collaboration: An Assessment of State, Local, and Program Initiatives on Behalf of Persons with Long-Term Mental Illness (Final Report/Draft)*. Philadelphia, PA: Matrix Research Institute.

Rice, D. P., S. Kelman, L. S. Miller et al. 1990. *The Economic Costs of Alcohol and Drug Abuse and Mental Illness*. Report (1985) submitted to the Office of Financing and Coverage Policy, Alcohol, Drug Abuse, and Mental Health Administration, U.S. Department of Health and Human Services. San Francisco, CA: Institute for Health and Aging, University of California.

Rubenstein, L. R. 1993. Director, Bazelon Center for Mental Health Law, Washington, DC. Remarks at Americans with Disabilities Act, Mental Illness, and Employment, a workshop sponsored by the Office of Technology Assessment, U.S. Congress, 21 April.

Scallet, L. J., and C. F. Rohrer. 1990. *Analysis: Americans with Disabilities Act and Mental Health*. Washington, DC: Mental Health Policy Resource Center.

Schmidt, J. R. 1993. Former Director, Fountain House. Personal communication.

Solomon, M. L. 1993. Is the ADA "Accessible" to People with Psychiatric Disabilities? *Journal of Rehabilitation Administration* (August): 109–117.

Tashjian, M. D., B. J. Hayward, S. Stoddard et al. 1989. *Best Practice Study of Vocational Rehabilitation Services to Severely Mentally Ill Persons*. Washington, DC: Policy Study Associates. Prepared for the Rehabilitation Services Administration, U.S. Department of Education, April.

U.S. Congress, Office of Technology Assessment. 1992. *The Biology of Mental Disorders*. OTA-BA-538. Washington, DC: GPO.

———. 1994. *The Americans with Disabilities Act, Employment, and Psychiatric Disabilities*. Washington, DC: GPO.

U.S. Department of Health and Human Services. 1991. Report for Public Health Service, Substance Abuse and Mental Health Services Administration, Center for Mental Health Services, Community Services Program. *Reasonable Accommodations for People with Psychiatric Disabilities*. Prepared by J. Parrish, March.

U.S. Department of Labor. 1982. *A Study of Accommodations Provided to Handi-*

capped Employees by Federal Contractors, Final Report. Prepared by Berkeley Planning Associates, Contract No. J-(-E1-0009). Washington, DC: GPO.

U.S. Equal Employment Opportunity Commission. 1992. *A Technical Assistance Manual on the Employment Provisions (Title I) of the Americans with Disabilities Act.* Washington, DC: GPO.

————. 1993a. Staff communication, 14 October.

————. 1993b. Staff communication, 10 November.

Wallace, C. J. 1993. *Psychiatric Rehabilitation: Summary for NIMH.* Draft report.

Washington Business Group on Health/Institute for Rehabilitation and Disability Management. 1992. *The Annual Review of Disability Management.* Ed. K. A. Kirchner and K. A. Tanasichuk. Washington, DC: Washington Business Group on Health.

Wells, K. B., A. Stewart, and R. D. Hays. 1989. The Functioning and Well-Being of Depressed Patients: Results of the Medical Outcomes Study. *Journal of the American Medical Association* 262: 914–919.

Wolf, J., and S. DiPietro. 1992. From Patient to Student: Supported Education Programs in Southwest Connecticut. *Psychosocial Rehabilitation Journal* 15: 61–68.

10 Mental Disabilities, Equal Opportunity, and the ADA

NORMAN DANIELS

Mental and physical disabilities achieve parity in the legal protections afforded them through the Americans with Disabilities Act (ADA), at least on paper if not in practice. No such parity in health care benefits was recognized in President Clinton's Health Security Act, or in any of the alternatives, even though members of the Benefits and Ethics Working Groups advising the White House Health Care Task Force urged parity. Instead the plan only promised that "future savings" in the system would be used to establish parity of benefits early in the next millenium ("and the check is in the mail"). Strong arguments for parity in both contexts derive from a commitment to protecting fair equality of opportunity. In both settings, it is the impairment of opportunity that matters, not whether its etiology lies in mental rather than physical disease or disability (Daniels 1985).

In what follows, I shall explore in more detail whether other key features of the ADA, especially as it is applied to mental disabilities, are adequately explained or justified by a principle assuring fair equality of opportunity. I will argue that the ADA is a reasonably good legislative approximation to what is required to implement such a principle. My interest in the issue is in part theoretical: showing that a general principle can provide a unified view of our commitments in two areas of public policy strengthens support for it. But the issue is also of practical interest, because the rationale for legislation affects its application and interpretation. Specifically, I shall focus on three issues.

The first concerns the strength of our commitment to provide work opportunities to the mentally (and physically) disabled, even where there are significant costs involved in reasonable accommodation. In some cases, employers may be obliged to ignore modest decrements in relevant talents and skills, decrements that would have been grounds for replacing a nondisabled employee. Can this strong commitment to allowing the mentally disabled to work be explained by a commitment to fair equality of opportunity? Or do we need to posit a "right to work" (Kavka 1992)? Is the obligation to assure access to work to people with disabilities a general social obligation or one that specifically falls on employers? Does the scope of the obligation match the distribution of its burdens?

The second issue concerns the relationship between our commitments to provide protection of employment opportunities for the mentally disabled and our commitments to provide them with income support. Does the strong commitment embodied in the ADA to protecting the opportunities to work of those with disabilities imply some special responsibility on their part to work? What is the relationship between entitlements to work opportunities and entitlements to income support for those with disabilities? How should we mesh our commitments to protecting opportunity and to providing income support, given that these commitments may derive from different principles of distributive justice?

The third issue concerns the difficulty of drawing boundaries, especially in many cases of mental disabilities. Talents and skills are "normally" distributed across a population, and ordinarily we think employers are free to make decisions about hiring and promotion based on their judgments about how different employees manifest the relevant talents and skills. But some mental disorders adversely affect talents and skills, for example, interpersonal social skills that might be important in many jobs. If a "normal" person simply has trouble "relating" to others, it is the employer's prerogative to make appropriate hiring and firing decisions. But if difficulty in interacting with others is the result of some mental disorder (e.g., something given an appropriate place in DSM-IV or subsequent revisions), then the ADA requires judgments about whether the employee is "disabled" yet "otherwise qualified," and about what reasonable accommodation involves. Similarly, in health care contexts, the diagnostic category can place a deficit in social skills in a special category. Insurers may then be obliged to provide assistance (e.g., treatment for shyness) that would not be available to the "normally" shy person. How similar, however, are these contexts in which third parties are obligated to take special steps on behalf of those with mental disorders? Should the same set of conditions trigger health care and employment protection obligations?

Fair Equality of Opportunity and Disability Rights

The standard account of disability rights rests, quite plausibly, on a commitment to assuring everyone equality of opportunity. Historically, protection for people with disabilities against workplace and educational discrimination followed and was modeled on equal opportunity legislation aimed at racist and sexist practices at work and in schools. The historical analogy seemed obvious and appropriate. Race and sex were widely used to determine access to jobs and educational opportunities in ways that have no relationship to the "morally relevant" grounds for distributing those goods. Talents and skills, including personality and character traits, are relevant grounds for awarding employment and educational opportunities because they have a reasonable relationship to being able to perform well, that is, effectively or productively. But race and sex have no relationship to being able to perform well at the required educational or employment tasks. Any practice that involves differential impact by sex or race should therefore be scrutinized very closely to see if it meets the stringent conditions on exceptions to the general rule. Legislation aimed at sex and race discrimination had to sweep away the many rationales and excuses that had been developed to justify discriminatory practices.

Disability legislation was aimed at a similar historical problem and rested on a similar underlying philosophical analysis. Because of discriminatory stereotypes, those with disabilities were kept out of jobs they could perform as well as those who were not disabled. In many cases, the disability was just as "morally irrelevant" to job or educational placement as race or sex, but it was being used to justify exclusion or reduced access. These employment and educational practices were supported by widely held stereotypes that ascribed a broad range of reduced capabilities to those whose disabilities were quite narrow and specific. The parallel to racist and sexist stereotypes is widely recognized.

To some extent, antidiscrimination legislation of all kinds looks backwards. It aims to correct for the historical effects on current practices of past attitudes and practices. It is a legacy of past attitudes that keeps us from being color-, or gender-, or disability-neutral now. Still, there is some difference between the case of disabilities and that of race and sex. Unlike race, which never has, and sex, which almost never has any real (as opposed to imagined) effects on capabilities to perform a job, mental and physical disabilities have some real effects. We can imagine (if only imagine) a more perfect world in which the legacies of past discrimination are eliminated and in which issues about race and gender bias disappear. But issues about placement of people with disabilities would remain to the extent that there were measurable effects on job- or education-related capabilities.

To that extent, legislation protecting the job rights of those with disabilities also looks forward: it addresses a residual problem we will always face. The legislation says we must make "reasonable accommodation," at some social cost, to provide employment opportunities to people with disabilities who are "otherwise qualified" to perform "the essential tasks" involved in jobs or educational slots. We cannot be disability-neutral but must instead wear corrective lenses that keep us from perceiving those social costs as an excuse to ignore or perpetuate barriers against people with disabilities. Of course, once we have invested in making the workplace more accessible to people with disabilities, the incremental cost of employing them will be reduced, at least for many disabilities.

The ADA forces us to accept the costs of reasonable accommodation. Focusing on this point and these costs should not mislead us into thinking that all accommodation is costly—some is not at all. Furthermore, except in many rigidly defined assembly-line or service jobs, employers generally make some accommodation to the needs and preferences of workers, and they do not generally look at these adjustments as costs. Nor should it mislead us into ignoring some important benefits, such as the benefits to others that come from increasing diversity in the workplace. Some well-managed corporations emphasize these benefits in motivating managers and employers to accept the changes required by the ADA. But these benefits of diversity are not the motivation or the rationale for the ADA. They would not justify entitlements, rooted in talk about fair treatment, that are at the heart of the ADA and other antidiscrimination legislation. Focusing here on the obligation to accept the costs of reasonable accommodation derives from thinking about the underlying issues of justice and its burdens; but although I focus on the burdens of justice, I am aware that there are also benefits from promoting diversity.

The burden of "reasonable accommodation" may lead some people to think that disability rights in the ADA take us beyond the scope of a principle assuring equality of opportunity. Reasonable accommodation asks us—actually, it requires employers, who pass these costs along to consumers—to ignore some inequalities in capabilities, including some effects on talents and skills, even though ignoring them actually affects productivity or otherwise increases costs. The cost increases may result from modifications in the workplace, in job structures, or from modest (acceptable) decrements in performance. Truly neutral consideration of abilities would require no such reasonable accommodation for the effects of disabilities. If equality of opportunity simply required us to consider only relevant characteristics, then it might seem not to carry us as far as the ADA and earlier legislation do toward reasonable accommodation.

A suitable appeal to plausible interpretation of equality of opportunity can, however, justify the reasonable accommodation requirement. Consider first the "reasonable accommodation" we must make in the case of race or sex. If sexist or racist practices have distorted the development of the talents and skills of women or minorities, then some accommodation must be made. We would not be protecting equality of opportunity if we simply ignored the impact of unfair social practices and formally made point-by-point comparisons of existing talents and skills. We are obliged to commit social resources to rectifying the distortions caused by these practices; we are obliged to seek *fair* and not merely *formal* equality of opportunity (Rawls 1971). Suddenly becoming color- or gender-neutral, without considering the varied effects of unjust practices on real opportunity, is insufficient. The costs we must bear do not only take the form of compensatory training programs aimed at restoring talents and skills to the levels that would have existed in a nonsexist, nonracist environment. We must also ignore the costs that derive from altering expectations of employers and coworkers, as well as from clients and customers. Simply calculating whether a female or minority employee is as productive ''at the margin'' as a competing white male hides existing biases behind the formally ''neutral'' calculation.

Many of the incremental costs of adding disabled workers to a workplace that is acclimatized to bias against the handicapped are strictly analogous to the costs of rectifying sex and race bias in the workplace. This is more obvious in the case of physical than mental disabilities. Modifying a workplace to make it accessible to a physically handicapped worker is much more costly than building an accessible workplace from the start. Counting the costs of modification as part of the ''inefficiency'' of hiring the handicapped understates what protecting equality of opportunity requires. So, too, altering job descriptions so that they reflect essential functions, or reassigning tasks so that job structures are more accessible to people with disabilities— modifications that may be necessary for the mentally disabled—may involve transition costs that should not count as true inefficiencies. We calculate the costs of protecting equality of opportunity not simply from the perspective of present structures and present costs, but from the perspective of what a fairer work context would have involved, had we been concerned with equal opportunity from the start.

There may be a significant residue of cases, especially when we consider the effects of mental disabilities, where the costs of making reasonable accommodation cannot simply be accounted for by appeal to what a fair ''baseline'' would have involved, had the workplace adequately assured equality of opportunity from the start. A person with mental disabilities may require modest concessions on the job—more frequent breaks, release time for counseling, or shifting job responsibilities—that involve extra costs, even from the perspective of a workplace that already was structured to protect equality of opportunity. Hiring or retaining the mentally disabled worker under these conditions—as opposed to hiring or retaining the slightly more efficient nonhandicapped worker—might be a reasonable accommodation, but it would seem to involve ''more than equal'' opportunity. Or can this case, regardless of whether it is hypothetical or rare, be accommodated within a concern about equality of opportunity?

To see why I believe it can be accounted for, we should back away from workplace contexts for a moment and think about how a commitment to equality of opportunity operates in the context of health care (Daniels 1985, 1988). Disease and disability both impair the range of opportunities open to individuals. To characterize the scope of this impairment, consider the array of plans for their lives that reasonable people in a given society might choose, given their talents and skills. This broad array of opportunities is the "normal opportunity range" for a given society. A given individual, with a particular set of talents and skills, occupies a subspace of the normal opportunity range. Each person has a fair share of the normal opportunity range, determined by her talents and skills. When people are diseased or disabled, their opportunities shrink to occupy only a part of this fair share. A commitment to equality of opportunity, however, is a commitment to keeping people functioning as closely as possible to normal, so that their shares of the normal range are as close to their fair share as possible, given reasonable resource constraints. Health care systems and institutions should be designed with that goal in mind. The principle of distributive justice governing their design should be the principle of fair equality of opportunity, construed in this way as a principle protecting the range of opportunities open to people.

A commitment to equality of opportunity leads us to accept somewhat greater costs to protect the range of opportunities of those who are most impaired as compared to those who already enjoy more of their fair shares of opportunity. Though we are not committed to pouring all of our resources into the most impaired cases—we do not "maximin"—we also do not simply calculate to most efficient allocation of medical resources (Daniels 1993). We give some, but not full, priority to treating sicker or more disabled patients—or that is what a commitment to protecting equality of opportunity seems to require. (It does not tell us, however, just how much priority to give; see Daniels 1993.) The loss of efficiency here—we do not allocate resources so that they maximize medical benefits at the margin—is a reasonable accommodation to the demand of equality of opportunity. We go an extra distance to bring those whose opportunities are most impaired or threatened as close to normal functioning as we can. Of course, health care settings are not competitive in the same way job competition is, even where we must make resource-allocation decisions among different categories of patients competing for scarce medical services or dollars. Still, it is instructive to see that a commitment to equality of opportunity in the health care setting has an analogue to reasonable accommodation in the employment setting.

The interpretation of equality of opportunity appropriate to health care contexts has the goal of keeping people functioning as normally as possible (Daniels 1985, 1988; Rawls 1993). This conception of our commitment has some bearing on how we should think about the residual problem of reasonable accommodation for people with disabilities in workplace settings. Keeping the people with disabilities functioning as close to normally as possible in the workplace setting may require that we take modest extra steps to open employment doors. We go beyond strict or formal comparison of the mentally handicapped to equally capable nonhandicapped workers, even if doing so involves a trade-off between protecting their opportunities and efficiency that is somewhat steeper than the one we otherwise must make. (The argument here suggests there should also be special vocational rehabilitation or other services to fill in the gap between the limits of health care and reasonable accommodation on the job. I shall not discuss this issue here.)

I believe there is no deep compromise with principle in making this extra concession. One way to think about it is that we make up in the employment sphere for what we cannot quite accomplish in the health care sector. To see this point, we need to think about how concerns about equality of opportunity fit together with other concerns about distributive justice. The account I have sketched of equal opportunity (Rawls 1971; Daniels 1985) accepts the existing distribution of talents and skills, corrected for unjust social practices, as an inevitable source of inequality. Economic redistribution *should* (following Rawls) aim at making those whose life prospects are worst end up as well off as possible. But this only *mitigates* the effects of the distribution of talents and skills on equality; it *does not eliminate* them. (Others argue that the demands of equality or equality of opportunity require more forceful or direct efforts to equalize capabilities and eliminate the disadvantage that would otherwise come from the natural distribution of talents and skills; see Sen 1990, 1992; Cohen 1989.) Accepting the existing distribution of talents and skills and its effects, combined with appropriate redistribution, thus puts that distribution of talents and skills to work in a way that tends to maximize the benefit of those worst off in marketable talents and skills. There is nothing sacred, however, about the existing distribution of talents and skills. The modest compromise with efficiency involved in reasonable accommodation thus is equivalent to slightly redistributing the talents and skills, or altering their market value, albeit at some cost. We put those with disabilities closer to where they would have been had they had no disability. Since we cannot make this correction in the sphere of health care, we do the next best thing in employment. Of course, this is only rough justice, but it recognizes the special importance of work opportunities in our lives.

Although I have argued that we can explain the reasonable accommodation requirement by appealing to an appropriate account of equal opportunity, some may think we should look elsewhere for such a justification. I want briefly to consider one alternative, Kavka's (1992) valuable discussion of a strong "right to work," which he claims gives an account of the employment rights of people with disabilities. Kavka argues that people with disabilities have a right to work with these five features:

1. They (but not other workers) have a right to employment rather than just an income stream (call this the *special right*).
2. They have a right to nondiscrimination.
3. They have a right to compensatory training and education.
4. They have a right to reasonable accommodation, where that involves some societal investment to make the workplace more disability-friendly.
5. They have a right to tie-breaking uses of preferential treatment in placement practices.

Taken by itself, the special right of those with disabilities (but not others) to employment, as opposed to an income stream, is at once too strong and too weak. It is too weak because, by itself, it would only assure access of people with disabilities to some job or other, perhaps a quite minimal job commensurate with the abilities of the handicapped worker. To make the right to work resemble the much more robust requirements of the ADA, features 2–4, and possibly 5, must be added to the special right. But these additional features of the right to work do not depend on the special right. They cannot be derived from it, nor can they be derived from the appeal Kavka makes to the importance of self-respect in trying to establish the special right. Some of the additional features, including reasonable accommodation, can, however, be given plausible foundations by appealing to a developed account of fair equality of opportunity, or so I have argued.

The special right Kavka claims for those with disabilities is also too strong. By this I mean two things. First, it goes beyond the scope of the disability rights we recognize in the ADA. The ADA carries no implication that it is more important to provide work to people with disabilities than it is to people without disabilities; its primary concern is to level the playing field. (Of course, this does not show that Kavka is wrong and the ADA right. It only shows how what he argues for is much stronger than what is needed to justify features of the ADA.) Second, and more important, Kavka's special right goes beyond the employment rights we ought to claim for the handicapped and can reasonably justify. To see this, consider Kavka's central argument.

Kavka's argument for this strong right to work, especially the special right, turns crucially on the relationship between working and self-respect. Kavka argues, correctly I believe, that working has a fundamental impact on self-esteem, especially in cultures like ours that attach so many other awards to work. Following Rawls (1971), he views the social bases of self-respect as a primary or basic good, and argues that contractors (whether Rawlsian, acting from behind a veil of ignorance, or Hobbesian, acting without a veil) would insist on securing that good for themselves through the design of social institutions. Taken so generally, the argument might provide some basis for explaining the importance of keeping people at work, including those with disabilities, rather than simply providing them with income streams. It supplements, in other words, the argument I offered earlier for accepting the costs of reasonable accommodation.

But Kavka argues more specifically that work is more important to the self-respect of people with disabilities than it is to people without them. It is more important, he speculates, because those with disabilities have fewer other ways to sustain self-esteem. Consequently, he argues, as social contractors we would give priority to putting our disabled future, or possible, selves to work over our nondisabled future selves. Here I believe Kavka draws on speculative psychological claims that cannot support his conclusion. Is self-respect sustained better when preferential treatment in access to jobs is our policy than when equal opportunity is assured? This very matter is the focus of sociological debate in the context of affirmative action programs regarding race and sex. Critics of preferential treatment argue that it undermines self-respect because it raises doubts about the ability of those who obtain jobs or educational opportunities.

The more secure inference from this argument about self-respect is that keeping people with disabilities at work is *just as important* as providing work to others. Consequently, equal opportunity requires reasonable accommodation. Abandoning Kavka's special right to work thus still leaves us with a strong defense of the features of disability rights provided by the ADA.

One qualification is needed to the argument so far. The obligation to guarantee equality of opportunity is a social obligation, and translating this social obligation into obligations that fall on different individuals or groups is complex. In the health care context, this implies an obligation to assure access to appropriate health care regardless of ability to pay, and the fairest way to distribute the burden of that obligation would be through progressive tax-based financing. In employment and education settings, the social obligation imposes a duty on employers and educational institutions not to discriminate against people with disabilities. The ADA also, however, imposes a duty to provide "reasonable accommodation," which implies that some costs will be borne by employers. Assuming these costs are passed on to consumers, there is a dispersion of the burden; if all employers bear some burdens, we may suppose the dispersion of the burdens to consumers will be widespread, though it is less likely to be as progressive as it would be if it were subsidized by taxes. A subsidy to employers who make more expensive accommodations to the handicapped would be a way to create further incentives to keep the mentally disabled at work, but the administrative burden of such a program, plus its visibility in public budgets, may constitute reasons why the strategy was not adopted when the ADA was passed.

Income Support and Disability Rights

What relationships hold between our obligations to support those who cannot work by providing them with income support and our obligations to assure people with disabilities access to work? When there are significant barriers to work for the disabled, because of discrimination or because reasonable accommodation is lacking, then there is clearly more need for income support for those with disabilities. Presumably, if more people with disabilities work, then there is less need for income support. Very generous income support for those who do not work would also have some negative impact on the willingness of people with disabilities to work, especially those whose prospects are for lower wages.

These interactions between support for disability rights and income support are not particularly interesting, however important they are from the point of view of institutional design. Two quite different moral principles underlie our commitment to disability rights and income support. Whereas disability rights rest on a commitment to a principle protecting fair equality of opportunity, or so I have argued, income support policies rest on other principles of distributive justice. Minimally, they can be thought of as social insurance protecting us against short-term disruptions of income (e.g., for temporary disabilities or other short-term unemployment). But they also reflect a concern to constrain the lifetime inequalities in income and wealth that can emerge in a society because some people are unable to work for protracted periods. Equal opportunity and income-support principles are not completely independent: lack of income support undermines equal opportunity, and lack of equal opportunity leads to unfair income inequalities. Clearly, we need both principles at work and institutions to embody them. We cannot say that because we are protecting equal opportunity, we need not provide income support, or vice versa. We must comply with both types of principles and cannot substitute compliance with one for compliance with the other. Though we are committed to both, there are the (uninteresting) interactions I noted.

Some people believe that a more interesting relationship between disability rights and income support surfaces when we meet our social obligations to improve work prospects for those with disabilities. They ask, Don't the disabled have a responsibility to work now that discriminatory barriers are lowered? Can we reduce access to income support or make it contingent on serious efforts to secure work?

We should be leery of the presuppositions behind these questions. The fact that we failed in the past to provide equal opportunity for people with disabilities did not make our *obligation* to provide income support greater: it only made the *need* for it greater. Similarly, providing generous income support does not relieve us of the obligation to protect equality of opportunity, though it may lower the demand of those with disabilities (or malingerers) to work. So too, protecting the work rights of people with disabilities does not make our obligation to provide income support less, though it may reduce the need for it. Similarly, I do not think people with disabilities "owe" us something more, in the form of a greater responsibility to work, simply because we now aim to protect opportunity in ways that we always should have. Their responsibility to work is neither greater nor less than the responsibility of anyone else.

The serious danger in thinking that the responsibility of people with disabilities to work increases as society meets its responsibility to protect opportunity is that we will overestimate the success of our efforts to protect opportunity. If we overestimate the improvement in access to work, we will underestimate the need for income support. In our eagerness to cut back on income support, we will then hold people with disabilities responsible for failing to meet their obligation to work. This is blaming the victim. We must avoid it. At the same time we cannot ignore whatever real work disincentives are created by income support and whatever real abuse occurs because of malingering and fraud. Those are the mundane issues of institutional design. Meeting our obligations to protect the opportunities of those with disabilities does not create these mundane problems, and the real relationships between equal opportunity and income support are the ones I described.

Mental Disabilities and Boundary Issues

I want to consider two objections to my claim that a principle providing for fair equality of opportunity gives a unified account of rights to health care and disability rights. The first objection is that the conditions that trigger treatment and employment protection differ significantly. How can they then be encompassed by the same principle? The second objection is that by treating disease and protecting people with disabilities, we in fact draw arbitrary distinctions that ignore other ways in which equal opportunity is ignored in health care and employment contexts. I conclude with a comment on the difficulty of establishing parity in the protections afforded to mental and physical disabilities.

Although I have appealed to a fair equality of opportunity principle in both health care and work disability contexts, eligibility for treatment or protection is triggered by different criteria in these domains. A departure from normal functioning that makes someone eligible for medical treatment may not count as a disability for purposes of the ADA. Many illnesses have an impact on normal functioning, and thus on the range of opportunities open to an individual, without, for example, impairing a "major life function." For example, a treatable mental condition may be transitory (e.g., a bout of depression), or it might be long-lasting but limited in its impact (e.g., a phobia). Thus many treatable mental illnesses or disorders will not constitute ADA-protected disabilities because of their limited effect on functioning, especially in the workplace. Similarly, a condition might trigger disability rights but not access to medical treatment, for example, because no effective medical treatment is available for it. Similarly, since the ADA allows the perception that a disabling condition is present to trigger ADA protections, there are many other cases where eligibility for medical treatment would not follow from the presence of an ADA-protected "disability." Here the antidiscrimination component of the ADA protects the worker even where there is a "misdiagnosis" of disability.

These differences in the eligibility requirements for medical treatment and ADA protection do not undercut the claim that both share the same general function of protecting equality of opportunity. Rather, the difference reflects differences in the means and context in which this function can be carried out in health care and employment settings. Once we think about it, identical eligibility requirements or triggers for treatment and employment entitlements would be totally inappropriate given these differences.

The issue of perceived disabilities aside, we might suppose that a more fully developed medical technology would eliminate the need for many of the protections afforded by the ADA. Suppose we could cure all mental illness, restore normal functioning to quadriplegics, grow new limbs for amputees, or replace enzymes that enhanced the intelligence of the mildly retarded. In this fantasy, much of what we consider disability would be eliminated, and we could narrow the scope of the ADA dramatically. This suggests that much of what we do through the ADA for mental and physical disabilities corrects for what we cannot do through health care. Where we cannot cure, we must compensate for loss of functioning and keep people functioning as close to the levels they would enjoy if we could do more medically. Though there is some divergence between the conditions that trigger medical entitlements and those that trigger employment protections, both sets of protections serve the same general purpose: keeping functioning as close to normal as they can. Employment protections are invoked where our limited capabilities mean we could not eliminate the need for them through health care interventions.

The second objection is that certain "hard cases," or boundary problems, confound the appeal to equal opportunity in employment contexts. These hard cases can arise for both physical and mental disabilities, but the latter seem particularly difficult to resolve. Consider first a hard case involving a physical disability: a disabled worker with reduced motor capability may be somewhat slower than a nondisabled worker at certain tasks. In the absence of the disability, the employer might have preferred to replace a worker who was so slow at those tasks. Nevertheless, reasonable accommodation might require retaining the disabled worker. In effect, the protection keeps the disabled worker in place at some cost in order to keep her functioning in life as close as possible to the level she would have enjoyed had she not been disabled. Here the protection is compensatory. We do not accommodate the "normal" worker who is just plain slow.

More complex cases arise for mental disabilities. A "normal" but irascible worker, or a very shy, withdrawn, or lethargic but otherwise "normal" worker, might be replaced by an employer for lack of social skills in certain jobs. If equally irascible, shy, or lethargic workers have mental diseases or disorders that qualify them as "mentally disabled," however, their employers may have to provide them with "reasonable accommodation." Is there some inequity here? Why should a compromise of performance be excused and compensated for in one case and not the other?

This problem may seem particularly hard at the extremes. Suppose two workers are seriously lacking in certain social skills. One has a mental disorder that triggers ADA eligibility—his shyness (or irascibility) is the result of a bipolar condition, for example. The other, however, is just as shy (or irascible), but we find no mental disease or disorder. He is just at the extreme of the normal distribution for shyness (or irascibility). Since the lack of skill is seriously disadvantaging in exactly the same way, then it seems troublesome that one is protected but the other not.

The very same problem arises in health care contexts. If a bipolar patient was extremely shy, we might provide insurance coverage for group therapy to address the shyness, even though we might not provide such coverage for an otherwise normal but equally shy person. The rationale would be that we were treating an effect of the disease. Similarly, very short children with diagnosable growth hormone deficiency are eligible for reimbursement for growth hormone treatment; this counts as "treatment." But shortness that results from just being at the extreme end of the normal distribution for height would not be reimburseable; this counts as mere "enhancement." In these cases, we are particularly troubled because the suffering or disadvantage in each case is similar for those eligible for treatment and those not. It seems arbitrary to treat in one way those people who have a biologically based condition we call "disease" and in another way those whose biologically based condition is "normal"—even though they suffer or are disadvantaged identically.

Despite the challenge of such hard cases, the treatment/enhancement distinction should play a role in deciding what obligations we have to provide medical services, and I think an analogous distinction can be defended in the case of employment rights for people with disabilities. To show that this distinction is not arbitrary from the point of view of justice, despite the hard cases, I shall argue that it fits better than alternatives with the approach I have taken toward fair equality of opportunity. This approach (call it the *standard model*) helps to specify a reasonable limit on the central task of health care, and its analogue does the same for disability rights.

I have argued that health care services aim to restore people to the range of capabilities they *would have had* without disease or disability, given their allotment of talents and skills. The *standard model* for thinking about equality of opportunity thus takes as a given the fact that talents and skills and other capabilities are not distributed equally among people. Some people are better at some things than others. Accordingly, we assure people *fair* equality of opportunity if we judge them by their capabilities while ignoring "morally irrelevant" traits like sex or race when we place people in schools, jobs, and offices. Often, however, we must correct for cases in which capabilities have been misdeveloped through racist, sexist, or other discriminatory practices. Similarly, by preventing or treating disease and disability, we can correct for impairment of the capabilities people would otherwise have. Reasonable accommodation for people with disabilities further corrects for the impairment of capabilities that we cannot correct through medical treatment. The standard model does not call for us to eliminate all differences in capabilities through medical enhancement, only those that result from disease and disability (Daniels 1990; Sabin and Daniels 1994, Daniels 1996). Similarly, it does not call for "reasonable accommodation" of all differences in capabilities among unequally skilled workers; we provide reasonable accommodation only for the decrements that can be attributed to the disability for "otherwise qualified" workers.

This limitation of the standard model can appear arbitrary. Our capabilities are themselves the result of a natural and social lottery, and we do not "deserve" them. We just are fortunate or unfortunate in having them. We can mitigate this underlying arbitrariness *somewhat* as follows. Those who are better endowed with marketable capabilities are likely to enjoy more goods such as income, wealth, and power. If we constrain inequalities in these goods so that those who are worst off do as well as possible, considering alternatives, then social cooperation will work to the benefit of all (Rawls 1971). Still, this constraint does not eliminate all inequalities in the capabilities people have and thus in the opportunities they enjoy, especially since we are enjoined to judge people in light of their capabilities. If our egalitarian concerns require that we strive to give people equal capabilities, wherever technologically feasible, then we should not settle for mitigating the effects of relying on equality of opportunity as standardly understood (Sen 1990, 1992; Cohen 1989). Rejecting the standard model pushes us toward leveling all differences in capabilities; from that perspective, the distinction between treatment and enhancement has no point.

From the perspective of the standard model of fair equality of opportunity, however, it is reasonable to limit the task of medical services to restoring people to normal functioning and thus to the range of opportunities they would have had absent disease or disability. In the standard model, the treatment/enhancement distinction retains its point. For purposes of justice, it is enough that the line between disease or disability and its absence is *uncontroversial* and *ascertainable through publicly acceptable methods,* such as those of the biomedical sciences, for the general run of cases. Being able to draw a line in this way allows us to refer counterfactually in a relatively clear and objective way to the range of opportunities a person *would have had* in the absence of disease and disability; it facilitates public agreement. My claim that we have obligations to provide health care services that meet people's medical needs, within resource limitations, thus derives from accepting the standard model for thinking about fair equality of opportunity. Abandoning the treatment/enhancement distinction would push us toward a much more radical form of egalitarianism. Dropping the distinction does not just open the door to growth hormone therapy for short normal children, eliminating one anomaly. It begins a cascade of changes in the scope of medicine that would forever change its face and might threaten the social consensus that gives medicine the strong moral grip it has on us and our resources.

It might be thought that we do not need to adopt such an extreme position if we abandon the notion of disease or disability. If extreme shortness or shyness could be considered a handicapping condition, then we might still be able to appeal to the standard model of equality of opportunity (Allen and Fost 1990). Growth hormone therapy would simply move people into the range of capabilities they would have had were they not handicapped. This compromise approach does not seek full equality in capabilities, only the end of handicapping disadvantages.

There are serious objections to dropping the reference to disease or disability in drawing this version of the treatment/enhancement distinction. First, we need a clear notion of "handicap." Specifying the shortest 1% as handicapped will itself seem arbitrary after the first cycle of therapies creates a new group of shortest people. Not treating the newest group would then seem arbitrary in light of a new set of hard cases. Second, it will now be medicine's task to eliminate all comparable handicapping conditions. In our racist society, this means black, brown, or red skin. Should we eliminate melanin or oppose discrimination? Although the compromise approach does not seek equality of capabilities, it vastly expands the function of medicine, and by medicalizing social problems, it risks losing whatever consensus exists on the moral importance of meeting health care needs.

The problem raised for the treatment/enhancement distinction by our hard cases is similar to the kind of problem all rules face when their justification derives from the fact that general conformity to them is on the whole either better or fairer. We can almost always describe hard cases in which the very reasons that lead us to adopt a rule to cover the general case also lead us to think the rule is nonoptimal or unfair when applied to them. Though troubling, hard cases do not always count as counterexamples that force us to reject the rule. Sometimes we must swallow the discrepancy between the particular case and the general run of things if we want a generally better or fairer distributive scheme.

Employment rights as specified in the ADA similarly rest on an appeal to the standard model of equal opportunity. Reasonable accommodation is given only for those with disabilities, not for those whose capabilities—whose talents and skills—put them at a market disadvantage. Hard cases in employment contexts retain a residual arbitrariness, just as they do in medical contexts, but the alternative is a radical egalitarianism aimed at leveling all differences in capabilities, with radical consequences for productivity. The leveling approach is no more plausible or feasible in employment than in medical contexts.

I shall conclude by returning to my starting point, the issue of parity—on paper, in law—between the treatment of mental and physical disabilities. Mental disabilities pose more difficult problems than physical ones. They force us to steer a narrow course between the Scylla of "otherwise qualified" and the Charybdis of "disabled." To show that a mental disorder constitutes a disability, we must show that it impairs a major life function. For many mental disorders, the impact on social skills has its primary effect on work. It is not possible to point to its effects on mobility, hearing, or seeing, the major life functions affected by physical disabilities. But showing that the disability has an impact on work makes it more difficult to show that someone with mental disabilities is "otherwise qualified" to work. Distinguishing essential and nonessential tasks may be harder when the job requires some level of social skills or some degree of "reliability."

For similar reasons, what constitutes reasonable accommodation may be more difficult to determine for mental than physical disabilities. Reasonable accommodation may require, for example, more extensive restructuring of job requirements or provision of breaks and other supports than for many physical disabilities. Here social prejudice against mental disabilities—strong biases and degrading stereotypes—is particularly difficult to guard against. It is much easier to moralize about mental disability than physical disability, easier to blame the victim. It is easier, for example, to imagine that if someone were more cooperative or tried harder, his performance would improve, and he would need less accommodation. These features of mental disabilities and the strength of social prejudice concerning them gives us strong reason to demand objective assessment of performance, essential tasks, and costs of accommodation.

The point of the comparison is the suggestion that real parity between mental and physical disabilities exists only on paper, despite the best intentions behind the ADA. The fair equality of opportunity account nevertheless provides a basis for diligent insistence on reasonable accommodation and the attempt to achieve real parity.

References

Allen, David B., and Norman C. Fost. 1990. Growth Hormone Therapy for Short Stature: Panacea or Pandora's Box? *Journal of Pediatrics* 117: 16–21.

Cohen, G. A. 1989. On the Currency of Egalitarian Justice. *Ethics* 99: 906–944.

Daniels, Norman. 1985. *Just Health Care,* New York: Cambridge University Press.

———. 1988. *Am I My Parents' Keeper? An Essay On Justice Between the Young and the Old.* New York: Oxford.

———. 1990. Equality of What: Welfare, Resources, or Capabilities? *Philosophy and Phenomenological Research* 50 (supp.): 273–296.

———. 1993. Rationing Fairly: Programmatic Considerations. *Bioethics* 7(2, 3): 224–233.

———. 1996. *Justice and Justification: Reflective Equilibrium in Theory and Practice.* New York: Cambridge University Press.

Kavka, Gregory S. 1992. Disability and the Right to Work. *Social Philosophy and Policy* 9(1): 262–290.

Rawls, John. 1971. *A Theory of Justice.* Cambridge: Harvard University Press.

———. 1993. *Political Liberalism.* New York: Columbia University Press.

Sabin, James, and Norman Daniels. 1994. Determining 'Medical Necessity' in Mental Health Practice: A Study of Clinical Reasoning and a Proposal for Insurance Policy. *Hasting Center Reports* 24(6): 5–13.

Sen, Amartya. 1990. Justice: Means vs. Freedoms. *Philosophy and Public Affairs* 19: 111–121.

———. 1992. *Inequality Reexamined.* Cambridge: Harvard University Press.

Epilogue

RICHARD J. BONNIE AND JOHN MONAHAN

Fair treatment of persons with work disabilities related to mental disorders will depend in part on the quality of knowledge in this field. The studies assembled in this book highlight five areas that should be addressed in the next generation of research.

First, research must include the experience of workers with diagnosed mental disorders. As noted earlier, the available research on work disability concerning people with mental disorders tends to focus on the population of individuals with the most serious or severe mental disorders, most of whom are not in the labor force. For this reason, the research tends to focus on clinical aspects of vocational rehabilitation of this population and on access to SSI/SSDI benefits. The most important challenge for research on work disability relating to mental disorder is to learn more about the experiences of people with disorders who *are* in the workforce. Interesting qualitative studies have emerged (e.g., Scheid and Anderson 1995), but we do not yet have systematic data on this population. Nor do we yet have systematic information about the difficulties confronted by people with mental disorders in the workplace or about the responses of employers to requests for accommodation. In this regard, research on mental disorder and workplace disability is significantly eclipsed by comprehensive empirical studies of work disability associated with mental retardation (Blanck 1994).

Second, issues regarding work disabilities should be studied from a public health perspective. To whatever extent work disability can be ameliorated by vocational rehabilitation or by workplace accommodation, the workers' well being will be enhanced, and the social costs of mental illness will be reduced. Ultimately, however, the loss of productivity and the cost of social support attributable to work disability can be most dramatically reduced by preventing the onset or exacerbation of serious mental disorder. Untreated mental and

emotional disorders in youths and young adults exact a high toll in diminished
social functioning in later life. This is the central lesson emerging from the
National Comorbidity study. Initial reports have already shown that 7.2 million people in the United States prematurely terminated their educations because of the early onset of psychiatric disorders (Kessler, Foster, Saunders,
and Stang 1995). Subsequent reports are bound to show that reduced employability and vocational success are also predicted by early onset psychiatric
disorders. In short, work disability attributable to mental disorder can be
substantially reduced by broader access to early interventions and treatments
for mental disorders in youth and young adults.

Third, the study of mental disorder and employment should be integrated,
both conceptually and empirically, with the study of mental disorder and
unemployment. Obviously, research will concentrate on one context or the
other. But the development of legal and social policy would benefit if researchers used a conceptual framework that encompassed the participation of
people with mental disorder in competitive employment, in subsidized or
otherwise supported employment programs, and in "entitlement" programs
based on work disability. Longitudinal research, following over time the
work careers of persons with mental disorder, would be most valuable in this
regard.

Fourth, from the perspective of mental health law, one of the most intriguing issues embedded in work disability legislation concerns the use of
these laws to provide leverage in the treatment process. For example, the
practice of designating treatment providers as representative payees under the
SSI system provides an opportunity to link the recipient's access to SSI
benefits to compliance with treatment requirements (Cogswell 1996). The
prevalence of this practice and its efficacy have not been adequately studied.
Similarly, as mentioned in chapters 7 and 9, it is likely that some employers
are "accommodating" employees with psychiatric disabilities by linking continued employment to compliance with recommended treatment. The prospect
of "coerced" treatment has troubled mental health advocates and consumers.
It should be mentioned, however, that therapeutic leverage has long been
used for employees with alcohol problems under the auspices of Employee
Assistance Programs. The extension of this approach to people with psychiatric disabilities requires careful study, both empirically and legally (Berg and
Bonnie 1996).

Finally, issues regarding work disability should be seen from a comparative
perspective. While the United States may be in the lead in according workplace rights to citizens with disabilities, there is no reason to believe that it
has achieved similar prominence in actually integrating persons with mental
disorder into the workplace. The experience of other countries relating to

mental disorder, work disability, and the law may yield important lessons for American law and policy (Doyle, 1995).

References

Berg, J., and R. Bonnie. 1996. When Push Comes to Shove: Aggressive Community Treatment and the Law. In D. Dennis and J. Monahan, eds., *Coercion and Aggressive Community Treatment: A New Frontier in Mental Health Law*. New York: Plenum.

Blanck, P. 1994. Employment Integration, Economic Opportunity, and the Americans with Disabilities Act: Empirical Study from 1990–1993. *Iowa Law Review* 79: 853–939.

Cogswell, S. 1996. Entitlements, Payees, and Coercion. In D. Dennis and J. Monahan, eds., *Coercion and Aggressive Community Treatment: A New Frontier in Mental Health Law*. New York: Plenum.

Doyle, B. 1995. *Disability, Discrimination and Equal Opportunities: A Comparative Study of the Employment Rights of Disabled Persons*. London: Mansell.

Kessler, R., C. Foster, W. Saunders, and P. Stang. 1995. Social Consequences of Psychiatric Disorders. Part 1. Educational Attainment. *American Journal of Psychiatry* 152: 1026–1032.

Scheid, T., and C. Anderson. 1995. Living with Chronic Mental Illness: Understanding the Role of Work. *Community Mental Health Journal* 31: 163–176.

INDEX

Accommodation, reasonable: for aberrant behavior, 271; ADA exemption from, 224–29; ADA response to mental health and physical disabilities, 125–27, 233–34; costs, 284–85; for psychiatric disabilities, 213–17. *See also* Americans with Disabilities Act, 1990 (ADA); Employers

Adams v. Alderson (1989, 1990), 217

Adverse selection: effect in insurance market, 165; effect on disability insurance, 165–66

Affective disorders, 29, 38–39

Alcohol and drug disorders, 38–39

American Medical Association (AMA), *Guides to the Evaluation of Permanent Impairment,* 153, 158, 187–91

Americans with Disabilities Act, 1990 (ADA): ability theme, 218; accommodation for persons with psychiatric disabilities, 125–27; accommodation mandate, 178, 203, 205–6, 211–17, 233, 263–73; as antidiscrimination statute, 1, 3, 9, 48–49, 225–29, 261, 292; as civil rights legislation, 203–4; direct threat standard, 210–11, 224–29; disclosure issue, 212; employee awareness of, 258–59; employer violation of, 203–4; employment and enforcement provisions, 203, 205; equal treatment concept for disabled, 222–23; existence of disability under, 203; hypothetical parity of disabilities under, 281;

ideal type of disability, 223–24; impact on labor force participants, 200–201; intent and goals, 1, 3, 25, 199–201; limitations on employers' interviews, 246–47, 263; paradigm of disability and work, 204–5; protection against discrimination under, 225–29, 261; relation to disability insurance and workers' compensation, 184–86; rights under, 57; supported employment services, 271–72; unintended consequences of, 222. *See also* Accommodation, reasonable; Disability rights; Equal Opportunity Employment Commission (EEOC)

Antidiscrimination law: Americans with Disabilities Act, 1, 3, 9, 48–49, 225–29, 261, 292; Rehabilitation Act, 3, 9

Antidiscrimination laws: limitations of, 283

Anxiety disorders, 29

August v. Offices Unlimited, Inc. (1992), 206

Beauford v. Father Flanagan's Boys' Home (1987, 1988), 206

Benefit determination: for mental and physical disabilities, 187–89; using AMA *Guides,* 187–91

Brief Psychiatric Rating Scale (BPRS): checklist, 72; focus on symptomatology, 93

Buckingham v. U.S. Postal Service (1993), 214